The Hidden
BHAGWAN

Editing by Ma Deva Sarito, Ma Prem Lisa (Cantab)
Typing by Ma Devaprem, Ma Dharma Pratito
Design by Ma Dhyan Amiyo
Production by Swami Satyadharma, B.A.,
Swami Prem Pablo, M.A.

Published by The Rebel Publishing House GmbH
Venloer Strasse 5–7, 5000 Cologne 1, West Germany

Copyright © Neo-Sannyas International
First Edition

Printing by Mohndruck, Gütersloh, West Germany

Splendor
SHREE RAJNEESH

All rights reserved

No part of this book may be reproduced or transmitted in any form or by any means electronic or mechanical including photocopying or recording or by any information storage and retrieval system without permission in writing from the publisher.

Distributed in the United States by
Chidvilas Foundation, Inc., Boulder, Colorado

Distributed in Europe by
Neo-Sannyas International, Zurich, Switzerland

ISBN 3-89338-019-1

Talks given
to the
Rajneesh International University
of Mysticism

Table of Contents

Session 1
Trust is the Bridge
Between You and Existence   1

Session 2
Just Be Indifferent
To the Mind   13

Session 3
Don't Make Life
A Question-Answer Game   23

Session 4
Who Is Preventing You?
Join the Dance!   39

Session 5
This Moment
Is More Than Enough   53

Session 6
Only Fools
Choose to be Somebody   65

Session 7
Preparing
For the Last World War   75

Session 8
The Taste of Your Being   85

Session 9
Papal Politics:
Organized Superstition   95

Session 10
Enlightenment
Is Not An Experience   107

Session 11
A Noah's Ark
Of Consciousness   119

Session 12
Life Itself
Is A Miracle   133

Session 13
Truth
Is Not Divisible   143

Session 14
No Time Left
For Any Device   155

Session 15
This is the Last Dance 167

Session 16
Love
Is Always an Emperor 177

Session 17
Watchfulness…
Your Gift to Yourself 189

Session 18
Inside You
God is Hidden 201

Session 19
At the Maximum
You Disappear 211

Session 20
Your Longing
Is the Seed 223

Session 21
The Greatest
Misfit in the World 233

Session 22
What More
Do You Want? 245

Session 23
Love…
Not a Relationship
But a State of Being 257

Session 24
All Our Doings
Are Disturbances 269

Session 25
The Watcher
Is Always in the Now 279

Session 26
Life's Aim
Is Life Itself 289

Session 27
Harmony
Is Your Reality 301

Introduction

This book is not just a book, it is a journey—call it a pilgrimage if you will, a pilgrimage in search of that indefinable something that all of us, at some time or another in our lives, feel as missing. Whether we choose to pursue this missing "something" or not is another question—but all of us have felt it.

In "the old days," in legends, or in the fairy tales we heard as children, the adventure of the pilgrimage, the search, was an exciting reality. Then, for most of us that adventure disappeared, along with the rest of our childhood dreams. We grew up, and did what a "grown-up" was expected to do. And it wasn't so exciting after all. But…

You go on missing something—something that you had known but you have forgotten—a faded memory, a lost remembrance. And the gap is not only a gap, it is a wound—it hurts, because you had brought something with your birth into the world and you have lost it in this crowded universe…

Bhagwan Shree Rajneesh, who spoke these words to an audience of disciplines and friends in India, is an extraordinary human being, difficult to introduce in words that the world, and particularly the Western world, understands. The East at least has a language for the phenomenon of one who is no longer "missing something," of one who has really *grown up* and not just got older, of one for whom all search and questioning has disappeared into discovery. But this language of the East does not translate very well into the language of the West, which is based on science and anti-science, the material world and the world of superstition, Karl Marx and the Virgin Mary. Neither Christianity nor science has a real concept of meditation, of enlightenment. So even though you can find these words in the dictionary, you will not find their meanings there. And you will certainly not find out about Bhagwan. But the language of the East, its tradition of a spirituality which renounces the world as *maya,* illusion, doesn't encompass Bhagwan either. He is a category unto himself, and you have to go to the source to be introduced.

His discourses have been published in hundreds of books, each of which speaks in its own unique way to the seeker in each of us.

This series of talks carries a particular sense of urgency: in 1987, the dreams of childhood seem further away than ever. The newspaper headlines tell of a mad race between religious fanaticism, political cunningness and ecological devastation, to see which will finish off the planet first–and Bhagwan makes the situation startlingly clear: *Before the outside world is destroyed by your politicians, enter into your inner world. That's the only safety left, the only shelter against nuclear weapons, against global suicide, against all these idiots who have so much power to destroy. You can at least save yourself.*

And, as always with Bhagwan, he also lights up a way out of the jungle–shows us that the snake over there we are so frightened of is just a dead branch, warns us of the trap hidden beneath the grasses strewn across the path, gives us a hand across the rapids and points out the beauty of the foliage along the way.

He invites us on a pilgrimage, to rediscover that missing "something"…to at least save ourselves, and in that process perhaps to re-create anew the planet which gave us birth:

Religion is basically the search for childhood: the same innocence, the same joy in things, the same fearlessness–those magical eyes, that heart that was able to dance with the trees, the heart that was enchanted with the moon and the stars. That space in which existence was nothing but sheer glory, pure splendor…

Ma Deva Sarito
Poona, India
September, 1987

Session 1

Trust is the Bridge Between You and Existence

*Millions of people are born, live their time and die,
but without knowing why they were born,
without knowing why the opportunity of life was given to them,
without even knowing who they are,
from where they come and to where they are going,
what their destiny is.
A life of such meaninglessness is at the most
a kind of vegetation, without consciousness, without awareness,
without ever knowing the hidden splendor of your being.*

March 12, 1987
Evening

Beloved Bhagwan,

A circle seems to be complete.
I feel myself arriving at a place I had left in my childhood,
living an innocent, poetic, ecstatic life.
The whole universe was my family.
Then – first out of trust, then out of fear – I allowed society to take over.
Now all has peeled off.
I have walked through the pain, the fear is gone, the ambition is gone.
Knowing about this whole journey with open eyes
I am sitting under the sky drinking the sweet splendor; day and night.
Bhagwan, there seems to be no darkness, no end, sometimes not even me.

Deva Pratito, it rarely happens that one attains his childhood again. It should happen more. It should happen to everybody because without its happening, your life remains incomplete.

You go on missing something – something that you had known but you have forgotten – a faded memory, a lost remembrance. And the gap is not only a gap, it is a wound. It hurts, because you had brought something with your birth into the world and you have lost it somewhere. And it seems impossible to find it in this crowded universe. But unless it happens, your life has been in vain, a misery, a suffering, a futile longing, a meaningless desire, a thirst that you know cannot be quenched.

Deva Pratito, you are blessed. And remember always to pray to the existence that everybody should be blessed in the same way.

You are saying, "A circle seems to be complete." It is complete – don't say it *seems* to be complete. "I feel myself arriving at a place I had left in my childhood, living an innocent, poetic, ecstatic life. The whole universe was my family. Then – first out of trust and then out of fear – I allowed society to take over."

This is the greatest crime that society commits against every child. No other crime can be greater than this. To spoil a child's trust is to spoil his whole life because trust is so valuable that the moment you lose trust, you also lose your contact with your own being.

Trust is the bridge between you and existence. Trust is the purest form of love, and once trust is lost, love also becomes impossible.

But every child's trust is being exploited. He naturally trusts his parents and because of his trust, they go on giving him beliefs which are poisonous, a personality which is false, an ego which will deprive him of his own soul; beliefs, thoughts, scriptures, which are going to hinder his intelligence, which are going to prevent his search for truth, which are going to make him part of some stupid, organized religion.

I call every organized religion stupid, because true religion can never be organized. True religion is always individual, it has nothing to do with the crowd. A Jesus can be religious but not the Christians. The Christians are only carbon copies. They have forgotten their own originality, their own individuality.

Jesus was not following anybody. He was not imitating anybody. That was his *fault*, that he did not allow the society to exploit his trust. He did not allow the crowd to reduce him into a false personality. He remained an individual.

He risked his life but he did not compromise with the society. It was better to die on the cross than to live as a hypocrite. At least on the cross he was true, authentic – himself.

In the crowd, he would have lived, but not his own life. He would have been a cog in the machine – without any individuality, without any intelligence of his own, without any realization of truth, significance, beauty and the immense grace of existence.

He could have saved his life but in fact, *that* would have been crucifixion. He accepted being crucified – that was saving his life – fearlessly, trusting in existence, without any anger against the crowd. Even at the last moment on the cross, he was praying for the crowd: "Father, forgive them. They know not what they are doing. They are unconscious people. One cannot expect from unconscious people anything more."

He was only thirty-three; a long life was ahead of him. But this is the beauty of the man, that he sacrificed that long life which would have been meaningless, false, pseudo, for something authentic, real – without any complaint, without any grudge against anybody.

First, the parents exploit the child because he cannot even conceive that they will be deceiving him – and it is not that the parents deceive the child intentionally. They are unconscious. They have also been deceived by their parents.

Every generation has been corrupting every new generation. The parents don't know whether God exists or not, but they pretend before the child as if God exists; they take him to the church, or to the synagogue, or to the temple. Neither they know nor their rabbis and their bishops and their priests know.

It is a very mad world.

Blind people are leading other blind people.

And nobody raises the question: where are we going and why?

From the very beginning I refused to believe in anything unless I was convinced. Everybody was irritated with me – and I was not doing any harm to anybody. They wanted me to go to the temple. They wanted me to touch the feet of somebody they thought was a saint.

I said, "I don't have any objection. I can touch his feet. I can even touch his head, but at least I must know why I am doing it. What qualities has this man got?"

And the replies I got were so ridiculous... "Because this man has renounced the world."

So I said, "That simply proves this man is a coward. He's an escapist. And if he has renounced the world then what is he doing here? This too is the world!

"He may have left his house but now he's staying in somebody else's house. He has simply renounced his responsibilities. He has left his wife and his children. The children will become beggars, the wife will become a prostitute, and who is responsibile for it? And this man has become a parasite, because he is not doing anything. His whole job is to let people touch his feet."

My father stopped taking me. But I would follow him and he would say, "Listen, you are not to come with me."

I said, "I am not coming with you. And this road does not belong to you. I don't know where you are going and I don't even want to know. Neither do you need to be worried about me. It is just coincidence that you happen to be ahead of me and I happen to be behind you."

He would stop. I would stop. He said, "This is not good, creating unnecessary fuss in the marketplace."

I said, "*You* are creating, I was walking silently. I have not raised a single question. Why have you stopped? And if you can stop without my permission, why can't I stop without your permission? It is a government road."

And finally I would reach wherever he was going, and as we were coming near the temple, or near the place where some saint was staying, he would start persuading me, "Okay, you have come but keep quiet."

I said, "If I see something stupid, I cannot keep quiet. I need honest answers."

He said, "It seems I will have to stop going to the temple, going to the saints – just because of you!"

I said, "It does not matter, I can go without you. And I will create *more* trouble because these people you are worshiping are the ugliest people I have seen."

The Hindu saints have such big bellies that one has to decide whether the man has the belly or the belly has the man. And these are the people who have renounced the world! So I used to ask: "What is the matter with his belly, is he pregnant?"

The simple fact is, the people who renounce sex start eating more and more, as a substitute. Food becomes their obsession. These big bellies of Hindu saints are nothing but symbolic of repressed sex.

And you are worshiping these psychologically sick people. I don't see any light in their eyes, I don't see any grace in their faces. I don't see any authority in their words. They quote scriptures. Their whole "being" is within inverted commas – they don't know anything on their own.

Gautam Buddha may have known, but to repeat his words does not mean that you are also a knower. Those words can be repeated by a parrot, too. But the parrot cannot become a buddha.

I would go with my grandfather to the temples, and I would see people worshiping dead, stone statues – what kind of humanity have we created – just because somebody has said that "This statue is the statue of God."

Nobody has seen God. No photographer has even taken a single photograph. How have these sculptors managed to make these statues? Just pure imagination.

Gautam Buddha died twenty-five centuries ago, and his first statue was made after his death, five hundred years later. There was not even an eyewitness alive. And you will be surprised to know that it was at the time when Alexander the Great came to India, and all Gautam Buddha's statues have the face of Alexander the Great!

Alexander was a beautiful man, young and powerful. He attracted the painters, the sculptors, and he became the prototype for Gautam Buddha, for Mahavira, for the twenty-four *teerthankaras* of the Jainas. None of them have the Indian face; the face is Greek.

But my grandfather would say, "Don't talk such things. If somebody hears, they will think that I have brought you basically to create trouble."

I said, "You are wrong. You have not brought me, you have come with me. I was coming myself. From where have you got the idea that you have brought me? And unless somebody proves to me that these statues are of Buddha, or Mahavira, why should I be expected to worship them? In fact, they should be removed! They are statues of Alexander the Great, one of the maddest men the world has known – who had the ambition to conquer the whole world.

"And these people – Buddha and Mahavira and others – were against ambition, against desire. They renounced their kingdoms, and what a strange fate: instead of their own statues, statues of Alexander are being worshiped in all the temples of India."

But naturally parents are powerful, more knowledgeable, and children are helpless, innocent. You can go on stuffing into their heads any nonsense. And by the time they mature, that nonsense will have become so deep-rooted that they will be ready to fight for it, they will be ready to kill for it or be killed for it.

What are religious wars? People are fighting about such fictions – "God." None of them has known God, neither the Christians nor the Mohammedans, but they are fighting that their god is right and your god is wrong.

Simplified, they are saying, "We are right. You are wrong." And that would be far more clear, that it is a fight of egos, it is not a religious war. It is not a crusade. Everybody wants to prove his ego to be right, and that can be proved only if he proves that everybody else's ego is wrong. Then he attains to a superiority, he becomes higher, holier.

So first, it is the simple trust of the child. And second...your observation, Pratito, is absolutely correct. Second, it is fear.

The parents can punish you; they can deprive you. Teachers can punish you. You have to accept whatever is being said by those who have power of some kind. In this way, everybody has been distracted, derailed from his natural path. And he has moved in a direction which was not meant for him.

That's why there is always anxiety, anguish and a deep sadness. This sadness is existential: unless you can be your natural self, the spring will never come to you, the flowers will never blossom in your being, love will never grow.

You will never know the glory of life and the splendor of consciousness.

You are saying, "Now all has peeled off." This is my whole work here – just peeling the onions. Peeling to the point where nothing remains – just spaciousness and silence.

Because an onion is nothing but layers and layers and layers, and when the final layer is taken off, your hands are empty.

In those empty hands descends the whole glory, the whole kingdom of God.

You have not to be standing in the way, you have to give way so that God can enter in.

You have to open the windows and doors so that fresh winds can come in and the life-giving sun rays can dance inside and the room becomes alive.

Your beliefs, your traditions, your scriptures, your religions – all are closing your being from all sides. No fresh air, no sun rays, no fragrance coming with the air, no life dancing inside you with the sunrays – how can you be happy? How can you be blissful? You have carved a grave for yourself. Alive, you are living inside the grave. Anybody who is a Christian or a Hindu or a Mohammedan or a Buddhist, is living in a grave. He is no more alive.

It is good that you were courageous enough

to drop all the layers of the onion.

"I have walked through the pain." Yes, there is pain because all those beliefs, thoughts, philosophies, have become so much part of you that it is not like taking your clothes off – it is something like taking your skin off. It is painful.

But this pain is worth it. It is almost the pain of a surgery, to remove the cancer from your soul. And once you have passed through the pain, the fear is gone, the ambition is gone.

Pratito, your observation is immensely significant for everybody, because all ambition is out of fear. All ambition is out of an inferiority complex, because you are afraid to be yourself. You want to be somebody else – a president of a country, a prime minister of a country, the richest man...and people find different ways because so many people cannot be the president, cannot be the richest, cannot be the prime ministers. Then they create a Rotary Club.

Man's stupidity knows no limits. In a Rotary Club, the presidents go in rotation. Everybody becomes the president, everybody's ambition is fulfilled. But the Rotary Club chooses only the topmost people from every profession. What about others? They create a Lions Club! And there are many other clubs. Their whole function is to give you some solace, that you are a president, that you are a secretary, that you are not just nobody.

The Hindu *shankaracharyas*, who are equal to the Christian popes, call themselves "world teachers" – *jagat guru*. I used to live in a place – Raipur. And I was surprised that a man in that city called himself Jagat Guru, the "world teacher." And he was not a shankaracharya.

Even the shankaracharyas are not *jagat guru*, because the whole world does not recognize them as masters. Even the pope, who has the greatest number of followers in the world – seven hundred million people – cannot call himself a world teacher. And this man was living just close by my house. So one day, I went there.

He was having a massage session; one of his disciples was massaging him. So I asked him, "I heard so much about you; just one problem has been puzzling me. How did you become the world teacher, Jagat Guru?"

He said, "It is a long story."

I said, "Howsoever long it is, you tell it."

And it turned out to be the shortest story I have heard! The whole story was that the man who was massaging him, was named Jagat. And this was his only teacher, and he was his only disciple, so somebody suggested, "Why don't you call yourself Jagat Guru?" And the idea was really very fulfilling! He started calling himself Jagat Guru.

I said, "This is absolutely logical. In fact, the shankaracharyas are not Jagat guru, *you* are. But you were saying the story is very long – the story is so short, only two persons!"

Man is in search of being *somebody*.

He cannot allow himself just to be himself.

Just to be himself means *nobody*.

I was a professor in a university, and just near my quarter lived the head of the economics department. And I was wondering: he was an Indian but his name was Doctor Gilbert Shaw. This is a strange name because in India...*Gilbert Shaw?*

Finally, I introduced myself to him. And I asked him, "Just one enquiry I have, that's why I have come to you. How come you have got such a strange name, Dr. Gilbert Shaw?"

He became serious. But I said, "You will have to tell me. Otherwise, I am going to come every day and I will make it known to everybody else in the unversity: 'Ask how this man has become Gilbert Shaw.' So you simply tell me."

He became afraid – he said, "You don't tell anybody because I have been here for two years and nobody has enquired. The reality is, my name used to be Gither Sahai. But when I went to London for my Ph.D., I changed to Gilbert Shaw. And when I came back...it looks more prestigious. Just the name seems to be impressive to people – Gilbert Shaw. Gither Sahai...there are so many Gither Sahais." Gither is one of the names of Krishna, and Sahai is his caste.

Seeing thousands of people, I have come to know such sick minds. Even changing the name, giving it some color so that it looks Western – as if he is the son of George Bernard Shaw, or at least some faraway relative.

People want to be somebody. But it is out of fear. The fear is that nobody knows you; whether you exist or not makes no difference to the world. Whether you have been here or not, nobody will remember.

People are not interested in living but being remembered.

What use is it to be remembered when you are dead?

"...Knowing about this whole journey with open eyes I am sitting under the sky drinking the sweet splendor day and night. Bhagwan, there seems to be no darkness, no end, sometimes not even me."

There is no darkness.

Darkness is only less light.

Our eyes are not capable, but there are animals, owls, who can see in the night – it is their day. In the morning comes their night, because their eyes are so delicate that they cannot open their eyes in the hot sun rays. So the whole day long, they are in darkness and the whole night they are in light. The difference between darkness and light is only of degree.

It is the same as the difference between coldness and hotness: the same thermometer can show you how much is the temperature. Is it cold or is it hot? – the difference is only of degrees. Wherever you see opposite things, remember: the difference is only of degree. There is no opposition anywhere. There is nothing contradictory.

And certainly there is no end, because there is no beginning. Existence has always been there, is there, will be there, and we are part of it. Forms may have changed, but the essential reality remains the same.

And you say, "Sometimes not even me." What is happening sometimes will soon become a permanent recognition that you are not. Only existence is.

But the first glimpses have started coming to you. You are right, the circle is complete. You are again becoming innocent, full of wonder. This is the rebirth Jesus used to tell of – "unless you are born again, in this very life, you will not attain the kingdom of God."

Before death comes, everybody has to become a child again. Then there is no death; then you die consciously, knowing perfectly well that only the body which has become old and useless, is being renewed. You are moving your house.

The only problem in attaining to your childhood again is that what, because of trust and because of fear, you have accepted from the family, from the society, from the church, from the school – all that has to be dropped.

It needs courage.

But what you drop is meaningless, and what you gain is so tremendous in its truth, in its beauty, in its joy, that it is worth it to drop everything and become an innocent child again.

My definition of sannyas is: the struggle to become a child again. Of course, the second childhood has a great difference from the first childhood: the first childhood was ignorant, and the second childhood is innocent. The demarcation point is very difficult. But once understood, it is simple.

The ignorant child looks innocent but he will lose his ignorance soon. He will have to become knowledgeable. As he grows, he will have to attain all kinds of knowledge just to survive in the society.

But the second childhood comes after you have known everything and known the futility of it and have dropped it. It is not ignorance – it is just a totally different kind of consciousness.

It is awareness.

You will not fall again into the trap of knowledgeability. The first was only negative; the second is something positive.

Ignorance means absence of knowledge.

And innocence means presence of wonder.

A young woman is going to marry a Greek man. The night before the wedding, her mother takes her aside. "Now look," the mother tells her daughter, "Greeks are a little strange. If he ever tells you to turn over, I want you to get out of bed, pack your clothes and come back home to me."

So the couple get married and everything is fine for the first two years.

Then one night, while they were in bed, the man says to the woman, "Sweetheart, roll over now."

She gets very upset, gets out of bed, puts her clothes on and starts packing her suitcase. As she's ready to leave, the confused man says, "Darling, wait a minute. What is the matter?"

Holding her tears back, she says: "My mother told me that you Greek men are strange, and that if you ever told me to roll over I was to get my clothes on, leave you and go home to her."

"But honey," says the man, "don't you want children?"

Beloved Bhagwan,

Again, You invite us to kill the Buddha when we meet him on the path.
You said that the master is the last attachment
and You want me to drop this too, in order to be totally free.
Oh my beloved, the problem is not that I love You too much:
I can kill You out of love, with no pain at all. But the real problem is,
that I like You too much! I like Your eyes, I like Your hands, I like Your beard,
I like Your face, Your profile. And I like the way You walk,
the way You talk, the way You laugh.
I like everything about You, Bhagwan – except for Your watches, of course.
For all my life I've been in search of beauty:
I have photographed the most beautiful women and the most beautiful men in the world,
but never, never have I come across a being who contains both:
the fragile beauty of a woman and the austere grace of a man.
How could I possibly kill You, if I like You more than any sunset, any temple,
any painting, any poem, any woman, any river, any sculpture;
more than anything I have ever seen?
And You must know my hidden secret too:
For I keep coming back in the body to please my eyes only.
How in heaven could I deprive my eyes of the vision of You,
of the ultimate grace of form, in this unaesthetic world?

Sarjano, your question is not a question. It is a statement. The only thing questionable in it is about my watches. So I can say to you, if I meet you on the way, take away my watch.

That will be enough. Moreover, they are not mine, they belong to sannyasins who want me to use them while they are here. And then they can take them back, and they become something precious to them. I don't own anything – even my dresses are not my own. They are also made by sannyasins.

And I agree with you, I don't like these cheap watches myself. But where to find richer people than sannyasins? If you have some idea, either you can inform me or if you can manage, you can bring the right watch, one that you like.

You are an Italian Sarjano, so especially for you I have a joke here.

An Italian ship has been out at sea for months and all the crew is missing the delight of female company. Everyone is becoming more and more irritable. Everyone, except the captain.

The crew begin to notice that the captain does not seem to suffer from the same frustrations that they do. So they decide to spy on him and find out his secret. That night, they creep down to his cabin and look through the keyhole.

They see him enjoying himself with a

beautiful and very lifelike inflatable doll.

So when the captain is not in his cabin, they all take turns to go down and enjoy the favors of this magnificent piece of modern engineering.

When the ship docks in Amsterdam, the captain goes back to the shop in the red-light district where he bought the doll. "Good morning, captain," says the attendant. "Are you satisfied with our product?"

"Ah, yes," replies the captain, "She is magnificent! And she is so lifelike that I even got gonorrhea from her."

Beloved Bhagwan,

Can You say something about the difference in the quality of silence between melting with You, melting with my beloved and melting alone?

Anand Michael, melting with your beloved is the easiest because it is very superficial and very momentary. It is mostly physical. Your mind remains chattering inside and your being remains uninvolved in it. Just a peripheral melting, you can call it.

Melting with your master is more difficult. Because it is not melting between two peripheries but between two centers. It is melting of two consciousnesses. It is melting of two souls in one organic whole. The ego has to be completely dropped. The mind has to be utterly silent. And it is not something momentary.

Once you have melted with your master, you have melted. There is no going back.

And the third is, melting alone. That is the most difficult – almost impossible. Because melting alone, you don't even have an excuse.

Melting with your beloved, there is an excuse – you love her. And melting needs the other. Melting with the master is difficult but not impossible; the other is still there, and you are melting with the consciousness of the other.

But alone, what will you be melting in? I am saying it is the most difficult – or perhaps impossible. There is only one possibility and that is, if you know how to melt with the master, you and your master's consciousness will become one. Then you are alone. Then you cannot say, "We are two." There is no "I," there is no "thou."

If you mean by "alone" this state of oneness, then melting is possible. Then melting will be with existence itself.

But one should start learning melting with the beloved. One should always learn from the easiest. If you are going to learn swimming, swim in shallow water. Don't immediately jump into the ocean.

When you are capable of melting with your beloved in love, then it is possible for you to melt with the master in trust. Trust is the higher quality of love.

And if you become capable of melting with the master, then the master becomes a door to the whole existence. Then you can try to melt alone.

Then, too, you are not melting alone; it only

appears to you that you are melting alone. You are melting into the universe itself. Because the existence is not present as the other – as your beloved or the master – it seems you are alone. But you are never alone. The existence is surrounding you from everywhere. You are almost like a fish in the ocean. The ocean is invisible, but you can try to understand it: you are breathing every moment, existence, in and out. Every cell of your body is breathing existence in and out. Every pore of your body is inhaling, exhaling.

You are eating food, which is your nourishment, without which you are going to die. In the food, you are eating the sun rays, the moon rays, the faraway stars and their effects, the earth. In all that is coming in fruits, in anything that you are eating, you are eating existence. You are breathing existence.

You are not alone. Because all this is not visible, you can *think* you are alone.

And once you have experienced the joy of melting into the master, heart-to-heart, center-to-center, then this third step is also possible, even though I call it impossible.

The impossible also can become possible if you go in the right way – step by step.

Hence I am not against love between a man and a woman. I want it to be as deep and as total as possible because that will prepare you for the second step, the melting with the master.

One who has never been able to melt in love with a woman or with a man, will be incapable of melting with the master. He does not know even the langauge of melting. He does not know even the most superficial experience of it. So start from the simplest.

The master is almost in the middle between you and existence. If you can melt with the master in total trust, in absolute surrender, you will find inside the master there is no one, but pure nothingness, a golden absence. A soundless music. A silence which is not of the graveyard but of a garden.

This will prepare you. The master and the merging in him is the greatest discipline in the world. It will prepare you to melt with existence itself. It will give you encouragement and it will give you a small taste...because the master appears from the outside as an individual but as you melt in him, you find that there is nobody. He was just a window into existence.

Now the impossible can become possible.

You can melt alone. You can simply close your eyes and melt with existence – with the sun, with the rain, with the wind, with the trees, with the birds. You can simply spread yourself all over the existence.

There is a difference of quality in all these three silences. There is also some similarity.

Two lovers melting have a faraway echo of the ultimate melting with the universe. Melting with the master, you have come very close; the distant sound is no longer distant. And as you melt in existence, you are melting in that distant music itself.

So there is a similarity and there is a difference, but the difference is not of quality. The difference is only of degree.

All the religions of the world have been telling humanity that there is a difference of quality, that when you love a woman and when you love a master and when you love God, there are differences of quality. I reject the whole idea, categorically. There is only a difference of degree.

Because the old religions believed in a qualitative difference, they wanted you to renounce the wife, the husband, because unless you renounce, you cannot attain to a different quality of silence.

I don't say to you to renounce anything. I simply say that these are three steps to the same temple. Even the lowest step belongs to the same temple, and is as absolutely necessary as the second step, as the third step. With the third step, you have entered into the temple.

Nothing has to be renounced.

Everything has to be deepened.

Everything has to be experienced as totally and as intensely as possible.

A Hollywood movie queen who had been married many times was to get married once again and went to her doctor to ask for a face lift. The doctor was not keen on doing it.

"I am sorry madam, you have had it done so many times that I do not think you should have it done again."

"Ah, please doctor, I am getting married again and he is much younger than me. I must look my best at the wedding."

"Alright, I will do it but it is definitely the last time!"

After the operation she looked in the mirror, "That's funny, doctor. I never had a dimple before."

"That is not a dimple madam, that is your navel. If I was to lift your face again, you would have to shave."

Okay, Vimal?

Yes, Bhagwan.

Session 2

Just Be Indifferent To the Mind

*It depends on you, how much indifference
you can create towards the mind,
how much you can be watchful.
The mind will become slowly, slowly rejected.
It will stop doing its things,
because now nobody is interested.
For whom to do all the circus?*

March 13, 1987
Morning

Beloved Bhagwan,

Over the past twelve years since I met You,
as flowers of joy and meditation have opened in my heart,
I've also been aware of a dark shadow waiting by the side,
ready to strangle my growth, and imprison me in its cold grip.
Sometimes it has been only half-seen, sometimes almost absent.
Now, in the last month,
it has leaped with colossal force to the front of my consciousness
and revealed itself as my jealousy and resentment.
I am so jealous and resentful of the people around me whom I see
as close to You and more privileged than me.
I feel like I'm drowning in this darkness.
If I can keep it back in the day, it comes in the night.
Please, Bhagwan, kick me out of this space.
My own light feels so small and helpless.

Prem Christo, the shadow is your old personality. It happens to almost all meditators: a point comes when you have to depart from your personality and recover your individuality, your authentic being.

But associations are very old. The personality may have been there for many, many lives. And to have a divorce from the personality...the personality feels hurt, and for a time it follows you in the hope that you will again get identified with it.

But it is only a shadow. It cannot strangle you; it can only give you threats. So don't be taken in by its threats – tell it to strangle you!

Neither can it drown you, but it is making a last effort before it will disappear completely. Up to now it was trying mildly; now it is becoming more and more terrible. It is coming in front of you and giving some meaning to itself. It is creating feelings of jealousy and resentment, which are absolutely absurd.

Here, nobody is closer to me than anybody else. There is no question of jealousy, resentment – against who?

I will read your question: "Over the past twelve years since I met you, as flowers of joy and meditation have opened in my heart..."

This shadow comes only when there is a fear of its being dropped. The non-meditator never feels it. The non-meditator is totally identified with it; he thinks he *is* it. It is only because meditation has opened your heart and flowers of joy have blossomed in your being, that the personality is feeling immensely afraid. The time of its death is very close, and it will struggle for survival. Even shadows try to survive.

And it has been with you for so long that it makes you feel guilty: now that you are being happy and joyous and meditative, you are leaving her! And when you were in misery, in anguish, in anxiety, you used her – naturally there is anger, resentment, jealousy.

Those are the old strategies of the ego. They used to work in the past, but now that flowers of meditation have blossomed in your heart, those old strategies cannot work.

"I have also been aware of a dark shadow waiting by the side...." It is no one other than your discarded falseness, your discarded hypocrisy, your discarded past identity. "...ready to strangle my growth and imprison me in its cold grip. Sometimes it has been only half-seen, sometimes almost absent. Now in the last month it has leaped with colossal force to the front of my consciousness and revealed itself as my jealousy and resentment. I am so jealous and resentful of the people around me whom I see as close to you and more privileged than me."

The shadow is impressing you. There is nobody who is closer to me than anybody else, and there is nobody who is more privileged. You have just to understand a simple thing: one thousand people cannot sleep in my room; otherwise I will have to get out!

And not to give anybody the idea that somebody is more close to me, I sleep alone. Nobody sleeps in my room. Naturally, a few people who bring my food will appear to you as closer to me, but it is only appearance. Those who love me are equally close to me and equally privileged. And it is just functional that a few people will be doing things – somebody will be cleaning my room. Now, one thousand people cleaning my room will make it more dirty. Too many cooks cannot be allowed in the kitchen; otherwise they will kill me.

So you have to be a little more rational and see that your old identity is putting wrong ideas in your head. If you get impressed by those ideas, then there is a possibility that the old shadow will take back its place.

You have to drop jealousy and resentment. Just being my sannyasin, you are so privileged that the whole world can be jealous of you. Just being in meditation, you can create jealousy in others.

That's what happened in the commune in Oregon, in America. Five thousand people being so happy, so blissful, continuously singing and dancing – it made the whole gang of American politicians antagonistic, because people started asking them: "These people have nothing but a desert, a vast desert, one hundred twenty-six square miles. In that desert, for forty years nobody had even tried to grow something...."

It was for sale for forty years, for three generations, and nobody had even bothered to purchase it, at any price. What you are going to do with a desert? And even when our sannyasins purchased it, the topmost real estate agent wrote a letter to me, saying that "Perhaps your people are not aware that a desert cannot support you. You cannot become self-sufficient. There is still time – stop them from purchasing it."

And he wrote in the letter, "This is for the first time...I am a real estate agent. My work is to persuade people to purchase things, but I can see that you are getting into great trouble. The fight with the desert will be ongoing, neverending."

But we made even the desert an oasis. The first day I entered the commune, there was not even a single bird anywhere, not a single deer. And that whole part of Oregon is full of deer – but what will they do in the desert?

But as our people started working and creating reservoirs for water, planting trees, cultivating – within five years so many birds started coming on their own, and the population of deer became so thick...and they understood perfectly well that these people were nonviolent.

In America, ten days every year are allowed for shooting deer. In those ten days all the deer surrounding the desert would enter the commune. That was a safe place, because we did not allow any hunter to enter the commune.

And once a deer had come in and found people who were nonviolent, they became so friendly that sometimes they started creating trouble. You would be driving and they would stand just in front of your car. You could go on honking your horn and they would behave just like your wife – they were not going to move. They knew that you would not hurt them, even by hitting them with the car. You had to get out and push them to the side.

But the politicians of Oregon became very much disturbed, because people who had the same kind of land had lived for centuries in poverty. They could not believe what kind of miracle had happened that we were working so hard, and still we had energy enough in the night to dance and sing and enjoy.

My attorney in America, Niren, is here. Just the other day he told me that now the politicians who destroyed the commune illegally, without any reason, are repenting. They are repenting because...the attorney general of Oregon, Frohnmeyer, was the number one enemy of the commune. He was supported by the whole state of Oregon just because he was opposing us, and the stupid fellow could not understand that once we were gone his support would also be gone. Now he has been defeated.

The governor of Oregon, Atiyeh, was also getting support from people because he was against us. As far as I am concerned, I will say they were amateur politicians. They did not understand a small thing: they should have continued harassing us, but not destroyed the commune. The whole of Oregon's population would have been behind them.

Now Atiyeh is gone. These two men destroyed the commune, and the day the commune was destroyed and closed, I told people: "These politicians will repent because they are in power because of us. Once we are gone, their power will be gone too."

Frohnmeyer, the attorney general, was hoping to become governor; there was so much support. Now he is not even the attorney general. Somebody else has defeated him. And when we were there a very competent man – far more educated in law, has many degrees, Ph.D.'s and D.Litt.'s in law – was defeated by Frohnmeyer only on one point: because that man was not against us. He made a political mistake by making a statement that "I don't see why these people should be harassed. They are not doing any harm to anybody." And that became the cause of his defeat. Against that man, Frohnmeyer was nowhere close – the man was an authority on law. But Frohnmeyer was victorious in the election. And now they are all gone. It is a very strange world.

In Oregon there is a law that if somebody lives there for twenty days, he becomes able to participate in the voting. They were afraid of us, so they were changing the law, which for more than a hundred years they had never thought of changing. For that, seventy-five percent of the peoples' signatures were needed.

When we were there, they had collected almost fifty thousand signatures. But as the commune disappeared, nobody was interested in giving them signatures. The campaign had been going very well. But it was going well because of us – that, they could not understand. Once we were not there, people said, "What is the need?

The law has been there for years and there has been no trouble and the people you were afraid of are gone."

They were so much afraid – as if we were going to take over Oregon! Because just jokingly I had said, "We are going to take the whole universe. What about Oregon? – I am not interested in small things."

Now those politicians who had become great leaders have fallen back into the nobodies. Now they must be repenting, and remembering....

Niren was saying that there is a possibility: "If you want to come back we can get the commune again, because the defeated politicians will support us. And now everybody understands that our presence is necessary for people who are in power to remain in power."

But I said, "Now, to start again in that desert from ABC – I am not interested."

I feel compassion for Frohnmeyer, and for Governor Atiyeh – poor fellows. They proved to be retarded, not understanding the ways of politics. I am not a politician but I can see it clearly: in politics you should not destroy your enemy completely. You should go on threatening him – that's enough – because by his presence, there is immense support to you, from all those people who are afraid.

Prem Christo, it is just a political strategy of your personality, of your old mind – which you are discarding, and getting into a new space, a new consciousness. The old mind will try in every way to imprison you. This is its strategy, to create resentment, jealousy. Once you get caught in jealousy and resentment, soon you will be back in the old prison.

And this is the last effort. Your old mind is putting everything at stake, so you have to be very alert.

Nobody is closer to me than anybody else. And there is no need for you to feel resentment against those people, who functionally have to be in my house. Or if you want me to start cleaning the house and the bathrooms, taking care of the library, taking care of the garden, I can do that. But then I will not be able to come in the morning to meet you, or in the evening to meet you.

In these mornings and evenings, if your heart rejoices with me, you are as close as anyone can be.

And you all can be as close as existence allows. There is no need to feel resentful about anybody. It only hurts you, not the person to whom you are resentful.

Don't hurt yourself. And this shadow is going to disappear, you just have to be a little courageous, intelligent, alert.

You are lucky to be here. In the whole world there are five billion people. Out of five billion people, a few people are fortunate to be again in the golden atmosphere of a living master, of a Gautam Buddha.

I will tell you a small joke.

Marty was walking down the street when he saw his friend and yelled to him, "John, how are you?" John replied, "Don't call me John. Call me Lucky."

"Why should I call you lucky?"

John proceeded to tell him that he had been standing on the corner of 52nd Street and Third Avenue, when he stepped off the curb just as a two-ton safe fell from the twentieth floor. It landed right where he had been standing an instant earlier.

Marty said, "My God, you certainly are lucky! That will be your name from now on."

A few weeks later they bumped into each other again, and Marty said, "Lucky, how are you?"

To which came the reply, "Don't call me Lucky. Call me Lucky Lucky."

Marty said, "Tell me now, why I should call you Lucky Lucky?" and he was told that Lucky had been bumped from a flight to Miami that was later hijacked to Cuba.

Marty agreed, "You certainly are Lucky, Lucky."

The next time they met, Marty shouted, "Lucky Lucky, how are you?" to which he replied, "Don't call me Lucky Lucky. Call me Lucky Lucky Lucky."

Marty said, "Why?"

Lucky Lucky Lucky said, "Just last week I took my girlfriend to a hotel room for a martini, and we made such a commotion that the chandelier over the bed came down and landed right in her lap."

Marty said, "But what's so lucky about that?"

To which came the reply, "Ten seconds earlier, it would have cut off my head!"

Prem Christo, you are lucky, lucky, lucky, lucky – four times lucky. Don't feel jealous, don't feel resentful.

Beloved Bhagwan,

My mind, the monster, distracts me even when I'm sitting in discourse.
It simply takes over and thinks all sorts of silly thoughts
and by the time discourse is over
I get the feeling I missed another golden opportunity to be with You,
drink from You, tune in with You.
This leaves me very, very sad.
What can I do?

Nishigandha, everybody has cultivated his mind for so long, for centuries, that it has got deep roots in you. You cannot destroy it in one day, it will take a little time.

And if you become depressed that you are losing the opportunity then it will take even longer. What is missed is missed.

Never look backwards. Nothing can be done about it. If you miss a train, the second train will be coming. There is no point in crying and weeping and making a fuss because you have missed the train. One understands that what has happened, has happened: now be more alert so that you don't miss the second train. And also be alert that you don't catch the wrong train.

I have heard...three professors were standing on the platform and got involved in a deep philosophical discussion, and then they suddenly realized the train had left. So they ran – two of them managed to enter the last compartment. Only one was left behind, who was standing there with tears in his eyes.

A porter was watching all this. He came to the third man and he said, "Many times people miss – I work here – but there is no need to cry. Within just half an hour another train will be coming. You can catch that train."

He said, "You don't understand the situation.

Those two fellows had come to see me off! In a hurry they got into the train – and they have taken my luggage too! What am I going to do with the train that is coming? First I have to get the luggage....

"And those two must be crying inside the train. They were not going anywhere; they had just come to see me off. But it was all such a hurry, so sudden, that everybody forgot who had come to send off and who was going...we all belong to the university's philosophy department."

It happens almost to everybody, so take it naturally.

You say, "My mind, the monster..." Don't call it "monster," because that creates a hate relationship.

Just as there are love relationships, there are hate relationships. People are not aware about their hate relationships.

I am reminded: In the freedom struggle of India, Mahatma Gandhi and Muhammad Ali Jinnah were arch enemies. Jinnah was asking for a separate country for Mohammedans, Pakistan, and Gandhi was insistent that the country should remain one: "Mohammedans and Hindus and Christians and Jains have always lived together – there is no need for Mohammedans to have a separate country. And why cut the country into parts?"

But Jinnah was very stubborn and he said, "Unless you agree to the separation, India will never become free, because Mohammedans will not agree to that freedom."

And finally, in 1947 Gandhi had to agree, seeing that either you remain a slave forever or you divide the country: "It is better to divide the country; at least both countries will be independent." The country was divided and in 1948 Mahatma Gandhi was shot, assassinated – of course by a man from Poona. Poona is a fertile land for murderers.

I am telling this because Jinnah was sitting in his garden in Karachi, Pakistan, talking to his secretary about some official work and suddenly a friend came running in and told Jinnah what had happened: "Gandhi has been assassinated!"

Nobody had seen tears in the eyes of Jinnah in his whole life. He was a very strong, stubborn, very logical, very rational man. The shock...his friend and his secretary could not believe it. He should be happy; his arch-enemy is dead – but there were tears.

He stood up, went inside the house, and told the friend, "Now I will not be living much longer either. Only today I realized how much I was related with Mahatma Gandhi. Without him, the whole world seems to be empty. We have been fighting our whole lives, and I never recognized that this fighting has also created a deep relationship. Without him I am almost half dead. All my joy for living is finished."

Up to that day Jinnah never used to have bodyguards, because he could not believe that Mohammedans, for whom he had been fighting his whole life, could make an attempt on his life.

The next day, Karachi was surprised: he had four people with loaded guns around him wherever he went. And somebody asked him what happened, because he used to go alone even in the market. There was no need even for a single bodyguard. He said, "If Hindus can kill Mahatma Gandhi, who has been fighting for them his whole life, what is the difficulty? Mohammedans can kill me.

"I am already half dead, and now I cannot trust Mohammedans. Gandhi, who was loved and worshiped as a great soul, as a *mahatma*, has been killed by Hindus themselves. I was never loved as a great soul, as a mahatma. In fact Mohammedans have never thought that I am a proper Mohammedan," because he never used to do the five prayers every Mohammedan is supposed to do. He never used to go to the mosque. He was a very ultra-modern man.

He was never in any way a man who can be considered a Mohammedan. He was educated in the West. He was not interested in the holy *Koran* – he was just born into a Mohammedan family, that was all. And strangely enough, just within one year, he died.

He started dying the same day Gandhi was assassinated.

Hate is also a relationship, just as love is a relationship.

And psychology is now absolutely certain that the energy of love and hate is not different. It is the same energy: standing upside down it becomes hate, standing right side up it becomes love – it is the same energy. That's why it is not very difficult – a friend turning into an enemy, an enemy turning into a friend.

Psychology has become aware of one more very significant thing: that you hate the same person you love. So there is a constant change: in the morning you love, in the afternoon you hate, in the evening you love, in the night you hate – just like a pendulum of a clock, your mind goes on moving between love and hate.

Don't call your mind the "monster" because you are creating a hate relationship. And relationship is relationship, whether it is love or hate.

Just be a silent watcher.

"The mind distracts me even when I am sitting in discourse."

So let him distract; you simply watch. You don't interfere. You don't try to stop, because any kind of action on your part is going to give energy to the mind. So whenever you can manage, you listen, and whenever mind wanders and takes you away, go easily with the mind. There is no harm.

It will look strange to you that I am saying go with the mind easily. Just be watchful – without condemning the mind, without abusing the mind – just be watchful that the mind is going somewhere else. And you are in for a great surprise.

It will take a little time, but slowly, slowly the mind will not wander so much. You will have a few gaps to listen to me; then those gaps will become bigger. And because you are not creating any relationship with the mind – of love or hate – you are becoming indifferent to mind.

Gautam Buddha has made it a meditation. He called it *upeksha* – indifference. Just be indifferent to the mind, and it won't be a disturbance for long.

And it is worthwhile to wait and not be in a hurry, because the very hurry will make your mind more stubborn. If you want to push it away, it will come back with force. You just let it do whatever it wants to do. It is none of your concern, this way or that. Suddenly a watchfulness arises. It takes a little time.

It depends on you, how much indifference you can create towards the mind, how much you can be watchful. The mind will become slowly, slowly rejected. It will stop doing its things, because now nobody is interested. For whom to do all the circus?

Just a few days before...my sister is here; her son had come. Now he is married and has children. The moment I saw him I remembered. It must be twenty years ago...they used to live in Kanva. The chief minister of Madhya Pradesh was also from Kanva. He wanted to meet me and he invited me to have dinner with him, so my brother-in-law took me in his car. And this boy was very small, he may have been five years old.

He also went with us. He was sitting on the front seat by the side of his father; I was in the back seat. My brother-in-law got out of the car and told me, "I will go and look, and make arrangements, and inform him that you are here, so he can come out and welcome you."

It took a long time. The minister was phoning somebody in the capital of Bhopal. The little boy fell asleep and struck his head on the steering wheel. I saw it, I heard it, but I started looking out of the window. He looked at me. I did not give any attention to what had happened. He tried two or three times to look at me: whenever he would look at me, I would look out of the window, so he thought: "It is useless."

When we went back home, after two hours, as he got out of the car he started crying. I said, "What has happened? Why are you crying?"

He said, "It happened two hours before! I had hit my head on the steering wheel. But you are strange: whenever I would look at you for some consolation, you would not look at me. So I thought, what is the point of crying? This man will not even say anything, and even if I cry or weep, my father is out. Now we are back and my mother is here. Now I can cry."

"But," I said, "two hours ago?"

But I could see his argument, it was right. If there is nobody to pay attention to you, what is the point in crying? At home everybody is going to pay attention. Then to make a fuss and cry...although now he is not hurting; it had happened two hours before.

And just a few days ago he was here, and I remembered. Now he has a child of the same age.

Mind is nourished by your attention, for or against.

You just be indifferent; look out of the window.

"It simply takes over and thinks all sorts of silly thoughts and by the time discourse is over I get the feeling I missed another golden opportunity to be with you." Don't call them "silly" thoughts. These adjectives are dangerous: "monster" mind, "silly" thoughts. You are taking great interest in it. Maybe you are against it, but the interest is there.

Be utterly indifferent. It is a golden key. And slowly, slowly the mind will start remaining silent.

And afterwards you repent that "I have missed another opportunity." Never repent about the past because that is again wasting the present. First you wasted the past; now you are wasting the present.

If you have wasted the golden opportunity to be with me, now don't waste the golden opportunity to be with the sun, to be with the moon, to be with the trees. It is the same opportunity.

The whole thing boils down to one single point: be silent. And everything becomes a golden opportunity.

But you are taking attitudes. You are saying, "This makes me very, very sad." You are in a vicious circle. First the mind takes you away; it is a "monster," all its thoughts are "silly." And when you are leaving here, you become sad, and you start condemning your mind.

There is no need to be sad: it is mind's nature, and what has gone is gone. What is available herenow, don't make it sad for that which is dead. On the contrary, make it so joyful that you can take revenge for the past too. Dance and sing so that what has been lost in the past moments is gained in the present. By sadness you cannot gain it, but by being joyous you can gain it.

And a few days or a few months are nothing much. In the long, long eternity they are just like small seconds.

Nishigandha, a Frenchman staying at an

English country house for the weekend was attracted to a debutante, and without much difficulty, seduced her. Several months later they met by chance at a very select society ball. He stepped forward with outstretched hand, but she walked straight past him without acknowledgement. As soon as he could, the Frenchman cornered her and said, "Surely you remember me?"

"Of course I do young man, but you are not to assume that in England a one-night frolic constitutes an introduction."

In a way she is right. Just a one-night frolic cannot be an introduction. The reality is that you may be living with your wife for thirty or forty years – even then you are strangers, you are not introduced to each other yet.

You have lived with the mind for centuries, for many, many lives, yet you are not introduced to it. You don't know its workings, you don't know its strategies. The repentance afterwards is also part of your mind; the sadness afterwards is also part of your mind. So you are moving in a vicious circle: first you miss the opportunity, then you abuse the mind, call the mind names: it is a "monster," the thoughts are "silly," then you become sad. And this whole game is of the mind.

You have to detach yourself and be a witness. Let the mind do whatsoever it is doing, but don't get identified with it. It is not you. You are pure awareness.

You are just awareness.

If you can remember only this much.... Gautam Buddha has used the words *samma sati* – right remembrance – and the mind will disappear with all its silliness, sadness, monstrosity. A single thing you have to keep: a remembering that "I am not the mind." You are not to say to yourself, "I am not the mind." The moment you say it, it becomes part of the mind, because language belongs to the mind. You have to remember it without any language, just a feel: I am not the mind.

I am using words because I have to tell you, but you are not to use words. You have just to be aware and remember without using language.

The mind will go. It has always happened. You cannot be an exception.

Okay, Vimal?

Yes, Bhagwan.

Session 3

Don't Make Life A Question-Answer Game

*This is the place where philosophy and authentic mysticism
take separate paths.
Philosophy goes after questions, answers,
and never reaches any conclusion.
Mysticism simply drops the mind, because it is
nothing but a question-creating mechanism,
and moves into silence. And the most amazing thing in life
is that then, when there is no question,
you have found the answer.*

March 13, 1987
Evening

Beloved Bhagwan,

You took my heart and now it is too late;
I am enjoying aloneness and laziness so much that sometimes I think
there must be something wrong with me.
I feel I am at the beginning of a new journey,
and there is a question that keeps on coming up:
what is the difference between being a watcher,
and the feeling of "I am not that"?

Prem Anugraho, it is not true that I have taken your heart. You have given it to me. If I had taken it, it would not be too late; because you have given it to me, it is certainly too late!

The master takes nothing from the disciple. The disciple gives everything, including himself. The master gives an opportunity for you to give. And it is a joy and a bliss to give your heart. Nothing can be more precious a present, and there is no other way to show your gratitude.

But in any case, your heart is gone!

And you are saying, "I am enjoying aloneness and laziness so much that sometimes I think there must be something wrong with me." There is.

Enjoying aloneness is perfectly right, but enjoying laziness is not right. Laziness is a negative state. One should be overflowing with energy. One should be at ease, but not lazy. One should be relaxed, but not lazy.

Laziness and easiness look so alike that it is very easy to misunderstand which is which. If you are enjoying your aloneness, it cannot be laziness because laziness always feels a certain guilt, a certain feeling that "I am doing something that I should not be doing," that "I am not participating in existence." Laziness means you have dropped out of the creativity of the universe – you are standing aside while the universe goes on creating day in, day out.

You are misunderstanding laziness for easiness.

My whole teaching is: take everything with absolute relaxation, with ease. Whether you are doing something or not, that is not the point. You must be overflowing with energy even when you are not doing anything. These trees are not doing anything, but they are overflowing with energy. You can see that in their flowers, in their colors, in their greenery, in their freshness, in their absolute naked beauty in the sunlight, in the dark night under the stars.

Life is not a tension anywhere except in the minds of humanity. To take life with ease, without any tension, without any hurry – that is not laziness, that is easiness.

I am reminded of one of the very learned scholars of Bengal. His name was Ishwar Chandra Vidyasagar. He was going to be awarded the highest prize that the British Empire had in India, for his scholarship.

But he used to live in a very simple way, and his friends forced him – "It won't look right standing before the viceroy in the Parliament House, before all the members of the parliament and all the other dignitaries. We will make a beautiful dress for you, we will bring you good shoes." He was reluctant, but they were insistent, so finally he agreed.

But there was uneasiness in his mind; in his heart, there was not total acceptance. To change your style of life just because you are going to receive an award from the hands of the viceroy looked to him like a compromise. It was against his pride.

Tomorrow it was going to happen, and he was walking on the sea beach with a disturbed mind: whether to follow the advice of his friends or just to go the way he always lives?

At that very moment he saw a man come running. And just in front of him, a very rich Mohammedan was also walking on the beach – the man said to the rich man...which Vidyasagar heard; he was just four feet behind him. The man said, "What are you doing here? Your palace is on fire!"

The rich man said, "Okay," and he continued to walk with the same ease, as if nothing had happened.

The man who had brought the news said, "Have you heard it or not? Your palace is on fire, everything is burning, and there seems to be no way to save anything."

He said, "I have heard; now you go and do whatsoever you can. First I will have to finish my evening walk, and then I will be coming."

Vidyasagar could not believe it. His whole house was on fire – and he had the most beautiful palace, rich, with many antiques. He was a lover of paintings and statues, and his palace was almost like a museum. People used to come to see it, to visit it. And just to go around his palace inside used to take hours, because there were so many art treasures to be seen. Everything is on fire, and the man says that he will first finish his evening walk!

And he continued at the same pace. There was no hurry, there was no tension. Vidyasagar could not believe his own eyes, and the thought arose in him: "Here is a man who knows how to live in utter ease. Whatever happens in the world is not going to change him even a little bit. And here I am – just for an award from the viceroy, I am going to change my whole lifestyle. They are going to cut my hair, put it in shape, cut my beard and put it in shape, and I have agreed! No, I am going to be just as I am."

And he thanked the rich man. "You have saved me." The rich man said, "I don't understand – how have I saved you?"

Vidyasagar explained. "I was going to change my whole dress, shave my beard and cut my hair...and just to be respectable, to look rich, just to take an award. And your house – I have been many times in your palace. Your whole life's collection of great paintings and other art pieces are on fire, and you are not disturbed at all.

"That's why I say you have saved me: I am going tomorrow just the way I am. You have taught me the greatest lesson of my life: that one can take everything easily, one just needs a certain acceptance that whatever is happening is happening, and whatever people can do they are doing. What more can I do?"

The man completed his evening walk, and then he went towards his home, but with the same pace. Vidyasagar followed him just to see what else would happen. There was a big crowd; almost everything was burning. All their efforts had failed.

The rich man also stood in the crowd, just as others were standing. Others were very tense, in great anxiety, in a great hurry – what to do? how to save? – and he was standing there, just a witness, as if it were somebody else's house and somebody else's art collection that was burning.

This is not laziness. This is a tremendous centering of being, such a groundedness that you can take everything at ease.

There is no need to think that "there must be something wrong with me." Just change that word "laziness" and everything is right with you.

Words mean much. Just a few days ago, I was informed that in the Soviet Union there are many Mohammedan countries...and religion is banned by the communist party of the Soviet Union. Each child is taught atheism from the very beginning. So the Mohammedans have been in trouble – what to do?

The month of *Ramadan* comes, when for thirty days they fast in the day and eat in the night. To do it will be a sure indication that you are acting against the government – you are still following a religion. They have simply changed the name; they call it "the month of dieting," and now there is no problem. Dieting is not prohibited. Fasting is prohibited.

A Mohammedan is expected by his religion to pray five times a day. And his prayer is such that it looks like an exercise: he bows down, gets up, bows down, touches the earth, gets up again, and inside he is reciting his mantra. Now they are still doing it; now they call it "exercise." It keeps your body and mind fit – the soul you cannot talk about; just the mind and body. In the Soviet Union the soul does not exist, it is against the policy of the government, but nobody can prevent you from doing exercises. Even if you do them five times a day, it is not a criminal act, and it is not religious. And it is good for the body and for the mind.

Just changing words.... And you will see that every word has a certain connotation with it. Laziness has a very negative, condemnatory connotation. But to be at ease is a beautiful phenomenon – relaxed, at home, centered, without any tension and without any anguish. Just because of that word "laziness" the idea is arising in you: "there must be something wrong with me." Nothing is wrong with you.

"I feel that I am at the beginning of a new journey and there is a question that keeps on coming up: What is the difference between being a watcher and the feeling, 'I am not that'?"

The difference is great, but very subtle. When you say, "I am not that," you are not a watcher in that moment. These are the two alternatives: "I am that" – a thought passes in your mind and you say, "I am that." This is a thought. Or you say, "I am not that." That too is a thought. Just because it is negative makes no difference.

But there is a watcher beyond both: "I am that"..."I am not that"...both are watched by a consciousness which is beyond.

The watcher is simply a mirror.

It does not say anything, it simply reflects.

The watcher knows no language, knows no concepts. It is pure awareness, it is just seeing.

Just think of a newly born baby: He will also

see the light in the room, the beautiful colors on the walls. He will also see the doctor, the nurses, the father, but he cannot say, "This is light, this is a beautiful color; this is red, this is green, this is the doctor, this is the nurse, this is my dad." But he is seeing all. He is purely a watcher.

But he cannot name anything, he cannot verbalize anything. How can he say, "This is red"? because he has never known it before, and nobody has told him that this is red. How can he think that this is light? because he knows nothing about light or darkness. And how can he make a difference between the doctor and the father, and how can he make any difference between men and women? These differences have to be learned.

But his eyes are open, and he has the freshest eyes that he will ever have in his life, the best clarity. They are just mirrors, reflecting everything that is around. There is no word, no explanation, no language, no mind.

The same is the situation of the watcher. You again become a newly born child.

At the innermost core of your being you are always a watcher.

So you can say, "I am not that" – the watcher is lost. You have come back to the mind. Only mind speaks in you.

Except mind, nothing speaks in you.

Your heart does not speak, your being does not speak. Only the mind speaks. Your heart feels, your being knows, but there is nothing to be said.

But Anugraho, questions will go on coming. In the mind, questions arise just as new leaves come out of trees. One question disappears, another question comes up. Mind is a factory for producing questions.

If no question arises, then the question will be: "What is happening? No question is arising, something must be wrong."

You have to be aware that mind *is* the question. What form it takes is immaterial. And if you follow behind the question you will be moving on the path of philosophy. You will find answers, and each answer will bring ten more questions. And this will go on spreading. The philosophical mind never comes to any conclusion. His whole life he thinks – question after question – and every time he finds some answer. But the moment the answer arises, it brings more questions with it. There is no end to questioning.

This is the place where philosophy and authentic mysticism take separate paths. Philosophy goes after questions, answers, and never reaches any conclusion. Mysticism simply drops the mind, because it is nothing but a question-creating mechanism, and moves into silence. And the most amazing thing in life is that then, when there is no question, you have found the answer.

There may be thousands of questions, but there is only one answer, and that answer is your awareness. It is not in the form of an answer, it is in the form of an experience: suddenly a great silence descends upon you. Everything becomes calm and quiet. And without any words, without any knowledge, there is knowing. Knowing that you have arrived home, that now there is nowhere to go.

If you look at the history of man...from the very primitive man, the same questions have been asked. Answers have become more and more sophisticated, but no answer destroys the question. The question has an immense capacity to survive all answers: it comes back again in a new form.

You ask who created the world. Your organized religions say God created the world, and the mind immediately asks who created God – the answer is nullified.

And if somebody says, "Number one god created the universe; number two god created number one god; number three god created number two god"...that will be ludicrous, because finally the last god will have the same question: who created him? The question has an immense capacity to survive all your answers, howsoever sophisticated.

The path of the mystic is totally different from the path of the philosopher. The mystic does not try to find answers for the questions. He simply understands one thing: that until he goes beyond mind, questions will continue; no answer can help.

But the moment you are beyond the mind, all questions disappear, and in that disappearance you have found the answer – without words, without language, you have become a knower. You have become knowing itself, not knowledge. This state is the state of the watcher.

So don't say, "I am not that." There are schools which teach that – when you see something in the mind go on saying, "I am not that. I am not the body, I am not the mind, I am not the heart; I am not this, I am not that." But the watcher is beyond all your negations, just as he is beyond your positive assertions.

Remain silent; don't say anything. If some thought floats in the mind, let it float. The way you allow a cloud to float in the sky – you don't start shouting, "I am not that." Your mind is also a sky, a screen. Things pass. You simply watch.

As Adam wandered about the Garden of Eden he noticed two birds up in the tree. They were snuggled up together, billing and cooing. Adam called to the Lord, "What are the two birds doing in the trees?" The Lord said, "They are making love, Adam."

A little while later he wandered into the fields and saw a bull and cow going at it. He called to the Lord, "Lord, what is going on with that bull and cow?"

And the Lord said, "They are making love, Adam."

And Adam said, "How come I don't have anyone to make love with?"

So the Lord said, "We will change that. When you awake tomorrow morning things will be different."

So Adam lay down beneath the olive tree and fell asleep. When he awoke, there was Eve next to him. Adam jumped up, grabbed her hand, and said, "Come with me. Let's go into the bushes." And so they went. But a few moments later Adam stumbled out, looking very dejected, and called to the Lord, "Lord, what is a headache?"

You cannot end questions. Something or other is going to be there – if nothing else, then a headache. Since Adam asked this – "What is a headache?" – The Lord has disappeared, saying, "This idiot is not going to allow me even to rest. He will be coming again and again – 'Lord, what is this? Lord, what is that?'" Since then, nobody has known where the Lord is!

Don't create an unnecessary headache for yourself. Just be a silent, relaxed watcher. The headache will disappear – and the head too! And you will find such a freedom and such a spaciousness, as if the whole sky has become available to you.

Beloved Bhagwan,

Someone once told me the saying:
"All that you put into the lives of others comes back into your own."
It has been with me ever since, and I feel it to be true.
Can You please talk about this? It keeps coming up a lot for me.

Prem Kendra, the saying is true. All that you put into the lives of others comes back into your own, for the simple reason that the other is not so "other" as you think. No man is an island; we are all joined together.

On the surface both my hands seem to be separate. But if I hit my right hand with the left hand, do you think the pain is going to be just confined to the right hand? The left hand is not separate. If the right hand suffers, sooner or later the left hand is going to suffer too. It is not possible to hurt someone and remain unhurt, because the other is not so other as he appears. Deep down in the roots we are one. So when you slap somebody's face, you are slapping your own.

People like Jesus, when they say, "Love your enemy just as you love yourself," are not just teaching ordinary morality. They are stating a very fundamental truth: the enemy is also part of you, as you are part of the enemy. Love the enemy as you love yourself.

Gautam Buddha used to say to his disciples, "After each meditation when you are feeling blissful, full of joy, peace, silence...shower and share your silence, your peace, your blissfulness with the whole of existence – with men, with women, with trees, with animals, with birds – with all that is, share it.

"It is not a question whether someone deserves it or not. The more you share it, the more you will get it. The farther your blessings reach, the more and more blessings will shower on you from all directions. Existence always gives you back more than you have given to it."

One man who was a very great admirer of Gautam Buddha raised his hand and said, "There is one question. I can share my blessings, my joy, with the whole existence. Please just allow me one exception: I cannot share with my neighbor. He is so disgusting – the very idea of sharing my joy with him makes me sick." And he said, "Just one exception I am asking. I am ready to share with all the animals, all the insects, all the birds, all the trees, everything – just that one neighbor who is so nasty. You don't know about it; otherwise you yourself would have said, 'You can have a few exceptions.'"

Buddha said to the man, "You don't understand what I am saying. *First* you have to share your joy with your neighbor; only then you will be able to share your joy with the whole existence. If even your neighbor is not your neighbor, then how can the birds and the animals and the trees can be your friends and your neighbors? So you first practice just that exception – forget about the whole universe. If you can succeed in sharing your joy with your neighbor, there is no problem. You are already ready to share your joy with everybody else."

Perhaps in the same situation, Jesus may also have said, "Love your neighbor just as you love yourself." It looks very strange that he makes these two statements: "Love your enemy just as yourself," and "Love your neighbor just as yourself." George Bernard Shaw joked about it and said, "It is because they are not two persons; they are the same person, the enemy and the neighbor. There is no need to make two statements. One statement will do, because they are not separate persons."

Kendra, this is the essential of all religiousness: that we should be able to share unconditionally all that grows in our being, all the flowers and all the fragrance. To be miserly about it is dangerous. In the ordinary world, the economics is that if you give something to someone, that much less will be with you. And if you share everything with everybody, you will be a beggar. But in the higher economics of life, just the opposite law functions: if you hold things to yourself, you will destroy them. They are delicate. They need freedom. They need wings and they need to be allowed to go into the sky.

The more you give your love, your compassion, your blessing, your joy, your ecstasy, the more you will find that the whole existence has become so generous to you that streams of love and joy are running towards you from all directions. And once you have known the secret – that by giving you don't lose, but you get more, a thousandfold more – your whole life structure goes through a transformation.

But even in our so-called religious and spiritual life, people are as miserly as they are in the ordinary life. They don't know that the laws of ordinary life are not applicable to the higher dimensions of being.

A famous story about a Zen nun is: She had a beautiful golden Buddha, a very artistic, aesthetic statue of Buddha, made of pure gold. And the nun used to carry the Buddha wherever she would go. Buddhist monks and nuns have to go on moving for eight months in the year, except the four months of rain. So from one temple, from one monastery to another....

She was staying in one of the temples of China – she had gone to travel to Chinese temples and monasteries and that temple has ten thousand statues of Buddha. It is a unique temple in the whole world. Ten thousand statues...almost the whole mountain has been cut into statues and made into a temple; perhaps it has taken centuries to build it. She was staying there.

And this had been her constant worry: Every morning when she worships her golden Buddha, she puts flowers, sweets, burns incense – but you cannot depend upon the wind, upon the breeze. The fragrance arising out of the burning incense may not reach the golden Buddha's nose, it may move in any direction. In that temple there were ten thousand other Buddhas, and the fragrance was going to other Buddhas' noses. And this was intolerable; this was too much. She was feeling very hurt, that her own poor Buddha is not getting any incense, and all these vagabonds... "And my Buddha is golden and they are just stones. And after all my Buddha is *my* Buddha."

This is how the mind functions: it is so possessive, it cannot even see that they are all statues of the same man. Which nose is getting the incense does not matter – it is reaching the Buddha. But *"my* Buddha" – the old possessive mind continues.

So she devised a small method: she brought a bamboo, a hollow bamboo, and cut it into a small piece. She will burn the incense, and put the bamboo on top of it. One side will take the incense smoke in, and the other side she will put on the nose of her golden Buddha – almost like making him smoke! But that created a problem: her Buddha's nose became black. That disturbed her even more.

She asked the high priest of the temple, "What should I do? My poor Buddha's nose has become black."

He said, "But how did it happen?"

She said, "I feel very embarrassed to say, it is my own doing." And then she explained the whole thing.

The priest laughed. He said, "All these are Buddhas here. One Buddha, ten thousand Buddhas – to whom it reaches does not matter. You should not be so miserly, so possessive. Buddha cannot be *yours* and cannot be *mine*. The nose of the Buddha has become black because of your possessiveness."

And the priest said to her, "We are making each other's faces black because of our possessiveness. If we could give without even thinking to whom it reaches.... Because to whomever it reaches, is part of the same existence as we are part of – it reaches to us."

Kendra, don't go on thinking about it as a proverb that is true. You are saying, "It keeps coming up a lot for me." It is not something to contemplate; it is something to do and to experience.

Just make somebody joyful and see – your heart immediately becomes light. Let somebody laugh, and something of the laughter enters in you, becomes part of you. Let somebody be blissful...help somebody to enjoy life more totally, and immediate is the reward. Existence is always cash. It does not depend on checks, drafts – it is always cash. Here, you do something and immediately comes the reward or the punishment.

Rather than thinking about it, whether it is true or not, try it. It is one of the truest axioms for transforming your life.

In giving small things, people think of a thousand things. You just look at the beggars. If you are alone, moving on the road, the beggar will not ask you for anything, because he knows you are alone; your respectability is not at risk. He will catch hold of you in the marketplace, where you cannot refuse. If you refuse, everybody will say, "Don't be so unkind, don't be so cruel."

Even the beggar knows the psychology: if the man is alone, he will give you a lesson, rather than giving you something: "You seem to be young, you seem to be healthy. You should be working – not begging."

The same man in the society will immediately give, and give more. He will feel resentful, but he wants to impress the people around him that he is a very generous man, and the beggar knows. The beggar also knows that he has befooled you: you have not given to him or to his poverty, you have given to your respectability, to your generosity.

People say "We will give only to worthy people, to deserving people." These are strategies for not giving. Otherwise who is unworthy? If existence accepts him, and the sun does not deny him light, and the moon does not deny him its beauty, and the roses do not deny him their fragrance...if the existence accepts him, who are you to think whether he is worthy or unworthy?

His being alive is enough proof that existence accepts him as he is.

Any conditional giving is not a giving at all. Every giving has to be unconditional. And every giving has not to ask even gratitude in response. On the contrary, the giver should feel grateful that his gift has not been refused. Then giving becomes a tremendous ecstasy. This is how your heart grows, how your consciousness expands, how your darkness disappears, how you become more and more light, more and more close to the divine.

Anything that appeals to you, don't let it remain in the mind; let it come into your actions.

Only the action will give you the proof whether it is right or wrong. Arguments can prove what is wrong as right, what is right as wrong.

In Greece, before Socrates, there used to be a great school of thinkers called *sophists*. They were strange people. Their ideology was that there is nothing true, nothing untrue, nothing good, nothing bad – it all depends how sharp is your argument. Sophistry was the art of argumentation.

These sophists used to move from town to town in Greece to teach people the art of argumentation. And they were so certain, that they used to take half of their fee before, in advance, and half they would take when you won your first argument with someone.

Zeno, one the very sharpest minds the world has known, went to be a disciple in the school of sophists. He deposited half of the fee and said, "The other half I will never give."

The master said, "You will have to give the other half – because how are you going to find out whether you have become really argumentative or not?"

He said, "I am not going to argue with anybody. But that is not a question right now. First you teach me."

Two years of teaching and the master could see that Zeno was a genius, far ahead of the master himself. His teaching was complete, and the master said, "Now you can go and argue with someone. Challenge anybody, and your victory is sure."

But Zeno said, "I am not going to argue with anybody. Even if somebody says in the day that it is night, I will say, 'Yes, it is night.' I am not going to argue, because if I win in any argument, then I have to pay half the fee to you. That I am not going to do."

Almost a year passed and he did not argue with anyone. The master even sent many people to provoke him to argumentation, but he would always be willing to accept whatever you said. You say, "God exists" and he says, "Yes, God exists." You say, "God does not exist." He will say, "God does not exist, I am in absolute agreement with you. The question of argument does not arise."

Finally the master, who himself was a great arguer, thought of a strategy: he should bring him to the court, sue him, because he has not paid his half fee. His idea was, "If I win, he will have to pay the fee. If he wins, then outside the court I will say, 'Now give me my fee; you have won your first argument.'"

But Zeno was also *his* disciple. He thought, "If he wins, I will tell the court that this was the agreement, that when I won my first argument, then I would pay him. Now I have lost my first argument: according to our agreement he has won the case, but I cannot give him the fee.

"And if by chance I win, I know that outside the court he will ask, 'Give me the fee.' And I will say, 'Come inside the court, because I cannot go against the law of the country. It will be a contempt of the court; the court has given me victory.'"

And the very thing happened. Zeno argued very well. And the master wanted him to win, so he argued in such a way that Zeno would win. The court decided that Zeno was victorious.

Outside the court the master said, "Now give me my fee."

Zeno said, "Then come inside the court: I will give you the fee if the judge says that I have failed in arguing. And I cannot go against the court – that will be a criminal act, a contempt of the court." Zeno never paid the half fee.

Zeno himself became a great teacher in his own right, but he used to take the full fee in advance! He said, "I cannot commit the same mistake my master committed."

Don't make life a question of argumentation, or truth a question of arguments, or love a question of arguments, or joy a question of arguments. Live, experience, because that is the only way to know. Argument is not the way to know.

Knowing is only through experiencing.

A nun dies and goes to heaven. St. Peter says to her, "I'm sure you have led a virtuous life, Sister, but before I can let you into heaven, you must answer one question. The question is: what were Eve's first words to Adam?"

"Boy," says the nun, "that's a hard one."

"That's right!" says St. Peter.

Don't make life a question-answer game. Make it more authentic, and anything that feels right to you, try to experiment with it.

There are millions of people who know what is right, millions of people who know what is good, millions of people who know what has to be done.

But they just know, they never try to transform their knowing into action, into actuality.

And unless your knowledge becomes your actual experience, it is simply a burden and not a freedom. It keeps you loaded with good thoughts, but good thoughts are useless. Unless they grow within you, they have roots in your heart, they are part of your being, they are simply wasting your time and your life.

Don't be like the crowd that exists on the earth. They all have beautiful theories, beautiful dogmas, great philosophies, magnificent theologies, but all in their heads. They have not tasted anything, and they will die without actually knowing anything. Their whole lives will be simply a long desert where nothing grows, where nothing happens, where nothing is realized.

And I say unto you: Unless God is realized, your life has been a wastage. And that is your capacity, your potential – the realization of the divineness of existence. Just a little taste and your whole life will become full of such glory, such ecstasy, such splendor that you cannot even dream about it.

Beloved Bhagwan,

In nature, spring comes, summer follows, and then autumn and winter.
Each time they are different, never the same;
but the phenomenon of the spring, summer, autumn and winter
is always coming regularly. The sun always rises in the morning....
Beloved Bhagwan, are there also
basic phenomena in the world of truth which occur regularly?
If so, can you please talk about them?

Shantidharm, it is true about nature: "Spring comes, summer follows, and then autumn and winter. Each time they are different, never the same; but the phenomenon of the spring, summer, autumn and winter is always coming regularly. The sun always rises in the morning...."

"Are there also basic phenomena in the world of truth which occur regularly?" No. Nature is autonomous, more mechanical than the world of consciousness. In nature there is no freedom, no choice. The sun cannot say, "I am going for a few days' holiday." Everything has to move absolutely mechanically. That's why the sun goes on rising from the east. Otherwise, in millions of years, it must have become tired and bored. It may have thought sometimes to rise from the west, or from the south, or from the north – or not to rise at all.

Nature is following a fixed routine. Consciousness is, intrinsically, freedom. So in the world of consciousness there is no regularity.

Sometimes it happens at one point of history that there are a dozen enlightened people. For example, it happened at the time of Gautam Buddha. Just at the same time there was Lao Tzu in China, and Chuang Tzu and Lieh Tzu; in Greece, there were Socrates, Pythagoras, Heraclitus, Plotinus; in India, Mahavira and eight other teachers of the same status. And perhaps in other countries...in Iran there was Zarathustra.

That was twenty-five centuries ago. Suddenly a tremendous spring came – so many enlightened people, such a cool breeze, such calmness, such consciousness. The earth was so fragrant that in India we called that age "the golden age." Never before or after has man reached to such a peak of consciousness. And then for centuries it was just a dark night.

Then in the middle ages, again there was an explosion: Kabir, Dadu, Nanak, Farid, Mansoor, Jalaluddin Rumi, and many others in China and Japan of the same quality of enlightenment. And then again the spring did not come. There seems to be no regularity.

On the contrary, there seems to be one thing: that whenever there is one enlightened person, then many people's consciousness is triggered. One person's enlightenment becomes an evidence and a proof of your hidden splendor, of which you were not aware.

But that man's splendor makes you confident about yourself – because you are also a human being, belonging to the same state of consciousness. He has discovered himself, while you have remained asleep. He has become awakened, while you have not been alert that it is dawn and time to wake up.

One thing is certain: that whenever one person is there, then in many places; many people – perhaps in faraway places; it does not matter whether those people are close to that person – wherever there are boundary cases, people who are just lightly asleep, a small shaking and they will wake up. So whenever there is one enlightened person, many people around the world start waking up. He triggers a process in the whole universe.

But there is no regularity. It is not that in every century there will be so many people enlightened, or every year there will come a season when people will become enlightened. There is no season, no spring for enlightenment. One can become enlightened any time.

But if somebody is already enlightened, your enlightenment becomes very easy. He has already broken the ice, he has already made a footpath. All that you need is a little courage to go alone, leaving the crowd behind.

The crowd is fast asleep, and I think it will remain asleep forever. Sleep is comfortable, dreams are beautiful – why bother to be awake? Because with awakening comes responsibility, with awakening comes freedom. With awakening, suddenly you find yourself alone with the whole world condemning you.

It happened in the beginning of this century, an actual case: In Mexico, in a faraway part of the mountains, there lived a small tribe of three hundred people who were all blind. It was very strange. Not a single person had eyes; all were blind.

One young scientist heard about the tribe and went there to find out the reason. And then he was even more surprised, because every child was born with eyes – not blind – but within three or four months' time, he would become blind.

The young scientist discovered that there was a fly in that forest, and its bite was making young children blind. And that fly was so common a fly, that it was almost impossible to keep your eyesight. But the poison of that fly was able to make a person blind only before he was six months of age. After that he was strong enough, and the fly could not affect his eyes, but six months were enough.

So, for six months some babies remained with eyes – a few for five months, a few for one month, a few for a few days – but by the sixth month, almost all the babies went blind. The scientist had discovered the fly, he had found the poison, and while he was discovering all this, he was trying to make people understand that they were blind. And they all laughed – because he was such a minority, one man, and they were three hundred, and they all said, "You are hallucinating, you are dreaming. Eyes don't exist."

While he was working with the tribe, he fell in love with a blind girl. She was so beautiful, but neither she was aware of her beauty, nor anybody else was aware of her beauty. Although she was blind, still the young man fell in love with her, and he proposed to be married to her. But the society refused.

The society said, "We can allow our daughter to be married to you if you become blind, just as we are blind. We will have to take your eyes out. So you can think it over, and tomorrow you can tell us your decision."

The young man was very much in love with the girl, but still he thought, "This is a strange bargain, to become blind – because these eyes are what has made me aware of her beauty. Losing these eyes, it does not matter whether she is beautiful or not. And I have come here to convince these people that their eyes can be cured, because they were born with seeing. Just a certain poison has destroyed their vision; perhaps we can find some antidote and they can be able to see again."

Rather than being ready for that...they were not ready to go to the city, out of their mountains. They were asking that the young man should become blind. In the night, he escaped.

The crowd is blind. And to have eyes in this crowd is to be condemned, is to be crucified.

The greatest crime in the eyes of the crowd is somebody becoming enlightened. That man disturbs your peaceful sleep; he starts trying to wake you up. He starts destroying your superstitions; he starts fighting against your ideologies, which are keeping you asleep; against your beliefs which are covering your eyes; against all kinds of your religious, social, and political dogmas, which want you to remain as you are because it is in their favor to exploit you, to enslave you.

Enlightenment is possible for everybody, but the crowd prevents it. Only a few daring people, courageous of spirit, follow the path alone into the unknown. They need somebody – at least the footprints of somebody, that somebody has gone ahead of them; at least somebody calling from the peaks of consciousness: *charaiveti, charaiveti.* That was Buddha's word – keep on coming, keep on coming. Don't stop.

So once in a while....

But the phenomenon is not regular, and cannot be regular. About consciousness, nothing can be mechanical. Everything is spontaneous.

Man's sleep is such that sometimes it is unbelievable. His unconsciousness is such that one wonders how he can go on being so unconscious. Because of this unconsciousness he suffers all kinds of misery, anxiety, fear, slavery, exploitation. He loses all his dignity, all his humanity. He misses all the joys of life, all the songs and all the dances.

And he goes on doing things which he knows are not right, but he seems to be almost incapable of getting out of the routine. You know anger is not right, you know it is simply torturing yourself for somebody else's fault. There is no logic in it, and you have suffered so much – but again you will do it.

Unconsciousness is very deep. And consciousness is a very small part, so unless you have great courage to use that small part of consciousness to transform the whole of your unconsciousness, it seems almost impossible to become enlightened. But seeing one man becoming enlightened creates a longing in you, a thirst in you, a trust in you that it is possible – a challenge to your sleeping humanity, that "you have slept long enough and it is time to know what awakening is." What Gautam Buddha experienced or Socrates experienced, is your birthright too.

Eunice and Frank were marooned on a small island in the middle of the ocean, the only two survivors of a shipwreck. Eunice was a virgin and a strict Catholic, but after a couple of months, Frank convinced her that they were never going to be rescued. Eunice finally relented and gave up her virginity.

After two years, Eunice became so ashamed of what she was doing that she killed herself.

A couple of years after she died, Frank became so ashamed of what he was doing that he buried her.

How you are going to respond to a situation is unpredictable. In a way that is a privilege, a prerogative of human beings, that they are unpredictable. But in a way it is a very dangerous privilege.

Still, it is good that man does not become mechanically enlightened, because then enlightenment will not be your glory but just a season. The season comes and people become enlightened; next year, again, when the season comes, people will become enlightened. But it is not your glory.

Your glory is in your effort to attain the ultimate truth. Your glory is to know your being on your own.

The only thing in life that is unpredictable is enlightenment. Everything is predictable: when you are young you will fall in love, when you are old, you will die. Almost everything that happens to everybody will happen to you. Enlightenment is the one thing that does not happen to everybody, although everybody is capable – but very few people use the opportunity.

Blessed are those who use the golden opportunity of becoming enlightened, because they prove everybody's birthright and everybody's ultimate growth, ultimate flowering.

Okay, Vimal?

Yes, Bhagwan

Session 4

Who Is Preventing You? Join the Dance!

*It can become a great revelation to you, and a revolution,
if you look inwards and start dropping everything
of which you feel ashamed.
And accept your nature as it is, not as it should be.
I do not teach any "should."
All shoulds make human mind sick.*

March 14, 1987
Morning

Beloved Bhagwan,

Of my many fears, the one of which I am most aware is that of intimacy.
I am like a hit and run driver in my relationships with people.
Could You speak to me of my fear of intimacy?

Ramaprem, everybody is afraid of intimacy. It is another thing whether you are aware of it or not. Intimacy means exposing yourself before a stranger. We are all strangers – nobody knows anybody. We are even strangers to ourselves, because we don't know who we are.

Intimacy brings you close to a stranger. You have to drop all your defenses; only then, intimacy is possible. And the fear is that if you drop all your defenses, all your masks, who knows what the stranger is going to do with you?

We are all hiding a thousand and one things – not only from others but from ourselves – because we have been brought up by a sick humanity with all kinds of repressions, inhibitions, taboos. And the fear is that with somebody who is a stranger – and it does not matter, you may have lived with the person for thirty years, forty years; the strangeness never disappears – it feels safer to keep a little defense, a little distance, because somebody can take advantage of your weaknesses, of your frailties, of your vulnerability.

Everybody is afraid of intimacy.

The problem becomes more complicated because everybody *wants* intimacy. Everybody wants intimacy because otherwise you are alone in this universe – without a friend, without a lover, without anybody you can trust, without anybody to whom you can open all your wounds. And the wounds cannot heal unless they are open. The more you hide them, the more dangerous they become. They can become cancerous.

Intimacy is an essential need on the one hand, so everybody longs for it. But he wants the *other* person to be intimate, so that the *other* person drops his defenses, becomes vulnerable, opens all his wounds, drops all his masks and false personality, stands naked as he is. And on the other hand, everybody is afraid of intimacy – with the other person you want to be intimate with, you are not dropping *your* defenses.

This is one of the conflicts between friends, between lovers: nobody wants to drop his defenses and nobody wants to come in utter nudity and sincerity, open – and both need intimacy.

Unless you drop all your repressions, inhibitions – which are the gifts of your religions, your cultures, your societies, your parents, your education – you will never be able to be intimate with someone.

And *you* will have to take the initiative.

But if you don't have any repressions, any inhibitions, you don't have any wounds either. If you have lived a simple, natural life, there will be no fear of intimacy, but tremendous joy – of two flames coming so close that they become almost one flame. And the meeting is tremendously gratifying, satisfying, fulfilling. But before you can attempt intimacy, you have to clean your house completely.

Only a man of meditation can allow intimacy to happen.

He has nothing to hide.

All that was making him afraid that somebody may know, he himself has dropped. He has only a silence and a loving heart.

You have to accept yourself in your totality – if you cannot accept yourself in your totality, how can you expect somebody else to accept you? And you have been condemned by everybody, and you have learned only one thing: self-condemnation.

You go on hiding it. It is not something beautiful to show to others, you know ugly things are hidden in you; you know evil things are hidden in you; you know animality is hidden in you. Unless you transform your attitude and accept yourself as one of the animals in existence…. The word "animal" is not bad. It simply means alive; it comes from *anima*. Whoever is alive, is an animal.

But man has been taught, "You are not animals, animals are far below you. You are human beings." You have been given a false superiority. The truth is, existence does not believe in the superior and the inferior. To existence, everything is equal – the trees, the birds, the animals, the human beings. In existence, everything is absolutely accepted as it is; there is no condemnation.

If you accept your sexuality without any conditions, if you accept that man and every being in the world is fragile…life is a very thin thread which can break down any moment. Once this is accepted, and you drop false egos – of being Alexander the Great, Mohammed Ali the thrice great – if you simply understand that everybody is beautiful in his ordinariness and everyone has weaknesses…. They are part of human nature because you are not made of steel.

You are made of a very fragile body. The span of your life is between ninety-eight degrees temperature and one hundred and ten degrees temperature: just twelve degrees of temperature is your whole span of life. Fall below it, and you are dead; go beyond it and you are dead. And the same applies to a thousand and one things in you.

One of your most basic needs is to be needed. But nobody wants to accept it, that "It is my basic need to be needed, to be loved, to be accepted." We are living in such pretensions, such hypocrisies – that is the reason why intimacy creates fear.

You are not what you appear to be. Your appearance is false. You may appear to be a saint but deep down, you are still a weak human being with all the desires and all the longings.

The first step is to accept yourself in your totality, in spite of all your traditions, which have driven the whole of humanity insane. Once you have accepted yourself as you are, the fear of intimacy will disappear. You cannot lose respect, you cannot lose your greatness, you cannot lose your ego. You cannot lose your piousness, you cannot lose your saintliness – you have dropped all that yourself. You are just like a small child, utterly innocent. You can open yourself because inside, you are not filled with ugly repressions which have become perversions.

You can say everything that you feel authentically and sincerely. And if you are ready to be intimate, you will encourage the other person also to be intimate. Your openness will help the other person also to be open to you. Your unpretentious simplicity will allow the other also to enjoy simplicity, innocence, trust, love, openness.

You are encaged with stupid concepts, and the fear is, if you become very intimate with somebody, he will become aware of it.

But we are fragile beings – the most fragile in the whole existence. The human child is the most fragile child of all the animals. The children of other animals can survive without the mother, without the father, without a family. But the human child will die immediately. So this frailty is not something to be condemned – it is the highest expression of consciousness. A roseflower is going to be fragile; it is not a stone. And there is no need to feel bad about it, that you are a roseflower and not a stone.

Only when two persons become intimate are they no longer strangers. And it is a beautiful experience to find that not only you are full of weaknesses but the other, too...perhaps everybody is full of weaknesses.

The higher expression of anything becomes weaker. The roots are very strong, but the flower cannot be so strong. Its beauty is because of its not being strong. In the morning it opens its petals to welcome the sun, dances the whole day in the wind, in the rain, in the sun, and by the evening its petals have started falling. It is gone. Everything that is beautiful, precious, is going to be very momentary.

But you want everything to be permanent. You love someone and you promise that "I will love you my whole life." And you know perfectly well that you cannot be even certain of tomorrow – you are giving a false promise. All that you can say is, "I am in love with you this moment and I will give my totality to you. About the next moment, I know nothing. How can I promise? You have to forgive me."

But lovers are promising all kinds of things which they cannot fulfill. Then frustration comes in, then the distance grows bigger, then fight, conflict, struggle, and a life that was meant to become happier becomes just a long, drawn out misery.

Ramaprem, it is good that you are aware of your greatest fear, that it is of intimacy. It can become a great revelation to you, and a revolution, if you look inwards and start dropping everything of which you feel ashamed. And accept your nature as it is, not as it should be. I do not teach any "should." All shoulds make human mind sick.

People should be taught the beauty of *isness,* the tremendous splendor of nature. These trees don't know any ten commandments, the birds don't know any holy scriptures. It is only man who has created a problem for himself.

Condemning your own nature, you become split, you become schizophrenic – and not just ordinary people, but people of the status of

Sigmund Freud, who contributed greatly to humanity, about mind. His method was psychoanalysis, that you should be made aware of all that is unconscious in you. And this is a secret, that once something unconscious is brought to the conscious mind, it evaporates. You become cleaner, lighter. As more and more unconscious is unburdened, your consciousness goes on becoming bigger. And as the area of the unconscious shrinks, the territory of the consciousness expands. That is an immense truth.

The East has known it for thousands of years, but to the West, Sigmund Freud introduced it – not knowing anything of the East and its psychology; it was his individual contribution. But you will be surprised: he was never ready to be psychoanalyzed himself. The founder of psychoanalysis was never psychoanalyzed.

His colleagues insisted again and again: "The method that you have given to us – and we all have been psychoanalyzed – why are you insisting that *you* should not be psychoanalyzed?"

He said, "Forget about it." He was afraid to expose himself. He had become a great genius and exposing himself would bring him down to ordinary humanity. He had the same fears, the same desires, the same repressions.

He never talked about his dreams; he only listened to other people's dreams. And his colleagues were very much surprised – "It will be a great contribution to know about your dreams" – but he never agreed to lie down on the psychoanalyst's couch and talk about his dreams. Because his dreams were as ordinary as anybody else's – that was the fear.

A Gautam Buddha would not have feared to go into meditation. That was his contribution – a special kind of meditation. And he would not have been afraid of any psychoanalysis, because for the man who meditates, by and by all his dreams disappear. In the day he remains silent in his mind, not the ordinary traffic of thoughts. And in the night he sleeps deeply, because dreams are nothing but unlived thoughts, unlived desires, unlived longings in the day. They are trying to complete themselves, at least in dreams.

It will be very difficult for you to find a man who dreams about his wife, or a woman who dreams about her husband. But it will be absolutely common that they dream about their neighbors' wives and their neighbors' husbands. The wife is available, he is not supressing anything as far as his wife is concerned. But the neighbor's wife is always more beautiful; the grass is greener on the other side of the fence. And that which is unapproachable creates a deep desire to acquire it, to possess it. In the day you cannot do it, but in dreams at least, you are free. Freedom of dreaming has not yet been taken away by the governments.

It won't be long – soon they will take it away, because methods are available, already available, so that they can watch when you are dreaming and when you are not dreaming. And there is a possibility some day to find a scientific device so that your dream can be projected on a screen. Just some electrodes will have to be inserted in your head. You will be fast asleep, dreaming joyously, making love to your neighbor's wife and a whole movie hall will be watching it – and they used to think that this man is a saint!

This much you can even see; whenever a person is asleep, watch: if his eyelids are not showing any movement of his eyes inside, then he is not dreaming. If he is dreaming then you can see that his eyes are moving.

It is possible to project your dream on a screen. It is also possible to enforce certain dreaming in you. But at least up to now, no constitution even talks about it, that "People are free to dream, it is their birthright."

A Gautam Buddha does not dream. Meditation is a way to go beyond mind. He lives in utter silence twenty-four hours – no ripples on the lake of his consciousness, no thoughts, no dreams.

But Sigmund Freud is afraid because he knows what he is dreaming.

I have heard about one actual incident. Three great Russian novelists – Chekhov, Gorky and Tolstoy – were just sitting on a bench in a park and gossiping...and they were great friends. All were geniuses; all created such great novels that even today, if you want to count ten great novels of the world, at least five will be from the Russian novelists – before the revolution. After the revolution, they have not created a single novel which has the quality of genius. Now, it is under government instruction. The government is the only publisher; the government scrutinizes, and the people who scrutinize know nothing of art. They are bureaucrats.

The police commissioner of Poona was just asking that before my lectures are published, he should scrutinize them – and what does a police commissioner have to do with meditation? – but that is happening in Russia, and because of that, in seventy years' time after the revolution, they have not been able to produce a single great novel. But before the revolution, Russia was at the top in creativity. These three people are still to be counted as great novelists.

Chekhov was telling about the women in his life. Gorky joined; he also said a few things. But Tolstoy remained silent. Tolstoy was a very orthodox religious Christian...you will be surprised to know that Mahatma Gandhi in India has accepted three persons as his masters, and one was Tolstoy.

And he must have been repressing so much...he was one of the richest men in Russia – he belonged to the royal family – but he lived like a poor beggar, because "blessed are the poor and they shall inherit the kingdom of God," and he was not willing to give up the kingdom of God. It is not simplicity, and it is not desirelessness – it is too much desire. It is too much greed, it is too much instinct for power. He is sacrificing this life and its joys because it is a small life...and then for eternity he will enjoy paradise and the kingdom of God. It is a good bargain, almost like a lottery, and certain.

He was living a very celibate life, eating only vegetarian food...he was almost a saint. Naturally, his dreams must have been very ugly, his thoughts must have been very ugly, and when Chekhov and Gorky asked him, "Tolstoy, why are you silent? Say something!" he said, "I cannot say anything about women. I will say something only when one foot is in the grave. I will say it, and jump into the grave."

You can understand why he was so much afraid of saying anything – it was boiling within him. Now, you cannot be very intimate with a man like Tolstoy.

Intimacy simply means that the doors of the heart are open for you, you are welcome to come in and be a guest. But that is possible only if you have a heart which is not stinking with repressed sexuality, which is not boiling with all kinds of perversions, which is natural – as natural as trees, as innocent as children. Then there is no fear of intimacy.

That's what I am trying to do: to help you unburden your unconscious, unburden your mind, to become ordinary. There is nothing more beautiful than to be just simple and ordinary. Then you can have as many intimate friends, as many intimate relationships as possible, because you are not afraid of anything. You become an open book – anybody can read. There is nothing to hide.

Every year, a hunting club went up into the Montana hills. The members drew straws to decide who would handle the cooking and also agreed that anyone complaining about the food would automatically replace the unlucky cook.

Realizing after a few days that no one was likely to risk speaking up, Sanderson decided on a desperate plan.

He found some moose droppings and added two handfuls to the stew that night. There were grimaces around the campfire after the first few mouthfuls, but nobody said anything. Then one member suddenly broke the silence. "Hey," he exclaimed, "This stuff tastes like moose shit – but good!" He is not complaining. In fact, he is appreciating!

You have so many faces. Inside, you think one thing; outside, you express something else. You are not one, organic whole.

Relax and destroy the split that society has created in you. Say only that which you mean. Act according to your own spontaneity, never bothering about consequences. It is a small life and it should not be spoiled in thinking about consequences here and hereafter.

One should live totally, intensely, joyously and just like an open book, available for anybody to read it. Of course you will not make a name in the history books. But what is the point in making a name in the history books?

Live, rather than think of being remembered. You will be dead.

Millions of people have lived on the earth and we don't know even their names. Accept that simple fact: that you are here for only a few days and then you will be gone. These few days are not to be wasted in hypocrisy, in fear. These days have to be rejoiced.

Nobody knows anything about the future. Your heaven and your hell and your God are most probably all hypotheses, unproved. The only thing that is in your hands is your life – make it as rich as possible.

By intimacy, by love, by opening yourself to many people, you become richer. And if you can live in deep love, in deep friendship, in deep intimacy, with many people, you have lived rightly, and wherever you happen to be…you have learned the art; you will be living there, too, happily.

I am reminded of one English philosopher, Edmund Burke. He was very friendly with the archbishop of England. Whenever Edmund Burke used to deliver a talk in the university, the archbishop used to come and listen to him. It was worth listening – each of his statements was coming with his wholeness, with great authority.

But he never went to listen to the archbishop on Sunday in the church. The archbishop said, "At least you should come one time. I always come to listen to you."

Edmund Burke said, "You come to listen to me because whatever you know is not your knowledge – it is all borrowed, and you are not certain of it. Whatever I say is my experience, and I give every evidence and proof and argument for it. I can stake my life for my statements. You are just a parrot. But because you have asked, I will come next Sunday."

So the archbishop prepared a really beautiful sermon, thinking that Edmund Burke will be present, so the sermon has to be as great as he can make it. But he was surprised. Edmund Burke was sitting in the first row but there was no emotion on his face. He could not judge whether he liked it, disliked it, agreed with it, or disagreed with it. He was very much puzzled.

As the sermon ended, Edmund Burke stood

up and he said, "I have a question to ask, a very simple question. Your whole sermon was, in a condensed form, that the people who live a virtuous life according to your Christian ideology, and believe in Jesus Christ, will go to heaven after this life. Those who do not believe in Jesus Christ and live the life of a sinner, will fall into eternal hell after this life.

"My question is," said Edmund Burke, "that if a person is virtuous but does not believe in Jesus Christ, what will happen? He is good. His life is a life to be praised but he does not believe in Jesus Christ – where is he going to be? Or, a man who believes in Jesus Christ but is a great sinner – where is he going to be? You missed mentioning two very important points; your sermon was half. And I was waiting to see whether you were aware of these two possibilities or not."

The archbishop thought for a moment – the question was really dangerous. If he says the good people are going to heaven whether they believe in Jesus Christ or not, then Jesus Christ and the belief in him become superfluous, non-essential. And if he says those who believe in Jesus Christ – even if they are sinners – will go to heaven, then sin is being approved by the church itself.

He was in a very muddled situation. He said, "Your question needs some time for me to think it over. Just give me seven days. Next Sunday, I will answer it."

For seven days, he tried all the scriptures, tried this way and that way, but...the question was simple...and he was caught in a dilemma. He could not sleep those seven days, because how is he going to face Edmund Burke and his congregation? And whatever he says seems to be wrong: either it goes against Jesus Christ or it goes against a virtuous life. He repented that he ever invited that fellow to come to the church!

He went early in the morning to the church, before the congregation came. He still did not have any answer. He thought, "In the early morning, when there is nobody in the church, I will pray to Christ himself to just show me the light, give me the answer. Because not only my prestige is at stake, his prestige is also at stake."

Seven days, continuously worrying, not sleeping...he was bowing down before the statue of Jesus Christ. He fell asleep, and he saw a dream. Naturally, because for seven days only one thing had been in his mind, the dream was also connected with it.

He saw himself sitting in a train, and he asked, "Where are we going?" Somebody said, "This train is going to heaven." He had a great relaxation, and he said, "That's perfectly good. Perhaps this is Jesus Christ's doing, so that you can see for yourself who goes to paradise and who does not go."

As he reached the station of paradise, he could not believe – it looked so rotten. He entered inside paradise. The people he met were almost corpses, walking. He recognized a few saints and he asked them, "I want to ask one question: where is Gautam Buddha? because he never believed in Jesus Christ or in God, but was one of the most moral men you can conceive of."

The saint said, "He is not here."

"Socrates? He was also not a believer in any god, but was a man of great virtue."

"He is also not here."

And he said, "Why does this whole paradise look like a ruin? And saints look like the dead; there seems to be no joy. I used to think that angels go on singing with their harps. I don't see any angels, any harps, any song, any dance – just a few dull and dead saints sitting under the trees."

And whoever he asked, said: "Don't bother us. We are tired."

Just an idea came into his mind at that moment that perhaps there is a train going to hell, also. So he rushed back to the station, and the train was standing at the platform, ready to leave for hell. He entered the train, and as the hell started coming closer, he was even more puzzled. The wind was fragrant with flowers. There was so much greenery, lush green. The station was so beautiful – he had never thought that a station could be so beautiful. And people looked so happy, so joyous. He said, "My god, is there something wrong or what?"

He enquired, "Is this really hell?"

They said, "It used to be. Before Gautam Buddha, Socrates, Epicurus, Mahavira, Lao Tzu, people like these came here, it used to be hell. But now they have transformed the whole place."

He entered hell and he could not believe – it was sheer joy! The very air was full of blissfulness. And there was dancing and there was singing, and he asked somebody, "Where is Gautam Buddha?"

They said, "Do you see in the garden, he is watering the roses."

"And where is Socrates?"

And they said, "Socrates is working in the field."

"Where is Epicurus?"

They said, "He just passed by you. The man who was dancing and playing on the guitar was Epicurus."

At that very moment, the shock was too much – he woke up. He said, "My god! What a dream!"

And people had started arriving – particularly, Edmund Burke who was sitting in the front seat already, waiting for the answer.

The poor archbishop said, "I have not been able to find the answer. But I have seen a dream which I will describe to you, and you can conclude the answer from the dream."

He described the dream. Edmund Burke said, "Now *you* conclude also! The conclusion is clear: that wherever good people are, there is paradise. It is not that good people go to paradise – wherever good people are, it becomes paradise. And wherever stupid people and idiots are – they may be great believers in God and Jesus Christ and the *Holy Bible*, it does not matter – even paradise becomes a ruin. It becomes a hell."

I have loved this incident very much because this is my approach, too. If you are simple, loving, open, intimate, you create a paradise around you. If you are closed, constantly on the defensive, always worried that somebody may come to know your thoughts, your dreams, your perversions – you are living in hell.

Hell is within you and so is paradise.

They are not geographical places.

They are your spiritual spaces. Ramaprem, cleanse yourself. And meditation is nothing but a cleaning of all the rubbish that has gathered in your mind. When the mind is silent and the heart is singing...just listen to these birds.

You will be ready, without any fear but with great joy, to be intimate. And without intimacy, you are alone here amongst strangers. With intimacy you are surrounded by friends, by people who love you. Intimacy is a great experience. One should not miss it.

But before you can become unafraid of intimacy, you have to be totally clean of all the garbage that religions have been pouring into you, all the crap that for centuries has been handed over to you. Be finished with it all, and live a life of peace, silence, joy, song and dance. And you will transform...wherever you are, the place will become paradise.

Beloved Bhagwan,

Everybody around is blissing out
and this is the first time it is not happening to me.
I want to feel You again and get lost. Right now, the connection
is like a fragile, thin thread felt in some rare silent moments
or shown by my tears.
I'm still full of fear and also getting older.
You gave me the name Pravira – do I still have a chance this lifetime?

The chance to be transformed remains with you to the very last breath of your life. But the problem with you is that you are more concerned that others are being so blissful, that so much is happening to them, and you are comparing.

Comparison always brings misery, and misery becomes a great hindrance for anything to happen to you. So the first thing is: if it is happening to many people, drop the old habit of comparing and being jealous. On the contrary, make it a point that "If it is happening to so many people, it is going to happen to me also. Because they are just like me."

We are all human beings. Nobody is superior and nobody is inferior. If it is not happening to you, you must be creating barriers so it cannot happen. The first barrier is comparison.

The second barrier is...you say, "I want to feel you again...." The moment you start desiring something, desperately longing for something, your very desiring and longing becomes a barrier.

It is something to be understood by everybody: when people come to me for the first time, they don't have any expectations, and things are very easy. Miracles are triggered in their being. But the next time they come to me, they come with expectations. Now the whole psychological set-up has changed: first they had come without any expectations, just available, just to see whether something happens or not. Now they come with a determined desire that it *should* happen. It has happened before, why is it not happening now?

It has happened before because you were in a totally different space. You were not desiring it; it happened in your innocence. Now you are no longer innocent – you are full of desire, full of wanting. And with desire and wanting there is comparison on the side, that "It is happening to others." So you are creating misery around yourself.

There is no need to compare, for one thing. You should rejoice that it is happening to so many people. They are also part of us. If it is happening to them, you should join the dance.

Rather than being in competition and hiding in a corner with tears because it is happening to everybody; everybody is dancing...who is preventing you? Join the dance!

And if you want to cry, let the tears be of joy that so many people are happy – even if you are not happy, then too, it is something to be rejoiced. Rejoice for others.

And drop the idea that it should happen to you again. The moment you drop the idea, it will start happening because you are again innocent.

It is something that perhaps almost everybody

must have felt: There are times when you remember somebody's name but you cannot say it. You say, "It is just on the tip of my tongue! I know him, I know his name. I know that I know...." But what is the problem? Then why don't you say it? You say it is just on the tip of the tongue – just push it out a little! But the more you try, the more it becomes difficult. It can drive you crazy because you know...you *know* that you know, it is on the tip of the tongue and my god, what has happened?

But tired with the effort, you go into the garden, start watering the plants and suddenly it is there. When you were trying, it was not there. When you forget all about it and start doing something else, suddenly it is there. There is a deep psychological fact in it: When you are tense and trying hard to remember something, your consciousness becomes very narrow. And in that narrow space, the name that you want to remember...you feel it is there but it is being hindered by many other things, other memories. And the passage has become so narrow that it cannot get out of that passage.

You forget about it; you start doing something else. Your consciousness relaxes. It becomes wider, the narrowness is gone. And with a wide consciousness, the name can find a way out. With a narrow consciousness, it is very difficult – so many other memories, so many other names are hindering the way.

The same happens with blissfulness, silence, peace, joy. You have known it, and because you have known it, you want to know it again. Now it has become a desire, and you are tense that it is not happening and everybody else is enjoying. So you are full of tears, you think something has gone wrong.

Nothing has gone wrong; you just have to understand. Drop the desire, so that you are again back in the same space in which it happened before – there was no desire – and join the dance, join the song.

Blissfulness is very contagious.

If you join the people who are joyous, you will suddenly feel that your own joy, which was asleep, has awakened. And then tears are not wrong – you can dance, you can sing, and you can have tears of joy.

But tears of misery...and particularly in this place – you can go to any church. Whenever you want to be miserable, the churches are basically meant for that. Entering a church you suddenly become sad. You cannot laugh in the church, you cannot dance.

And look at poor Jesus, hanging on the cross. Just seeing him and his long, British face.... I have always wondered why he was born in Judea. England was the right place! I don't think that he ever laughed in his life, he was so serious....

And naturally, you cannot expect a man to laugh when you are crucifying him. Even the sculptors and the painters cannot paint him laughing, otherwise it will look so absurd – "Is it a joke? Is it a real cross?" So he is, poor fellow, keeping his face very serious – in tune with the cross. The whole atmosphere in the church is created by Jesus and his crucifixion.

So whenever you want to be miserable...once in a while, one enjoys being miserable, it feels good. Go to some Catholic church. Weep and cry – that is allowed. Just don't laugh in between. Don't even smile.

Because the American government is pressuring the Indian government that sannyasins from other countries should not reach me, I have told my sannyasins, "Use all the colors. It was only a device; it has worked. In five years we made the movement international. Now there is no need."

But whenever you apply for a visa, be very

serious. Be Catholic! You can even have Jesus Christ on the cross hanging around your neck – they will not suspect that you could be my sannyasin. But if you look joyous, smiling, happy, blissful – feeling great that you are going back to your master – they will prevent you.

Just pretend a little bit.

You are saying, Pravira, "I am still full of fear, and also getting older." In getting older, there is no problem – everybody gets older. Since the day you were born, you have been getting older. It is not a new problem.

Just understand one thing: getting older is a natural phenomenon. Let it happen – you cannot prevent it. Grow up. That is *not* natural; that needs your conscious effort to be silent, to be peaceful, to be joyful. Then getting older is one thing, and growing up is a different thing. Getting older is horizontal and growing up is vertical.

And I have given you the name "Pravira." Pravira means one who is very courageous. And the greatest courage in life is to live totally, in spite of all the priests and all the people who want you not to be joyous, not to be living totally.

And as far as you are asking, "Do I still have a chance this lifetime?" I cannot say anything about this lifetime but I can say you have the chance just *now*. Why postpone it for the lifetime? Because the older you get, the less is the possibility of being dead. Have you ever thought about it? At the age of ninety, very few people die. At the age of a hundred, even less people die. At the age of a hundred and twenty, nobody dies. So getting older is not a problem. People die at seventy, seventy-five, and then the number starts getting less and less. By the time they have made the century, then they don't die.

So don't be worried about getting older. Just be concerned with this moment, and this space that is being made available to you.

And I still say you are courageous enough to take the jump. Drop your desire, drop your competition. Start singing and dancing, and suddenly you will find the climate has changed. The spring has come to you.

But it always comes when you are not asking for it.

Existence gives you everything; just don't ask.

It gives only to the emperors, not to the beggars.

There are three big game hunters in the jungle in Africa: an American, an Italian and a Polishman. Suddenly they are captured by cannibals and brought before the chief.

The chief tells them, "By tribal custom, I am required to allow each of you a chance to escape. And I have to give you any weapon of your choice. However, I must warn you: If we catch you, we are going to skin you and make a canoe out of you."

Before they even get a chance to get their breath, the chief points to the American and asks, "You are first. What do you want?"

The American says, "I want a gun."

The chief hands him a gun and the American takes off into the jungle. Well, pretty soon the gun runs out of bullets and the natives catch up to him. They shoot him with poison darts and within five minutes they skin him and make a canoe out of him.

The chief points to the Italian. "You are next. What do you want?"

The Italian says, "I want a horse."

The chief looks at him and says, "Well, that's not really a weapon but if you want a horse, I will give you a horse." So the Italian rides off into the jungle. However, he is very quickly surrounded by a thousand natives on all sides. The natives shoot him with poison darts, skin him and make a canoe out of him.

Finally, the chief looks at the Polish guy. "What do you want?"

The Polish guy says, "I want a fork."

"A fork? what do you want a fork for?"

"Look," said the Polish guy, "you said I could have anything I wanted. Now give me a fork, alright?"

"Okay, okay," says the chief, "here is a fork."

Immediately the Polish guy takes the fork and starts stabbing himself all over.

The chief stares at him and exclaims, "What are you doing?"

The Polish guy laughs at him and says, "You are not going to make a canoe out of me!"

Just a little intelligence...and that much intelligence you can find even in a Polack. And I certainly believe that you are not a Polack. You must have more intelligence.

Don't destroy yourself unnecessarily because others are happy, because so much is happening to them and you are tense because something has happened to you before and you want it to happen again.

Something much more beautiful will happen to you if you can drop this tension and this desire and this competition.

Okay, Vimal?

Yes, Bhagwan.

Session 5

This Moment Is More Than Enough

*All that matters is that we all reach our home,
that our wandering stops, that our anguish and anxiety,
our tensions disappear.
All that matters is that we come to the center of our being
where we can be utterly relaxed – in joy, in peace,
in blissfulness and in great gratitude towards existence.
I know no other prayer.*

March 14, 1987
Evening

Beloved Bhagwan,

Is it possible that for some, melting with the master comes first,
and all else follows? Or are You after all my beloved as well as my master – even though
I am not sleeping in Your room!?
Just with a move of Your arms, fire spreads from deep within my body
and giggles of pure delight, lightness and joy follow
like ripples in its wake.
Sometimes a moment of Your silence, or the impact of just a few of Your words,
carries me straight into infinite space.
Bhagwan, I feel that any melting that I have known so
far is out of my melting in Your love – and that melting with You
is easier for me and more possible than melting with any other man has been.
I have never melted in a total orgasm with a man, however beloved.
Yet You say this has to come first, before any melting with You.
Beloved Master, I am scared to expose all this,
but tell me: have I not known any melting at all?

Prem Arup, the physical world has definite laws without any exception. But the spiritual world has no laws as such, because there are always exceptions. That is part of the freedom of the spiritual area of our being. So whatever I say about the spiritual growth, always remember: there are exceptions, because it is a freedom of consciousness.

It is freedom from laws, too. When I use the word *law* in the spiritual realm, I simply mean that generally, it happens that way. But that does not mean that it *only* happens that way. What is the first step to one person may not be the first step to another person. What is the second step to one person may not be the second step to another person. Spirituality recognizes your individuality and your uniqueness.

In the physical world, there are no exceptions because there is no consciousness and there is no freedom. Trees are not struggling for freedom, the stars are not struggling for freedom – they are not even conscious about the phenomenon. Not even the whole of humanity is striving for spiritual growth. Millions of people are not even aware that there is much more to life than they can ever imagine or can ever dream. They go on living as if they are under a physical, mechanical law.

My whole effort here is to break the ice for you, to make a space available for you so that you can see: you have every possibility to go beyond laws, rules, regularities. And no two persons' spiritual growth is going to be the same, because no two persons are in any way the same. They are all unique individuals. And as you become more and more alert, you will also become more and more unique. At the highest peak of consciousness, you are absolutely like yourself alone. There has never been anybody like you before, nor will there be anybody afterwards. Existence does not repeat.

Many people have wondered why, after twenty-five centuries, millions of Buddhist monks – who have been striving hard, sincerely, honestly – have not been able to produce a single Gautam Buddha. And it is not only true about Gautam Buddha; the same is true about Socrates, the same is true about Kabir, the same is true about Jesus, the same is true about Nanak.

You can, at the most, imitate. You can act the role in the drama of life – but it will not be an authentic and existential growth in you, but only a parrot-like repetition. The reason why there has never been another Socrates, another Buddha, another Chuang Tzu, another Kabir, is not that people have not strived.

People have strived; millions of people have strived hard. And I want to say to you: it is because of their striving that they missed being themselves. They never became Buddhas, they never became Meeras. They never became Kabir, they never became Nanak. On the contrary, because they were trying to become somebody, they missed becoming what they were destined to be.

This whole world would have been tremendously beautiful if we had accepted a simple phenomenon – that each individual is unique. Hence, there can be no organized religions. Religion is of the individual, absolutely private, absolutely personal. It is a dialogue between the individual and existence, without any mediator.

You cannot become anybody else but yourself. And there is no need. If you grow and bring your whole potential to become actual, you will produce flowers which have never been known before. You will produce a fragrance for the first and last time, a fragrance of its own kind. You will be a historical phenomenon. Each individual has that capacity, but because all cultures and all teachings are driving people to become somebody else, they are destroying humanity. This whole humanity lives in such misery for the simple reason that nobody is allowed to be himself. Nobody is accepted just as himself and respected. Everybody is being humiliated.

You may not have thought of it this way: to tell you to become a Jesus is to humiliate you. It is insulting. To tell you to become a Gautam Buddha is to destroy your dignity, is to take away your pride of being a human being. You are being forced to be carbon copies.

When you have the right and the potential to be the original, why should you be a carbon copy? But all the organized religions and your so-called leaders have been misleading you. And because you cannot become yourself, life becomes nothing but misery and anguish.

Just think of a rose bush: If the roses are condemned and the rose bush is asked to produce lotuses, you will create insanity in the rose bush! It cannot produce lotuses, it is not in its potential. It is not in its seed, it is not meant to be.

But fortunately, there are no priests corrupting the rose bushes, no political leaders, no educationists trying to impose ideals on the rose bushes. That's why rose bushes are still happy, still have a dance, still bring beautiful flowers, great fragrance. And the rose bush is not jealous at all of any lotus. There is no question of any jealousy. A lotus is a lotus. A marigold is a marigold, and they are all needed.

Existence would be very poor if everybody were a Gautam Buddha. Just think for a moment: everybody has become a Jesus Christ, carrying his own cross on his shoulders. Then everything else will stop! You have just to carry your cross all your life. In fact, it will be difficult to find a Judas because he himself will be carrying his own cross. It will be difficult to find the priest to crucify you; you will have to manage it yourself. There will not even be a crowd to see it, because they have to do *their* work. They have to dig the ground, put their cross up, and crucify themselves. Perhaps people will make contracts with each other: "You crucify me, help me to arrange my crucifixion, and I will help you with your crucifixion." Or there may be some agencies who do the work.

But it will be a very poor world where everybody is alike. The variety makes it rich, and the variety should be respected.

Prem Arup, you need not be worried. If things are happening differently to you, it is perfectly right. All I want is that things should be *happening*. Which step comes first and which comes last in your journey does not matter.

All that matters is that we all reach our home, that our wandering stops, that our anguish and anxiety, our tensions disappear. All that matters is that we come to the center of our being where we can be utterly relaxed – in joy, in peace, in blissfulness and in great gratitude towards existence. I know no other prayer.

All your prayers are false – there is only one prayer which is authentic, and that prayer is when you have arrived home and you feel tremendous gratitude towards existence that it not only gave you life, it gave you love, it gave you meditation. It gave you fellow travelers, it gave you masters, it gave you directions, dimensions to move in, and it gave you the courage and the intelligence. Only gratitude is the right prayer. If you are asking something, you are complaining. It is not prayer.

Prem Arup, you are asking, "Is it possible that for some, melting with the master comes first – and all else follows?" Yes, it is absolutely possible.

You are saying, "I feel that any melting that I have known so far is out of my melting in Your love." The question is not in whose love the melting happens; the important thing is that the melting happens, so that the ego dissolves and you are left alone with your unique consciousness. In melting, your truth does not melt – only the false. So who becomes the excuse is absolutely nonessential and unimportant. What is important is that your ego dissolves. You are, and there is no sense of I-ness.

So if it is happening, you need not be worried, need not be concerned that perhaps something is growing wrong because you are not following the steps in the sequence I talked about. In the world of consciousness, the deeper you will enter, the more you will be an exception.

The problem comes from the mind, which has been conditioned and is always waiting to raise questions to disturb your peace, to disturb your silence. And man has lived in such insanity – and goes on living in the same insanity....

Just the other day, I was telling you a joke which I knew was crude...but man is far more crude. The joke was about a Catholic nun and a man who find themselves on an island, shipwrecked. They are the only survivors.

For two years, they wait for someone to rescue them, but nobody comes. Then finally, the man pursues the nun, saying: "Forget all about the world. Forget all about your vows of celibacy and this and that. Let us start living, because there is nobody coming to rescue us."

So they started making love. A bit reluctantly, the nun finally agreed. After all, a nun is also a woman. His idea finally entered the heart of the woman, because all your religion is only in the head; it never reaches to your heart. It never reaches to your body, it never reaches to your biology.

They were making love for two months and then the woman started feeling very guilty, because her conditioning was such that she has betrayed Jesus Christ, she has betrayed her religion. A nun is a bride of Jesus Christ, and this ugly fellow...but she is stuck with him on this island. She felt so bad about it that she committed suicide.

Two months after her death, the man started feeling that what he was doing was very bad. He was making love to the dead woman. He felt so bad...but a man is after all a man, and he was not a religious man. He buried the woman. Out of feeling bad, he buried the woman.

One of my friends informed me that it was a very crude joke. And just today, I received a press clipping: In Pakistan, a man has been caught red-handed – he has pulled out a dead woman from the grave and he was making love to her.

Now what do you say? And that man is not an exception. It is a fact recorded by history that Cleopatra – perhaps one of the most beautiful women, at least mythologically; but she was a historical person – was raped after she died. And she was raped not by one man but by many men. According to custom, for three days, the body had to remain outside the grave. In those three days, she was attacked again and again in the night by a group of people and raped. She was dead.

My joke may seem crude to you but in fact, I am trying to tell you actual facts about your inhumanity to other human beings, your barbarousness, your ugliness. In a joke, you think, "It is just a joke." I am trying my best to make it as little crude as possible. But it is a strange world....

Holland has denied me entry on one ground: that I have been speaking against homosexuals, and that hurts the feelings of homosexuals. My entry is refused by the parliament of Holland and the reason is that I have been speaking against homosexuals. One cannot even speak against perversions!

Just now, a few governments have informed how many people are suffering from AIDS. Not all the governments of the world – for example, the governments of the East are completely silent, because before you can declare it, you will have to test millions of people. India has a population now of nine hundred million people who would have to be tested.

But from those few governments who have given the numbers of people who are suffering from AIDS, the total is ten million. And their doctors have said that by the end of this century, there will be one hundred million people suffering from AIDS. If ten million people are suffering from AIDS, then what do you think? How many people will be involved in homosexuality?

And when I had said for the first time that two thirds of humanity will die from AIDS, all the journalists laughed about it. Now the doctors are saying that at least seventy percent of people in some areas of the world could die from AIDS. That is a bigger percentage than I had predicted. My prediction was only two-thirds; that was sixty-six percent. They are talking now of seventy percent. But everybody is taking a very hopeful and optimistic attitude – and there are hundreds of other countries which are not exposing themselves, not reporting how many homosexuals they have and how many people are suffering from AIDS.

There may be no need of a nuclear war. AIDS may finish the whole humanity. But I was prevented from entering Holland because I have spoken against homosexuality – as if homosexuality is also a religion. Now, religious feelings are hurt; I have been sued again and again in courts because I have been hurting people's religious feelings. Soon, I think homosexuals will be suing me through the courts. People who are suffering from AIDS will be suing me through the courts, saying that "This man is hurting our feelings." So rather than saying simple facts and data, I try to indicate through my jokes, the reality. Don't take my jokes nonseriously!

You can take everything else that I say nonseriously, but not my jokes. They contain something which cannot be said directly. It will hurt you.

Just the other day, American Catholic priests have come up with an idea. I was telling you that Mohammedans in Russia are calling their fast "dieting" because fasting is against the communist government. And fasting is a religious thing so they have changed it to "dieting." They are calling their prayers, "physical exercises."

But this is nothing compared to what the American Catholic priests have come up with: they have declared that "Celibacy does not prevent us from homosexuality – celibacy includes the idea that we should remain unmarried." That is the meaning of celibacy according to their spokesman: "Celibacy means that we will remain unmarried. At the most, celibacy means we will not make sexual contacts with women, but there is no idea that celibacy prevents monks and priests from homosexuality."

These are your religious leaders! And on these religious leaders you have depended for centuries, to guide you to spirituality.

Everywhere Catholic priests have been caught abusing small children. Homosexuality is rampant. In one monastery in Europe, half the monastery is homosexual, so they have divided the monastery in two parts. They have raised a wall: the homosexuals are separate, and those who are backward and don't understand human freedom...homosexuality is part of human freedom.

A few of my sannyasins have come to me. They belonged, before they came to me, to the women's liberation movement and they told me, "The women's liberation movement is very much against you because you have been condemning lesbianism, and you are converting many liberation women into sannyasins." And their liberation consists in hating men! Rather than being in love with a man, they will be in love with women only. The man has to be boycotted. And if you say anything, it hurts their feelings. They are angry.

It seems almost impossible to say anything significant. That's why I find jokes an indirect way of telling you things, because nobody can sue me in the court for telling a joke. A joke is after all, a joke.

A man decides that he wants to become a monk. So he goes to the monastery and is informed that before he can become a monk, he must pass two tests: "First," says the head monk, "We will put you in a cell for six months. You will have nothing to eat or drink but bread and water. And each entire day must be spent reading *The Bible*.

"Then," he continues, "should you pass the first test, you will be ready for the second test. For this, we put you in a room and take off all your clothes. We then tie a little bell to your male member and then we walk a nude nun through the room. Should that little bell make any sound at all, I am afraid you will be deemed unfit to join the monastery."

So they put him in a cell with nothing but bread and water and he does nothing but read *The Bible* for six months. At the end of this time, he is once again brought before the head monk.

"Are you ready for the second test?" asks the

head monk. "I am," says the man.

He is taken into a room and stripped down. They put the little bell on him, then they walk a nude nun through the room.

Well, right away his bell starts ringing.

The monk says to him, "I'm sorry, but I'm afraid you must leave."

"Wait a minute," says the man. "Are you going to tell me that *every* priest in this monastery has passed this test?"

"Every one," says the chief monk.

"Before I will agree to leave," says the man in defiance, "I demand proof. I want to see ten monks pass this test."

"All right," says the head monk. They get ten monks in the room, undress them, line them up, and put bells on them.

The nude nun then walks through and there is nothing but dead silence. Except of course for the first man's bell, which is ringing like crazy. As a matter of fact, it rings so hard that it falls off. When the man bends over to pick it up, all the other ten bells ring.

Now there are governments who are making laws against homosexuality but no government is daring to make celibacy a crime – which is the root cause.

Homosexuality is only a symptom. Make celibacy a crime and then homosexuality will disappear on its own accord.

But rather than making celibacy a crime, celibacy is still thought to be holy and spiritual. Homosexuality has to be condemned as a crime, because of the fear of AIDS. But by declaring anything criminal, have you ever been able to stop it?

Your jails go on becoming bigger, their number goes on increasing. Your crimes go on increasing. As your laws increase, more than your laws, your crimes increase. And it has been the idea in the past that if you punish a criminal, then other people will be prevented from committing the same crime – which has been found to be psychologically nonsense, because nobody is prevented.

In England, in the middle ages, they used to beat thieves in the middle of the town, naked – a hundred lashes, two hundred lashes, until they would fall unconcscious. Their whole body covered in blood...and thousands of people would come to see it; it was free entertainment. But England's parliament finally decided to stop it. And the reason why they stopped it was: they were punishing a thief and because the crowd was so much involved and so much concentrated on looking at the man being beaten – naked, blood flowing out from all over his body – and there were at least a dozen people who were cutting their pockets! So the whole idea, that beating a thief will prevent other people from stealing, was absolutely nonsense. In fact, they were using the opportunity to cut people's pockets.

And you send people to jails. When they enter, they are amateur; when they come out they have graduated from the university. All that your laws and your jails teach the criminals is one thing: that committing a crime is not a crime, but being caught is a crime. So just be more alert, more artful, more articulate so that you are not caught. And jails are perfect universities, where there are very experienced and seasoned criminals who will train you, who have been there for their whole life, coming and going.

When I was put in the first jail in America, in that area there were six small cells, each cell for two persons. And the man who was the sheriff of the jail had read me, and was very careful: he took every care that was within his capacity to make my three days in his jail as comfortable as possible.

He removed all the people from the cells who were smokers. He brought into all the cells, people chosen from six hundred inmates in the jail – the best people, the most understanding ones, intelligent, educated. He cleaned all those six cells, because he knew that I am allergic to smell.

I enquired of those inmates – "You seem to be very at ease here." Somebody was very old, sixty years; somebody was fifty...nobody was below thirty. They all said, "Outside life is difficult, a constant struggle. And because people know we are criminals, employment is difficult. Even our families don't want us back because they lose respectability because of us. So whenever we are released, we commit a small crime in such a way that we can be caught immediately. So back we are in the jail! And the jail is the perfect place – no worry about employment, food is supplied on time, medical care is available, clothes are available. Everything that is needed is given and all our friends are here. Outside we feel alone.

"Our society is totally different, and here we have such experienced criminals, so wise that just to sit with them and learn is a great education. Once a person enters jail, he comes out a seasoned criminal, graduated. He has learned many things that he had never known before and now it becomes more difficult to catch him."

Condemning homosexuality as a crime will drive homosexuals underground. Right now, it is better not to make homosexuality a crime, because people are ready to go for the test. Once it is a crime, people will stop going for the test or they will start bribing the doctor. They may have AIDS and they will bribe the doctors. In that bribe, they are saved and the doctor is also saved because no doctor wants, in his hospital, patients suffering from AIDS. But then those people are free in the society, spreading the virus – which spreads like wildfire.

But I was amazed that a cultured country like Holland should prevent me from having just a tourist visa because I had been speaking against homosexuality and AIDS and celibacy.

Man is more barbarous than you ever conceive him to be. And man has done to other men such cruel acts that are unbelievable – and in the name of beautiful words: God, religion, nation, race.

My effort here is to make you aware, in every possible way, what kind of humanity we have – and how to transcend it, because it is not only outside you, it is also inside you. You have been brought up by this mad society so they have given all kinds of mad ideas to you.

And nobody seems to bother that man's life can be such a joy, and it is going down the drain every day – from bad to worse. But at least for my people, I would like you to remember: if you can do only one thing, everything else that is ugly will disappear from your life and everything that is beautiful will come on its own. And that simple thing is: learning to be silent, learning to be meditative, being a watcher, being natural and yet alert and conscious of whatever you are doing, of whatever you are thinking.

Consciousness and nature – and just be easy and relaxed and you can get rid of this whole madness, in which man is rushing so fast that it seems it won't take much to destroy life on this planet. Perhaps this is the last century. We may not be able to see life after this century. This beautiful earth will become just a dead graveyard.

So remember: whatever I say, don't think that it is something like an absolute law. I am saying it in a very general way; then you have to adjust it to your individuality. You have to make out of it your own discipline, your own religion, your own path.

Beloved Bhagwan,

Sometimes, remembering You,
it feels that Your longing for me is much bigger than my longing for You.
Sometimes, saying hello to a tree or looking at a mountain or a star,
it feels that they are whispering:
"Don't forget that we love you." Am I imagining, or is it true
that all existence wants of me is to open myself
to all dimensions of its love?

Deva Parigyan, rather than being concerned whether what you are experiencing is imagination or reality, you should enjoy each moment with totality and intensity, not holding anything back. You are not doing that. If you were doing that, the question would not have arisen. I will read your question so that you can understand: "Sometimes, remembering you, it feels that your longing for me is much bigger than my longing for you."

Why should my longing for you be bigger than your longing for me? I don't have any longing at all – for you, or for anybody else. This idea is arising out of your ego. You want it that way: my longing should be bigger for you than your longing is for me. But you are not aware that this is the game of the ego and you are being befooled by it. I don't have any longing at all. All that is past, far away. All longings have disappeared. Your longing for me will also disappear, and only then is there a possibility of meeting. Longing is a barrier, desire is a barrier.

I don't have any longing. That does not mean that I am hurting you, don't misunderstand me. It has nothing to do with you; it is just explaining to you my situation. In my heart, there is no longing. It is completely fulfilled. If I die this very moment, I will die in utter contentment because nothing is left which is incomplete.

I have nothing special to do tomorrow.
I have not postponed anything.

For thirty years continuously I am living in the moment, neither looking backwards nor looking forwards. Just this very moment is enough. It is so much, so overwhelming that I am absolutely grateful to existence for *this* moment, and I don't have time to think about the next moment.

When the next moment comes, I will live it.

But your ego must be telling you that my longing is bigger than your longing for me. I want your longing also to disappear, so we can meet with each other without any longing, without any desire, without any expectation.

The meeting with the master happens only when there is nothing else between them – just a pure meeting of two consciousnesses, of two flames. For no reason at all – just for the sheer joy.

You are saying, "Sometimes saying hello to a tree or looking at a mountain or a star, it feels like they are whispering, 'Don't forget that we love you.'" Again, your ego seems to be the center. Just as my longing has to be bigger than your longing, even the mountains and the stars and the trees are telling you, "Don't forget that we love you." It is not that you love them. Your ego is feeling very nourished.

You are saying, "Am I imagining?"

This question would not have arisen at all. It arises only when you are imagining. Do you ever think that you are imagining this meeting here? Do you ever think you are imagining these lights here? Do you ever think you are imagining my words, my being, my presence? No, the question arises only when you are imagining.

And it is certainly imagination that mountains and rivers and trees say to you, "Don't forget that we love you." That's how you distort everything. I have been telling you: love the mountains, love the trees, love the stars, because by loving, your consciousness will expand.

But you are doing just the opposite: you are imagining that the whole existence is in need of you. They are all begging you, "Don't forget us. Without you, what will happen to us? The whole existence will become a widow." The rivers will cry, the mountains will mourn, the stars will commit suicide.

Again, you are saying: "Is it true that all existence wants of me is to open myself to all dimensions of its love?" But you are not saying even once that you have to love the existence. Again, you are saying that "Existence wants me to open so that it can love me." The ways of the ego are very subtle. But howsoever subtle they are, if you are a little alert, a little intelligent, you can catch hold of the ego.

You were not here; the existence was here and perfectly happy. The stars were not missing you, neither the mountains nor the rivers. And one day, you will not be again and the existence will continue its celebration, its dance, its song. It will not miss you. But don't feel hurt. You have not done anything that you should be missed.

The existence misses Gautam Buddha even today, the existence misses Socrates even today. The last words of Socrates to the judges were, "When I am gone, then you will miss me. And your names will be remembered only because of me. Otherwise, nobody will remember even your names. But right now, you are deaf and blind."

Love the existence so much that certainly when you leave, the whole existence misses you. But what have you done to be missed? You have been only exploiting existence. You have been only destructive to existence. Do you think you have contributed to the beauty of existence a little bit more?

Have you made its music a little deeper? Have you joined in its dance and made it a little juicier? What have you done? Have you added your silence to the silence of existence? Have you raised the consciousness of humanity by raising your consciousness? Then certainly, it will miss you.

But to raise your consciousness, you will have to drop this ego and you will have to drop all this imagination and you will have to drop this mind which is playing tricks with you.

Mind is so tricky and plays such games, so convincing to you. That's why the whole humanity goes on living in misery.

Two Jews meet on a train. One asks the other if he has the time.

No answer.

Again he asks. Again, no answer.

Eventually, he taps him hard on the knee and almost shouts his question, and the other at last tells him the time.

"And why did it take you so long, if I may ask?"

"Well, it is like this. We will get talking. We will become friendly. When we get to Vienna, I will ask you to come home with me to have a bite to eat and you will meet my daughter. She is beautiful and you are a nice-looking chap and you will fall in love and you will want to get married and quite frankly, I don't want a son-in-law who has not got a watch."

Such long range thinking! But everybody's mind is doing such things.

Beware: imagination is not going to help. Howsoever beautiful it is, it is just a soap bubble.

Deva Parigyan, meditate more. First get in touch with your own being, then only you have the right to say hello to the trees. Then only you know the language of how to talk with the mountains and the clouds and the stars and the rivers, because their language is silence, and unless you know that language, how can you talk with them?

And in silence, there is no talking involved but still a dialogue happens, a deep understanding without words, a transfer of energy without language. Trees will not say anything and you will not hear anything but between you and the being of the tree, there will be a transfer of energy – not of language. And only then you will know that you have to love if you want love to be showered on you.

Yes, mountains can love, rivers can love, trees can love, clouds can love. But before they love you, you have to learn how to love – how to love this whole existence, how to respect life, how to have a reverence for all that is.

To me, this is authentic religion: reverence for all that is. And then certainly, you will be showered with flowers which nobody will see, but you will understand. And certainly you will find you are needed.

And it is one of the greatest joys in existence: to be needed by existence, to know that you are fulfilling something essential by being here.

But don't start with imagination – start with meditation. Begin with meditation, and let your meditation make you so silent that you can join with existence in its eternal silence.

There are experiences which are beyond words. Don't try to imagine those great experiences, because your imagination can become a barrier.

Only silence is the bridge.
The mind is the barrier.
The no-mind is the bridge.

Beloved Bhagwan,

What is meant by a spiritual ego?
Is spiritual greed one of its symptoms? Is it curable?

Anand Tarangini, the spiritual ego is not something different from the ordinary ego. Somebody feels his ego because he has money, somebody feels his ego strengthened because he has political power. Somebody feels ego because he has great respectability. But the ego is the same. Somebody feels that he is spiritual – he's a great saint, holier than you – that is also the same ego. You can call it "spiritual ego" but spiritual ego is a contradiction in terms.

I have heard a story. There were three monasteries in the mountains. And one day, three monks, from each of the monasteries, just by chance met on the road.

One of them said, "You have beautiful monasteries. But as far as our monastery is concerned, you cannot compete with us in our austerity."

The second said, "We know your monastery; its discipline is arduous, your austerity is great. But nobody can compete with us as far as learning is concerned. Our monastery is full of scholars, great scholars."

Both looked at the third man. He said, "You are both right. One monastery is very perfectionistic in its disciplines, austerities, and the second is certainly full of great scholars. But we are the tops in humbleness."

"Tops in humbleness...." You can see the contradiction. There is no such thing as spiritual ego. Yes, there is such a thing that ego can exploit any direction of life: it can be religious, it can be spiritual, it can be financial, it can be political. It can be scholarship, it can be beauty, it can be physical strength. Ego is capable of exploiting anything. But spiritual ego is simply an impossibility because spirituality arises in you only when the ego dissolves. Either you are an egoist or you are in the world of the spirit, you can't be both together. They don't have any coexistence.

And you are asking, "Is spiritual greed one of its symptoms?"

Any greed – material or spiritual – is simply greed. Greed means you want more and more and more; there never comes a time when this continuous hankering for more, stops. So whether you are in search of more spirituality or more money or more power, it does not matter.

But in fact, about spirituality, you should understand that the same contradiction again arises: you become spiritual only when this desire for more and more disappears, when you are utterly satisfied and contented as you are, when there is no "more" goading you...because the "more" creates the future. "More" means tomorrow is needed.

For the spiritual person, this moment is more than enough. He is utterly grateful for whatever is allowed to him. His contentment cannot be disturbed by any desire for more.

And you are asking, Anand Tarangini, "Is it curable?" It is a very strange question. Do you want to get rid of the ego or do you want to cure it? If you want to cure it, then you are in a wrong place. Here, we simply chop the head off! We know only one cure: a simple surgery.

What do you mean by "curable"? Do you want your ego to become more healthy? stronger? more powerful? But that will be destructive to your spirituality. That will be against your inner growth.

The ego is your enemy, not your friend. The enemy has to be destroyed – completely destroyed. Not to be cured, but killed!

Okay, Vimal?

Yes, Bhagwan.

Session 6

Only Fools Choose to be Somebody

*Religion has been raising human consciousness for centuries.
Whatever man is now, whatever little consciousness he has,
the whole credit goes to religion.
Politics has been a curse, a calamity;
and whatever is ugly in humanity, politics is responsible for.
But the problem is that politics has power;
religion has only love, peace and the experience of the divine.*

March 15, 1987
Morning

Beloved Bhagwan,

Prime Minister Rajiv Gandhi is going to hold a national debate
on the need for separating politics from religion.
We would love to hear Your vision on this question.

Anand Maitreya, politics is mundane – the politicians are the servants of the people. Religion is sacred – it is the guide for people's spiritual growth. Certainly, politics is the lowest as far as values are concerned, and religion the highest as far as values are concerned. They are separate.

Rajiv Gandhi wants religion not to interfere with politics; I want politics not to interfere with religion. The higher has every right to interfere, but the lower has no right.

Religion has been raising human consciousness for centuries. Whatever man is now, whatever little consciousness he has, the whole credit goes to religion. Politics has been a curse, a calamity; and whatever is ugly in humanity, politics is responsible for.

But the problem is that politics has power; religion has only love, peace and the experience of the divine. Politics can easily interfere with religion; and it has been interfering all along, to such an extent that it has destroyed many religious values which are absolutely necessary for the survival of humanity and life on this earth.

Religion has no mundane power like nuclear weapons and atom bombs and guns; its dimension is totally different. Religion is not a will to power; religion is a search for truth, for God. And the very search makes the religious man humble, simple, innocent.

Politics has all the destructive weapons – religion is absolutely vulnerable. Politics has no heart – religion is pure heart. It is just like a beautiful roseflower: its beauty, its poetry, its dance makes life worth living, gives life meaning and significance. Politics is like a stone, dead, but the stone can destroy the flower and the flower has no defense. Politics is aggressive.

Rajiv Gandhi is putting things upside down. He wants religion not to interfere with politics. Politics should have the whole monopoly to enslave humanity, to reduce men to slaves, to destroy their freedom, to destroy their consciousness; to convert them into robots so that the politicians can enjoy the power and the domination.

Religion is the only problem for the politicians. It is beyond their reach and beyond their understanding. Religion is the only area where politics should not interfere at all, because religion is the only hope.

Politics, for centuries, has been just killing, destroying people – the whole history of politics is the history of criminals, murderers. In three thousand years, politicians have created five thousand wars. It seems that inside the politician, the barbarous instinct is very powerful; its only joy is to destroy, to dominate.

Religion creates a problem for it, because religion has given the world its highest peaks of consciousness – a Gautam Buddha, a Jesus, a Chuang Tzu, a Nanak, a Kabir. These are the very salt of the earth. What has politics given to the world? Genghis Khan? Tamerlane? Nadir Shah? Alexander? Napoleon? Ivan the Terrible? Josef Stalin? Adolf Hitler? Benito Mussolini? Mao Tse-tung? Ronald Reagan? – these are all criminals. Rather than being in power, they should be behind bars; they are inhuman.

And they are spiritually sick people. The will to power and to dominate arises only in the sick mind. It arises out of the inferiority complex. People who are not suffering from an inferiority complex do not care about power; their whole endeavor is for peace, because the meaning of life can be known only in peace – power is not the way. Peace, silence, gratitude, meditation – these are the basic constituents of religion.

Religion cannot be allowed to be dominated by stupid politicians. The situation is as if sick people are trying to dominate the physicians, directing what they should do and what they should not do. Accept it – the sick people are in the majority, but that does not mean that the physician should be dominated by the majority. The physician can heal the wounds, can cure the sicknesses of humanity. Religion is the physician.

Politicians have done enough harm, and they are leading the whole of humanity towards a global suicide. And still Rajiv Gandhi has the nerve to say that religion should not interfere – when the whole of life on this planet is in danger! Not only man, but the innocent birds and their songs, the silent trees and their flowers – everything that is alive.

Politicians have managed to create enough destructive power to destroy life from the earth; and they are continuously piling up more and more nuclear weapons. In fact, three years ago there were enough nuclear weapons to destroy every man seven times, to destroy this whole earth seven times, or to destroy seven earths. A man dies only once; there is no need to accumulate so much destructive power.

The whole of politics depends on lies.

Just the other day – I could not believe that any man who is sane can make such a statement – Ronald Reagan made a statement. He was denying before the Senate, continually, that any weapons were being given to a few countries. And now investigation has shown that he was lying – lying for two years continually. Destructive weapons have been given to poor countries – and not in a small measure, a great lot. Now the facts are there and Ronald Reagan had to make a statement, and the statement he has made, made me laugh – so ridiculous.

He said, "In my heart, I still know that

whatever I said was the truth. But the facts that have been discovered say that it was a lie. I still believe in my heart that I have been speaking the truth." He is accepting the facts, and still, simultaneously, saying, "I still believe in my heart that whatever I was saying was true, although the facts are proving it wrong."

Politicians live on lies; politicians live on promises – but those promises are never fulfilled. They are the most unqualified people in the world. Their only quality is that they can manage to befool the poor masses – or, in poor countries, they can purchase their votes. And once they are in power, they forget completely that they are servants of the people; they start behaving as if they are the masters of the people.

What do they know about the inner world of man? What do they know of blissfulness, of godliness? Still, they want religion not to be allowed to interfere with politics. What about them? They should be allowed to interfere with religion? Is the lower going to dominate the higher? Is the mundane going to dominate the sacred? That will be the ultimate misfortune for humanity.

As far as I can see, all politicians should be meditators, should know something of the inner world. They should be more conscious, more compassionate, should know the taste of love. They should know the experience of the silence of existence, and the beauty of this planet, and the gifts of existence. And they should learn to be humble and grateful.

Religion should be the teacher of all the politicians. Unless politicians have something of religiousness, there is no future for humanity. Religion *has* to interfere with the politicians. Without religion interfering with the politicians...the politicians are blind, they don't have eyes; they are deaf, they don't have a silent mind to listen to the truth.

But why is Rajiv Gandhi concerned that religion and politics should be separated? Politics is a small thing. Religion is man's whole evolution. Politics should be only a minor part of the vastness of religious experience. There is no need for any separation. But the politician, as he is in power, becomes so egoistic that he cannot think of going to those humble, simple, but wise people.

The problems go on increasing; the politicians have proved impotent to solve them. But they will not go to the people who can give them direction, who can give them advice because they have the clarity.

I am not a politician. I have never voted in my life and I am not going to vote – ever – because what is the point of choosing between two chimpanzees, just because they are holding different flags? just because they have different symbols? Chimpanzees are chimpanzees.

They need a deep respect for religion, for religious people, because one thing is certain: religious people are not going to fight the elections – no religious person is going to beg for votes. Basically, he has no desire to fulfill his ego and to cover up his inferiority complex. In his silence, in his peace, in his blissfulness, he has known the ultimate superiority. Now there is nothing more than that, nothing higher than that. He has become a temple; his god is within his being.

The politician lives on war, lives on creating riots, lives on disturbance – these are his nourishment.

Adolf Hitler has written in his autobiography: "Unless you have enemies, you cannot become a great leader. Even if you don't have enemies, create the fiction that your country is in danger, because when people are afraid they are ready to become slaves. When people are afraid they are ready to follow politicians."

Although he was an insane person, once in a while he made statements which are very significant. He has said, "The greatest leaders of humanity are born in times of war." So unless there is a great war, you cannot be a great leader; just to fulfill the desire of being a great leader, you have to kill millions of people.

And he is right: in days of peace, people don't need to follow; people don't make the leader almost a god, so that his word becomes the law.

Politicians try in every way to keep countries afraid. China is gathering nuclear weapons on its boundary with India; Pakistan is gathering armies on its boundary with India – the Indian politicians go on insisting this is so. In Pakistan, they go on insisting that India is gathering armies on its boundary; in China, they go on insisting that India is preparing nuclear weapons. In the parliaments, they go on saying, "We are not creating anything" – but that is an absolute lie.

The Chinese leader has to keep the people of China afraid. The Indian leader has to keep the Indian people afraid. The Pakistani leaders have to keep the Pakistani people afraid.

In your fear is their power.

The more they make you afraid, the more powerful they are. Outside the country they go on creating fictions, and inside the country they also continue: Hindu and Mohammedan riots, riots between Hindi-speaking and non-Hindi-speaking people. They want you to continue fighting for anything – any trivial thing. If you are engaged in fighting, they are in power. If you stop fighting, their power disappears. This is an ugly game.

It is one of the duties of religious people to keep themselves above politics and lead the people towards creative values, towards more humanity. In fact, if religions understand one thing – that the whole of humanity is one, and there is no need for any nations – all these pygmy politicians will disappear.

But the strangest thing is that politicians go on saying that religion and politics should be separate. Why? Why should truth be separate from politics? And why should love be separate from politics? Why should meditative consciousness be separate from politics? Why should a prayerful heart be separate from politics?

Yes, I understand that it should be separate in the sense that it is higher. And the politician is in need of psychological treatment and spiritual treatment, and he should go to the religious people for advice. That was the situation in ancient India. We have seen those days; those golden days are still alive in memory. There was a time when kings would go to the forest to pay their respects – to beggars, who had nothing – and to ask for advice.

Kings used to touch the feet of those who had realized themselves, because even their blessing can transform you. Politics is functional; it is utilitarian. But it has no way of transforming man into higher consciousness. And, particularly in reference to India, it has been such an ugly situation. It hurts.

Mahatma Gandhi used to say, before freedom, that the first president of India would be a woman – and not only a woman, but she would be a sudra, from the lowest untouchables.

But as freedom came, he forgot all the promises that he had been talking about and the power game started again in the old style. Pandit Jawaharlal Nehru was a brahmin; he was not a woman and he was not a sudra. Again, the brahmin becomes the power, and for forty years, one family of brahmins have been dominating India. They have made it almost their personal dynasty. It is no longer a democracy.

Just look at the facts: What was the hold of Mahatma Gandhi over the Indian people? He was pretending to be religious – he was not a religious man – pretending to be a Hindu saint, because Hindus were in the majority and they were going to rule the country. That's why he was insistent that India should remain undivided, because in an undivided India, Hindus will be in power; nobody can take the power from the hands of the Hindus because everybody else is in a minority. Nobody looks at Gandhi's politics: he was using even religion for ugly ends.

Doctor Ambedkar wanted a separate vote for the untouchables, and I am in absolute agreement with him for the simple reason that for five thousand years these people have been oppressed, exploited; their whole dignity as human beings had been destroyed – and they are one-fourth of the Hindu population. And they do the ugliest jobs; they should be respected, they should be honored for that. But on the contrary, even their shadow is untouchable. If the shadow of an untouchable falls on you, you have to take a bath immediately to purify yourself.

Ambedkar was absolutely right to ask for a separate vote for the untouchables so that they could be certain of having one-fourth of the members in parliament. Otherwise, they will never be able to be represented in the parliament; they will never be able to change the five-thousand-year-old, ugly laws created by Manu.

There are great criminals, but Manu seems to top them all. Adolf Hitler was very respectful of Manu; Friedrich Nietzsche was very respectful of Manu – not of Gautam Buddha – and Manu has been a curse to this country. He has taken all humanity from millions of people; they are living like animals.

Ambedkar was absolutely logical and right in saying that they should be given a separate vote, but Gandhi started a fast unto death for Ambedkar to take back his movement; otherwise, Gandhi will not eat until he dies. Now this is absolutely illogical. Because you convince people by fasting, it does not mean that you are right. It is blackmail, it is threatening: "I will commit suicide if you don't agree with me."

Naturally, the whole country was pressurizing Ambedkar: "Take back your movement; otherwise Gandhi's death will prove very dangerous to you and to the untouchables. They will be burned alive. Their villages will be burned; the Hindus will take revenge because the untouchables have killed Gandhi." Ambedkar tried as long as possible, and finally gave up, seeing that perhaps if Gandhi does die.... Although this is no argument.

If I were in Ambedkar's place, I would have told Gandhi, "You can die because your death is not an argument. It is as stupid a story as I have heard."

A very ugly man wanted to marry a beautiful girl – and he was the age of the girl's father. And he tried the Gandhian methodology: he took his mattress, lay down in front of the house of the girl and declared a fast unto death unless her father agreed to give his daughter in marriage to him. Now everybody was in sympathy with the poor man: "He is dying...what a great lover! We have only heard about these lovers in stories, and he's actually a Majnu, a Farhad, a Mahival."

The father was in great distress; the girl was in great fear. The whole day, the house was crowded and they were shouting: "His death will be dangerous for you. The man is not being violent: he is being nonviolent, a religious man, fasting."

Somebody suggested to the father of the girl, "You go to some old Gandhian to find out what to do."

The Gandhian said, "There is no problem. There is one ugly prostitute, very old.... You just give her a hundred rupees and she also takes her mattress and lies down by the side of the man, saying, 'I will fast unto death unless you marry me.'" In the night, the man rolled up his mattress and escaped! These are not arguments....

But Ambedkar was forced to take back his movement, and went to Gandhi with a glass of orange juice to break his fast. This is using religion in the service of politics. No religious man can do that.

The idea of India remaining whole and one was also nothing but politics being used in the service of Hindus, so that Mohammedans or Christians or Jainas or Sikhs will never be able to be in power. Hindus will remain in power – they are in the majority.

Jinnah, the man who created Pakistan, was not a religious man at all; but he also used religion. He created the movement for Mohammedans to have a separate country; otherwise they could not be in power, ever. Suddenly he became a great Mohammedan, a great religious man. And in the name of religion, it was all politics: neither Mahatma Gandhi was religious nor Muhammadali Jinnah was religious. But both wanted power.

Since then, forty years have passed – what have the politicians done to this country? When it became independent, the population was only four hundred million. They have not even been able to prevent the population explosion – which is going to kill the country without any nuclear weapons. Now the population is more than double: nine hundred million people! And by the end of this century, India will have the greatest population in the world. Up to now, it has been China, but China is behaving more scientifically and trying to reduce its population. By the end of this century, one in every four men will be Indian.

And what are the politicians doing? They are afraid to say anything to the people in favor of birth control, in favor of abortion, because their whole interest is not whether this country survives or dies; their interest is that they don't want anybody to be hurt. People have their prejudices, the politicians don't want to touch their prejudices because they need their votes. If they hurt their prejudices, these people are not going to give them their votes.

Only a religious man with a clarity of vision, who does not need the votes of the people, can say the truth. Politicians can only say beautiful lies, consoling lies, just to get your votes. The religious man has nothing to get from you; on the contrary, speaking the truth can be dangerous to his life – it has always been so. Whenever truth is spoken, the man who has spoken it has been crucified. Politicians need power, not crucifixion.

The world needs more religious people who are ready to say the truth even if it means crucifixion. The religious man is not afraid of being crucified, for the simple reason that he knows there is no death. At the most they can destroy his body – but his consciousness, his soul, his god within, will go on living.

Religion should have a higher status, and religious people should be listened to. Parliament should continually invite religious people to give them some ideas on how to solve the problems of the country, because they themselves seem to be absolutely impotent in solving anything. Problems go on growing. But the ego of the politician wants nobody to be higher than him.

But whether you want it or not, the religious person *is* higher than you. You cannot bring transformation into people's consciousness – he can.

Certainly, religion should not step down from

its sacredness into the trivial matters of politics. So I agree with this point: religion and politics should remain separate. The distance is big. Religion is a star in the sky and the politicians are creatures crawling on the earth. They *are* separate; there is no question but that they should be separate. But politicians should remember that they are functioning in mundane matters. And that is not the true goal of humanity.

Religious people are making every effort to raise humanity – its consciousness, its love, its compassion – to a point where wars become impossible, where politicians cannot deceive people, where their lies and their promises can be exposed. This is not interfering with politics – this is simply protecting the people from the exploitation of politicians. The separation is already there. Who has given Rajiv Gandhi the idea that religion and politics are not separate?

Politics is something that belongs to the gutters. Religion belongs to the open, clean sky – just like a bird on the wing, flying across the sun to reach to the very center of existence.

Certainly religious people cannot be participants in politics; but politicians should learn to be humble – their power should not make them blind. Power corrupts and absolute power corrupts absolutely; and all politicians are corrupted by their power. And what power do they have? They can kill you – their power is the power of a butcher; nothing glorious, respectable.

The religious man has a totally different quality of power. It is in his presence; it is in his great love and reverence for life; it is in his gratitude to existence.

We should not forget that the lower should remain within its own limits. And the wise people of the country should be asked to address the parliament as often as possible on problems which politicians cannot solve – don't have even the brains to solve.

But Rajiv Gandhi's intentions are totally different. He wants politics to be the only power dominating everybody, religion included, and that religion follow the dictates of the politicians.

I absolutely condemn the idea. Religion cannot follow the dictates of the politicans. Politicians should learn, should listen to the advice of the religious people. The problems are so small that any man of intelligence and good will can easily solve them. But the politician does not want to solve them; he only talks about solving them because his power is dependent on how many problems you have. The more problems you have, the more miserable you are, the more powerful he is.

To the religious consciousness, the more joyful you are, the more loving, the more rejoicing.... He wants your life to be songs and to be a dance. Because that is the only way we should worship the source of life – with our joy, with our songs and with our dances.

Beloved Bhagwan,

Before I came to Poona this time, I was just a nobody.
But sitting in front of You every day, reading people's questions,
a feeling arose of being somebody,
and that there was no need for me to ask any questions.
But the other night in darshan,
when You raised Your arms and stopped the music in front of me,
You caught this somebody in his mind.
Now, instead of feeling fine about being a nobody,
I feel like a very stupid somebody. Please will You explain what is happening to me?

Vimal, that is the difference between the politician and the religious man. The politician feels he is somebody, and the religious man feels that he is nobody.

But to be a nobody is to be divine, because you have dropped your ego and you have allowed God to enter in you. When you are somebody, you are just an ugly ego, and you have closed the doors for God to enter within you – because God and your ego cannot exist together. They are just like darkness and light: you cannot have them both.

Either you have light...then there is no darkness, and that is the state of a nobody. He is spacious, without any tensions, without any anxiety, without any anguish; just a tremendous silence prevails over his heart. There is a song without sounds in his being; there is a poetry without any words. Nothing moves, and still everything is dancing.

It is good that you have experienced both: now it is up to you to choose. Only fools choose to be somebody – that means you are limiting yourself, encased, imprisoned. Being a nobody means you are as vast as the sky; perhaps even the sky is not the limit.

So it has been a good experience for you, and I will keep an eye on you so that you don't become somebody. I am not very reliable – I can even hit you on your head. Just as I stop the music, if I see somebody is arising in you, I will stop it too. Just a good hit on your head....

So be careful: remain a nobody. It is so beautiful to be nobody, anonymous, just like a newborn child with no name, no fame, but tremendous innocence, great joy, eyes full of wonder and freshness. To be nobody is an absolute necessity on the path. The moment you become somebody, you become frozen. As you allow yourself to be nobody, the ice starts melting and the river starts flowing – flowing towards the ocean. That is the goal of us all.

Just a joke for you, Vimal, because when you laugh totally – in those moments you cannot be somebody. The people who are somebody are very serious; they never laugh, they don't even smile. Only people who are nobody can enjoy the great blessing of laughter. And I have been watching: when you laugh totally, you are no longer there – only laughter. Every cell of your body has become just a dance.

So don't hold yourself back, because this is not a serious place. It is for the gamblers, for the drunkards, for all kinds of good people who can relax and who can laugh and who can dance, and who don't care what the world thinks about them. At the most they will think you are mad – so what? Madness is better than politics. You are not going to harm anybody. And mad people are always joyous, not worrying about anything in the world.

A man with a poodle goes into a bar. After ordering a drink, he tells the bartender that he would like to buy some cigarettes. But the bartender replies that they have run out.

So the man says, "That's alright, I will just send my dog across the street to get some." He reaches into his pockets for the money, and discovers that the smallest bill he has is a twenty. He puts it in the dog's mouth and tells the dog, "Boy, run across the street and get me some cigarettes. And don't forget to bring the change." Immediately the poodle runs out the front door. A man sitting at the bar says to the dog's owner, "Say, that dog is really something!"

"Sure," says the man, "he can do all sorts of stuff. He is an amazing dog."

Just then they hear the loud sound of tires screeching. The man runs out into the street, and sees a car stopped right in front of his dog, who is making love to another poodle, right in the middle of the road.

"Hey," says the man to his dog, "what is going on? You never did anything like this before."

The dog looks up at him and says, "I never had twenty dollars before."

Okay, Vimal?

Yes, Bhagwan.

Session 7

Preparing For the Last World War

*Before the outside world is destroyed by your politicians,
enter into your inner world.
That's the only safety left, the only shelter
against nuclear weapons, against global suicide, against
all these idiots who have so much power to destroy.
You can at least save yourself.*

March 15, 1987
Evening

Beloved Bhagwan,

Since peace was officially restored to the world at the end of World War Two, what have the politicians been doing?

Anand Maitreya, there has never been any peace. There have been only two periods in history: the period we know as war, and the period we call peace, which is a cover up – in reality it should be called preparation for another war. The whole history consists only of two things: war and preparation for war. And you are asking me, "Since peace was officially restored to the world at the end of World War Two, what have the politicians been doing?"

The politicians have been doing exactly what they have always been doing: creating more conflict, more unrest, more discrimination, more destructive weapons – and preparing for the third world war.

Once, Albert Einstein was asked: "You, being the scientist who discovered atomic energy, must be able to inform us what is going to happen in the third world war."

Einstein had tears in his eyes and he said, "Don't ask me about the third world war – I do not know anything about it. But if you want to know about the fourth world war, I can say something."

The journalist who was asking the question was immensely surprised and amazed: The man is not saying anything about the third world war, says he knows nothing about it, but he is ready to say something about the fourth world war? He asked excitedly, "Then please tell me about the fourth world war."

Einstein said, "Only one thing can be said about it – that it is never going to happen."

The third world war will be the last world war. For this last world war, politicians have been preparing since peace was officially restored after the second world war.

The politician and his game are the ugliest things you can conceive of. We are facing a dark night, and I am reminded of the old saying that "When the night is darkest, the dawn is very close by." But I hesitate to say that this dark night that is surrounding us will have any dawn to it.

I will just tell you exactly what has been happening since 1945 – and people are kept in absolute ignorance; they are not aware that they are sitting on a volcano which can erupt any moment. They are kept engaged in trivia, and the real problems are kept hidden as if they don't exist.

Since 1945 there have been one hundred and five wars fought in sixty-six countries – all of them in the Third World. One is necessarily tempted to ask, "Why in the Third World?" America and the Soviet Union both have gone so far ahead in developing destructive weapons, that the weapons used in the second world war are out of date. For them, they are of no use. They have to be sold somewhere; some market is needed, and the market is possible only if there is war.

America goes on giving weapons to Pakistan. Then, naturally, India goes on taking weapons from the Soviet Union. And this has been happening in the Third World: one country purchases out-of-date material from the Soviet Union; then its enemy purchases from America. This is good business.

And they don't want these people to stop wars, because otherwise, where are they going to sell these weapons on which they have spent billions of dollars? And these poor countries and their politicians are ready to purchase them, although their people are dying of hunger – seventy-five percent of their budget goes towards war.

On the average, each war has lasted three and a half years. So who says peace has been restored? One hundred and five wars in sixty-six countries, each war lasting at least three and a half years – and you call it peace?

These wars caused sixteen million deaths. In the second world war, there were also millions of deaths. Since the second world war, which is the time of peace, sixteen million people have been killed in wars – and still you go on calling it peace?

But the politicians are so cunning, and people are so blind that they will not look around at what is happening. They will go on fighting about small things: which district should remain in which state? Belgaum is a district here; should it remain in Maharashtra? – because it is a boundary district between the states of Karnataka and Maharashtra. There are people belonging to both languages, and they have been killing each other continually for three decades – and just a small thing cannot be decided.

In fact, nobody wants to decide it. Otherwise, what is the problem? Just a small plebiscite, a vote under neutral observation, and people can decide where they want to be. There is no need for killing each other. But it seems politicians are deeply interested in trouble continuing somewhere or other, so that they are needed.

Sixteen million people have been killed, and yet in every school and every college and in every university, they go on repeating, "We are living in a period of peace." In fact, the world war was almost more peaceful!

The majority of the wars have been in Asia. It is one of the strategies of the powerful nations and their politicians that they should fight always in some other country; the Soviet Union and America should fight in Afghanistan. So the people of Afghanistan are killed; Afghanistan becomes a graveyard, and America and the Soviet Union are both profited by selling weapons. They are sending their experts, their weapons; they are training the Afghanis, and Afghanis are killing other Afghanis. One side has weapons from America, the other side has weapons from the Soviet Union.

Nine million civilians have been killed in conventional wars since Hiroshima. In ancient times, civilians were never killed. It is absolutely absurd: if your armies are fighting, the people who are fighting in armies may be killed, but now there seems to be no sensibility, no reasonability – nine million people who are civilians are killed. There may be small children, women, old people – who have nothing to do with the war, who may be reading in their schools, who may be working in their factories, or who may be cooking in their kitchens.

Just a few days ago Ronald Reagan, for no reason at all, attacked Libya – he bombed the civilian parts of Libya. His target was Kaddafi, and because Kaddafi has three houses inside the city, all his three houses had to be bombed. And in bombing his houses, other houses were burned and bombed. And just now, investigators have come to know that while the bombing was going on, professional killers were searching inside Libya for Kaddafi because it was possible he might not be killed by the bombs, he might not be in his own house.

So they were bombing the civilians, and professional killers were searching inside Libya to find Kaddafi. They could only kill Kaddafi's daughter. And neither Kaddafi nor the Libyans have done anything wrong against them.

And it is a coincidence that the day England allowed Ronald Reagan to use England as a base for bombing Libya, the parliament of England did not allow me to stay at the airport, in the lounge, for six hours – because I am a dangerous man! And Ronald Reagan is allowed to use England to bomb an innocent country which has done no harm to him.

This is as dark a night as humanity has ever faced.

The current war budget is around seven hundred billion dollars per year. Every year, fifteen million people die from malnutrition and disease, and every year seven hundred billion dollars are spent on warfare.

Every minute, thirty children die for want of food and inexpensive vaccines and every minute one point three million dollars of public funds are spent on the world's military budget.

It seems we are not interested in life anymore; we have decided to commit suicide. Man has never been in such a suicidal mood – ever, in the whole of history.

Two hundred and fifty million children have not received even a basic education. A single nuclear submarine equals the annual education budget for one hundred and sixty million school-age children in twenty-three developing countries. Just one submarine! And there are thousands of submarines moving around the ocean all over the world – American and Russian both – and each submarine has nuclear weapons six times more powerful than all the weapons that were used in the second world war. And they are so costly that we could have provided our children with education and food, nutrition. But our interests are not there.

These are the politicians who don't want to be interfered with, who want absolute control of humanity – nobody above them.

The world's forests are disappearing at the rate of eighteen to twenty million hectares a year – an area half the size of California, and California is one of the biggest states in America. Within the next twenty to thirty years, all the tropical forests will be gone; and the implications are tremendous because these forests are supplying you with oxygen and life. If these forests disappear at the rate they are disappearing, mankind will be at a loss to find enough oxygen – from where?

And on the other hand, whatever carbon dioxide you exhale, these forests inhale. If these forests were not there...already there is a very thick layer of carbon dioxide continuously accumulating in the sky, just on the twenty-mile boundary where the atmosphere ends. And because of that carbon dioxide, the temperature of the atmosphere is rising. It is already four degrees higher than it has ever been.

If all the forests disappear, the temperature will become so high that it will do two things: firstly, it will become impossible for life to survive; secondly, all the ice at the north and the south poles, on the Himalayas and the Alps and other mountains, will start melting because of the heat. And this will raise all the oceans by forty feet. It will flood all our cities, all our countries; it will drown almost the whole earth – and this is not a flood that is going to recede.

But these politicians go on doing it. Just a few months ago I was in Nepal. Nepal is the poorest country in the world, but rather than dropping its arrangements for war, it has sold its forests – eternal forests of the Himalayas – to the Soviet Union. And the Soviet Union has cut whole mountainsides and left them dry. And for what? To create more newspapers.

What is the need of so many newspapers? It is almost the same news every day, and now that we have got far better media systems, the newspaper is out of date – there is radio, there is television. Why do you go on clinging to newspapers and destroying all the forests? Just because all the politicians, presidents and prime ministers need their pictures on the front page; their speeches, which are simply bullshit, to be published – without any consideration of what harm they are doing.

During the same period, the world population is expected to increase thirty to forty percent, from five billion to seven billion. This population growth alone will cause requirements for water to double in nearly half the world. Food is another thing...even water will become difficult, because the requirement will be double and we don't have that much water for drinking.

In addition, the United Nations reports say that globally, twenty million hectares a year of farm and grazing land are being reduced to zero productivity. More than one thousand plant and animal species become extinct each year – a rate that is expected to increase. One and a half to two million people in developing countries suffer acute pesticide poisoning annually, and pesticide-related deaths are estimated at ten thousand per year.

Officers of India's planning commission reported recently: "We in India are on the verge of an enormous ecological disaster, with our water reserves drying up. What is happening in Africa is going to happen in India within a few decades."

Your population goes on growing, your land goes on becoming more barren, your water supply is becoming less and less, and because forests have been cut, the rivers that go through Nepal to Bangladesh are creating, every year, such floods as have never been seen before. Thousands of people are dying, thousands of villages simply disappear – because those thick trees were making the rivers flow slowly. Now that there are no trees, the rivers come with such force that the ocean is not ready to absorb that much water so quickly. The water starts returning and that returning water creates the floods that happen in Bangladesh.

Neither Indian politicians nor Nepalese politicians are ready to stop cutting the trees.

Nobody is interested in human life. Nobody is interested in finding out what our priority should be.

A poor country like India has so many newspapers, so many magazines, which are absolutely unnecessary. And that newsprint paper does not grow in the fields, does not fall from the sky; you have to cut trees. Trees that have taken one hundred fifty years, two hundred years to grow, disappear. And what do you gain from your newspapers?

Politicians are the real criminals – not the criminals who are in your jails. It would be a far better world if there was an exchange: all the politicians in the jails, and all the criminals in the politician's positions – they would prove more human.

The politicians go on hiding facts as long as possible, as if by hiding facts you can change anything.

Now many countries are not declaring how many homosexuals they have. Families are not declaring that the person who has died, has died from AIDS. They are bribing doctors to get certificates that he has died of a heart attack, or of cancer – because the family is more worried about its respectability, about what people will think: "Somebody has died of AIDS in your family?"

But hiding the fact means...that man had a wife; he may have transferred the disease to the wife and if there are children, they may be born with the disease – and nobody will know it and they will go on spreading it all around.

The disease is not an ordinary sexual disease – anything that comes out of your body, even your tears, carries the virus. If a child is crying, and just out of kindness and compassion you wipe the tears of the child, there is a danger you may be getting AIDS. Saliva carries the virus, and the whole of humanity is being kept in darkness: kissing should be stopped now – completely!

There is only one small part of humanity – the people who live in Siberia, the Eskimos – they are the only people in the whole of history who have never kissed. And when for the first time they saw Christian missionaries kissing, they could not believe it: "How dirty these people are, mixing saliva with each other! Are they human beings or some kind of monsters?"

Their way is far more scientific and far more hygienic. They don't kiss just to show love – because it can be not love, but death – they rub noses with each other; that looks very clean, unless you have a cold.

The other day it was accepted that ten million people are suffering from AIDS right now; and this is not a definitive report because countries like India have no way of knowing – nor the means to know. Only very developed countries have come to know that ten million people are suffering.... Perhaps at least one hundred million people are suffering in all these backward countries.

For example, in Africa, AIDS is more prevalent than anywhere else. And it was never made known that Africans are not homosexuals, but they have a strange perversion: they make love to women, but not from the front.

There are people around the world, in small villages, who even make love to animals – and they have given AIDS to animals! And now animals are spreading that AIDS through their milk, through their meat. Things have gone beyond human control.

No doctor wants...even if he comes to know that his patient has AIDS, he does not want to tell the patient because then the patient will insist, "Treat me!" There is no treatment. So the doctor tries, "You have some other disease," and sends him to some other expert because being in contact with the AIDS patient the doctor is in danger, the nurses are in danger. The whole staff is in danger.

In one of the reports I saw about jails…thirty percent of the people in jails are homosexuals. And that does not seem to be an accurate report. It must be the minimum that jail authorities have accepted – because people who are living in jails for twenty years, thirty years, and cannot come in contact with women, are bound to force homosexuality on each other.

The simplest thing would be…. There are separate jails for women – why should they be separate? The prisoners should live in a mixed way, with women and men together, and then AIDS and homosexuality can be avoided. But politicians will not say anything about it, simply because of fear. Their whole object is to say only things which people like, only things which don't go against people's prejudices, their traditional mind – because they depend on people's votes.

That's why I said that religious people should always be consulted by the politicians; their advice should be given every possible attention. But Rajiv Gandhi says that politicians should not be interfered with by religious people. Religious people can be interfered with by politicians – about that, there is no question. This is an unfortunate thing, but it goes on and on, and time is very short.

I used to be very hopeful. Still, I go on hoping against hope that perhaps, in a very dangerous situation, man may awaken. But there seems to be a sadness in my heart because I can see that if nothing is done, then this century is going to be our end.

And not only *our* end, but the end of the whole of existence's dream of creating consciousness. It has been successful only on this planet. There are millions of stars and each star has dozens of planets; only on this small planet has the miracle happened that not only life exists – consciousness exists; not only consciousness exists, but there are people who have reached to the ultimate peak of consciousness: a Gautam Buddha, a Socrates, a Pythagoras, a Chuang Tzu.

Life disappearing from this small planet will make the whole universe so poor that it will take millions of years to come again to this state where consciousness can become enlightened.

My sadness is not about myself. I am absolutely contented. Death cannot take anything from me. My sadness is concerned with the whole of humanity, because their death will take away any opportunity of their becoming enlightened, of their becoming blissful, of their knowing meaning and significance.

They have lived in darkness. Are they going to die in darkness too?

I would like my people, at least, not to waste time in postponing their own growth, because politicians are absolutely prepared to destroy each other – to destroy all and everything. Their lust for power has come to the climax. Before they succeed in committing a global suicide, at least *you* should have known the god that exists within you.

You should spread your joy and your silence and your laughter to anybody you come in contact with. You cannot give a better gift to your friends, to your acquaintances, to your lovers, to your children.

The time is very short and the work is tremendous, but if you have courage, the challenge can be accepted. Don't depend on politicians; they cannot do anything; they are not even aware of where they have been leading humanity – into what darkness.

Beloved Bhagwan,

I am now gone – good for nothing;
sorry to say, don't expect anything from me.
Koti koti pranam.

Gyan Asanga, I will tell you a small, beautiful story. Just before Ninakawa passed away – he was a great master – the Zen master Ikkyu visited him. "Shall I lead you on?" Ikkyu asked. Ninakawa was dying and Ikkyu said, "Shall I lead you on?"

Ninakawa replied, "I came here alone and I go alone. What help could you be to me?"

Ikkyu answered, "If you think you really come and go, that is your delusion. Let me show you the path on which there is no coming and going."

With his words, Ikkyu had revealed the path so clearly that Ninakawa smiled and passed away.

Gyan Asanga, where are you going? You say, "I am gone – good for nothing." That is true. You have proved definitively that you are good for nothing. Nothing is wrong in it...but where are you going? because there is nowhere to go!

We are always here and always now. Neither we go nor we come. All going and all coming is only dreaming, so just wash your face with cold water and wake up! You have not gone anywhere, you are just sleeping in your bed.

And you are saying, "Sorry to say, don't expect anything from me."

You amaze me! Who has ever expected anything from you, good for nothing? So don't be worried about it.

Just remember one thing that Ikkyu said to Ninakawa: "If you think you really come and go, that is your delusion. Let me show you the path on which there is no coming and no going" – just awakening.

A young nun said to her mother superior, "I was out walking in the garden last night and the gardener took me, threw me to the ground, and well, you know.... Can you give me penance?"

"Go and eat ten lemons," said the mother superior.

"But that won't cleanse my sins away."

"I know, but it will wipe that contented grin off your face!"

So Gyan Asanga, first get up, wash your face and eat ten lemons! I think that is not too much to ask. You can do that and if you cannot, there are many people here who will force you to do it – till your grin is gone!

And to whom are you saying this *Koti koti pranam? Koti koti pranam* means millions and millions of goodbyes. You are not going anywhere. I am not going anywhere. Stop talking in your dream! *Koti koti pranam!*

Beloved Bhagwan,

Can You please comment on
this beautiful poem by Rumi which I love so much:
Outside, the freezing desert night.
This other night inside grows warm, kindling.
Let the landscape be covered with thorny crust.
We have a soft garden in here.
The continents blasted, cities and little towns,
everything becomes a scorched blackened ball.
The news we hear is full of grief for that future.
But the real news inside here is
there's no news at all.

Devaprem, the poem by Mevlana Jalaluddin Rumi is beautiful, as always. He has spoken only beautiful words. He is one of the most significant poets who are also mystics. That is a rare combination; there are millions of poets in the world and there are a few mystics in the world, but a man who is both is very rare to find.

Rumi is a very rare flower. He is as great a poet as he is a mystic. Hence, his poetry is not just poetry, not just a beautiful arrangement of words. It contains immense meaning and points towards the ultimate truth.

It is not entertainment, it is enlightenment. He is saying, *outside, the freezing desert night. This other night inside grows warm, kindling.* The outside is not the real space for you to be. Outside, you are a foreigner: inside, you are at home. Outside, it is a freezing desert night. Inside, it is warm, kindling, cozy.

But very few are fortunate enough to move from the outside to the inside. They have completely forgotten that they have a home within themselves; they are searching for it but they are searching in the wrong place. They search for their whole lives but always outside; they never stop for a moment and look inwards.

Let the landscape be covered with thorny crust. We have a soft garden in here. Don't be worried about what happens on the outside. Inside, there is always a garden ready to welcome you.

The continents blasted, cities and little towns, everything becomes a scorched, blackened ball. The news we hear is full of grief for that future.

These words of Rumi are more significant, meaningful, today, than they were when he wrote them. He wrote them seven hundred years ago, but today it is not only a symbolic thing, it is going to become the reality: *The continents blasted, cities and little towns, everything becomes a scorched blackened ball. The news we hear is full of grief for that future. But the real news inside here is there's no news at all.*

This last sentence depends on an ancient saying which says: No news is good news. I was born in a very small village where the postman used to come only once a week. And people were afraid that he may be bringing a letter for them; they were happy when they found that there was no letter. Once in a while, there was a telegram for someone. Just the rumor that somebody had received a telegram was such a shock in the whole village that everybody would gather there – and only one man was educated enough to read. Everybody was afraid: A telegram? That means some bad news. Otherwise, why should you waste money on a telegram?

I learned from my very childhood that no news is good news. People were happy when they received no news from their relatives, from their friends or from anybody. That meant everything was going well.

Rumi is saying: *The news we hear is full of grief for the future. But the real news inside, is there's no news at all.* Everything is silent and everything is as beautiful, peaceful, blissful as it has always been. There is no change at all; hence, there is no news.

Inside it is an eternal ecstasy, forever and forever.

I will repeat again that these lines may become true in *your* lifetime. Before that happens, you must reach within yourself where no news has ever happened, where everything is eternally the same, where the spring never comes and goes but always remains; where flowers have been from the very beginning – if there was any beginning – and are going to remain to the very end, if there is going to be any end. In fact, there is no beginning and no end, and the garden is lush, green, and full of flowers.

Before the outside world is destroyed by your politicians, enter into your inner world. That's the only safety left, the only shelter against nuclear weapons, against global suicide, against all these idiots who have so much power to destroy.

You can at least save yourself.

I was hopeful, but as the days have passed and I have become more and more acquainted with the stupidity of man...I still hope but just out of old habit; really my heart has accepted the fact that only a few people can be saved. The whole of humanity is determined to destroy itself. And these are the people...if you tell them how they can be saved, they will crucify you. They will stone you to death.

Going around the world, I still laugh, but there is a subtle sadness in it. I still dance with you but it is no longer with the same enthusiasm as it was ten years ago.

It seems that the higher powers of consciousness are helpless against the lower and ugly powers of politicians. The higher is always fragile, like a roseflower; you can destroy it with a stone. That does not mean that the stone becomes higher than the roseflower; it simply means the stone is unconscious of what it is doing.

The crowds are unconscious of what they are doing, and the politicians belong to the crowd. They are their representatives. And when blind people are leading other blind people, it is almost impossible to wake them up; because the question is not only that they are asleep – they are blind too.

There is not time enough to cure their eyes. There is time enough to wake them but not enough time to cure their eyes. So now I have confined myself completely to my own people. That is my world, because I know those who are with me may be asleep, but they are not blind. They can be awakened.

Okay, Vimal?

Yes, Bhagwan.

Session 8

The Taste of Your Being

There is such a synchronicity in existence.
You become graceful, the whole existence becomes graceful;
you become silent, everything else becomes silent.
A song arises in you, and all around the birds start singing;
you dance, and you see the whole of existence
is dancing with you, hand in hand.

March 16, 1987
Morning

Beloved Bhagwan,

What is religion?
What is Your opinion on organized religion?

Anand Maitreya, religion is the highest flight of human consciousness – it is the individual search for truth. The inner truth cannot be made an object of common knowledge.

Each one has to go within himself; each time, it is a new discovery. It does not matter how many people have attained awakening, realization; the moment *you* attain it, it will be absolutely fresh – because it cannot be borrowed.

The search basically consists of knowing your interiority. You have an outside, and no outside can exist without an inside: the very existence of the outside is proof of an inner world.

The inner world consists of three layers: thoughts are the most superficial; feelings are deeper – and then is the being, which is your godliness. To know one's own godliness, to know one's own eternity, is the basic search of religion.

All your senses lead you outside: eyes open to look outside, ears hear what is happening outside, your hands can touch what is outside. Senses are the doors to go out – and always remember, the door that takes you out, can also take you in. It is the same door from which you go out of your home and through which you come back in; just the direction changes.

To go out, you need open eyes. To come in, you need closed eyes, all your senses silent. The first encounter is with the mind – but that is not your reality. Although it is inside your skull, it is not you – it is the reflection of the outside. All your thoughts are reflections of the outside.

For example, a blind man cannot think about colors because he has not seen colors – hence the reflection is not possible. The blind man cannot even see darkness; and because he has never seen light or darkness outside, there is no possibility of any reflection. The blind man does not know whether there is darkness or there is light – both words are meaningless. And if you analyze your thoughts, you will find they are all triggered inside you by outside reality – so they are basically of the outside, reflected in your inner lake of consciousness.

But because of these thoughts...and they are a tremendous crowd in you; they go on accumulating, they create a China wall. You have to go beyond your thoughts. And religion knows only one method – there are different names, but the method is one: it is watchfulness, it is witnessing. You simply watch your thoughts, with no judgment, no condemnation, no appreciation – utterly aloof; you just see the process of thoughts passing on the screen of your mind.

As your watcher becomes stronger, thoughts become less – in the same proportion. If the watcher is ten percent of your energy, then ninety percent of your energy is wasted in thoughts; if your watcher becomes ninety percent, then only ten percent remains in thoughts. The moment you are one hundred percent a watcher, the mind becomes empty.

This whole process is known as meditation.

As you pass through the thoughts, you will come to the second layer which is inside you – of feelings, of your heart, which is more subtle. But by now, your watcher is capable even of watching your moods, your sentiments, your emotions, your feelings – howsoever subtle they may be. And the same method works in the same way as it worked with the thoughts: soon there will be no sentiments, no feelings, no moods. You have gone beyond the mind, and the heart. Now there is utter silence; nothing moves. This is your being; this is you.

The taste of your being is truth.

The beauty of your being is the beauty of existence.

The silence of your being is the language that existence understands. And just settled in being, you have come home.

The wandering is finished.

The struggle is finished.

At ease, you sit silently within yourself.

A great hidden splendor is revealed to you: you are not separate from reality, you are one with it. The trees and the moon and the stars and the mountains are all part of one organic unity; you are also part of that organic unity – you become part of God.

Religion is man's highest achievement.

Beyond religion, there is nothing – but there is no need either. Your being is so abundant, so overflowing with bliss, silence, peace, understanding, ecstasy, that for the first time, life becomes really a song, a dance, a celebration. Those who do not know religion, don't know celebration.

But organized religion is a totally different affair, so I have to make it clear to you that authentic religion is always individual. The moment truth is organized, it dies; it becomes a doctrine, a theology, a philosophy – but it is no longer experienced, because the crowd cannot experience. Experience happens only to individuals – separately.

It is almost like love. You cannot have organizations of love – so that you need not bother; the organization will take care, the priest will love on your behalf. But that's what has happened to religion. Each time a man discovers the truth, immediately one of the most cunning parts of humanity, the priests, surround him. They start compiling his words; they start interpreting his words; and they start making it clear to people that if you want to know truth, you have to go via them – they are agents of God. They may call themselves prophets, they may call themselves messengers; they may choose any name, but the reality is, they are self-appointed agents of God. They don't know God, but in the name of God, they exploit humanity.

Organized religion is another form of politics. Just as I have always condemned politics as the lowest activity of human beings, the same is my attitude about organized religions. You can see it: the priests and the politicians have always been in conspiracy against humanity. They have been supporting each other. They have divided things between themselves so that your worldly life belongs to the politician, he is the ruler there, and your inner life belongs to the priest, he is the ruler there.

One sometimes feels so amazed...it seems unbelievable, that even in the twentieth century the pope could declare, a few months ago, that to communicate with God directly is a sin. You should go through the priest, the right channel – because if people start going directly to God, confessing to God, praying to God, the millions of priests will be unemployed. They don't do anything; their whole function is to deceive you. Because you don't understand the language of God, and you are not so evolved, just for some fee – a donation to their church or to their temple – they will do the job for you.

All those donations go in the pockets of the priests. They don't know anything about God, but they are very learned – they can repeat scriptures like parrots. But their inner desire is not for God, not for truth – they are not seekers, they are exploiters.

I have heard...a priest bought two parrots and he taught them, with great hardship, beautiful statements of Jesus Christ. And everybody was really amazed – the parrots were so accurate. He made small beads for them so they were constantly praying, and he also found small bibles for them.... So they were always keeping their bibles open, and moving their beads. Although they could not read, they had already crammed everything. The priest would open the page and say, "Twelfth page," and they would start reading it – not that they were reading; they had memorized it.

The priest was very pleased and he felt it would be good to have one more parrot. Rather than learning the bible and the beads, he could be taught to give whole sermons. He found a parrot, and the pet shop owner said, "Your wish will be fulfilled; this parrot is the most intelligent I have ever seen."

But he was not aware that it was a female parrot. And as the parrot was put in the same cage as the two parrots who were moving their beads and reading the bible, they both looked at the female parrot, and one parrot said to the other, "George, now drop those beads! Our prayers have been heard."

Your priests are no more than parrots – and their prayers are for power, for prestige, for money. They are politicians in disguise; they are doing politics in the name of God – the politics of numbers. There are now seven hundred million Catholics; naturally the pope is the most powerful religious man in the world.

Every religion has been trying to increase its population by different methods. Mohammedans are allowed to marry four women so that they can produce four children per year. And they have been successful: they are the second largest religion after Christianity.

Organized religion is only a content-less, meaningless word; hidden inside is the politics of numbers. And you know perfectly well – as the election comes near, your politicians start going to see the *shankaracharya*. For five years, nobody goes to visit the shankaracharya, but when the election comes near, then the prime minister goes to visit the shankaracharya. He goes for a pilgrimage to the temples, high and deep in the mountains of the Himalayan range. For what? Suddenly, a great religious urge has arisen...which subsides as the election ends.

These people need votes; they have to pay respect to the leaders of religions. And a shankaracharya feels great that the prime minister is touching his feet. And the followers of the shankaracharya, the Hindus, feel that "our prime minister is a very religious person."

When the pope comes to India, even the president and the prime minister with his whole cabinet, stand in line at the airport to receive him. For what? The third largest religion in India is now Christianity, and to pay respect to the pope means all the votes of the Christians will be yours.

Organized religions – whether it is Christianity or Hinduism or Mohammedanism – have not been seekers of truth. In two thousand years, what truth has organized Christianity added to the statements of Jesus? So what is the need of this organization? It is not increasing religiousness in the world, it is simply repeating what Jesus has said – which is available in books for anybody to read. In twenty- five centuries, how many Buddhists have searched for the truth, or have found the truth? – just a long line of parrots repeating what Gautam Buddha has found.

And you should be reminded that Gautam Buddha was not part of any organized religion; neither was Mahavira part of any organized religion, nor was Jesus part of any organized religion – they were individual seekers.

Truth has always been found by individuals. That is the privilege of the individual, and his dignity.

Organized religions have created wars – just like politicians have done. Their names may be different...politicians fight for socialism, for communism, for fascism, for nazism, and organized religions have been fighting for God, for love, for their concept of what truth is. And millions of people have been killed in the clashes between Christians and Mohammedans, between Christians and Jews, between Mohammedans and Hindus, between Hindus and Buddhists. Religion has nothing to do with war; it is a search for peace. But organized religions are not interested in peace, they are interested in becoming more and more powerful and dominant.

I condemn the organized religions in the same way I condemn the politicians – they are nothing but politics. So when I said to you that religious people should be respected, honored – the politicians should go to them for advice – I was not talking about organized religions; I was talking only about religious individuals. And a religious individual is neither Hindu nor Christian nor Mohammedan. How can he be? – God himself is not Hindu, not Mohammedan, not Christian. And the man who knows something of the divine becomes colored with his divinity, becomes fragrant with godliness.

In the ancient East these religious people were our highest flowers, and even kings and emperors used to go to them to touch their feet and to be blessed – to ask their advice on problems which they were unable to solve.

If we want the world to remain alive, we have to bring back our ancient childhood days when the religious person had no interest of his own. That's why his eyes were clear, his heart was pure love, his being was nothing but a blessing. Whomsoever came to him was healed, his problems were solved; he was given new insights into rotten old problems.

Organized religions should disappear from

the world – they should drop this mask of being religious.

They are simply politicians, wolves hiding themselves in the skin of sheep. They should come into their true colors; they should be politicians – there is no harm in that. And all the time they *are* politicians, but they are playing the game in the name of religion.

Organized religions don't have any future. They should drop their disguise and come truly out in front as politicians, and be part of the political world so that we can find the authentic religious individual – who will be very rare. But just a few authentic religious individuals can lead the whole world towards light, towards immortal life, towards ultimate truth.

Beloved Bhagwan,

I have been living in America while You have been traveling around the world.
Now I have come here to Your mystery school,
to enjoy You for a few weeks before I continue my life in the West.
Bhagwan, I feel You so strongly inside of me
that I don't experience the ache of being physically away from You.
I am savoring every moment of being in Your presence while I am here,
yet I don't feel a longing to stay.
Is it possible for the marketplace to actually be *my* mystery school for now?
Is there anything that I can do for You out there?
You are the center of the cyclone, Bhagwan.
I am so grateful, and I love You.

P rem Sunshine, the love between the master and the disciple is not of the physical; hence space makes no difference. You can be far away on another star, but your heart will be still beating with me. That is the only closeness, the real closeness; otherwise, you can be sitting by my side and still you may be wandering somewhere on some other star.

I am not interested in your physical body, where it is; I am interested in your being, that it is centered. I am interested in your love – that it reaches to as many people as possible.

The marketplace is perfectly the right place for anyone who wants to grow spiritually. In the past, the fallacy was to renounce the marketplace and run away to the mountains. But if your mind has not changed, even in the mountains it will be thinking of your business, of your wife, of your children. If some traveler comes by, you will be hankering to know what is happening there. If your mind remains the same, it does not matter that you have renounced a palace.

I was traveling in the Himalayas and I saw a very beautiful bodhi tree. I was tired, and it was time…I have never in my whole life missed a good two hours' sleep in the afternoon. It was very cool and the shadow was thick, so I was just going to lie down, and a man came, saying, "You cannot lie down here."

I said, "What is the problem?"

He said, "This is my tree, and I have been living under this tree for five years."

I said, "You look like a sannyasin."

He said, "I am; I am a Hindu monk."

I said, "You have renounced the world?"

He said, "Yes, I have renounced everything."

"Well," I said, "What about this tree? – it is still yours. The shadow is so big, we can both rest underneath it. And I will not be disturbing you because I will be sleeping, and I don't snore – unless I decide to."

He said, "What do you mean?"

I said, "If you snore, then I will snore loudly. I cannot snore while I am asleep, so I have to pretend that I am asleep – and I will snore loudly unless you stop your snoring. If you don't snore, there is no problem: there is a lot of space here, and I am going on my way after just two hours.

"But I must say to you, that you have left the world, but the world is still within your heart. The very idea of *'my* tree' is not different in any way from *my* kingdom, *my* palace, *my* wife. It is not a question of what you are claiming as *mine*; the question is that you are possessing."

Humanity has to face two problems from the past. People renounce the world, but nothing is renounced. You can leave your house, you can leave your wife, you can leave your friends, you can leave your money – but where will you leave your mind, and how will you leave your mind? And if you can leave your mind, then there is no need to go anywhere; then your very house becomes the temple, because the real question is transcending the mind. These monks who left the world lived in a very illusory idea that they were no longer concerned about the world. They missed the chance to grow.

Secondly, living in a mountain cave you may not get angry, because anger needs somebody to provoke it; there is nobody to provoke you….

I have heard…a man lived for thirty years in the Himalayas, and he had gone there because of his too-angry mind; his mind was so angry that when he was in anger he was almost mad. One day he had pushed his wife into the well, and then as he became aware of what he had done, he decided that now he would renounce this world. And for thirty years anger never happened, because there was no wife, no children, no customers, no friends, no enemies – there was nobody. Slowly, slowly, his fame spread to the plains: "A man has been living for thirty years in the caves, and we have never seen such a silent man."

There was going to be a great fair, the *Kumbha Mela*, in Prayag – it happens every twelve years. It is the biggest gathering in the whole world; millions of people come. A few people went to this silent monk, saying, "Now all the great saints and monks are coming to the fair to give their teachings to the people who are going to participate in it. It is time you came down: you have not come down for thirty years; now you are ripe." It was very ego-fulfilling, this invitation.

He came down to the plains. As he entered the crowd of millions – and they did not know anything about him – somebody stepped on his feet, and all those thirty years disappeared. He grabbed the man by his neck and he said, "You idiot, don't you see that I am a saint?" It was very difficult to take him away, he was going to kill the man. He was the same man who had killed his wife thirty years before. It was not such a great crime; the crowd was so thick that if somebody stepped on your feet, it was not intentional. But it made him aware of one thing: that even thirty years in the Himalayas had not changed him a little bit.

So this is the second problem. Your real test is in the world – whether you are becoming silent or not; whether you are becoming more loving and compassionate or not; whether you are growing spiritually or not.

Sunshine, go to the marketplace, but remember not to get lost in it. Remain a watcher. It is very easy to get lost.

You have asked me, "Is there anything that I can do for you out there?"

Only one thing I expect from all of you: to be yourself, to discover your inner beauty, your purity of consciousness, your hidden splendor – and spread it to as many people as possible. People are miserable. Help them to laugh a little, to sing a little, to dance a little.

I don't want missionaries. You are not to spread my teachings – I don't have any anyway – but you have to spread the joy, the blissfulness, the silence that you have felt here. Don't let it become just a faded memory. And you are going to the greatest marketplace in the world, to California. You will have to be very watchful. If you can remain untouched by California and all its stupidities…I have been thinking to call the saints "California- returned."

Just take a joke from me; laugh and help others to laugh….

An American traveling in the United Kingdom was riding in a train with an Englishman and an elderly English lady with her pet Pekingese. They had traveled only a short distance when the dog threw up all over the American's trousers. Instead of apologizing, the English woman fondled her dog and comforted it, saying, "Poor, itsy-bitsy doggy has a little tummy ache."

A few miles later the dog raised its leg and pissed all over the American. Again the English woman consoled her dog, saying, "Poor itsy-bitsy doggy has a cold in the bladder."

A short while later the dog shat all over the Yank's other things. Exasperated, the American stood up, grabbed the dog and threw it out of the window.

At this point the Englishman commented, "You Yanks are a peculiar lot. You speak the wrong language, you live on the wrong side of the ocean, and you, sir, threw the wrong bitch out of the window."

Beloved Bhagwan,

As the years have gone by since I took sannyas, my love has changed its quality.
At first I felt a certain excitement;
now there is a deep coolness and I feel relaxed within myself.
This is accentuated when I sit in front of You in meditation.
As I am writing this, a certain little voice inside bubbles up and says,
"Yes, everything is fine."
Beloved Bhagwan, is this little voice a figment of my imagination,
my mind playing tricks?

Yoga Videh, I have been watching you. I have seen you becoming more silent, more peaceful. A certain grace is arising in your eyes and on your face. In the beginning I used to see that it was even difficult for you to sit for two hours – you were tossing and turning. Now all that is past; you sit almost like a marble statue. This shows the inner centering.

So whatever you have heard is not a figment of your imagination. I also say to you: Yes, everything is fine. But don't be satisfied with what you have attained. There is much more – infinitely much more. As you go deeper and deeper, you will find more and more treasures; and unless you come to the feeling of immortality, eternity, remember that the journey has not ended.

You will come across beautiful spaces which are so enchanting, so magical that one thinks, what more can there be in life? – so much bliss, so much benediction – but don't stop. Everybody has to discover his eternity, that "I am part of a life that knows no death." And it is not far away if you go on and on.

Whatever happens, be grateful to existence and move on.

Charaiveti, charaiveti – this was one of the constant messages of Gautam Buddha. Whenever sannyasins came to relate to him their state of mind, their consciousness, he would always say, "Everything is fine, but *charaiveti, charaiveti*. Continue, continue going on and on and on, because I know there is much more to be discovered."

Remember the fragrance of the beautiful words of one of the great Zen masters, Ryokan:

With no mind, blossoms invite the butterfly.
With no mind, the butterfly visits the blossoms.

There is no cerebral activity in it. The flowers are not thinking and planning how to invite the butterfly. With no mind, in their silence, is their invitation.

With no mind, blossoms invite the butterfly.
With no mind, the butterfly visits the blossoms.
When the flower blooms, the butterfly comes.
When the butterfly comes, the flower blossoms.

There is such a synchronicity in existence. You become graceful, the whole existence becomes graceful; you become silent, everything else becomes silent. A song arises in you, and all around the birds start singing; you dance, and you see the whole of existence is dancing with you, hand in hand.

Says Ryokan,

I do not know others, others do not know me.
Not knowing each other we naturally follow the way.

There is no need of knowledge, because nature has its own wisdom. If you don't interfere with nature and its wisdom, everything goes as it should go.

I do not know others, others do not know me.
Not knowing each other we naturally follow the way.

Whatever is happening to you Videh, just follow it, very naturally. Don't be in a hurry, don't bring your knowledge to improve upon it. Nobody can improve upon nature: when the spring comes, the flowers will come also – and there is no way to bring the spring, and without the spring the flowers won't come. So you go on the way you are moving. It is the right path, the easy path in your naturalness and spontaneity, and you will not be going astray. You will reach to the ultimate ocean where one merges with the eternal life.

Knowledge is really a very complicated phenomenon; you have to be like little children.

Little William went to his father and said, "Daddy, where did I come from?" The father started to stutter and stammer, but he realized that he had to tell his son the facts of life.

"Sit down, Willie," he said. At great length he described the whole business of creation, beginning with the birds and the bees. Then he went into the most graphic descriptions of human intercourse. He concluded at last, feeling limp and drained. He took a handkerchief and wiped the perspiration from his brow: "Okay, Willie, do you understand now?"

Willie scratched his head. "Not really, Dad. Henry says he came from New Jersey, but you have not told me where I came from."

His question is of a very innocent character, but the father is a knowledgeable person. He gives a whole discourse on how human beings are produced – and he is perspiring and stuttering and stammering. And the boy must be puzzled about what is going on? He has simply asked a simple question: Where did I come from? Such a complicated journey...and Henry has come from New Jersey.

Be natural, be simple, be innocent, and allow nature to guide you – it has never misguided anybody. Knowledge, on the contrary, has never been able to guide anybody to the ultimate goal, the ultimate peak of our experience, of our consciousness, of our blissfulness, of our enlightenment.

Okay, Vimal?

Yes, Bhagwan.

Session 9

Papal Politics: Organized Superstition

*All the organized religions
are basically depriving humanity of religion
because they are misdirecting you. They are always
directing you outwards – their God is far away in the sky.
And when you pray, folding your hands towards the sky, you don't realize that
there is nobody to hear you.
In fact, the one who is praying, the one who is
alive in you, the one who is breathing in you, is the god.
You have just to discover it.*

March 16, 1987
Evening

Beloved Bhagwan,

You are against the pope so much – is that because the Roman Catholic religion is the most organized religion?

Anand Maitreya, I am not against anyone – but I am certainly for the truth. Anything that goes against the truth, I am determined to criticize; it is a sacred duty as far as I am concerned. That the Roman Catholic religion is the most organized religion is only one of the reasons I am criticizing the pope so much. There are many other things, too.

I would like to give you all the implications of my criticism. First, the Catholic church in particular, and Christianity in general, is not a religion at all. To call it an "organized religion" is to use the wrong language. It is organized superstition.

In the twenty centuries after Jesus, Christianity has been defending all kinds of superstitions, and fighting against science, against any discovery of truth.

And the people who have been the leaders of this war between superstitions and science are the popes. In the first place, the popes down these twenty centuries have been declaring one thing: that they are infallible – which is an absurdity. But their logic is: they represent Jesus Christ, and Jesus Christ is the only son of God. So, in an indirect way, they are the vehicles of God – how can they be fallible?

But life is not logic. Your God itself is a fiction; Jesus Christ being the only begotten son is another fiction. And the infallibility of the pope is just ridiculous.

When Galileo discovered for the first time that it is not the sun that goes around the earth, but the earth that goes around the sun – he was very old, seventy-five or eighty, almost on his deathbed – he was dragged to the court of the pope. And the pope said, "Before you die, change that statement, because it goes against *The Bible*. And anything that goes against *The Bible* is automatically wrong, because *The Bible* is the word of God."

Galileo was a great scientist, and I have immense respect for a man who, even at the age of eighty, when he was dying, had such a beautiful sense of humor.

He said, "There is no problem. I will change it; I will write in my book exactly what God has written in *The Bible* – that the sun goes around the earth. But one thing I must make clear to you: neither the sun reads my book nor the earth reads my book. As far as reality is concerned, the earth will continue going around the sun.

"And why should you insist? Because I have every proof; I have devoted my whole life to the search, and all those who have a scientific mind are in absolute agreement with me. Sooner or later you will have to agree because one cannot remain against truth for long."

The pope said, "We cannot allow even a single statement to go against *The Bible* for the simple reason that if one statement becomes false, God's infallibility disappears. And if God himself is fallible, what about Jesus Christ? And what about the pope? And if God can write one thing wrong, who knows? – he may have written many things wrong. We cannot afford it."

For three hundred years, the popes have been fighting a hard battle against each and every scientific discovery of truth. Nobody can be victorious against truth, but they have tried their best. It is the only religion that has been fighting against science – that is one of the fundamental reasons why I criticize the pope.

Even today they go on fighting science, knowing perfectly well that each time they will be defeated, and that they are fighting a losing battle. And still, they go on declaring themselves infallible.

It is amazing that people can be so shameless. It is time they learned.

They crucified and burned Joan of Arc by the order of the pope, because he declared that she was a witch. Now on what grounds, what reasoning, what revelation? because the pope says it is so, it has to be right. The word of the pope is the law; the word of the pope is the truth. They burned a young, beautiful, courageous, intelligent woman who had fought for the freedom of the country and who had won the freedom of the country. And that was the reason for the jealousy – that a woman should become so prominent that even the pope is left behind.

She was burned because of jealousy; she had not committed any sin. The whole of Europe was shocked and slowly, slowly, people started raising their voices against her crucifixion; but it took almost three hundred years for people to be so strong about it that another pope declared Joan of Arc a great saint.

One pope burns her alive because she is a witch – she is in sexual relationship with the devil. And after three hundred years, another pope – his own descendant, his own successor, representative of the same Jesus Christ and the same God – declares that she was a saint. Her bones were taken out of the grave and worshiped, and a beautiful cathedral now stands in her memory. Now, nobody calls her just "Joan of Arc" – her name is "Saint Joan of Arc."

The pope goes on traveling around the world preaching that birth control is against God, that any method of preventing the birth of a child is anti-God – particularly in the countries of the East where people are so poor, and they are going to become poorer and poorer every day. But the pope's interest is not that man should live comfortably without hunger.

People should not die just because they

cannot even get water, cannot get food.

And you will be surprised to know that on one hand, the pope goes on talking against birth control methods, and on the other, the Vatican has a hidden factory where they create birth control pills – because it is good business; it brings millions of dollars.

You call such people religious?

He goes around the world saying that Christian priests and bishops and cardinals should not get involved in politics – because he wants politicians to be in favor of him. And it has been found that the same man sent one hundred million dollars to Poland, to a political party, to fight against the Communists.

Is this not politics?

And his interest in birth control is really to increase the population. Whatever consequences happen to people is not the problem. If people are poor and hungry, they can be easily converted to Christianity, and particularly the Catholic church. Their schools, their hospitals, their orphanages are nothing but factories for converting people into Catholics.

It is now a well-known fact that by the end of the century, almost half the population of the world will be dying of hunger. You cannot even conceive of the situation where one man out of every two will be dying. All around there will be corpses and there will be nobody even to bury them or to take them to the mortuary or to the funeral. In fact, dying will be better than living amongst those corpses.

The whole world will be stinking of death.

The popes don't seem to be interested in saving humanity. Their basic interest is how to get more and more people into their religion, because that is going to be their power. It is pure politics.

The whole Christian theology is based on such stupid ideas that to call it "religion" is just absurd. Jesus is born of a virgin mother. The whole of medical science is against it – it cannot be possible, but it is one of their fundamentals. If you remove it, the whole edifice of Christianity falls down.

They have not given the world any method for how to raise consciousness. They have not produced awakened and enlightened people; but they have caught seven hundred million people in the Catholic fold alone. These people are full of absurd beliefs – and even though they have eyes, they don't see; they have ears, but they don't hear. And if you say anything, immediately they are ready to crucify you. They are against the crucifixion of Jesus, but they are, every moment, ready to crucify you if you just tell the truth.

I said in one of my speeches, that *The Holy Bible* is the most unholy book in the whole world, because it has five hundred solid pages of pure pornography. One of my friends in America, hearing this, actually collected all those five hundred pages and published a book called the *X-Rated Holy Bible*. And now I have received a summons from Kanpur – ten Christian associations have made a case against me; that I am hurting their religious feelings.

I cannot believe that people are so blind. If anything is hurting your religious feelings it is your *Bible* – I have nothing to do with it. You should tell the government that *The Bible* should be banned, or it should be labeled and listed among the pornographic literature.

I am not saying anything myself. Those five hundred pages are there in *The Bible* and those ten associations at least could have looked in their *Bibles* to see what I am talking about; otherwise in the court they will look absolutely foolish.

Now, they are creating agitation in every country for homosexuality to be made a severe crime. And everybody in the world knows that Pope Paul the Sixth was a homosexual. Before he became the pope, he was the cardinal in Milan – and that was the talk of the town. The whole of Milan was surprised that he was always seen with his boyfriend – a young, beautiful man. Knowing this perfectly well...still he became the pope. And the moment he became pope, his boyfriend was called to the Vatican, and the boyfriend became the secretary. Ordinarily, the secretary becomes the girlfriend; here, it was just a little different...but the same story.

And it has never been denied by the Vatican; they could not deny it – it was so factual. But if you say it, that means you are against the pope. I am not against the pope. I am just in favor of truth.

But perhaps this kind of thing begins with the virginity of Mary and the birth of Jesus. I have heard...it is a story of the future, because this Polack pope seems to be very slow to die. Popes ordinarily have died within an average of one or two years at the most because by the time they become popes, they are always around the age of seventy-five, seventy-eight. And they must have been hoping that this Polack would also die – but they don't know Polacks. He has completely forgotten about dying; and he is enjoying his popehood so greatly – no other pope has ever done such things.

He is continuously touring around the world, and the Vatican is getting into debt: nine million dollars he has spent on traveling. The last time he went to Australia, just two days before him the British queen had also gone to Australia. More money was spent on the pope's visit to Australia than on that of the queen of England. And these are the people who say, "Blessed are the poor."

But finally, the Polack pope died and went to heaven with pomp and circumstance. At the pearly gates, Saint Peter stopped him and said, "Hey, you can't walk in just like that. Who are you?"

The pope answered, "Well, I am your very own representative on earth. I am the pope."

Saint Peter said, "Pope? My representative? I have never heard of you."

The pope, puzzled, said, "Ah, just tell God I am here. He will tell you to let me in."

Saint Peter yelled, "Hey, boss, a guy here says he is the pope. Do you know him?"

God answered, "Never heard of him." The pope said, "Strange, but ask Jesus. He knows me."

Saint Peter yelled, "Hey, sonny. There is a guy here says he is the pope. You know him?" Jesus answered, "No."

Saint Peter said, "Sorry, I can't let you in. Nobody around here knows you."

The pope said, "You can't turn me away like this. I am the pope himself. Ask the Holy Ghost. He knows me for sure."

Saint Peter yelled again, "Hey, spook! A guy here claims you know him. Says he is the pope."

And the Holy Ghost shouted, "The pope, sure I know him. He is the guy that spread those dirty rumors about me and Mary. Kick him out of here."

The whole religion is founded on a dirty joke.

Pope Paul the Sixth, who was the homosexual, was followed by Pope John Paul the First. He was an intelligent, liberal man who ordered an investigation of the cardinals and bishops who belonged to Masonic Lodges, which were outlawed by the Catholic church.

These Masonic Lodges have as their members only the wealthiest people of the world. They are secret societies doing secret rituals. They were outlawed by Christianity – no Christian priest, bishop or cardinal, or anybody officiating in any position, should be a member of any Masonic Lodge – because their secret rituals consist of sexual orgies and all kinds of ugly things. John

Paul the First ordered an investigation of the cardinals and bishops who belonged to these Masonic Lodges. He discovered that many top Vatican officials were Freemasons, and ordered that they be removed from office.

You see the hypocrisy? These are the same people who made the law that no Christian priest could become members of Masonic Lodges, but in the Vatican itself, the cardinals and bishops and archbishops were found to be members of Masonic Lodges. And because John Paul the First ordered that they be removed from office, the whole Catholic hierarchy and bureacracy turned against that intelligent man. In the whole history of Christianity, perhaps he was the only pope who had some intelligence, some humanity, some understanding.

At the same time, he ordered an investigation into the Vatican bank which would have shown that the bank was laundering hundreds of millions of dollars of Mafia heroin money every year.

These are your religious institutions. The Vatican bank itself, which is under the pope, is nothing but the greatest Mafia organization. Hundreds of millions of dollars of heroin money.... They go on talking and preaching against drugs, while behind the curtain they are dealing in drugs themselves.

He also ordered a meeting to announce that the church supported birth control. He was really a man of understanding – he wanted to call the pill the "Catholic pill." But before any of these orders could be carried out, he was found dead in suspicious circumstances.

He was murdered. Vatican officials said it was of a heart attack, but that is absolutely wrong because his own personal physician said he had a perfect heart – he had had no heart trouble, ever. And the most important thing was that his personal physician was not called. Instead, the Vatican officials ordered immediate embalming and refused to let his personal physician examine the body – even the dead body. They also refused a post-mortem. No death certificate was issued; even up to now, officially he is living because there was no death certificate issued for him.

After they had embalmed him, an autopsy was done. But once you embalm a dead body – once you take all the blood out of the body and fill it with chemicals – it becomes impossible to find whether it has been poisoned or what has happened. But the whole situation is very clear: insiders say that papers he was clutching in his hand when the body was discovered were the papers in which he had written his will. Realizing in the middle of the night that he has been poisoned, feeling that he was going to die, he may have tried to write his will. Or he may have tried to write what had happened to him, what had been done to him. But all those papers mysteriously disappeared, along with his medicine bottle and the will.

It has been thought that they mixed poison in his medicine bottle, and he drank the poison, thinking it was medicine. Once the poison started having its effects, he must have tried to write his will, and he tried to write that it seemed he had been poisoned and that he was dying. The people who found him first saw the will he was clutching in his hands.

And the most amazing thing is: even before his body was found, orders for embalming the body were given because the people who were in the conspiracy were aware that in the morning the embalmers would be needed, so every arrangement was made beforehand.

It was not an accidental death.

He was followed by Pope John Paul the Second, the Polack who prohibited all birth control methods except the rhythm method – even though the Vatican actually owned a company which made birth control pills. He also dropped the church law forbidding membership in the Freemasons. And he promoted Marcinkus, the head of the Vatican bank, to Archbishop, and made him part of his personal group. This is the man who was running all the Mafia heroin money through the bank.

In 1982 Archbishop Marcinkus was involved in a huge financial scandal after an Italian bank collapsed. One of his business friends was found hanged beneath a London bridge. And another colleague, who was in jail on charges of murdering a police commissioner, died from drinking coffee with cyanide. These were the people who could have been witnesses against Archbishop Marcinkus; these two people knew all the secrets – and both were killed.

A warrant for the arrest of the Archbishop had been issued, but the Vatican is a separate government – just eight square miles – and the Italian government has no power to interfere in the Vatican. And the pope was hiding the man inside the Vatican; the arrest warrant was waiting outside. These are your religious leaders.

The Polack pope also strongly reprimanded priests around the world for their involvement in politics, but he himself ordered one hundred million dollars of Vatican money to go to the Solidarity group in Poland who were fighting the communist government.

I am against organized religion because the moment anything becomes organized, it has its own vested interest. Then religion is forgotten – other things become more important. Truth and the search for truth need your total involvement; nothing else should be in the way.

Organized religion becomes a prison. It gives you ready-made doctrines, and your only function is to believe in them – whether they are reasonable, logical, or not. You are not supposed to experiment on your own because, who knows? – you may find something which goes against the official doctrine.

But official doctrine cannot become your enlightenment. The official doctrine can make you learned, scholarly – but it cannot make you wise, it cannot make you intuitive, it cannot make you aware of God.

I am criticizing the pope because he is not only the head of an organized religion, but also the head of a government. It is not much of a government, eight square miles, but still, he is being accepted as head of a country; he has his representatives in the U.N.; he has his ambassadors in different countries.

Religion is something so high, and politics is so low that one thing has to be remembered: whenever there is a mixture of something lower with something higher, it is always the higher which becomes polluted – not the lower. It is always the higher which loses its quality of being higher. The lower has nothing to lose; it cannot fall any more – it has already fallen to its uttermost.

Religion and politics should be separate.

And the moment religion becomes organized, it becomes politics. Hence religion should not be organized at all; it should be everybody's private, personal, intimate search.

At least some area of life should be left to the individual where he is totally free, without anybody else deciding for him, where he can open his wings like an eagle and fly across the sun – no chains, no bondages, no hindrances.

Religion blossoms only in a heart which is absolutely free of all doctrines, all beliefs, all churches, all mosques.

I want the whole world to be religious but not

Christian, not Catholic, not Hindu, not Mohammedan. Just to be religious is enough.

Can't you see these simple facts? Honesty is honesty – it is neither Christian nor Hindu. Truth is simply truth – it cannot be Mohammedan, it cannot be Christian. Love is simply love – it cannot be Eastern and it cannot be Western. Compassion is compassion – it does not belong to any race, to any country, to any climate; it is not dependent on any geography, or any history. These are the ingredients of a religious consciousness.

Meditation is simply so scientific that just as you accept physics without bothering about whether it is Hindu or Mohammedan, you accept chemistry without ever thinking whether it is Protestant or Catholic.... When you go to the doctor, you never bother whether the medicine is Hindu or Buddhist.

The inner reality is simply a pure silence: thousands of flowers blossom there but they don't belong to any organization. They are the reward of your own search, of your own inward-going.

All the organized religions are basically depriving humanity of religion because they are misdirecting you. They are always directing you outwards – their God is far away in the sky. And when you pray, folding your hands towards the sky, you don't realize that there is nobody to hear you.

In fact, the one who is praying, the one who is alive in you, the one who is breathing in you, is the God.

You have just to discover it. It is hidden in the layers of your false personality. Find out, in your innocence, and life becomes a sheer joy, a song without words, a dance, a celebration.

And at the very end of your celebration, there is nothing but tears of gratitude. I cannot think or conceive that those tears of gratitude belong to any religion.

They belong to the individual heart, overflowing with gratefulness towards existence.

Beloved Bhagwan,

The other morning before lecture, I suddenly felt an overwhelming urge to touch, with great gratitude, the floor where you walk.
In that moment, I heard again that voice – it still sounds like Your voice:
"If you can kiss in gratitude the place on earth where I have stepped...
I want to tell you, that I've stepped everywhere on this earth."
This is really too much, for I see myself in tears, kissing every spot on the earth.
And again that voice comes in me, or from me, whispering,
"If you can kiss in gratitude all the earth, and all that abides on the earth, you don't need me anymore."
Please, Bhagwan, tell me that I was just imagining, that it was just a dream.
You haven't said that to me, have You?

Sarjano, the idea is Catholic. You come from the country of the pope, and that fellow goes on kissing the earth wherever he goes – even in India, where kissing the earth means kissing cow dung. When he kissed it here, that very day I said, "He has tasted something of Hindu religion."

It is just your imagination, Sarjano. There is no need for your gratitude to be expressed in stupid gestures. Just being grateful, your eyes full of tears, your heart just melting and merging with existence, is enough. Kissing the earth is just an idiotic symbol; I could never have said anything like this to you. But you love me, and you are so full of me that even if you speak in your imagination, you may hear my voice.

But remember one thing: except for silence, everything else is your imagination – howsoever beautiful. Only your silence I can say has my support, because only in your silence are you close to the very center of existence. In absolute silence, you become the very center yourself. But remember to avoid any kind of imagination – *all* imagination – even beautiful imagination, apparently looking like the divine.

It happened once: I had a few Mohammedan friends and they were followers of a Sufi mystic. The mystic used to come to the city once a year to see his disciples, and they were continuously telling me, "This time when he comes, some way has to be found so that you both can meet."

I said, "There is no problem with it. I can be his host; he can be my guest. That will be the best thing because he is going to be here three days, so for three days we can be together."

They liked the idea. The most impressive thing to them in the Sufi mystic was that he saw God everywhere: he would see a tree and he would go and hug the tree and start talking to the tree. Almost in a trance, he would kiss the earth; he would hold your hand and kiss it and he would start talking in a trance and address you as "God! My Lord!" People were very impressed.

He came to stay with me. Before he could kiss my hand, I said, "Wait! Do you really see God in me or have you been imagining for years?" – because that is one of the traditions in the Sufis: you start imagining and slowly, slowly, the imagination becomes a reality.

He was shocked. There was a moment of silence – painful silence, because his disciples were there. But he was an honest man; he said, "Ah, at least thirty years ago I started on the path, and this was the path shown by my teacher: 'Look into everything for God.'

"In the beginning, it was difficult to see God in a camel, in a donkey, in a buffalo. But my master insisted: All these forms are gods; you don't have to judge them – your path is just to see God in everything, so that one day you can see God everywhere. And I succeeded in three years, and I started seeing God everywhere. Now I see God everywhere."

I said, "Just listen to me. For the three days you will be here, stop imagining. Just see things as they are: a table is a table, not God; a camel is a camel, not God; and a buffalo is a buffalo, not God – just for three days."

He was very reluctant and afraid and nervous, but he was staying with me, so I said, "I will remind you about this kissing and hugging – don't forget! After three days you can hug with a vengeance, because no tree can prevent how much you hug it. For three days...you can fill the quota afterwards, but for three days I will be constantly after you. You have to see things as they are."

There was no need for three days. Within just one day, in twenty-four hours, the god that had been there for thirty years, disappeared. In the morning, he was very angry at me. He said, "What have you done? I really see a table is a table! Just now I saw a man going by on a bicycle, and I saw neither the god in the man, nor in the bicycle. You destroyed my thirty years of practice."

I said, "Just think a little. If something that you have spent thirty years discovering was really true, then in one day it could not disappear. For thirty years you have lived in a hallucination – you created the hallucination, and the hallucination can be so strong that all doubts disappear. And thirty years is a long time."

I told him a story of Ramakrishna which is very rare in the history of mystics. After attaining enlightenement, nobody ever tries to look into other paths to see whether they also reach to enlightenment or not – there is no point. You wanted to reach here, you have reached – now what is the point of finding out whether other roads also reach here or not? But Ramakrishna had something tremendously significant on his mind, so he gave six months to each religion that was available in his vicinity; for six months he would practice the religion and forget everything else. Of course, he was already enlightened so the path was not a problem; in six months, he would reach back to the point of consciousness.

In Bengal, there is a small local group of a very strange religion: they believe that Krishna is the only man, and those who follow him are all women. They may be men, but that is only an illusion; in reality, except for Krishna, there is no other man – all are women. He is the lover and you are the beloved. In the night, the followers of that sect, men and women both, dress alike – like women. And even men sleep with a statue of Krishna in their beds – he is their husband.

Ramakrishna followed that path also for six months. For others it was just a ritual; they were born into that religion, just as you are born into Christianity, or Hinduism, or Jainism. You don't really care; it is just accidental that you are born into a certain religion and you follow it, but it is a formality – at the most.

But Ramakrishna was not going into those processes in a formal way: when he was following something, he was following it with totality and intensity. And almost a miracle was seen! Even in the day, he used the same clothes as women use in Bengal. Even the people of that sect told him, "In the day you can use men's clothes; otherwise it looks very awkward."

But he said, "When I follow something, I follow it totally. I cannot divide my day from my night. And I don't care about the world."

His breasts started growing; his disciples became very much afraid. So much intensity of projecting that even the doctors who came to know about it when they visited Ramakrishna and saw his breasts, could not believe it – because this was a physiological miracle. But his disciples whispered in the ears of the doctor, "This is nothing – he is having monthly periods!"

For six months continuously...his voice changed, it became more like a woman's. He started walking like a woman – which is very difficult; difficult because only a woman can walk that way. She has a womb inside her body and that womb gives a different kind of movement to the legs. Man has no womb inside; his legs have a different movement.

He started walking like a woman, speaking like a woman, his voice changed. And when the menstrual period started, then the disciples became really afraid. They said, "We have lost him. How can we get him back?" They tried to persuade him, but until six months was up, he was not going to change his path. They said, "This path is dangerous. We don't think that these breasts and this period are going to disappear even after six months. Your whole life you will be a laughingstock – and we are going to be laughingstocks because we are your disciples."

It took almost six months after he stopped for the change to take place again. Slowly, slowly, he became a man again – before that he had become a woman. Such a deep psychological projection.... It is through such projections that people are experiencing Krishna, Jesus, Buddha – and when they experience it, they see it.

And if you say to them that it is only an illusion, how can they believe you? Their illusion looks more real than you are. Mind has a capacity to project anything and make it appear almost real; or sometimes, if the mind is very powerful, even more than real.

But my path is not the path of imagination: It is the path that does not use the mind at all.

Imagination and projection and hallucination and illusion – they are all parts of the mind. My simple approach is transcendence of mind; so only when you start seeing absolute nothingness, utter silence, can you see that I am very close by.

In that silence, you have heard me; in that nothingness, you have seen me. But if you see something, if you hear something, then it is your imagination – you have fallen from the beyond, back into the mind.

Only one thing has to be remembered: the mind is the world – and going beyond the mind is the beginning of God.

Okay, Vimal?

Yes, Bhagwan.

Session 10

Enlightenment Is Not An Experience

*Enjoy the journey and enjoy all the scenes
that come on the journey – the trees, the mountains,
the flowers, the rivers, the sun and the moon
and the stars – but don't stop anywhere
unless your very subjectivity becomes its own object.
When the observer is the observed,
when the knower is the known,
when the seer is the seen, the home has arrived.*

March 17, 1987
Morning

Beloved Bhagwan,

Whenever You talk about Your surgery, or hitting people hard, I can sense what You mean by it. Yet in all these years I have never experienced it myself.
To me, You are like a potter:
I feel Your hands molding me, guiding me, leading me, strong and firm, but also with such tenderness and love as I have never experienced before.
It is such a joy to be formed by Your gorgeous hands.
Beloved Master, in my doubting mind a question arises:
can it really be true that You are guiding me ever so gently?

Prem Nandano, each individual needs a different treatment because each individual is so unique. On the path there can be no mass surgery. You are right that you have not been hit; you don't need it.

You are saying, "Whenever you talk about your surgery, or hitting people hard, I can sense what you mean by it."

Only people who are so unconscious that unless you hit them they cannot wake up...everybody is not so asleep, so unconscious. There are so many categories. A few people are just on the verge, where a small push by a loving hand will do the whole surgery; a small push and the bird is on the wing. There was a little hesitation; just that little hesitation has to be removed. A little fear of the unknown...and the only way to remove the fear of the unknown is to push you into the unknown. Because what is unknown to you is known to me; so on my part there is no question of any hesitation.

You say, "Yet in all these years I have never experienced it myself." You will never experience it. You are one of those fortunate people who need a very tender and loving treatment – a hit can destroy you, a hit can make you more afraid of the future and the unknown.

The master works according to the need of the disciple; each according to his need.

You say to me, "You are like a potter. I feel your hands molding me, guiding me, leading me, strong and firm, but also with such tenderness and love as I have never experienced before. It is such a joy to be formed by your gorgeous hands."

To you I am a potter, because to me you are a pot! Now, to hit a pot is to destroy it – and a very immature pot; you have not even gone through the fire test – that's why you have not experienced it.

But if you want to experience, it is up to you: just wait a little! Once you have passed through the fire and you have become hard and capable of receiving a hit...because the hit is also so beautiful, so loving, that you will forget all the tenderness and all the love that I am showing to you – it is out of pity. And when I strongly hit somebody – that too is out of love – my hit gives you dignity. It is a recognition of your strength, your integrity, your centeredness.

You are asking, "Beloved Master, in my doubting mind, a question arises: can it really be true that you are guiding me ever so gently?" I have to, you are fragile. But you will not remain fragile forever. And it is a spiritual surgery, not a butcher's shop.

Rejoice in whatever you are getting. The hits will also come in their right time. Perhaps they are also a basic need, finally – just as a child is born and the cord that joins him to the mother has to be cut, although it has been his life for nine months. And cutting this life source is the most shocking thing he will ever experience – unless he meets a master. Because to cut a physical cord between two bodies is not a very big thing, but to cut the cord between your consciousness and your body is certainly the biggest shock possible. It comes, finally – when the season is right, and the moment has arrived that you have to be taken out of your body, out of your imprisonment, and left totally alone in your tremendous freedom. This is called, in the mystic language, the second birth.

The first birth is from the mother's body.
The second birth is from your own body.
From the first birth, you become a personality.
From the second birth you become an individual.

The first birth is bound to lead you one day to death. The second birth only begins, and never ends. It leads you to immortality.

But whatever is needed at a certain time will be provided to you. That's why I don't give you a discipline. All the religions are doing that stupidity – they are giving disciplines, commandments, without even bothering about whom they are addressing. Because to one, something is a medicine, and to another the same thing becomes poison.

Unless you have the fortune of being with a living master, with whom you are related – not the way people are related to organizations, but with whom you are related individually, the way lovers are related, in personal intimacy – only then can care be taken, and you can be helped slowly, slowly, towards the final quantum jump.

I can also read in your question, between the lines, that somewhere you think you are missing the hits. Right now, any hit will be dangerous. Just wait a little more and you will get as big a hit...because what is the use of giving you small hits? I'm accumulating all your hits for a single hit: one hit and your head is gone! Be intelligent, and be patient.

Mrs. Harris stood before the chimpanzee cage and watched in frozen horror as one of the chimps picked up a peanut and placed it in his rectum, then pulled it out and ate it. The distraught woman rushed over to the zookeeper and said, "I thought chimpanzees were supposed to be the most intelligent animal next to man."

"That's right, lady," said the zookeeper.

"Then why is he doing that disgusting thing?" she countered.

"Well, some boy scouts were here yesterday and gave him peaches to eat. He had trouble passing the pits. Now he checks everything for size."

Beloved Bhagwan,

The other night when You talked about the false and the real,
I came to a place inside of me that could for the first time really understand You.
It was as if I was looking at myself from the outside,
as a body that was given to me but was not really "me";
then a layer of my personality that was also just a layer of falseness and not really "me".
And even further inside was a space that was very silent and beautiful,
but that couldn't be me either,
because it was neither masculine nor feminine,
nor could it understand any language of words – it was just a nothingness.
Beloved Bhagwan, if none of those three things are me,
then where am I?

Anand Disha, one of the most fundamental things to be remembered – not only by you but by everyone – is that whatever you come across in your inner journey, you are not it.

You are the one who is witnessing it. It may be nothingness, it may be blissfulness, it may be silence, but one thing has to be remembered: however beautiful and however enchanting an experience you come across, you are not it.

You are the one who is experiencing it. And if you go on and on and on, the ultimate in the journey is the point when there is no experience left – neither silence, nor blissfulness, nor nothingness. There is nothing as an object for you, but only your subjectivity.

The mirror is empty; it is not reflecting anything.

It is you.

Even great travelers of the inner world have got stuck in beautiful experiences, and have become identified with those experiences, thinking, "I have found myself." They have stopped before reaching the final stage where all experiences disappear.

Enlightenment is not an experience.

It is the state where you are left absolutely alone, nothing to know. No object, howsoever beautiful, is present. Only in that moment does your consciousness, unobstructed by any object, take a turn and move back to the source. It becomes self-realization, it becomes enlightenment.

I must remind you about the word "object." Every object means a hindrance – the very meaning of the word is "hindrance," objection.

So the objects can be outside you, in the material world; the objects can be inside you, in your psychological world; the objects can be in your heart, feelings, emotions, sentiments, moods. The objects can be even in your spiritual world. And they are so ecstatic that one cannot imagine there can be more. Many mystics of the world have stopped at ecstasy. It is a beautiful spot, a scenic spot, but they have not arrived home yet.

When you come to a point when all

experiences are absent, when there is no object, then consciousness without obstruction moves in a circle – in existence everything moves in a circle, if not obstructed – it comes from the same source of your being, goes around. Finding no obstacle to it – no experience, no object – it moves back, and the subject itself becomes the object.

That's what J. Krishnamurti, for his whole life, continued to say: that when the observer becomes the observed, know that you have arrived.

Before that, there are thousands of things in the way.

The body gives its own experiences, which have become known as the experiences of the centers of kundalini; seven centers become seven lotus flowers. Each is bigger than the other and higher, and the fragrance is intoxicating. The mind gives you great spaces, unlimited, infinite. But remember the fundamental maxim that still, the home has not come.

Enjoy the journey and enjoy all the scenes that come on the journey – the trees, the mountains, the flowers, the rivers, the sun and the moon and the stars – but don't stop anywhere unless your very subjectivity becomes its own object. When the observer is the observed, when the knower is the known, when the seer is the seen, the home has arrived.

This home is the real temple we have been searching for, for lives together, but we always go astray. We become satisfied with beautiful experiences. A courageous seeker has to leave all those beautiful experiences behind, and go on moving. When all experiences are exhausted and only he himself remains in his aloneness...no ecstasy is bigger than that, no blissfulness is more blissful, no truth is truer. You have entered what I call godliness; you have become a god.

Anand Disha, you are asking, "If none of those three things are me, then where am I?"

An old man went to his doctor. "I have got toilet problems," he complained.

"Well, let us see. How is your urination?"

"Every morning at seven o'clock, like a baby."

"Good. How about your bowel movement?"

"Eight o'clock each morning, like clockwork."

"So, what is the problem?" the doctor asked.

"I don't wake up until nine."

Anand Disha, you are asleep and it is time to wake up. All these experiences are experiences of a sleeping mind.

The awakened mind has no experiences at all.

Beloved Bhagwan,

A year ago, on March 15th, I was visiting friends in Santa Fe.
Early that morning, Mahamati and I were lying in the back of my van
when it was struck from behind. Following the impact I couldn't breathe.
My neck and back were aflame with pain, and I panicked.
My hand discovered my mala and the struggle dropped with the deep remembrance of
sannyas, and I relaxed to be aware for death.
Ironically, I began to get air, just a little, and told Mati
not to freak out if I dropped the body, because I was still intact.
In the hospital emergency room, we both, simultaneously, felt Your presence,
and ecstatically laughed, to the dismay of the doctors and nurses.
For seven weeks I was flat on my back, and my heart flowered as never before.
The spine was fractured in two places, and this whole year I have been lazy –
doing art, portraits of You, and a novel depicting my experiences with You.
Beloved Master, I am so grateful to find I can let go
when death knocks on my door, and I feel so fortunate to look into Your eyes once more.
Thank You.
Would You like to comment on my experience?
Was it really You who came to the emergency room, or just our let-go
to existence and life?

Atmo Shahid, my whole work – day in, day out – is going from one emergency room to another emergency room. I don't have any other work. I have so many people in the world, and they are so expert in creating emergencies, that I am running like crazy. Why do you think I have told you now to drop the mala and orange clothes? Because it is getting too much! – running, without any rest.

But whatever happened to you has been of great value; this is the preparation every sannyasin is going through.

Life has to be a joy, a dance, a celebration. And when death comes, it has to be welcomed with silence, with serenity – wholeheartedly, not holding anything back. This is a way to kill death itself.

If you have lived joyously, you will be ready to welcome death too – invite her for a dance! Death is powerful only over people who have never lived, who don't have the courage to relax peacefully in moments of death without any fear – because no accident, no disease, nothing can make even a dent in your consciousness; you are always intact.

But the problem with people is, they live their whole lives unconsciously – in such misery, anguish, anxiety, that it is almost necessary for them to remain unconscious. They find new ways to be unconscious: drugs...anything that makes them unconscious. But then when death comes, they fall into a deep coma. The very fear of death, the very presence of death makes them absolutely unconscious, without any anesthesia.

Only for these people does death happen. Otherwise, death is a fiction. It is just moving the house; your old house has become such that renovating it is more troublesome than moving into a new house. The moment the body comes to a point when it is no longer functioning organically – when its inner structure is fractured, when things are not happening as they should happen, when mechanisms have run to their full capacity....

Each child brings with himself at birth, the genes which tell his whole history. And soon it may become possible – it is almost possible now – in the reports of the scientists, they say that they can read the program of the first cells that begin your life. At least they will be able to know the great events in your life: when you will become sexually mature, at what age; when you will become old, when death will strike your body just to make you free.

Death is in the service of life. Life never dies.

But in unconsciousness you go on doing things that you are not clearly aware of why you are doing. You go on moving because everybody else is moving, but you don't know where you are moving and for what. You go on living because everybody else is living, but without any consciousness.

Why? Why should you wake up tomorrow morning and still go on breathing? Your whole past proves that it has been nothing but an exercise in futility, and you know perfectly well you will be repeating it as long as you are alive – unless by accident, you come across a man who is awake. And the awakened people have become so few, as centuries have passed, that it is almost improbable that you will come across an awakened person.

But only the awakened person can wake you up, shake you up; can give you a little consciousness of what you are doing: This is not life. This is only a slow death which will be completed in seventy or seventy- five years' time. You are dying every day, every moment.

The great masses of the world only know slow death.

Only very few people who have become awakened have known the tremendous tidal wave of life.

Just as the unconscious goes on dying, the conscious goes on becoming more and more alive. The unconsciousness only grows old; the conscious grows up, becomes mature, reaches heights of consciousness. It is in its seed in everybody, but the problem is how to challenge the seed, how to call to the seed: "Don't remain dormant!" Only the awakened person can create the presence in which your seed inside starts waking up.

It was a good experience, Shahid. You remained aware in the moment of death. Now don't take it for granted. You have to be aware each moment in life.

Sometimes, particularly in accidents, people become aware because the accident is such a shock that the unconsciousness disappears. But if they survive, the unconsciousness again starts gathering around them like a dark cloud and they start living a life which is meaningless, imitative, not knowing why.

Goldstein got a job in the sports section of a large department store. On his first day there, the store manager overheard him with a customer: "Look," said Goldstein, "these fish hooks are fifty cents each. But I can sell you three for a dollar."

"I will buy them!" exclaimed the customer.

"Now, you have fish hooks but you need a fishing line. This excellent nylon line normally costs two dollars for a hundred yards but I can give you two hundred yards for three dollars," said Goldstein.

"I will buy it!" exclaimed the customer.

"Now you have fish hooks and a line, but you need a rod. Here is a rod – normally costing one hundred dollars, but I can sell it to you for only seventy-five dollars," said Goldstein.

"I will buy it!" exclaimed the customer.

"Now you have fish hooks, a line and a rod but you need a fishing boat. Here is a boat normally costing eight thousand dollars but it is yours for five thousand dollars."

"I will buy it!" exclaimed the customer.

"Now you have fish hooks, a line, a rod, and a boat but you need a trailer to carry the boat on. Normally, this one costs two thousand dollars but it is yours for eighteen-hundred dollars."

"I will buy it!" exclaimed the customer.

"Now," said Goldstein, "you have fish hooks, a line, a rod, a boat and a trailer. All you need now is a car to pull your boat and trailer. Here is a car especially made for fishermen, designed to pull a boat and trailer – normally costing ten thousand dollars, but you can have it for eight thousand dollars."

"I will buy it!" exclaimed the customer.

After the customer had left with all his purchases, the manager went up to Goldstein. "Goldstein," he said. "I've been running this store for thirty years and never have I seen anyone making such an incredible sale. Starting with fifty-cent fish hooks and working up to a ten-thousand-dollar car!"

"What do you mean I started with fish hooks?" demanded Goldstein. "The man came in asking where he could buy tablets for his wife's period, and I told him that what he needs right now is a weeks' fishing holiday!"

This is your life.... Why are you doing things? Why are you buying things? How are you spending your life? You are not at all aware. You are just a sleepwalker, a somnambulist. Anybody can cheat you – the politicians are doing it, the priests are doing it, but in your unconsciousness it is absolutely natural. Only a conscious man cannot be exploited.

Only a conscious man really lives. And those who really live, die peacefully, silently, with a smile on their face. For these people who die with a smile on their face, there is no death – because deep down in in their consciousness there is an absolute certainty that it is only the body that is being dropped. Life has continued always, and will continue always.

Beloved Bhagwan,

At the moment, my life seems to be an endless dive into deep, dark valleys
of greed, jealousy, self-condemnation, deep pain, and feeling very lost.
Coming out of these valleys, I feel refreshed, more clear –
like after a thunderstorm in hot summer.
But the next valley follows soon afterwards. Are these dark valleys a sort of cleaning, and has
this to happen again and again?

Prem Vanshi, the question is: "At the moment, my life seems to be an endless dive into deep dark valleys of greed, jealousy, self-condemnation, deep pain and feeling very lost. Coming out of these valleys, I feel refreshed, more clear – like after a thunderstorm in hot summer. But the next valley follows soon afterwards. Are these dark valleys a sort of cleaning, and has this to happen again and again?"

As long as you wish.

Because these valleys are your creation. This is your creativity; they don't come from outside.

You have managed your life in such a way that these have become your constant companions: greed, jealousy, self-condemnation, deep pain. You cannot live without them, or you will feel very alone. However miserable they are, anyway it is your family. However ugly the mother is, no boy says that his mother is ugly.

The gaps between valleys are *not* your creation. The valleys that you create are so painful that you cannot tolerate them continuously. Once in awhile you want to be alone, and when you are alone you again feel fresh.

But just look at your logic: You are consoling yourself that these deep valleys of darkness are cleansing you. Those few moments between two valleys, you think are cleansing, refreshing, because of the valleys. You are indebted to all the nonsense that you are creating yourself.

What is the need of greed in life? Greed arises only because your present moment is empty, and to live in an empty moment hurts very much. To forget it you project greed into the future, thinking that tomorrow things are going to be better, a lottery is going to open in your name. But of course you have to wait for tomorrow, it cannot be just now – and tomorrow never comes. All that comes is always the present moment, which is empty.

Greed is because we don't know how to live the present moment in its total richness.

Just the other night I saw a small anecdote about a great Zen master, Ryokan. He used to live in the mountains in a small hut. Another Zen master was staying with him. The whole day passed, talking about poetry, painting, sculpture, music, and they both forgot about food.

He had to go to beg for his food in the town. By the evening, he became aware. He said, "I am sorry – to me it is not much, it is my usual habit. Sometimes I forget. But I am keeping you hungry, so I will go immediately and find something before the sun sets." So he rushed down the mountain and his friend waited and waited and waited for three hours. No sign...and he was feeling so hungry that he came out of the house – what has happened?

Has there been some accident?

And he could not believe his eyes: Ryokan was sitting outside the house under a tree with closed eyes, a great grace on his face, murmuring – almost in a whisper – new haikus, new poetries. The guest went there, shook him and asked him, "What happened about the food?"

Ryokan said, "My god! When I saw the sun setting, it was so beautiful that I could not move away from this tree. From this tree, the sunset is a golden experience. I had stopped only for a moment but the sunset and its beauty impressed me so much that I forgot all about food and all about you! But here are a few beautiful haikus…"

The guest said, "But haikus won't help. I cannot sleep with such hunger."

Ryokan said, "Wait – I will go. Although it is late, I may find something." And he rushed down from the hill towards the town. The whole night, the guest was tossing and turning, and coming out again and again to see what had happened to Ryokan.

In the early morning, when the sun was rising, the guest went out again – he had not slept a single wink. Ryokan was still sitting under the same tree – smiling and swaying and murmuring.

The guest said, "Ryokan, what about food?"

Ryokan said, "My god! When I reached the bottom of the hill, people were asleep and it was a fullmoon night. It was so beautiful, you would not believe. I have seen fullmoon nights before, but never anything comparable to this. So just to enjoy it a little, I sat under a tree – and I don't know when the night passed, but I have found some beautiful haikus….

"And living in this glory of the full moon…you can understand me, and forgive me. I forgot all about food. In fact, I was wondering, when the sun started rising – what am I doing here? So I returned to my tree, from where sunset, sunrise, both have such a divine splendor."

The guest said, "You will kill me! I am going."

Ryokan said, "But at least listen to my few haikus. They are not mine, truly. Some are given by the full moon, some are given by the rising sun, some are given by the birds singing in the trees. And life has been so rich and I was so nourished by it that even the idea of food never crossed my mind."

The guest left. He said, "You seem to be a madman!" But a man like Ryokan cannot have greed.

Each moment is so full of blessings, each moment is such an eternity of joy, each moment is such a dance of beauty. Greed arises, Vanshi, only because you don't know how to live herenow.

Greed is a postponement of life.

It is one of the most stupid things one can do, because it will land you in death and nowhere else.

And a man who lives totally in the moment – his heart full of songs, his presence radiating joy – how can he feel jealous? The whole world may feel jealous of him, but he cannot feel any jealousy. These are your wrong approaches to life, that greed and jealousy arise in you and create dark valleys. And then comes self-condemnation, because you know deep down that you are the creator of your greed, of your jealousy. But self-condemnation does not help. It makes things worse: you become depressed, you start feeling unworthy of life. You start feeling that you don't deserve even a single breath more, and that gives great pain.

You have not lived life at all.

Each moment has gone empty.

It is great pain, great anguish – but remember it is your creation.

When you become tired, and out of the tiredness there is a little relief, then you feel clean. No condemnation, no pain, no jealousy, no greed – but no energy either. You have spent all your energy in those idiotic fantasies. Because there is no energy, for a few moments, a few hours, you are left alone. It is peaceful. But this peace is not the authentic peace. It is the peace that rains on the graveyard; it is not the peace of the garden, full of songs and full of flowers.

And as you gather energy again, the old companions are back.

This wheel will go on rotating unless you understand and jump out of it. And the only way to jump out of it is to live each moment so totally that it brings such contentment, such fulfillment that you cannot be greedy. And you cannot be jealous, and you cannot be in self-condemnation, and you cannot feel pain.

Existence gives you one moment by one moment.

So if you know to live one moment totally, you know the whole secret of life.

An Irish worker used to take tunafish sandwiches to work every day, but a fellow worker noticed that each day he would take one bite and throw the rest away in disgust.

"But if you don't like tunafish," said his friend, "why don't you ask your wife to make something else?"

"Ah," said the Irishman, "it is not as easy as that. I have not got a wife, I make them myself."

Okay, Vimal?

Yes, Bhagwan.

Session 11

A Noah's Ark Of Consciousness

*Whatever you are doing, do it with such love,
with such care that the smallest thing in the world
becomes a piece of art.
It will bring great joy to you.
And it will create a world without competition,
without comparison; it will give dignity to all people;
it will restore their pride, which religions have destroyed.*

March 17, 1987
Evening

Beloved Bhagwan,

You tell us to be aware of everything – which means
to be a witness to everything, every act.
When I decide to be aware in work, I forget about awareness,
and when I become aware that I was not aware, I feel guilty;
I feel that I have made a mistake.
Could You please explain?

Manish Bharti, it is one of the basic problems for anybody who is trying to be aware while at work – because work demands that you should forget yourself completely. You should be involved in it so deeply...as if you are absent. Unless such total involvement is there, the work remains superficial.

All that is great, created by man – in painting, in poetry, in architecture, in sculpture – in any dimension of life – needs you to be totally involved. And if you are trying to be aware at the same time, your work will never be first rate, because you will not be in it.

So awareness while you are working needs a tremendous training and discipline, and one has to start from very simple actions. For example, walking: you can walk, and you can be aware that you are walking – each step can be full of awareness. Eating...just the way in Zen monasteries they drink tea; they call it the "tea ceremony" because sipping the tea, one has to remain alert and aware.

These are small actions, but to begin with they are perfectly good. One should not start with something like painting, dancing – those are very deep and complex phenomena. Start with small actions of daily routine life. As you become more and more accustomed to awareness, as awareness becomes just like breathing – you don't have to make any effort for it, it has become spontaneous – then in any act, any work, you can be aware.

But remember the condition: it has to be effortless; it has to come out of spontaneity. Then painting or composing music, or dancing, or even fighting an enemy with a sword, you can remain absolutely aware. But that awareness is not the awareness you are trying for. It is not the beginning, it is the culmination of a long discipline. Sometimes it can happen without discipline too. At least one story I remember....

A great swordsman, a great warrior, came back home and found that his servant was making love to his wife. According to custom, he challenged the servant – gave him a sword and told him to come out of the house and let it be decided; whoever remains alive will be the husband of the woman.

The servant did not even know how to hold a sword – he was a poor servant, he had never been trained in swordsmanship. He said, "Master, although you are following a convention, and respecting even a servant and giving him an opportunity, this is for you just a game. I don't know anything about swordsmanship. At least give me a few minutes so that I can go to the greatest master – who lives nearby in a monastery, a Zen monk – to have some clue."

The man agreed. He said, "You can go. And if it is needed, a few hours, or even a few days, or even a few months – you can get disciplined. I will wait for you."

He went to the great warrior, the Zen master. The Zen master said, "Even years of training will not help you. Your boss is just second to me in the whole country – you cannot hope to compete with him. My suggestion is: this is the right moment to fight."

The servant could not understand. He said, "What kind of puzzle are you giving to me: this moment is the right moment?"

And he said, "Yes, because you have one thing certain – your death. Now more than that you cannot lose. Your master has many things to lose: his wife, his prestige, his respectability as a warrior; he is a great landlord...all his money – his mind cannot be total while he is fighting. But you can be total. You *have* to be total – just a moment of unawareness and you are gone; you have to be totally alert. This is the right moment; don't bother about any discipline – you simply take the sword and go."

The servant came back within minutes. His boss said, "Have you learned anything?"

He said, "There is no need of learning anything. Come out of the house!"

And the way he shouted, "Come out of the house".... The boss could not believe what magical change had happened to his servant. As he came out, the servant, according to convention, bowed down to the boss; the boss bowed down to the servant. That is, in Japan, part of their culture; even with the enemy, you have to respect his dignity, his humanity, his divinity.

And then the servant started hitting the warrior – knowing nothing about swordsmanship. The warrior was at a loss, because where any expert would have hit, the servant would not hit because he had no idea; he would hit somewhere where no expert would have ever hit. And he was fighting with such totality that the warrior started moving backwards, and as the warrior started moving backwards, the servant gathered more courage. He was moving his sword without knowing why – to what purpose, or where he was hitting. And since it has been decided that his death is certain, now there is nothing to worry about – all worries belong to life.

Soon he cornered the master. Behind, there was the wall surrounding the master's garden. He could not move backwards anymore. He was so afraid of death, for the first time in his life, and he said, "Wait! You can have my wife, you can have my properties; I am renouncing the world, I am becoming a monk."

He was trembling with fear. Even he could not understand what happened. From where did this courage come? From where this totality? From where this awareness? But it can be only in such special situations that without any discipline, just the situation can create so much awakening in you.

Whenever I have read this story, I have always remembered Adolf Hitler. For five years continuously he was winning the war on all fronts, alone – fighting the whole world. And the reason he was winning the war was that he was not listening to the generals at all.

Fighting is an art; in the military you go through a long training. Hitler's advisors were not generals and experts in military science; his advisors were astrologers. They would tell him where to attack and where not to attack, and that was the reason that for five years he went on winning – because the other side was following military science. And if he had also listened to his generals, then there would have been no possibility for five years' of continual victory.

You will be surprised to know that finally Churchill had to call astrologers from India to find out where he was going to attack – because it is normal and common sense that wherever the enemy is weak, you attack at that point, and wherever the enemy is strong, you avoid that point until the very last. But the astrologers have nothing to do with the army or fighting; they consult the stars.

The enemy would be following military science and would be preparing at the weakest point, knowing that this would be the point where Adolf Hitler's generals would decide to attack. And Adolf Hitler would attack the strongest point of the enemy, where they were fast asleep…not even bothering – because no military scientist would ever suggest to attack at the strongest point. They were not prepared there; they were preparing at the weakest link.

In a haphazard way…the enemies were simply puzzled: What to make of it? He knows nothing of the army; he knows nothing of military science. But his not knowing was immensely helpful for five years until Churchill decided, in spite of himself – knowing that this is stupidity – that astrologers from India would come to London. And from that very day, Germany started falling apart – because now astrologers were against astrologers; it was no more a war between two armies. As stupid as Adolf Hitler was, Winston Churchill had found even greater idiots from India. Things changed – just within two months, Adolf Hitler was retreating.

Whenever I have come across the story of the Zen master and his servant, I have always remembered Adolf Hitler: he had absolute certainty about astrology, he was total in his action. Not even a single doubt crossed his mind, ever.

The same must have happened to the servant. When death is certain, fear disappears. Fear is only there because of death. But when death is certain and there is no way to avoid it, what is the point of being afraid? He became almost a man of total integrity – knowing nothing, but defeating the master who had been a victorious man in many combats.

But this can happen only rarely, in extreme conditions. In everyday life you should follow the simple course. First become aware about actions which do not need your involvement. You can walk and you can go on thinking; you can eat and you can go on thinking. Replace thinking by awareness. Go on eating, and remain alert that you are eating. Walk; replace thinking by awareness. Go on walking; perhaps your walking will be a little slower and more graceful. But awareness is possible with these small acts. And as you become more and more articulate, use more complicated activities.

A day comes when there is no activity in the world in which you cannot remain alert and at the same time, act with totality.

You are saying, "When I decide to be aware in work, I forget about awareness." It has not to be your decision, it has to be your long discipline. And awareness has to come spontaneously; you are not to call it, you are not to force it.

"And when I become aware that I was not aware, I feel guilty." That is absolute stupidity. When you become aware that you were not aware, feel happy that at least now you are aware. For the concept of guilt, there is no place in my teachings.

Guilt is one of the cancers of the soul.

And all the religions have used guilt to destroy your dignity, your pride, and to make you just slaves. There is no need to feel guilty, it is natural. Awareness is such a great thing that even if you can be aware for few seconds, rejoice. Don't pay attention to those moments when you forgot. Pay attention to that state when you suddenly remember, "I was not aware." Feel fortunate that at least after few hours, awareness has returned.

Don't make it a repentance, a guilt, a sadness – because by being guilty and sad, you are not going to be helped. You will feel, deep down, a failure. And once a feeling of failure settles in you, awareness will become even more difficult.

Change your whole focus. It is great that you became aware that you had forgotten to be aware. Now don't forget, for as long as possible. Again you will forget; again you will remember – but each time, the gap of forgetfulness will become smaller and smaller. If you can avoid guilt, which is basically Christian, your gaps of unawareness will become shorter, and one day they will simply disappear. Awareness will become just like breathing or heartbeat, or the blood circulating in you – day in, day out.

So be watchful that you don't feel guilty. There is nothing to feel guilty about. It is immensely significant that the trees don't listen to your Catholic priests. Otherwise, they will make the roses feel guilty: "Why do you have thorns?" And the rose, dancing in the wind, in the rain, in the sun, will suddenly become sad. The dance will disappear, the joy will disappear, the fragrance will disappear. Now the thorn will become his only reality, a wound – "Why do you have thorns?"

But because there are no rose bushes so foolish as to listen to any priest of any religion, roses go on dancing, and with the roses, thorns also go on dancing.

The whole existence is guiltless. And a man, the moment he becomes guiltless, becomes part of the universal flow of life. That is enlightenment: a guiltless consciousness, rejoicing in everything that life makes available – the light is beautiful; so is darkness.

When you cannot find anything to be guilty about, to me you have become a religious man. To the so-called religions, unless you are guilty you are not religious; the more guilty you are, the more religious you are.

People are torturing themselves as punishment, as penance. People are fasting; people are beating their chests with their fists till blood oozes from their chests. These people, to me, are psychopaths; they are not religious. Their so-called religions have taught them that if you commit anything wrong, it is better to punish yourself than be punished by God on Judgment Day – because that punishment is to be thrown into the abysmal darkness of hell for eternity. There is no escape, no exit. Once you enter hell, you have entered.

The whole humanity has been made guilty in

some measure or other. It has taken away the shine from your eyes, it has taken away the beauty from your face, it has taken away the grace of your being. It has reduced you to a criminal – unnecessarily.

Remember: man is frail and weak, and to err is human. And the people who invented the proverb, "To err is human," have also invented the proverb, "To forgive is divine." I don't agree with the second part.

I say, "To err is human and to forgive is also human." And to forgive oneself is one of the greatest virtues, because if you cannot forgive yourself, you cannot forgive anybody else in the world – it is impossible. You are so full of wounds, of guilt – how can you forgive anybody? Your so-called saints go on saying that you will be thrown into hell. The reality is, they are living in hell! They cannot allow even God to forgive you.

One great Sufi poet, Omar Khayyam, has written in his *Rubaiyat*, his world-famous collection of poetry: "I am going to drink, to dance, to love. I am going to commit every kind of sin because I trust God is compassionate – he will forgive. My sins are very small; his forgiveness is immense."

When the priests came to know about his book – because in those days books were written by hand, there were no printing presses.... When the priests discovered that he was writing such sacrilegious things, that he was saying, "Don't be worried, go on doing anything you want because God is nothing but pure compassion and love. How much sin can you commit in seventy years of life? – in comparison to his forgiveness, it is nothing."

He was a famous mathematician too, renowned in his country. The priests approached him and said, "What kind of things are you writing? You will destroy people's religiousness! Create fear in people, tell people that God is very just: – if you have committed a sin, you will be punished. There will be no compassion."

Omar Khayyam's book was burned in his day. Whenever a copy was found, it was burned by the priests, because this man was teaching such a dangerous idea. If it spreads among human beings and everybody starts rejoicing in life, what will happen to the priests? What happen to the saints? What will happen to their mythologies of hell and heaven and god? All will disappear in thin air.

At least with me, Omar Khayyam is one of the enlightened Sufi mystics, and what he is saying has immense truth in it. He does not mean that you should commit sin. What he means simply is that you should not feel guilty. Whatever you do – if it is not right, don't do it again. If you feel it hurts somebody, don't do it again. But there is no need to feel guilty, there is no need to be repentant, there is no need to do penance and torture yourself.

I want to change your focus completely. Rather than counting how many times you forgot to remember to be aware, count those few beautiful moments when you were crystal clear and aware. Those few moments are enough to save you, are enough to cure you, to heal you. And if you pay attention to them, they will go on growing and spreading in your consciousness. Slowly, slowly the whole darkness of unawareness will disappear.

A young man is about to be married so before his wife-to-be moves into their apartment, he has a man-to-man chat with his pet parrot.

"Now listen, buddy, there is this beautiful young woman whom I am about to marry and we are going to live together in this flat. She comes from a very good family and I want you to forget all about those dirty, four-letter words that you have picked up from living with me these past few years. If I hear you utter one dirty remark in front of her, I am going to sell you to the zoo. Got it?"

"Okay," says the parrot. "Got it!"

After the wedding, the couple are packing their bags for their honeymoon. There are suitcases all over the apartment, and after hours of struggle everything is packed – even the parrot's cage has a cover on it. But suddenly they discover that one shoe has been left out. The girl tries to push it into a large suitcase but it just won't go in.

So the husband says, "You will have to sit on top and I will push it in."

They try and try but it does not work. "Let's try it another way," says the wife. "Let's both be on top and push it in together."

At this point, the parrot pushes his covering aside and says, "The zoo be damned. This one I've got to see!"

He kept in control of himself so much, but there comes a point that even he has to go to the zoo. He says, "Let the zoo be damned, but this thing I have got to see." The curiosity...he could not believe that this kind of thing is possible.

In the beginning you will also find many times that perhaps it is not possible to be working and to be aware together. But I say unto you that it is not only possible, it is very easily possible. Just begin in the right way. Just don't start from XYZ; start from ABC.

In life, we go on missing many things because of wrong starts. Everything should be started from the very beginning. Our minds are impatient; we want to do everything quickly. We want to reach the highest point without passing through every rung of the ladder.

But that means an absolute failure. And once you fail in something like awareness – it is not a small failure – perhaps you will not try it again, ever. The failure hurts.

So anything that is as valuable as awareness – because it can open all the doors of the mysteries of existence, it can bring you to the very temple of God – you should start very carefully and from the very beginning.

And move very slowly. Just a little patience and the goal is not far away.

Beloved Bhagwan,

Please talk to us of tension and relaxation.
Usually, when I sit in front of You I relax all through myself.
I lose any alertness I may have.
When I am alert, there is a subtle tension which I need
to maintain this wakefulness. It winds me up like a spring
and then I feel horrible. How can I stay awake
without all this tension?
How to find the stillness, though busy?
I watch You move and sit with such joy.

Anand Trinda, it is the same question that I was answering, just written in a different way. If you have listened to my first answer, your question has also been answered. I will just tell a small anecdote.

One day a man from a small village in the mountains sees a tourist driving his car backwards up a narrow road towards the top of the mountain. The man stops him and says, "Why are you driving backwards?"

The tourist replies, "They told me that there is no room to turn a car around on top of the mountain."

The man says, "I have lived here all my life. I know there is enough space to turn around."

Half an hour later, he sees the tourist driving down again, backwards. He stops the car and says, "What are you doing now?"

The tourist replies, "You were right. There *was* enough room to turn around."

Whatever I have said is simple: Start being aware with day-to-day, routine actions, and while you are doing your routine actions, remain relaxed. There is no need to be tense. When you are washing the floor, what is the need to be tense? Or when you are cooking the food, what is the need to be tense? There is not a single thing in life which requires your tension. It is just your unawareness and your impatience.

I have not found anything – and I have lived in all kinds of ways, with all kinds of people. And I have always been puzzled: why are they tense?

It seems tension has nothing to do with anything outside you, it has something to do within you. Outside you always find an excuse only because it looks so idiotic to be tense without any reason. Just to rationalize, you find some reason outside yourself to explain why you are tense.

But tension is not outside you, it is in your wrong style of life. You are living in competition – that will create tension. You are living in continuous comparison – that will create tension. You are always thinking either of the past or of the future, and missing the present which is the only reality – that will create tension.

It is a question of simple understanding; there is no need of any competition with anybody. You are yourself, and as you are, you are perfectly good.

Accept yourself.

This is the way existence wants you to be. Some trees are taller; some trees are smaller. But the smaller trees are not tense – neither are the taller trees full of ego. Existence needs variety. Somebody is stronger than you; somebody is more intelligent than you – but in something, you also must be more talented than anybody else.

Just find your own talent. Nature never sends any single individual without some unique gift. Just a little search...perhaps you can play on the flute better than the president of the country can be a president – you are a better flautist than he is a president.

There is no question of any comparison. Comparison leads people astray. Competition keeps them continuously tense, and because their life is empty, they never live in the moment. All they do is to think of the past, which is no more, or project in the future, which is not yet.

This whole thing drives people almost abnormal – insane. Otherwise there is no need: no animal goes mad, no tree needs any psychoanalysis. The whole existence is living in constant celebration, except man. He is sitting aloof, tense, worried.

A small life, and you are losing it and every day death is coming closer. That creates even more angst – "Death is coming closer and I have not even started living." Most people realize only when they die that they were alive – but then it is too late.

Just live the moment.

And whatever qualities and whatever talents you have, use them to the fullest.

One of the mystics in India, Kabir, was a weaver. He had thousands of followers and still he continued to weave clothes. Even kings were his followers.

The king of Varanasi asked him, "Master, it doesn't look good, it makes us feel embarrassed. We can take care of you. There is no need for you to weave clothes and every week on market day, go into the market to sell your clothes. Just think of us: people laugh at us."

Kabir said, "I can understand your problem but I have only one talent and that is to weave beautiful clothes. If I stop doing it, who will do it? And God comes in different faces, in different bodies, to purchase clothes every week in the marketplace."

He used to address every customer, "Lord, be very careful of the cloth. I have been weaving it, not just like any other weaver – my songs are in it and my soul is in it. I have poured my whole being in it. Be careful, use it with tenderness and love and remember: Kabir has woven it especially for you, Lord." And it was not something that he was addressing to anybody in particular – any customer!

This was his contribution. He used to say to his disciples, "What else can I do? I am doing my best: I can weave, I can sing, I can dance – and I am immensely contented."

Whatever you are doing, if there is contentment and a feeling that this whole existence is nothing but the manifestation of godliness, that we are traveling on holy earth, that whomever you are meeting, you are meeting God – there is no other way; only faces are different, but the inner reality is the same – all your tensions will disappear. And the energy that is involved in tensions will start becoming your grace, your beauty.

Then life will not be just an ordinary, routine, day-to-day existence, but a dance from cradle to grave. And existence will be immensely enriched by your grace, by your relaxation, by your silence, by your awareness.

You will not leave the world without

contributing something valuable to it. But people are always looking at others, at what others are doing – somebody is playing the flute and you cannot, and immediately there is misery; somebody is painting and you cannot, and there is misery.

Whatever you are doing, do it with such love, with such care that the smallest thing in the world becomes a piece of art. It will bring great joy to you. And it will create a world without competition, without comparison; it will give dignity to all people; it will restore their pride, which religions have destroyed.

In my whole life, I have never judged any person. If God is happy with him, why should I be worried whether he is a thief or a murderer? Perhaps that is the function existence wants him to do. All that is needed is that he should do it with as much artfulness and as much intelligence as he can gather – with his totality.

Any act done with totality becomes your prayer.

Beloved Bhagwan,

Rocks easily destroy flowers.
The politicians and religions sense that enlightenment,
freedom and individuality threaten their power.
Is it fear alone that is the basis
of the dark use of intelligence to crush man's finest blossoms?
or is there an unconscious urge for "endarkenment" too?

Devageet, there is an unconscious urge for endarkenment too. It was only a hundred years ago that Sigmund Freud stumbled, in the unconsciousness of man, on a very strange instinct.

Man has been, for almost ten thousand years, working on himself, on his consciousness, but it was left to Freud to find a totally new idea. He himself was shocked, but when he came, across it again and again, in different patients, he had to give it recognition. And the idea was, that just as there is a lust for life, to balance it in the unconscious of the human mind, there is an instinct for death. Perhaps this was one of the great contributions of Sigmund Freud to human knowledge, and for the future transformation of man.

Slowly, slowly, then he started gathering facts, and now it is almost an established thing that in life, everything exists with its opposite balancing it. If there is a lust for life – that one wants to live – somewhere hidden, there is bound to be a lust for death. In certain situations, it may get a grip on you – that's why so many people commit suicide. Otherwise, suicide has no explanation.

Devageet is asking: "Rocks easily destroy flowers. The politicians and religions sense that enlightenment, freedom and individuality threaten their power. Is it fear alone that is the basis of the dark use of intelligence to crush man's finest blossoms? or is there an unconscious urge for 'endarkenment' too?"

There is; there has to be. Just as there is a longing for enlightenment, to reach to the highest peak of consciousness, there is certainly, parallel to it in the unconscious of human mind, a deep urge to drown oneself into darkness, into death.

It has been observed, although never made clear, by all the physicians of all the ages, that there are people who can be helped by medicine but it seems impossible to help them because they have completely lost the willpower, the will to live – completely. They don't support the medicine. But none of the physicians found the thing that Sigmund Freud discovered. Perhaps this had some sense in it: a man who loses the will to live is bound to replace it by something of its opposite – the will to die.

And now medicine accepts that the physician can only help by his medicines and other things, if the person wants to live. If the person has dropped the idea of living, then all those medicines are useless. Medicines don't cure you. Your will to live cures you – medicines are only a secondary help, a support. But if somebody has moved to the opposite pole – the instinct for death, for darkness – then no medicine can pull him out.

As I was reading the question, I thought about AIDS. Perhaps someday it may be found that AIDS is nothing but an unconscious desire to die; that's why scientists are unable to find any cure for it.

At this moment in history, Devageet's question becomes even more pertinent, because one wonders that seventy-five percent of the budget of the whole of humanity is being devoted to create destructive weapons – nuclear weapons, and half of humanity is starving. Thousands of people are dying without medicine, and millions of children are dying because they cannot get very inexpensive vaccines.

On the one hand, humanity is on the verge, just because of overpopulation, of dying of starvation; and on the other hand, all politicians in the world have only one desire: to become nuclear powers. Five countries are already nuclear powers, and by the end of this century, twenty-five more countries will be nuclear powers. Already, we have enough nuclear weapons to destroy humanity seven times.

It seems absolutely ridiculous now to go on piling up nuclear weapons. Billions of dollars are wasted on nuclear weapons while children are dying because they cannot get medicine, they cannot get food. By the end of this century, half of the population of the world will die from starvation; and the other half, perhaps, will die through nuclear warfare.

It seems it is not only one individual, but perhaps the whole of humanity that has lost the will to live, the will to be more conscious, the will to be more aware, the will to reach to the highest peak of enlightenment, to be a Gautam Buddha.

On the contrary, people are waiting to disappear into darkness, into death, because life is so meaningless and so futile. There seems to be no reason to go on living. For the first time, on a tremendous scale, millions of people are feeling meaninglessness. It is creating tremendous anxiety, and it seems death is the only cure. With death, everything will subside. There will be no problem, no anxiety, no struggle, no jealousy, no tension.

Perhaps, Devageet, your word "endarkenment" may become a contribution to our language, as the opposite of enlightenment. People have always lived unconsciously, but today, the unconsciousness has reached to such a point that even death is preferable to unconsciousness.

A Scotsman named Angus needed a new kilt. When he went to pick out some material at the store, he decided to purchase two extra yards of fabric to make a matching scarf for his girlfriend.

He then went home and made such a beautiful kilt that when he tried it on, and looked in the mirror, he forgot all about the scarf and thought, "I shall go right now and show this to my lady."

As he ran out of the door, a thread of the new kilt caught on the doorway, unraveling the garment. Eventually, Angus was running across the heather with his jewels dangling in the dew. He got to his girlfriend's house and knocked on the door.

As his girlfriend opened the door and looked him up and down, she said, "Hello Angus, so nice of you to drop in."

"Hello my bonny lass. And what do you think of this?" Angus said, pointing down to where he thought his new kilt was.

She said, "Ah Angus, it is just lovely."

Angus said, "That's right my pretty lass, and I have got two more yards at home to wrap around your neck."

Man has always lived in unconsciousness, but the darkness was never as much as it is today. There have been nights, but always the dawn has come. This time it seems to be doubtful whether the dawn will come or not.

I am not a pessimist, but I am no longer an optimist either. I used to be – now, I am simply a realist. And the reality is: perhaps we are very close to the end of this beautiful planet, with all its beauty, all its life, and all its great achievements. There seems to be no ray of hope from anywhere. And perhaps when I am saying this, it is not me who is saying it; perhaps it is existence itself who has lost hope about humanity and its future.

The only thing that I still go on dreaming for is my people. Perhaps the planet will not be saved, but those who have come to me, if they make a little effort to become conscious, to create a longing for enlightenment, at least they can be saved. But if you go on behaving like the masses of the world, you are also a lost case.

Immense responsibility rests on you because nowhere else in the whole world are people trying, even in small groups, to achieve enlightenement, to be meditative, to be loving, to be rejoicing. We are a very small island in the ocean of the world, but it does not matter. If these few people can be saved, the whole heritage of humanity, the heritage of all the mystics, of all the awakened people, can be saved through you.

If this planet dies, perhaps on another planet.... There are fifty thousand planets which can sustain life; perhaps civilization has to begin from ABC on some other planet. But who will be the pioneers? These dark masses, utterly unconscious, cannot be. Only a few chosen ones who have strived hard to make themselves deserving of light, of eternal life, of some experience of godliness – perhaps they will be the ones who will be starting a new civilization somewhere in the universe, on some new planet.

I have never said this before but, going around the world, I have felt such a wound in my heart that the people who need to be saved are the people who are creating every kind of barrier to being saved. Even to approach them has become impossible. And seeing the whole world, I started feeling that there is now only one possibility, and that is to create in the consciousness of those few who have come close to me, a Noah's Ark. It will not be a physical thing, but a Noah's Ark of consciousness which moves a small group of conscious people to another planet. That seems to be the only possibility to save the great heritage of humanity.

You cannot depend any longer on the politicians and on the priests, and on the masses who seem to be willing, deeply desiring, to die. Death seems to be the greatest desire in the world today, and because I have been talking about life and love and laughter, I have been condemned from every corner.

I can understand the reason: to spread the message of life, love and laughter amongst people who, deep down, are getting ready to commit a global suicide...this is very contradictory to them.

Perhaps we will have to meet on some other planet – this planet seems to be spent. And it is not new: planets are born, planets die; stars are born, stars die – so it is not something strange. And the preparations are going so well that it seems almost an impossibility for life to survive here on this earth. The whole blame goes on those vested interests which have kept humanity unconscious, and don't want man to become intelligent and conscious, alert and aware. Anyway, it seems too late.

The police were investigating the death of Markowitz, the dress manufacturer who had jumped from the window of his office. The detective decided to query Marlene, his lovely young secretary.

"Can you offer any explanation?" he asked the girl.

"Well, after working for Mr. Markowitz one month," she began, "I got a forty-dollar-a-week raise. At the end of the second month, he gave me a beautiful black necklace. At the end of the third month, he gave me a new Thunderbird, and a stunning Persian lamb coat. Then he asked me if I would be willing to make love, and how much I would charge him. I told him that he had been so nice to me, I would charge him only ten dollars, even though I was getting twenty from the other guys in the office. And that is when he jumped out of the window."

Okay Vimal?

Yes, Bhagwan.

Session 12

Life Itself Is A Miracle

*There are no miracles in the world
in the sense people think about miracles.
Otherwise everything is a miracle.
Just that we are here is a miracle;
just that the sun has again risen today is a miracle.
That roses bloom, that lotuses open,
that trees sway and dance in the wind – everything is a miracle.*

March 18, 1987
Morning

Beloved Bhagwan,

What happens to human consciousness
when the people of the world suddenly realize
they are in the midst of an unstoppable, devastating plague
that will kill most of the people they know?

Amrito, it depends on different people. For one who is absolutely conscious, nothing will happen; he will accept it, just as he has accepted everything else. There will be no struggles, no anxieties.

As he can accept his own death, he can accept the death of his planet too. And this acceptance is not in any way a kind of helplessness but on the contrary, just seeing the suchness of things – that everything is born, lives and has to die.

This planet was not here four billion years ago; then it was born. Perhaps it has lived its whole life. And anyway, even if the human mind manages to pull through this crisis created by the politicians, the planet cannot live long because the sun is dying. In four billion years' time it will have exhausted all its energy; and once the sun dies, this planet cannot remain alive. Our whole life energy comes from the sun.

The man of perfect awareness will simply accept it as a natural phenomenon. Just now, leaves are falling from the trees; the other evening, the wind was blowing strong and the leaves were falling just like rain. But what can you do? This is the law of existence. Everything comes into form and disappears into formlessness. So for the man who is awakened, there will not be any change in his consciousness. For the unawakened man there will be different reactions.

I have heard...a man was dying; he was very old, had lived his life – there was no need to be worried about death. It was getting dark as the sun had set. The man opened his eyes and asked his wife who was sitting by his right side, "Where is my eldest son?"

The wife said, "He is sitting just in front of me on the other side of the bed. Don't be worried about him; don't be worried about anything in this moment. Relax and pray."

But the man said, "And where is my second son?"

The wife said, "He is sitting by the side of your eldest son." And the old man who was almost on the verge of death started to get up.

The wife said, "What are you doing?"

He said, "I am looking for my third son." And the wife and the sons all felt how much he loved them. The third son was sitting just near his feet.

He said, "I'm here pappa. You relax, we are all here."

He said, "You are all here, and you want me to relax? Who is tending the shop?"

At the moment of death he is still concerned about the shop.

It is very difficult to predict how different people's unconscious minds will react. Their whole life will be reflected in their reaction, that much is certain. But everybody's life has moved through different paths, different experiences, and the culminating point is going to be different.

Death brings to the surface your essential personality.

Another old man was dying – he was a very rich man. His whole family was gathered there. The eldest son said, "What should we do when he dies? We will have to rent a car to take him to the graveyard."

The youngest son said, "He always longed for a Rolls Royce. In life he could not sit in one, but at least, dead, he can enjoy a ride – a one-way ride of course – to the graveyard."

But the eldest son said, "You are too young, and you don't understand a thing. Dead people don't enjoy anything. It does not matter to the dead person whether it is a Rolls Royce, or just a Ford. A Ford will do."

The second son said, "Why are you being so extravagant? Anyway, a dead body only has to be carried. I know a person who has a truck – it will be more comfortable, and cheaper also."

The third son said, "I cannot tolerate all this nonsense. What is the need to be worried about Rolls Royces and Fords and trucks? Is he going to be married? He is going to die. We will just put him outside the house where we put all our garbage. The municipal truck will take him automatically, no expense at all."

At this moment the old man opened his eyes and said, "Where are my shoes?"

They said, "What are you going to do with your shoes? You just rest."

But he said, "I want my shoes."

The eldest son said, "He is a stubborn man. Perhaps he wants to die with his shoes on. Let him have his shoes."

And the old man, as he was putting the shoes on, said, "You need not be worried about expenses. I still have a little life left; I will walk down to the graveyard. See you there! I will die exactly by the grave. It hurts me that you are all so extravagant; even in my life I only dreamt about a Rolls Royce, or some other beautiful car. Dreaming is inexpensive, you can dream about anything."

And, it is said, the old man walked to the graveyard, his sons and his relatives following him, and he died exactly by his grave – to save money.

The last thought in a dying man is very characteristic of his whole life, his whole philosophy, his whole religion. It is a tremendous exposure.

One of the followers of J. Krishnamurti – an old man and very respected in India – used to come to me because his son was attorney general of Madhya Pradesh, and the MP court is in Jabalpur. He used to come to visit his son, and whenever he was there he made it a point to see me if I was in the town. The old man had been Krishnamurti's follower for almost fifty years. He had dropped all rituals, all scriptures; he was absolutely convinced logically, intellectually, that Krishnamurti was right. I used to say to him, "You should remember, intellectual conviction, logical or rational conviction is very superficial. In times of crisis it disappears, evaporates."

But he used to say to me, "Fifty years – it cannot remain superficial."

One day his son came to me and said, "My father is dying and I could not think of anybody else whom he would like to have near him – he loves you so much. So you just come with me; I have brought the car, there is not much time."

So I simply went with him. As I entered through the door of his father's room, very silently his lips were moving. So I went in, also very silently, because I wanted to hear what he was repeating. He was saying, "Ram Ram Ram," the Hindu name of God. And for fifty years he had been saying there was no God.

I shook him. He opened his eyes, and he said, "Don't disturb me. This is no time for argumentation."

I said, "I am not going to argue, but just to ask: what happened to those fifty years? From where does this repetition of the name of God come? You insisted that there is no God."

He said, "That was okay at that time, but now that I am dying – and the doctors have said I cannot survive more than half an hour – just don't disturb me; let me repeat the name of God. Anyway, who knows? He may be. If there is no God, there is no harm in repeating his name. But if there *is* a God, and you don't die repeating his name, then you are on the blacklist. And I don't want to go to hell, I have suffered enough here on the earth."

I said, "That's what I was saying to you, that intellectual conviction is of no use."

He did not die; he survived. After three, four days I went to see him. He was sitting in the garden and I said, "What about that evening?"

He said, "Forget all about it. It was just a time of weakness, a fear of death that made me start repeating the name of God. Otherwise there is no God."

I said, "It means you need another experience of dying? This was your first heart attack: you survived – the second will be coming soon. At the most you can survive the second, but the third you will not be able to survive. And remember what you were saying to me."

He said, "Forget all that. I am absolutely certain there is no God."

I said, "Just let death start approaching near you, and immediately your superficial, intellectual convictions will disappear. This idea that there is no God is not your own, it is borrowed. It is not your own exploration; it is not your own insight; it is not part of your consciousness but only part of your mind."

People will behave differently.

You are asking: "What happens to human consciousness when the people of the world suddenly realize they are in the midst of an unstoppable, devastating plague that will kill most of the people they know?"

A few points can be certainly asserted. One, when the whole world is dying, all your relationships – your mother, your father, your girlfriend, your wife, your husband, your boyfriend, your children – do not mean anything. When the whole world is on the point of disappearing into death, into a black hole, the relationships that you have created in life cannot remain intact.

In fact, behind our relationships we

are strangers.

It makes one feel afraid, so one never looks into it. Otherwise, even when you are in the crowd, you are alone; even if your name is known to people, does that make any difference? You are still a stranger. And this can be seen...a husband and wife may have lived thirty years, forty years, fifty years together, but the more they live together, the more they become aware that they are strangers.

Before they got married they had the hallucination that perhaps they were made for each other, but as the honeymoon ends, that illusion disappears. And every day they start becoming distant and more distant – pretending that everything is all right, everything is fine, but deep down they know that their strangeness is untouched.

This whole world is full of strangers. And if it was going to disappear the next moment, if it was announced on all the radios and all the televisions, suddenly you would see yourself in your utter nudity – alone.

A small child had gone to the zoo with his father, and they were watching a very ferocious lion in his cage – he was walking up and down. The boy became very much afraid; he was not more than nine. He asked his father, "Dad, if this lion gets out and something happens to you...please just tell me what number bus I have to take to reach home!"

In such a situation he is asking a very relevant question. He cannot conceive that if something happens to his father, something will also happen to him; but in case something happens to his father and he is alive, he needs to know the number of the bus. The father was shocked that he was not concerned about him at all. Whatever happens to him happens – his concern is to know the number of the bus.

The very climate of death suddenly takes away all your masks, suddenly makes you aware that you are alone and all your relationships were deceptions, ways to forget your aloneness – somehow to create a family in which you feel you are not alone.

But death exposes without fail. And this is only about small deaths; if the whole world is going to die, all your relationships will disappear before it. You will die alone, a stranger who has no name, no fame, no respectability, no power – utterly helpless. But in this helplessness people will still behave differently.

An old man is about to have a date with a young woman; so he goes to the doctor, who prescribes him an aphrodisiac that will increase and prolong his libido. He takes his date to one of the best restaurants in town. When they have ordered their soup, he sends his date to powder her nose and then takes the waiter aside. "Put these pills into my soup," he confides in him, "just before you bring it out from the kitchen." The young lady comes back, but when, after fifteen minutes, the soup has not been served, the old man calls the waiter over. "Where is our soup?" he demands.

"It will be here in a few minutes," replies the waiter, "just as soon as the noodles lie down again."

At the time of death, the most important subject in the minds of people who are not conscious is going to be sex – because sex and death are two sides of the same coin.

Life is so full of mysteries: you will be surprised to know that when people are crucified, just as they are crucified they almost always ejaculate. Doctors have been thinking why, and they have come upon the explanation that those sperms, which are alive, seeing the situation – that the body is dead – rush out of it. Their life out of the body is only two hours, but in two hours they may find some other body, some other center.

First it was thought to be a very mysterious thing, that crucified people should ejaculate – but it is just as though your house is on fire and you start escaping out of it. Your sperms are living beings, and you are dying – why should they die with you? You have been just a house to them and the house is on fire – and everybody has the right to make an effort at least to save his life.

When the whole world is dying, most of the unconscious people who have been repressing their sexuality will think only of sex. They cannot think of anything else; all their interests and hobbies and religions will disappear – the world is dying, perhaps they can make love one more time before death destroys everything. They have been repressing their whole life's libido, the sexual urge, according to the priests, according to the society and the culture – and now it does not matter. Everything is going to disappear; they don't need any respectability, they don't care about religion.

One man was told by his doctor that this would be the last night in his life. "As the sun rises in the morning, you will be dead. Everything has been done, but nothing seems to succeed. What do you want? If you have any wishes to be fulfilled, you have one night."

The man simply rushed home. He told his wife, "This is my last night and I always wanted to make love to you with totality, but there were so many hindrances, inhibitions. And at this moment the only idea in my mind is, before I die, I should at least experience a total orgasm."

He made love. In the middle of the night he again nudged the wife and said, "The morning is coming close. I will never be able to see you again. If I make love one more time, it won't harm you."

So he made love a second time, and as he felt – because he could not sleep; when death is going to knock on your doors, how can you sleep? As the morning was very close he again nudged the wife and said, "Darling, just one time more."

The wife said, "Listen, you never think of others. You don't realize the simple fact that in the morning I have to wake up. You will be gone, that's okay, but I have to wake up – so just let me rest a little. And when you die there is going to be so much fuss, so much trouble – crying and weeping and all those things. You just go to sleep."

Once you know the person is going to die, suddenly the small thread of relationship breaks down.

The world disappearing into a black hole, in the ultimate death, perhaps may make people almost crazy, may bring out all their repressed sexuality, sensuality. But it will all depend on different individuals, how they have lived. If they have lived an uninhibited, natural life, each moment given its total share, then perhaps they will simply watch it – it is going to be the greatest tragedy, the greatest drama in the world. They will not do anything but sit silently and watch. But no general law can be established as to what people will do.

Only about the enlightened people can it be said, with absolute guarantee, that there will be no difference at all. They know that such is the nature of things. This is the whole approach of Gautam Buddha – the philosophy of suchness – that there is a time when the fall comes, and the leaves have to leave the tree.

When the spring comes there are flowers, and in the East particularly…the West has no idea about it; in the East it is not one creation, but every creation that goes into a de-creation – just as every man, after the whole day's work, goes to sleep in the night. This is a very potent idea. Each creation, after a time – they have even talked about the exact time, how long one creation lasts – goes into de-creation. It also needs rest. So for the enlightened person it is not anything unusual; it is part of existence itself. As the day has ended, the night will end also – and again the creation wakes up.

Modern physics is coming closer to the idea. First they discovered black holes: that in space there are strange black holes and if any planet or any sun comes close to the black holes it is pulled in and simply disappears. But science understands the balance in nature, so now they are saying that there must be white holes; perhaps the black hole is one side of the door, and the white hole is the other side of the door. From one side a planet or a star goes into the black hole and disappears from us, and from the other side, the white hole, a new star is born.

Every day new stars are born and old stars are dying; life and death is a continuous circle. If life is the day, death is the night – it is not against it; it is just rest, sleep, a time to be rejuvenated.

The man of understanding will not be disturbed by it. But the unconscious people will simply freak out, and they will start doing things they have never done. They have been controlling themselves and now there is no point in controlling, there is no need.

If it is known beforehand – which is not very possible, because with nuclear weapons it will take only ten minutes for the earth to disappear, so there is not much possibility that you will be informed in advance. Get ready! Just the shock of hearing on your radios or on your television sets that within ten minutes the world is going to collapse, you may get simply frozen, paralyzed – the shock will be so big and so unfamiliar.

Perhaps most of the people will die from shock, not from nuclear weapons. Just hearing that within ten minutes the whole world is going to die will be enough – the shock will destroy their fragile existence. So how people will behave is going to be only hypothetical.

Only about the enlightened ones I can say with absolute guarantee, on my own authority, that there will be no difference. If they are drinking tea, they will continue to drink tea; their hands will not even shake. If they are taking a shower, they will continue to take a shower. They will not be in shock; neither will they be paralyzed, nor will they freak out. Nor will they indulge in things which they have been repressing, because an enlightened man has no repressions in his being; he knows always only one word to say to nature – "yes."

They will say "yes" to the disappearing earth, to the ultimate death – they don't know the word "no." There is not going to be any resistance on their part; and they will be the only ones who will die consciously. And the one who dies consciously enters into the eternal flow of life; he does not die.

Those who die unconsciously will be born on some other planet, in some other womb – because life cannot be destroyed, even by nuclear weapons. It can destroy only the houses in which life exists.

Beloved Bhagwan,

You really are too much!
The other night You said that You don't do miracles,
but this morning, in front of my own eyes,
I saw old Maitreya levitating when You danced with him.
Isn't that a miracle?

Anando, I still say the same: I do not do miracles. But that does not mean that miracles don't happen. I was not doing anything, and Maitreya was levitating. I had to move quickly because if he levitates too much – he is old and may get hit with the ceiling.

A group of men gave a testimonial dinner to Goldberg, and after they had praised him for an hour, Goldberg finally got up to speak.

"Gentlemen," he said, "when I came to this town forty-one years ago, I walked down a dirt road with one suit of clothes, one pair of shoes, carrying a dirty old suitcase. And to show you what hard work can do, along with the great opportunities this country can offer, today I own three banks, five apartment houses and ten oil wells!"

Everybody applauded, and right after the dinner one salesman walked up to the old man and said, "Pardon me, sir, I would like to ask you a question. When you came here forty-one years ago with just that one suit, a pair of shoes and an old suitcase – what was in the suitcase?"

The old man said, "I had three million dollars in bonds and two hundred thousand dollars in cash."

Miracles only appear to happen; they do not really happen. When you are totally singing and moving with the energy of the whole, you still cannot levitate – but you can start hopping. That's what was happening: old Maitreya was hopping, and Anando was just behind him so she must have been afraid – What has happened to old Milarepa?... I called him Milarepa by mistake, because it was expected to happen to Milarepa, not to Maitreya!

For centuries it has been observed that when you are silent, joyous, and if you are sitting with closed eyes, you start feeling as if you are levitating. If you open your eyes you will find you are sitting on the ground. You have not levitated, but consciousness can move upwards and that can give you a feeling of levitation.

Thousands of seekers have felt levitation; it is not physical, but with closed eyes you will feel exactly as if your whole body is moving up. It is only your consciousness which is rising up, but you and your consciousness are so identified that unless you open your eyes you will not become aware that the body has not levitated – only the consciousness went higher than the body, beyond the body. It is a law of consciousness: just as things gravitate, consciousness levitates – it is simply balance. But there are no miracles.

I have heard that two rabbis and one bishop were very close friends. All three had gone to Israel for a holy pilgrimage, of course for different reasons. The rabbis had gone for their own religion – that is their holy land. And the bishop had gone because of Jesus Christ;

it is also the Christian holy land.

Now all three went to see Lake Galilee, where Jesus is supposed to have walked on water. They went in a boat on the lake, and the bishop said while they were on the lake, "Do you really believe that Jesus walked on the waters?" The rabbis looked at each other, winked their eyes and said, "Yes!"

The bishop said, "Can you do that miracle also?"

The rabbi said, "It is a very simple thing in these parts; it was nothing special, not a miracle." And the rabbi got out of the boat from his corner, and walked a few feet.

The bishop could not believe his eyes. The rabbi got in. The second rabbi also walked a few feet and he also came back. They said to him, "We are not Christians and we don't believe in Jesus, but as far as walking on this lake is concerned, anybody who lives around here can do it. Would you like to give it a try?"

The bishop said, "Certainly – since you two have walked, and I am a believer in Jesus Christ...." So he stepped out into the lake from his side, and the moment he stepped out he started drowning and shouting, "Save me, save me!"

Both the rabbis laughed, and they said, "Should we tell the poor boy about the stones – that he has stepped out on the wrong side of the boat? If you want to walk on water, there are rocks, hidden just under the surface!"

There are no miracles in the world in the sense people think about miracles. Otherwise everything is a miracle. Just that we are here is a miracle; just that the sun has again risen today is a miracle. That roses bloom, that lotuses open, that trees sway and dance in the wind – everything is a miracle.

You can choose between the two: either there are no miracles, or everything is a miracle. My preference is for the second, because the first is a very dry attitude towards life, and that attitude will make your life flat, without any mystery and without anything miraculous. My preference is the second.

Everything is a miracle: a seed turning into a sprout, growing into a huge tree, flowering, bringing fruits – it *is* a miracle.

Just the other day, Shunyo said to me that it is strange that old leaves are falling and new leaves have already arrived in the same place where the old leaves used to be; one has just fallen and a new leaf has started growing in its place, fresh and young....

Life itself is a miracle.

But I am not interested in miracles like Jesus walking on water, or bringing the dead back to life. Those are only fictions. It is strange...you can easily understand, if somebody walks on water, then he will be reported all over the world, in all the newspapers; he will make a mark in history. If somebody makes people come back to life historians cannot ignore such a person, and such a person cannot be crucified; he should be worshipped like a God.

But strangely enough, Jesus, who was a man of miracles according to Christians, was thought by his contemporaries to be only a nuisance, someone who should be destroyed. Not a single Jewish contemporary book, scripture or inscription even mentions his name. He is mentioned only by his four disciples in the New Testament. Other than those four gospels the whole of Judea did not bother about the man – and he was a man of such qualities, at least his name must have been referred to. Even if they were against him, as an enemy his name must have been mentioned. But there is no reference in any Jewish scripture.

This gave an idea to George Gurdjieff, and his

idea seems to be plausible. He used to say that Jesus Christ never existed; that there used to be a drama, and Jesus Christ was only an actor in that drama that was played year by year – just as in India, the story of Rama is played as drama all over the country every year. That drama became a reality, or was made a reality by a Christian priest to create a new religion. The fiction in the drama of Jesus Christ was perfect for creating a religion, and because they created the religion, the Jews stopped the drama.

That too is a hypothesis, but no Christian authority has refuted George Gurdjieff because they don't have any evidence except for those four gospels. And they are written by his own disciples and are not much different from each other; they are the same gospel written by four different people.

One thing is certain, even if Jesus was a historical figure, too much mythology and too much fiction have been added just to make him "the only begotten son of God." And it becomes more probable, because the same has happened to Gautam Buddha and to Mahavira – who were absolutely historical personages. There is so much reference to them in their contemporary literature, even in the literature of their enemies, that they cannot be said to be simply mythological.

But to make them superior human beings, supermen, the disciples went on adding new miracles. And that can be seen: the older the book, the less miracles there were; as new books were written, more miracles were added. From where were they getting those miracles? – because in the old literature those miracles are not there.

For example, in the oldest book about Gautam Buddha it was not mentioned that he was born when his mother was standing under a sal tree. To give birth to a child while standing is a very unfamiliar and very strange style. And not only that Gautam Buddha was born while she was standing – he stood on the earth as he came out of the womb. Not only that – he walked seven feet! And not only that, he declared, "I am the greatest awakened man in the whole history of man – past, present, and future."

To the superstitious these may seem miraculous, but to any reasonable man they are fictions, added to make Gautam Buddha a superman, a god – because unless you have a god, you cannot create a religion. All those miracles are cunning strategies to create religions.

Okay, Vimal?

Yes, Bhagwan.

Session 13

Truth
Is Not Divisible

*It is because of this that I emphasize that
religion is a private, personal and individual affair.
It cannot be organized.
The moment you organize it, you destroy it.
And if we want humanity to be religious,
then all the religions have to disappear.
They are the barriers.*

March 18, 1987
Evening

Beloved Bhagwan,

Let's reverse the question for once:
What have You learned being with us?

Sarjano, it is the last supper. Jesus has gathered all his disciples together and there is a great feeling of gloom in the air. A single candle lights the room. Everybody can sense that something momentous is going to happen and that this may be their last meal together.

Jesus pours out the wine and passes the glasses around and then divides up the food and personally serves his disciples. The candle burns low and at last, all the food is gone except for one hard-boiled egg.

Jesus says to Peter, sitting on his right, "Peter, my blessed disciple, would you like to eat this last egg?"

"Ah, no master," says Peter. You must have it."

Jesus then turns to his left and says, "John, my blessed disciple, would you like to eat this last egg?"

"Ah, no master," says John. "You must have it." Jesus asked all his twelve disciples in turn, and they all refused the last egg, saying that he, their master, must have it. Just then a gust of wind comes through the window and blows out the candle. The room is plunged into darkness and it is filled with an awesome silence.

Suddenly, there is a hideous scream. Someone lights a new candle, and everyone gasps as they see Jesus with his hand stretched out for the remaining egg – and embedded in the back of his hand, are twelve forks! But it was too late to learn....

I have learned much. One of the most significant things that I have learned is not to feel sad when you betray, not to feel sorry when you go astray – in fact, not even to expect that you have to trust.

The relationship between me and you has to be one-sided, only from your side, not from my side at all. You are here of your own free choice; you can move away just as freely as you had come. You love me – that is your decision. You can start hating me – that will also be your decision. I am absolutely unconcerned; only then is it possible not to feel hurt, not to feel wounded.

Jesus was betrayed only once, by one disciple. I have been betrayed continually for almost as much time as Jesus lived on the earth – thirty-three years. So many people I have trusted so totally have betrayed me so easily. There was a moment they were ready to die for me and just some small thing...if I was not fulfilling their expectation, which I have never agreed to fulfill, their love changes into great hate. The same person who was ready to die for me is ready to kill me.

So I have learned it the hard way that if you love, it is your decision. If you hate, it is your decision. I am almost non-existent as far as my side is concerned: neither am I a partner in your love, nor am I going to be a partner in your hate. This is a sad lesson but it is good that I have learned it long before.

If somebody assassinates me, at least I will not have any complaint, any grudge – because to love was his freedom, to hate is also his freedom. I am absolutely out of the relationship.

I will go on doing whatever I feel is needed for the growth of your consciousness. But people have been going on, changing...such stupid expectations and if they are not fulfilled...it seems as if they have come to me to change *me*, to transform *me*. They want me to be according to their idea of how a master should be.

I give you total freedom to be yourself. I never expect anything, any ideal to be imposed on you. I don't give you any commandments. And yet you go on carrying within your mind certain expectations that I have to fulfill, and if they are not fulfilled...and they *cannot* be fulfilled. Thousands of people are related to me. They have different ideals, different moral concepts. It is almost impossible – and even if it were possible, I am not a man to fit with those who are unconscious, who are themselves living in darkness.

You are here to go through a transformation. It is none of your business how I live, what I say, what I do – the moment you start thinking to change something in me, the bridge between me and you is broken.

And it is a one-sided bridge; I am not a partner in it. I know it is hard for you but your very question implies, Sarjano – perhaps you have not read it very consciously while you were writing it. You say, "Let us reverse the question for once." You cannot reverse it even for once. You are asking now, "What have you learned being with us?"

I have nothing to learn.

You are here only because of the fact that you have found a person who has nothing to learn – and particularly from you, who are groping in darkness, in unconsciousness, who are almost on the boundary line of insanity – any moment, just one step more and you are in a madhouse.

Neither from you, nor from anyone else.

And my whole approach is – and I have been insisting millions of times – that as far as truth or the ultimate reality is concerned, you cannot learn it from anybody else. And once you have known it, there is nothing that remains to be learned.

So I say to you: not even once can the question be reversed. I have not learned anything from you. You need not feel responsible for anything. Just being with you for all these three decades, it has not been a learning but simply a discovery: that there is nobody in the world who is so awakened that you can even call him a friend, so awakened that you can even call him, a beloved. This has not been a learning – this is simply a discovery, slowly slowly, as I have come to know human beings.

And as I went around the world, my discovery has become absolutely clear: this humanity has come to a dead end. To hope for anything from this humanity is sheer nonsense. Perhaps a few people may be saved – and for them I go on creating the Noah's Ark, knowing perfectly well that perhaps when the Noah's Ark is ready, there may not be anybody left to be saved. They may have all gone their own ways.

It rarely happens: never have so many people come in contact with anybody – either Jesus or Mahavira or Buddha – and never have so many people left Buddha, Mahavira or Jesus. It is significant to have some insight into it. Even Gautam Buddha, a man of immense insight, was ready to compromise on minor points with his disciples. And the disciple feels immensely happy if the master agrees with him – although the master agreeing with the disciple is like light agreeing with darkness, truth agreeing with that which is not true, life agreeing with death. But because Buddha, Mahavira, Jesus and other teachers of the past have compromised on minor points, very few people have left them.

I am an absolutely non-compromising person. Either you have to be with me absolutely… without expecting anything from my side, because I cannot agree on any smallest, most minute point if it is not true.

And truth is indivisible. You cannot say, "I may not have the whole truth…but a little bit, a piece of it, a fragment of truth." Truth is not divisible. Truth is almost like a circle. Have you ever seen a half circle? Perhaps you may have misunderstood: if you have seen a half circle, it is no longer a circle at all; the circle can only be full. The half is only an arc, it is not a circle. Just as the circle is indivisible, so is truth, so is life, so is existence, so is love, so is ecstasy.

Either you have it or you don't have it.

If you have it, there is no question of your being here. If you don't have it, then be absolutely clear that you don't have it, because living in the illusion that perhaps you have a little bit of it, is dangerous.

What can I learn from you? – being unconscious? Being greedy? Being jealous? Being violent? What can I learn from you?

As I have gone on discovering more and more people, my hope for humanity has disappeared. If you want to call it a learning, you can.

I don't see any future possible. And the time is so short before the curtain falls, that you should not waste it in unnecessary things. Your life has now to be absolutely devoted to the most essential thing, the most fundamental thing: to be enlightened has to be your single-pointed concentration.

Everything else has to be sacrificed for it, because you cannot even postpone it for tomorrow.

Tomorrow may never come.

Beloved Bhagwan,

Would You please comment on commitment and spontaneity.
Are they opposite poles of the same energy?

Prem Nirmala, commitment and spontaneity are certainly opposite poles, and of the same energy. Commitment is something like death; spontaneity is something like life. Commitment is something like darkness, and spontaneity is something like light.

Although they belong to the same energy as opposite poles, you have to start from being spontaneous. All the religions of the world want you to start from commitment, all political parties want you to start from commitment.

Commitment, if you start with it, is very dangerous. It is another name of slavery. It means you are saying and promising something which is not within your capacity. You are saying that "Tomorrow also, I will be the same." But who can say what tomorrow is going to bring?

Commitment means, "I will remain blind to anything else that can change my commitment." That's why every belief makes people blind. They have to keep their eyes closed, out of fear – they may see something which goes against their belief, their commitment.

Every year, the Catholic pope declares a black list of books that Catholics are not supposed to read. Reading them means a certainty of your going to hell. I was talking to a bishop in Nagpur, because a few of my books had been listed by the Catholic pope as not to be read by any Catholics; whoever reads them is paving his path towards hell. And this is not new, this is an almost eighteen-hundred-year-old tradition in the Catholic Church.

Before this century, they used to burn and destroy any book they decided was dangerous for Catholics. Now they cannot do that, but at least they can prevent the Catholics – who are a great majority in the world, seven hundred million people.

I simply said to the bishop of Nagpur, "At least somebody must have been reading my books; otherwise how do they decide? Either the pope himself must be reading, or some associate cardinals in the Vatican must be reading – without reading, you cannot decide that a book is dangerous to the Catholic belief."

He was in a dilemma: he could not say yes, he could not say no. Because if he says "Yes, somebody reads it," that means that person is bound to fall into hell. And if that person is not going to fall into hell, then the whole idea is ridiculous; then nobody is going to fall into hell. It is just to keep people's eyes closed: no facts should be allowed to be known to them that go against their belief.

Commitment demands that you lose your eyes, lose your mind, lose your reason, your logic, your intelligence, your consciousness. It is almost a living death. Never begin anything with commitment.

But such is the mystery of life.... Begin everything with spontaneity, with natural awareness, with no commitment for anything, but always ready and open and available to anything new that you come across on the path.

Only a spontaneous lifestyle can lead you to

your authentic being.

And this is the miracle: that once spontaneous living has led you to clarity of vision, to purity of intelligence – has destroyed all the darkness of your soul and has made everything light within you – then spontaneousness itself becomes commitment.

But it is not being imposed from outside, it is a growth within yourself. It is your experience to which you are committed; it is your understanding to which you are committed. You are committed to your own eyes, to your own consciousness, to your own intelligence, to your own experience.

This commitment has a beauty and an aliveness.

It is spontaneity becoming mature.

Spontaneity was like a child; commitment is maturity, crystallization. Just as nobody can start from the middle of life, or from the end of life – everybody has to start from the childhood. Although every childhood will reach old age, and every birth will reach death...but nobody can begin with death. And a life that has been lived with joy and dance and love – its crescendo, the death, will not be dark. It will not be an end of something but a new beginning, a new beginning of a higher spontaneity on another plane.

But religions have deceived humanity in such cunning ways. And unless you are very alert, it is difficult to understand in what ways they have deceived you. Spontaneity and commitment are two poles of the same energy, but there is one commitment – which is imposed from outside, which has not come as a flowering of your own spontaneity – that is a false commitment: your being a Christian, or a Hindu, or a Mohammedan, or a Jew is a false commitment. It has not grown within you, you have not lived up to it. It is not a maturity of your own consciousness, not a crystallization of your being, but something imposed from above by others.

It has no roots within you. That's why the whole world is full of religious people but there seems to be no religiousness anywhere. No religious values blossom, but just the opposite – humanity lives on an almost subhuman level.

Prem Nirmala, start from spontaneity. But no tradition, no culture, no civilization, will allow it, because they can control only dead people. And they can control through commitment.

The spontaneous person is beyond anybody's enslavement. And if the spontaneous person grows, he will come to a commitment – but that will be his own commitment to existence, between himself and existence. No other mediator, no priest, no pope, no imam, no shankaracharya is going to stand between him and this immensely beautiful existence, this great life, this divineness that is spread all over the world.

His spontaneity will bring him to a commitment, but that commitment will be out of his own freedom. It will have roots deep in his own being. He will not be a Christian – he can be a Jesus Christ. He will not be a Buddhist – he can be a Gautam Buddha. He will not be a Hindu, but he can be a Krishna; he will not be a Jaina, but he can be a Mahavira.

It is because of this that I emphasize that religion is a private, personal and individual affair. It cannot be organized. The moment you organize it, you destroy it. And if we want humanity to be religious, then all the religions have to disappear. They are the barriers.

There are three hundred religions on the earth. They are dividing human beings, giving them different commitments, and those commitments have nothing to do with the time, with the space in which we find ourselves.

When a commitment comes out of spontaneity, it is always timely, it is never dead – it is always growing with the changes that are happening every moment. It is just a riverlike flow, it is not frozen ice.

But it is very easy to deceive people because both the phenomena are so deeply interrelated. And people are living in such a deep sleep, without any alertness at all, that they cannot make the discrimination between such closely connected experiences.

But just a little turn makes all the difference. If you start from commitment, then you will never reach to spontaneity; you have started from death. But if you start from spontaneity, you will reach to commitment – and that commitment will not be death. Out of spontaneity, death cannot grow – only more life and more life and infinite life.

But you have to be alert, just a little conscious....

Two criminals were caught and went to jail. They became friends, and most of the day they were talking about how to escape. One morning, George looked so blissful that his friend Arthur asked, "Hey, what happened to you last night?"

"Well," said George, "first tell me how you spent the night."

"Okay," replied Arthur. "I had a beautiful dream: The gate opened by itself and I walked out. In the street, there was a racing bike with ten gears and I jumped on it and rode away. Great, was it not? But now, tell me about you?"

George answered, "In my dream, the door also opened and two very beautiful young girls came in, stripped, belly dancing."

At this point, Arthur could not hold back and said, "George, but why didn't you wake me up?"

"Impossible," replied George. "Don't you remember? You were gone on the bike!"

Our lives are not different from our dreams. Have you ever observed that even in your dreams, the dream also looks real? as real as the life when you are awake – perhaps more real because when you are awake, you can doubt.

You can doubt – right now you can doubt; perhaps this is real or perhaps it is just a dream.

There have been great philosophers in the world, like Shankara in the East, and Bradley in the West, whose whole philosophy consists of a single, significant statement: that the world is illusory. There is no way to prove that it is real. One thing is certain, that you can doubt it. But in the dream, you cannot even doubt. The reality of the dream is so tremendous that you cannot dream and wonder if perhaps it is a dream. No, the dream overwhelms you completely.

We are living, although with open eyes, in different dreams. And those dreams don't allow us the alertness to see simple things: how we are being exploited, how our dignity as human beings is destroyed, what very stupid and idiotic people become our religious saints – those who have no sharpness of intelligence. But we find strange excuses....

Just a few days ago, one young Jaina nun escaped from a Jaina monastery with a young man. The whole Jaina community in that area near Indore was in such a turmoil, and the turmoil became even more significant because the girl gave a statement to the press and wrote letters to her parents saying that "Now I am twenty-one years of age and I have the right to choose my lifestyle. I don't want to be a nun, and if you insist...." Because they were trying in every way to catch hold of her, to find where she was hiding. And Jainas are rich people. The government was supporting them, the police officers were supporting them.

She gave the statement to the newspapers: "If they insist that I have to remain a nun, then I will expose the reality, the inside story of the monastery and what is going on inside there. Nobody is following the teachings that they teach to the layman outside. There are all kinds of corruption. Monks, who are not supposed to have money, have accumulated money. Monks and nuns who are not supposed to have any sexual relationship are having sexual relationships. And I have been tortured in so many ways that if you insist, I will expose it to the whole world." She said, "My younger sister is still there. She also wants to come out of the monastery but she is only eighteen years of age."

But still, in India, money functions like miracles. They must have bribed the police, they must have bribed the magistrate. An arrest warrant was issued. Now, that girl has not done any harm to anybody – is she not free to have her own way of life? If she does not want to be a nun, has she to be forced to be a nun by the police and by the government and by the court? And the parents started fasting. These are ways of torturing people – people think these are ways of nonviolence, they are not. The father and mother started fasting in front of the monastery, and declared they would not eat unless the girl came back. Now, it is a very subtle way of forcing the girl to come back.

The prestige of the family, the prestige of the religion, the prestige of the monastery is at stake. But the girl must be courageous; she did not turn up. And before the police reached the place where she and the young man were hiding, they escaped from there. I hope they will come here, because they cannot find anywhere any shelter with dignity and respect. Wherever they go, they will be thought to be criminals.

In fact, she has done a really courageous act; she needs immense respect and honor. And their whole effort is to catch hold of her, alive or dead. The fear is what she is going to expose about the monastery – but every monastery is doing all those things.

I used to meet Jaina monks while I was traveling around India, and I was surprised. When I became intimate and friendly with a few Jaina monks and nuns.... They would close the door and they were hiding in their bags Coca Cola, Fanta, and they would offer it to me. I would say, "This is a miracle! From where have you got this? You are not supposed to keep these things...." They are not supposed to keep anything with them. They all had money, and they were all hiding their money. And they all had their agents everywhere who were bringing things – even in the night – for them to eat. And none of them was celibate.

I would love that girl to turn up here, because here we can give her total freedom to be herself. We don't have any belief system and we don't have any commitment. And from here, she can expose all that she has passed through.

Beloved Bhagwan,

Referring to the present situation of the world and of humanity, the famous psychiatrist, R.D. Laing, asks himself the question: "What to do when we don't know what to do?" Can You please answer him and all of us?

Chidananda, R.D. Laing is certainly one of the most sensitive psychiatrists of the world. In fact, he was responsible for sending Chidananda's mother, Pratiti, to me. She was Laing's patient for twelve years, and because he could not cure her, he sent her here to me. And it is because of Pratiti's coming here that Chidananda also came to the commune.

The very fact that Laing accepted that what psychiatry cannot do, meditation can do, shows immense sensibility and understanding. What he is asking is "What to do when we don't know what to do?" If he wants a really Eastern answer – and he is well-acquainted with the Western answers; they have all failed – the Eastern answer is in Basho's haiku:

Sitting silently, doing nothing,
The spring comes and the grass grows by itself.

R.D. Laing must have read this small haiku of Basho's. There are moments in life when you don't know what to do. But still you go on doing something as if all the answers need some kind of doing to find them, as if all the questions can be solved by doing. The whole of the East stands on a very different level. It says: the questions that cannot be solved by doing can only be solved by non-doing. Don't go on searching for something else to do; there are questions which cannot be solved by *any* doing. In fact, every doing will make them more complicated.

For example, if you are not falling asleep one night and you *want* to go to sleep, and you ask, "What to do?" and somebody suggests, "Do this mantra, do this chanting; count from one to a hundred and then backwards from a hundred to one," all these efforts will keep you awake. They are not going to help you to fall asleep because doing them needs awareness, not sleep.

I would say to you, forget all about sleep. What is wrong in it? If you are not able to fall asleep, enjoy it. Lying down in your bed, doing nothing, the night comes and sleep follows.

There are things which do not have to be done, which have to be allowed to happen. The West knows only one category of things: everything that has to be done. Unless you do it, how can it happen? But they are forgetting that there is a category which is not available to doing, which is available only to a state of relaxedness, of non-doing.

I have seen an American book on relaxation, and the title of the book is *You Must Relax!* The very word "must" makes even relaxation some kind of tremendous effort. And the book has sold millions of copies because America is one of the places where people suffer from sleeplessness the most.

Poor people cannot afford sleeplessness; it is a rich man's disease. Poor people snore perfectly, rich people suffer. Even sleep – which is so natural to all the animals, to all the trees – even *that* has become difficult for man, and the reason is that our whole day is full of doing. And the doing is so much that when we go to bed, the mind needs time to drop the habit – but before it can drop it, you start a new doing: methods of sleep. So you continue in the same rut of doing. You never touch a deeper layer of your being where all is relaxed, where all is at rest, where nothing moves...just eternal silence.

This is the time, certainly, to find the right answer for R.D. Laing's question: "What to do when we don't know what to do?" He is still asking, "What to do?" That is the Western conditioning of the mind. He should have asked, "What *not* to do when we don't know what to do?"

Doing has failed. Now let us try non-doing – and non-doing is another name for relaxation, another name for meditation.

Basho is absolutely right. The world has known great poets but perhaps none of them was a great meditator like Basho; hence his poetry is not just poetry, it is the very essence of his meditations. Each word contains immensities.

So when I repeat Basho's haiku, don't just listen to the words. Try to feel the content of the words, not the container – the words are only containers.

Sitting silently, doing nothing,
The spring comes and the grass grows by itself.

He has said everything about meditation, all the essential ingredients. It is not something that you have to do; it is something that happens. You have just to wait; it happens in its own time. When the spring comes, the grass grows by itself. And just sitting won't do, because you can sit and your mind can go on wandering around the world. Hence, he has added: "Doing nothing" – neither with your body, nor with your mind. Just sitting like a stone statue of Gautam Buddha, and waiting for the spring.... There is no impatience: it always comes, and when it comes, the grass grows.

The world has come to a point...and it has been brought to this point by the Western attitude of action, and always action, and condemnation of inaction. Now the East can be of immense help. Action is good, it is needful, but it is not all.

Action can give you only the mundane things of life. If you want the higher values of life, then they are beyond the reach of your doing. You will have to learn to be silent and open, available, in a prayerful mood, trusting that existence will give it to you when you are ripe, that whenever your silence is complete, it will be filled with blessings.

Flowers are going to shower on you.

You just have to be absolutely a non-doer, a nobody, a nothingness.

The great values of life – love, truth, compassion, gratitude, prayer, God, *everything* – happen only in nothingness, in the heart which is absolutely silent and receptive. But the West is too rooted in action. And there seems to be perhaps not enough time left for it to learn non-doing.

You will be surprised to know that India never invaded any country – and India was invaded by almost all the countries of the world. Whoever wanted to invade India, that was the easiest thing. It was not that there were no courageous people, that they were not warriors, but simply the idea of invading somebody else's territory was so ugly.

It is a surprising fact that one Mohammedan conqueror, Mohammed Gauri, invaded India *eighteen* times, and he was thrown back by a great warrior king, Prithviraj. Mohammad Gauri was driven back, but Prithviraj never entered his territory.

Prithviraj was told again and again, "This is going too far. That man will gather armies again in a few years, and again he will invade the country. It is better to finish him once and for all. And you have been victorious so many times – you could have gone a little further. He has just a small country by the side of India; you could have taken his country and...finished! Otherwise, he is a constant worry."

But Prithviraj said, "That would be against the dignity of my country. We have never invaded anybody. It is enough that we force him to go back. And he is such a shameless fellow that even after being defeated dozens of times, he again comes.!"

The eighteenth time when Mohammad Gauri was defeated, all his armies were killed, and he was hiding in a cave and thinking, What to do now? And there he saw a spider making its net. Sitting there, he had nothing else to do, so he watched the spider. It fell again and again. It fell exactly eighteen times, but the nineteenth time it succeeded in making a net, and that gave the idea to Mohammad Gauri: "At least one time more I should make the effort. If this spider was not discouraged after eighteen failures, why should I be?"

He again gathered his army, and the nineteenth time he conquered Prithviraj. Prithviraj had become old, and having fought his whole life, his armies were tattered, ruined. He was taken prisoner, handcuffed, chained – which was absolutely against the Eastern way of life.

When another king, Poras, was defeated by Alexander the Great, and was brought before him, chained, Alexander asked him, "How should you be treated?"

Poras said, "Is that a question to be asked? An emperor should be treated like an emperor."

There was a great silence for a moment in the court of Alexander. It was very appropriate for Poras to say this, because his defeat was not really a defeat; his defeat was through the utter cunningness of Alexander. Alexander had sent his wife to meet Poras – he was waiting on the other side of the river. It was the time when, in India, sisters would tie a small thread around the wrist of their brothers – and it was called *rakshabandhan,* a bondage, a promise that "You will defend me."

When Alexander's wife came she was received just like a queen should be received. Poras himself came to receive her, and asked, "Why have you come? You could have informed me – I could have come to your camp."

That was part of the Eastern tradition: by the time the sun was down, people would go into each other's camp – the enemy's camp – just to discuss how the day went, who died, what happened. It was almost like a football game – nobody took it that seriously.

But the woman said, "I have come because I don't have a brother. And I heard about this tradition here, so I want to make you my brother."

And Poras said, "It is a coincidence; I don't have a sister."

So she tied the thread and took the promise of Poras that "Whatever happens in the war, remember, Alexander is my husband; he is your brother-in-law, and you should not want me to be a widow. Just remember that."

There came a moment when Alexander's horse died as Poras attacked the horse with his spear, and Alexander fell on the ground. Poras jumped down with his spear, and the spear was just going to pierce Alexander's chest when Poras saw his own wrist with the thread. He stopped.

Alexander said, "Why have you stopped? This is the opportunity – you can kill me."

Poras said, "I have given a promise. I can give my kingdom, but I cannot break my promise. Your wife is my sister, and she has reminded me that I would not like her to be a widow." And he turned back.

Even this kind of man was treated by Alexander as if he were a murderer. And Alexander asked Poras, "How should you be treated?"

"You should treat me just as an emperor treats another emperor. Have you forgotten that just a second more, and you would not have been alive? It is because of your wife – the whole credit goes to her."

But it was a conspiracy. The East cannot think of such things. Mohammad Gauri imprisoned Prithviraj – and Prithviraj was the greatest archer of those times. The first thing Mohammed Gauri did: he took both of Prithviraj's eyes out.

Prithviraj's friend was also captured with him – he was a poet. Prithviraj told him, "You come with me to the court. Nobody understands our language, and I don't need eyes to hit my target – you just describe how far he is."

Mohammad Gauri was so afraid of Prithviraj that he was not sitting on his usual throne, he was sitting on the balcony; the whole court was on the ground floor. And Chandrabardai, the poet, described exactly how many feet high, how many feet away. "Mohammad Gauri was sitting...." He sang it in a song, and blind Prithviraj killed Mohammad Gauri just through that description. His arrow reached exactly to his heart.

But Chandrabardai was very much puzzled, because in Prithviraj's blind eyes there were tears. Prithviraj said, "It is not right of me, but he has forced to do me something which goes against our whole tradition."

The East has a totally different approach towards things. If the West learns something about the East, the most important thing will be that all that is great comes out of non-doing, non-aggressiveness – because *every* act is potentially aggressive. Only when you are in a state of non-doing are you non-aggressive. You are receptive, and in that receptivity, the whole existence pours all its treasures into you.

R.D. Laing's question is perfectly significant. Chidananda, send my answer to him also. He has been reading my books; he knows me perfectly well. And he has influenced in the Western psychological field; he is perhaps the most influential and most original figure today.

If he makes it a point, he can spread – rather than psychological, psychoanalytical, and psychiatric ideas – what the West needs: a deep understanding of meditation, of non-doing and of allowing existence to take its own course.

Okay, Vimal?

Yes, Bhagwan.

Session 14

No Time Left For Any Device

Man is so asleep he is almost in a coma,
and all his actions are arising out of this state of coma –
otherwise, there is no necessity for the world to end.
But we are carrying nuclear weapons within our souls.
The end is going to come because of our own ignorance,
our own deep sleep.

March 19, 1987
Morning

Beloved Bhagwan,

In the last few weeks You have been talking a lot
about the world running fast towards a dead end,
without showing any more hope that things will ever change.
On the other hand, up to one month ago,
You talked on the possibility that the presence
of two hundred enlightened people, or even one,
could save the world.
Why this shift of emphasis?
Did You give up on the other possibility? Did something happen
within the last few weeks that made Your vision change?

Chidananda, it is true that I have been talking a lot about the world running fast towards a dead end. The reason is, factually it *is* running towards an end. But it was running towards its end before, too. Now I want it to be absolutely emphasized on your consciousness, so that you stop postponing your own transformation. Man's mind is so stupid that if there is a little possibility to postpone, then he will postpone for tomorrow – unless he comes to a dead-end street where there is no way to go forward and he has to take an absolute about-turn.

But things in the world are not visible to you. You may go on sleeping and the world may die. It is urgent that you take it seriously that the world may not be there tomorrow.

You don't have time to waste for anything else other than your own awakening.

I still know if there are two hundred enlightened people in the world, the world can be saved; but I have never told you that just one enlightened man can save the world. It is a heavy load. One single enlightened man cannot carry it; two hundred is the minimum. But from where to bring those two hundred people? They have to be born amongst you – you have to become those two hundred people. And your growth is so slow, there is every fear that before you become enlightened the world will be gone.

You are not putting your total energy into meditation, into awareness. It is one of the things that you are doing, amongst many; and it is not even the first priority of your life.

I want it to become your first priority. The only way is that I should emphasize, deeply into your consciousness, that the world is going to end soon.

And if you are not awakened before its end, you will be lost in a long journey, because evolution will start from the very beginning on some other planet. On this planet it took four billion years for man to arrive. His life began in the ocean as a fish. On another planet, if this planet is destroyed, life will continue, but it will have to begin from the very beginning – and after four billion years you may be again a human being. It is a great risk to take.

Nothing has changed in the world; everything is going exactly in the direction of death – a little faster of course – and the moment of total annihilation is coming very close. It all depends on what your priorities are. If being awakened has become your priority, and you are ready to sacrifice everything for it, then there is hope.

I have told you the ancient story in the Old Testament – but that will not help today, the situation is so different. In the Old Testament there is a story about two big cities almost the same size as Hiroshima and Nagasaki. The names of those two cities were Sodom and Gomorrah. The people of those two cities had become so perverted, they were doing all kinds of unnatural, psychopathological actions. Their sexuality had totally gone astray. Those two places must have been the California of the Old Testament.

The story is that God tried hard to change those people. But to change anyone is a difficult task, even for a god – because the very idea that somebody is trying to change you creates a resistance, even if the change is for your good, even if there is no vested interest for the person who is trying to change you. But the very idea that somebody is trying to change you creates an unconscious resistance not to change.

Finally, God gave up the idea and decided to destroy those two cities because their very existence was dangerous. They could spread all their diseases to the whole of humanity. Sodom was so perverted that people were making love to animals; hence the word *sodomy*. Gomorrah had gone completely homosexual; heterosexuality had completely stopped. According to the Old Testament, God destroyed those two cities completely; but there is another version from Hassid mystics.

Judaism has produced one of the most essential lines of mystics, the Hassids. The orthodox Jews don't accept them – the orthodox can never accept the religious. But every organized religion has produced, on the margin, a rebellious group which is not organized, which has different interpretations and a different style of life. Hassidism is one of the most beautiful ways to find oneself and to find the reality of existence.

The Hassids have a different version because they cannot accept God destroying two cities; there must be some way to save them. Their story is that when God became determined to destroy them, one Hassid approached God and asked him one question: "You are going to destroy these two great cities, but have you ever wondered that there may be, in both cities, two hundred good people? They will also be destroyed, and this will not be a good precedent. Just for the sake of those two hundred, you have to change your decision."

God thought for a moment and he said, "I never looked at this side. Certainly there may be good people and they will be destroyed with the bad. No, if you can prove that there are two hundred good people, I will not destroy those two cities."

The Hassid said, "But suppose there are not two hundred, but only twenty – ten in each city. Will you destroy those good people? Does quantity mean so much to you, and not quality? What does it matter whether there are two hundred good people or twenty good people?"

God had to concede to the argument of the Hassid. He said, "Of course. Prove that there are twenty good people."

The Hassid said, "And if there is only one good man who lives six months in one city and six months in another city, what is your idea? Will you destroy those cities? Will it be a godly action? Ninety-nine percent of the people can be destroyed, if they are evil, for the one percent of good people; but one percent of good people cannot be destroyed to save the ninety-nine percent of evil people."

God said, "You are very persuasive. Okay, show me, where is the good man?"

The Hassid said, "*I* am the good man, and I live six months in one city to help people transform their ways of life, and six months in another city for the same purpose. What is your decision? Are you going to destroy me too? Is not one good man more valuable, has he not more weight than thousands of evil people?" And according to the Hassidic story, God had to concede not to destroy those two cities. Orthodox Jews don't believe in the story because it is not written in the Old Testament. The story may be a fiction, but I say unto you, it is truer than any truth. It may not be written in the Old Testament, but its logic is so clear that it cannot be false. It may not be historical, but it has a spiritual reality.

In the same way I have been telling you that two hundred enlightened people can save the world. Existence is very generous; it cannot destroy two hundred awakened people, who have reached to the highest peak of consciousness – which has taken four billion years of evolution. But *you* have to become those two hundred people! To wake you up, I have been insisting that the end is very close. And this time it is not a parable.

Jesus used it as a device, that the end of the world is very close and the last judgment day is very close. His disciples asked him at the time of his departure – before the enemies got hold of him and when it was certain that he would be crucified the next day, their last question was, "When will we be seeing you again?" He said, "In this very life, because the end of the world is very close – but do what I have told you."

And even Christians don't know what he has told them. The last night before he was caught they were in the mountains and he told his disciples, "This may be the last night we are together, and I am going to do my prayer. While I am praying behind the bush you should remain awake. It is absolutely essential, to support my prayer, that you are awake. Don't fall asleep."

In the middle of his prayer he came back – and almost all were fast asleep. He woke them up and said, "Have you not heard me? I had told you, you have to remain awake. Can't you remain awake just one night? – because I will not be here with you again. Even my death tomorrow cannot help you to remain awake?" They were very sorry. They said they would try, and he went again. This went on four, five times – he would come back and they would all be fast asleep.

According to me this was his last teaching: to remain awake. But Christianity has completely forgotten about it. And I have not seen a single commentary by Christians on the implications of why Jesus was so insistently saying, "Be awake!" He was trying his hardest because once he was gone, there was every possibility they would all fall asleep, just as the whole of humanity is asleep, and they would start doing in their dreams things that are not to be done. But things that are not to be done can be prevented only when you are aware, alert.

His last teaching was awareness, but the

disciples failed him – not only those twelve intimate disciples failed him, for two thousand years all his disciples have failed him. The very word "awareness" has disappeared from the Christian idea of transforming human beings. Jesus was continually saying, "The end is very close." That was a device – because if you feel that there is enough time, why not sleep a little more? What is the hurry? But if there is no time left at all, perhaps the shock of it may wake you up.

What was only a device to Jesus, to me is not a device. It is a reality. The world *is* going to end.

I have been giving you hope, because I have to do two things: on the one hand I have to make it clear to you that the world is coming to its final suicide; and on the other hand, I have to give you the hope that still there is a possibility at least for *you* to become awakened.

Your awakening is of tremendous importance; it has never been so important before – neither with Jesus nor with Gautam Buddha – because there was enough time. Time has run out. We are at the fag end of time.

To make you aware of the reality – so that you can make some effort to remain awake, to make some effort to be more conscious and not to get lost in trivia – is absolutely necessary. That's why my insistence will go on growing, because every day the end is approaching closer.

Man is so asleep he is almost in a coma, and all his actions are arising out of this state of coma – otherwise, there is no necessity for the world to end. But we are carrying nuclear weapons within our souls. The end is going to come because of our own ignorance, our own deep sleep.

I have heard...a Polack is crossing the Sahara desert on a camel. After two months alone with the camel, and dreaming of beautiful women, he starts to find the camel attractive and decides to make love to her. But as soon as he is ready, the camel stands up, walks a few feet away and stops. The Polack tries again, but again the camel stands up, walks a few feet away and stops. The Polack tries again and again with no luck.

One day he finds the remains of a plane which has crashed in the desert, and just nearby a young woman, unconscious, but still alive. For days he takes care of her and she recovers totally. One morning she comes to him, looking her prettiest, hugs him and tells him how thankful she is to him for saving her life. "You have been so sweet with me," she says, "and I like you so much that I'll do anything for you."

Looking at her beautiful face, the man says, "Would you really?"

"Yes," she says.

"Oh, I really appreciate that," replies the Polack. "Would you mind holding that camel for me please?"

Such is the situation of humanity. At least *you* have to come out of it – and you need a constant hitting on your head to remind you that the times are no longer ordinary. And there have never been, in the whole history of man, such dangerous moments as those through which we are passing. It is no time for quarreling, arguing about theological matters; it is not intelligent to console yourself that some miracle will happen and the world war will be postponed. It is not only the world war – the attack is multi-dimensional.

The ecology of the earth is breaking down.

There are thousands of submarines moving around the earth in the ocean – and each submarine is carrying nuclear weapons so powerful that even the whole energy that was used in the second world war is nothing compared to the energy of one submarine carrying nuclear missiles. The Soviet Union has its own submarines; America has its own submarines. Just by accident two submarines can collide, and the whole life on the planet will evaporate into smoke. And the politicians of the world are continually piling up more and more nuclear weapons.

The population of the world is growing so fast that just the growth of population will be enough to kill half of humanity out of hunger and thirst.

Sexual perversions have become so rampant that Gomorrah and Sodom look very outdated.

Ten million people around the earth already have AIDS – which has no cure. And this number of ten million people is not accurate, because many countries have not yet declared how many people there have AIDS; they don't have any way to find it out. For example India is not aware how many people are suffering from AIDS. Mohammedan countries are bound to have a very large number of people suffering from AIDS, because homosexuality has been there for thousands of years.

Even according to very moderate estimates, by the end of this century there will be one hundred million people suffering from AIDS. And when one hundred million people suffer from AIDS, that means at least one billion people must have been involved in homosexuality.

These are the multi-dimensional ways that death is approaching the earth.

Because we have cut so many forests, a thick layer of carbon dioxide has gathered on top of our atmosphere, miles away from the earth, where the air ends. The layer is so thick that it has already increased the temperature more than it has ever been on the earth; and that rise of temperature is melting the ice of the north and south poles. If that ice goes on melting – and there is no way to prevent it – all the oceans of the world will rise four feet higher. And all your big cities are ports; they will be flooded with water, will become unlivable.

If this carbon dioxide becomes a little thicker, then the Himalayas and the Alps, which have eternal snow which has never melted, will start melting. The Himalayas alone have so much ice that if it melts completely, it will raise all the oceans of the world forty feet higher. All your cities will be drowned, and this is not a flood that is going to recede.

One of the most dangerous things happening is that carbon dioxide is going to accumulate more and more. The trees go on inhaling carbon dioxide. If you cut the trees you are cutting two things: the supply of oxygen for your life, and the place for carbon dioxide to be absorbed. It is a double-edged sword – and absolutely unnecessary.

Man has been trying to reach to the moon and to Mars, and before that, we were never aware that where the air ends, miles above earth...all around the earth there is a thick layer of a certain gas, ozone, O_3, which is a very protective layer. Because of that ozone, life has been possible on earth. That ozone has only one function: it does not allow any sunrays which are destructive to life; it returns them. It allows only those rays which are life-giving.

Because of our rockets moving towards the moon and towards Mars, we have made holes, for the first time, in the layer of ozone. Now those holes are allowing in all the rays of the sun towards the earth – and death-rays are also included.

So when I say the end is not very far away, it is not like when Jesus says it – just a device. By the end of this century, you will see all these dimensions bringing death to you. It has to be emphasized: unless you become absolutely clear about death, you are not going to concentrate your whole energy on tranforming your being.

People change with difficulty; they find it easier to remain as they are – just like stones, like rocks. Change means a determined effort, a commitment to transform your energies, to take your being in an absolutely serious manner – it has not to be wasted in stupid things.

A famous playboy dies, and his best friends decide to celebrate with a mourning party. Late in the night someone suggests calling Hell in order to find out where he is. "But how can you call Hell?" someone asks.

"Well," the man answers, "I guess it is just a long distance call."

So they check the telephone book and find out all about outer space calls and then dial Hell. A few seconds later a very hoarse voice answers, "This is Hell. What do you want?"

Terrified by the devilish voice, they say, "We are looking for a friend."

"What is his name?"

"Peter Thompson."

"He is not here." And the devil hangs up.

Totally amazed and having dropped all reference to logic, they decide to call Purgatory. They dial Purgatory, and to their relief, the voice on the phone does not sound so terrible – more businesslike. They explain that they are looking for a dead friend who is not in Hell and who just died.

"Well," the voice answers, "he is not here, either. Try Heaven."

"But he was a playboy!" his friends reply.

"He has to be somewhere. Try Heaven."

So they dial Heaven, and a heavenly voice answers very softly and slowly, "Hello. This is Heaven. This is Virgin Mary. Can I help you?"

Very shy, they explain the whole story.

"No," says the beautiful voice, full of echo: "He is not here. Thank you for calling. Call again."

So every day they call Heaven, and every day they get the same answer. So they call again and again; and one week later, on Sunday morning, a very sexy, foxy, quick voice answers, "Hey, this is Mary. What do you want, guys...?"

Looking at each other and laughing, the friends agree: "He has arrived!"

Change is very difficult. A playboy will be a playboy, whether he is in hell or in heaven; he will go on doing his repetitive style of life.

Being alert means you have to stop being robots. Change your routines, move more consciously; let every act become an object of awareness. Then even these few years that are left are enough – more than enough. If you put your total energy into transformation, the destruction of the earth will not be your destruction. If you can die consciously, you have found the key to a higher life, to an eternal life, to a divine life.

Beloved Bhagwan,

What is this undercurrent of giggling in my heart
every time I feel that You are using the whole world
as a device for our growth, and that You are using us
as a device for the whole world?
Would You please comment?

Sarjano, you will have to stop your giggling in the heart. This is not a device. There is no time left for any device at all. Your giggling is simply a rationalization: you don't want to believe that the world is going to end because you don't want to change. You want me to say to you that this is only a device, so that you can relax – relax in your fixed pattern of life. But I cannot lie to you.

When I use something as a device, I tell you it is a device. But this is not a device, either to transform the world through you or to change you through the world. I am simply stating a very sad fact. Your giggling is nothing but an effort to erase the impact which I am trying to create.

Giggle about everything else, but not about your transformation. That giggling is your unconscious trying to deceive you, telling you something or other will happen, so you need not worry.

The unconscious does not want to disappear. Your unconscious is nine times more than your conscious; it is nine times more powerful too. And you have to be very alert not to be caught in the powerful unconscious; otherwise, it will close all the doors, all the possibilities, all the potentialities of transformation.

I am in absolute support of your giggling about everything in the world except the transformation that is needed within you. And the problem is that you are very serious about everything in the world, and only nonserious about your own interiority.

During his world tour, the Polack pope arrives in America. When he comes out of the plane, there is a big crowd standing on the runway waving flags, shouting, "Elvis, Elvis!"

The pope looks at them, full of holiness, kisses the ground and says mildly, "My children, look: I am not Elvis, I am the pope."

He enters the airport hall and notices a mass of people standing there, dancing, waving flags and shouting at him: "Elvis, Elvis!"

A little bit indignant, he blesses the people, and very softly he says, "Oh no, my dear sheep, I am not Elvis, I am the pope."

Later on, when he finally reaches his hotel, he can't believe his eyes: in the lobby, hundreds of people are crowded, waving flags, yelling, "Elvis, Elvis!"

A little bit puzzled now, he puts his hands together, makes a cross, smiles as divinely as possible and announces, "No, my beloved little lambs. No, I am not Elvis, I am the pope."

Centered again, he goes upstairs to his suite, opens the door and suddenly sees two beautiful naked women are lying in his bed, waving little flags, shouting ecstatically at him, "Elvis, Elvis!"

Immediately, jumping out of his clothes, he starts singing, "You ain't nothing but a hound-dog..."

Your unconscious is always there, so powerful that if it gets any chance – pope or no pope – the unconscious will be the winner. You have to make your consciousness so strong that the unconscious slowly, slowly becomes weaker and finally dies. That's the meaning of the enlightened man: one whose unconsciousness has disappeared, whose whole being is full of consciousness.

Whatever I am saying, it is my absolutely clear vision that the world is very close to its end. Don't giggle it away. Don't find rationalizations; they won't help.

There is no time to waste in any unconscious consolations. An immediate transformation is absolutely needed; it is an urgency which man has never faced before. In a way, you are unfortunate that soon there will be no future. In another way, you are very fortunate because this crisis is so big – perhaps it may help you to wake up.

Beloved Bhagwan,

Often, when I come to see You I want some kind of recognition:
a sign that You see me, that You know I exist – a look,
a hand gesture, perhaps to answer a question.
You never respond to this.
Feeling the tension and pain this longing causes in me,
I cry and then relax.
An opening is there and You look my way.
Bhagwan, must I always go through this way
of pain and tears to reach my inner being?
I am Jewish by conditioning – could that be part of it?

Prem Indivar, that explains everything – that you are Jewish by conditioning. But your question may be the question of many others.

You say, "Often when I come to see You I want some kind of recognition." This is one of the sicknesses of our souls. The whole existence recognizes you – the birds by their songs, the trees by their flowers, the sun by its rays, the moon by its beauty – they are all recognizing you.

Just you have forgotten. You want recognition in a human way; perhaps in language.

Existence is silent, its recognition is silent.

All that you have to know is to be silent to understand the recognition.

As far as I am concerned, I have given you recognition just by initiating you on the path of mysticism. I have not asked whether you are worthy or not, whether you deserve or not. I have recognized your potential spirituality without any examination, without any test.

You say "...a sign that you see me, that you know I exist – a look, a hand gesture, perhaps to answer a question." I know that you exist – and my whole effort is that you should *not* exist; that's why I go on avoiding seeing you! Because seeing you may give you energy and nourishment to exist, and that is not your true existence; that is your ego, you are suffering from an inferiority complex. I want you to drop this ego which is hungry for recognition. And the moment you drop it, immediately you will find there is recognition.

You say, "You never respond to this. Feeling the tension and pain this longing causes in me, I cry and then relax." If you have carefully understood your own question, it has the answer: You cry and then relax. "An opening is there and you look my way."

If you are relaxed the whole existence is tremendously happy. Not only am I looking at you, everything is looking at you. But the reason is your relaxation, the reason is your crying; your tears cleanse you, your relaxation does not allow the ego to form. And you have come to know the secret – that I look your way...

"Bhagwan, must I always go through this way of pain and tears to reach my inner being?" It all depends on you. If you love it, if you want it this way – only then do you have to go through pain and tears. Otherwise you can go through laughter and singing and dancing. The whole question is that in pain and tears, or in singing and dancing, the ego disappears – it is your choice.

I have heard, a man noticed a signboard on a restaurant saying, "You are welcome here, and you will feel absolutely at home. Come in; at least just give us one chance to serve you."

The man entered. The waitress came and he ordered four burnt chappatis. The waitress could not believe what he was saying – "Vegetable without any salt," and things like that. She said, "Are you joking?"

He said, "No." So she went, burned the chappattis, and brought the plates, feeling very weird about the whole thing – what kind of man is he? And then she asked, "Anything more?"

He said, "Yes, sit across from me and nag."

She said, "You seem to be a very strange fellow." He said, "I am not a strange fellow – just in front of your door, you say 'You will feel at home,' and I want to feel at home. That's what happens in my home: burnt chapatis, vegetables without salt, everything wrong – and finally my wife sitting across from me, nagging me. Because of her nagging, I cannot even say that the chapatis are burned, that there is no salt..."

It is up to you: both are possibilities. You can relax through pain and tears...but that is not a good choice. You can relax through singing, dancing, rejoicing – and relaxation will come. Try the other way.

You say, "I am Jewish by conditioning. Could that be part of it?" It certainly is. But once you have become a sannyasin, you are no longer Jewish.

A sannyasin is simply a human being. Your conditioning is there, but rather than continuing the tears and pain, start singing and dancing. Even if it feels a little difficult in the beginning, the conditioning can be changed; you can be unconditioned.

At the conclusion of the physical exam, the doctor summoned his patient into his office with a very grave look on his face. "I hate to be the one to break it to you, Fred," he said, "but I'm afraid you have only got six months to live."

"Oh my god!" gasped Fred, turning white. When the news had sunk in his heart he said, "Listen, Doc, you have known me a long time. Do you have any suggestions as to how I could make the most of my remaining months?"

"Have you ever been married?" asked the doctor.

Fred explained that he had been a bachelor all his life. "You might think about taking a wife," the doctor proposed. "After all, you will need someone to look after you in the final illness."

"That's a good point, Doc," said Fred. "And with only six months to live, I'd better make the most of my time."

"May I make one more suggestion?" asked the doctor.

When Fred nodded, he said, "Marry a Jewish girl."

"A Jewish girl – how come?" wondered Fred.

The doctor replied, "Then six months will seem like six lives."

It is your choice, but my suggestion is: you have been married to Jewish conditioning; now get divorced. Just be a human being, rejoicing, dancing, singing. And if tears come they have to be of joy, of blissfulness, of peace, of silence. And the moment you feel relaxed, ecstasy will enter within your being from all sides. The whole existence will recognize you, not only me.

Ecstasy can be explained in other words:

A recognition by the whole existence that you are needed, that you are beautiful, that without you existence will be poorer.

Okay, Vimal?

Yes, Bhagwan.

Session 15

This is the Last Dance

*To dance totally, all that is needed
is that we accept the reality only of this moment.
We will accept the reality of the next moment when it arrives, but we will not be
waiting for it.
All the religions have been teaching you to wait.
I am teaching you to live, to love,
to dance, to sing – and don't wait.*

March 19, 1987
Evening

Beloved Bhagwan,

While reading Your books and listening to Your tapes when I am alone, I become immensely happy and I weep, cry and dance in aloneness. But I can't express my feelings in the presence of others, even though I wish very much to do so. Please tell me what to do.

Kishor Bharti, it is one of the basic human problems, because our whole upbringing creates a split in our very mind. You have to show a face to the society, to the crowd, to the world – it need not be your real face; in fact, it *must* not be your real face. You have to show the face that people like, that people appreciate, that will be acceptable to them – their ideologies, their traditions – and you have to keep your original face to yourself.

This split becomes so unbridgeable because most of the time you are in the crowd, meeting with people, relating with people – very rarely are you alone. Naturally, the mask becomes more and more part of you than your very nature itself.

And society creates a fear in everybody: the fear of rejection, the fear of somebody laughing at you, the fear of losing your respectability, the fear of what people will say. You have to adjust to all kinds of blind and unconscious people. You cannot be yourself. This is our basic tradition all over the world, up to now, that nobody is allowed to be himself. It is because of this that the problem has arisen – it is everybody's problem.

You are asking, "While reading your books and listening to your tapes when I am alone, I become immensely happy and I weep, cry, and dance in aloneness. But I can't express my feelings in the presence of others, even though I wish very much to do so."

The moment the other is there, you are less concerned about yourself; you are more concerned about what his opinion will be about you. When you are alone in your bathroom, you become almost like a child – sometimes you make faces before the mirror. But if you become suddenly aware that even a small child is looking through the keyhole, you immediately change:

you become your ordinary, old self again – serious, sober, as people expect you to be.

And the most amazing thing is that you are afraid of those people and they are afraid of you – everybody is afraid of everybody else. Nobody is allowing his feelings, his reality, his authenticity – but everybody *wants* to do it, because it is a very suicidal act to go on repressing your original face.

You are not living; on the contrary you are simply acting. And because the whole world is watching, your centuries-long unconscious holds you back – not to express, not to come out of the mask of your personality. Everybody is hiding behind something false – it hurts.

To be dishonest, to be insincere to yourself, is the worst punishment you can give to yourself.

And you are not going to do something harmful to anybody – you just want to cry, and your tears will be of joy; you want to dance, and dance is not a sin, is not a crime. You simply want to share your blissfulness – you are being generous. Still, the fear is that people may not accept your blissfulness. Somebody may say it is false, somebody may say it is just acting, somebody may say you are hypnotized.

It is a strange thing that if you are miserable, nobody says anything to you. In a miserable society, you fit perfectly well. But where everybody is miserable, if you suddenly start dancing you fall out of tune with the crowd.

You want to express your joy but you are not courageous enough to be alone...but in fact, who cares? Perhaps people will think, once, that you are a little crazy – at the most – and once they have accepted that you are a little crazy, then there is nothing to fear.

And what is wrong in being called crazy? The world has known such beautiful, crazy people...in fact, all the great people in the world have been a little bit crazy – crazy in the eyes of the crowd.

Their craziness was expressed because they were *not* miserable, they were not in anxiety, they were not afraid of death, they were not worried about trivia. They were living each moment with totality and intensity, and because of this totality and intensity, their life became a beautiful flower – they were full of fragrance, love and life and laughter.

But this certainly hurts millions of people who are around you. They cannot accept the idea that you have achieved something which they have missed. They will try in every way to make you miserable. Their condemnation is nothing but an effort to make you miserable, to destroy your dance, to take away your joy – so that you can come back into the fold.

One has to gather courage. And if people say you are crazy, enjoy the idea. Tell them, "You are right; in this world, only crazy people can be happy and joyful. I have chosen craziness with joy, with bliss, with dance; you have chosen sanity with misery, anguish and hell – our choices are different. You be sane and remain miserable; leave me alone in my madness. Don't feel offended; I am not feeling offended by you all – so many sane people in the world, and I am not feeling offended."

It is only a question of a very short time. Soon, once they have accepted you as crazy, they will not bother you; then you can come into the full light with your original being – you can drop all your falsities.

I was a student in the university.... I had not chosen the university for itself but because of a professor who was so alive, so full of love, and so unafraid of the world. I had chosen the professor. And because he was in that university and he had invited me to join the university where he was teaching...and he said he would make every kind of facility possible for me.

He loved me immensely, because every year I used to go to that university for an inter-university debating competition; for four years continually I had been the winner. The very first year, he was one of the judges. He took me aside and told me, "I cannot say this to anybody else but I cannot keep it to myself either. I can only say it to you: I have given you a ninety-nine percent mark in the debate, and I am sorry, because I wanted to give you a hundred percent. But I could not gather the courage. Because people may think that I am prejudiced, I am favoring. I became afraid. But forgive me, because I have taken off one percent of the marks which were yours."

Each year he was one of the judges, and the fourth year, when I graduated, he invited me to join the university for my post-graduation. I said, "I am coming here just because of you."

He took me the very first day to the vice-chancellor, and on the way he told me, "Don't get into any argument – because this man, the old vice-chancellor, is very stubborn, and one has to be very diplomatic with him."

I said, "You can be diplomatic with him; I will be simply myself."

He said, "What do you mean?"

I said, "To be diplomatic means to be somebody else, diplomacy is another name of hypocrisy. You be diplomatic – I will be simply myself. And if the worst comes to the worst, at the most he will not grant me the money for two years' education, and he may not grant me other facilities – but just for those facilities, I cannot be dishonest to myself."

He said, "At least can you remain silent? Don't say anything; I will talk to him on your behalf."

I said, "I cannot promise, because if he says something stupid, I cannot resist the temptation to tell him that it is stupid."

He said, "I had never realized that you are such a tough person."

I said, "It is good to know from the very beginning. This is the first day; there is still a chance: you can simply tell me and I will leave."

"No," he said, "we will try." He took me to the vice-chancellor.

I always used to live in my own way, and the vice-chancellor had been a professor at Oxford, had lived almost his whole life in England, and had become almost a proper Englishman. He said something about my beard which I was just growing: "Why have you not shaved your beard?" My professor became afraid that this was the beginning of the end.

I said, "You are asking a wrong question; in fact, I should ask why you *have* shaved your beard – because I am not growing mine; it is growing itself. Your question is nonsensical – you could ask why have I not cut my fingers, you could ask anything. It is natural that a man should have a beard, *you* are being unnatural. You have to answer me – why have you been shaving your beard?"

My poor professor, who was sitting by my side, started nudging me. I had to tell him, "You stop nudging me. I don't care about all the facilities for which you have brought me to the vice-chancellor. In this moment, my only concern is that he should accept that he has asked a wrong question."

There was great silence for a moment, and the old man said, "In fact, you are logically right. And right now I don't have any answer, because nobody has ever asked this in my life – I have never thought about it."

I said, "It is your beard, and you have been cutting and cutting and shaving and shaving, perhaps for fifty years, without ever thinking about what you are doing." So I said, "Okay, you can have time. I will be coming every day at eleven o'clock when the office opens; you can meet me in front of the office. You have to find the answer."

But my professor said, "We have not come here to discuss the beard! It is a question of your further education, your post-graduation, and he is the man who can decide."

I said, "I don't care. For the present, my whole concern is to make him realize that he has lived an unconscious life."

The old man said, "From the beard you have reached to 'an unconscious life'?" He asked my professor, "What are the requirements? I will grant him a scholarship for two years." Free lodging, free boarding, he signed everything, and he said, "Just don't stand every day in front of my door! If you need anything, you simply come and tell me, and I promise that I will not ask anything – it was my fault."

So I said, "It is decided? Once you ask me a question, then that becomes my priority for that moment; whatever I have to sacrifice, I will sacrifice."

He said, "I promise, and your professor is the witness." But it was difficult for him – it would have been difficult for anybody, because I used to wear a robe without any buttons so my whole chest was exposed.... And the next time I went because I wanted to be allowed to take as many books as I wanted from the library to my room; the rule that only one book could be issued at a time, should not be applied to me.

He said, "We can talk about that, but where are your buttons?"

I said, "You are getting into trouble; you have forgotten your promise. In fact, *I* should ask again, that in a hot country like India...and it is summertime, and you are perspiring, and still you are using a necktie and wearing a coat? I don't use buttons because I want my chest to have the fresh breeze. Is it something wrong?"

He said, "It is not wrong."

I said, "Something immoral? Something against the rules of the university? Why should you be concerned about it? It is my chest, and I want it to have as much breeze as possible."

He said, "I forgot my promise. You are allowed to take as many books as you want. I will not even ask why you want so many books because I don't want to get into any argumentation. One thing is decided: it is better not to argue with you."

The first meeting that I attended in which he spoke was the birthday of Gautam Buddha. He was a very good orator, and a good actor too. When he was talking about Gautam Buddha, tears came to his eyes, and he said, "I have always felt that if I was in the time of Gautam Buddha, I would have gone and sat at his feet and learned the art of attaining more consciousness, of becoming enlightened."

I was sitting in the middle; I stood up. As he saw me standing, he said, "Have I said anything wrong?"

I said, "You have not only said something wrong, you are behaving very falsely. At least before your students you should not be so insincere. Whatever you have said, you don't mean; your tears are false."

All the professors of the university were present; the whole student community was present. They were all shocked that I would say before everybody, to the vice-chancellor, "You are insincere."

I said, "You have heard the name, Raman Maharshi?"

He said, "Yes, I have heard it."

"Have you ever been there to sit at his feet? – because he is of the same calibre and same consciousness as Gautam Buddha. And I can say with authority that even in Gautam Buddha's time you would not have gone to him. This century is also not without enlightened people. You have to take your words back."

People used to think he was very stubborn...but perhaps he had never met somebody so authentically sincere that it could bring his original face into the public. He wiped his tears and he said, "Perhaps you are right – I might not have gone. It was just oratory and nothing else; I did not mean it. In this whole gathering, perhaps you are the only person who is listening – not only to the words, but also to the meaning behind them.

"I would love you to take your dinner with me tonight, because I would like to discuss a little more. I have never come across anybody in my whole long life who has brought my original face before the crowd. And something is very strange – I don't feel angry at you; I simply feel a deep sadness about myself. Why can't I be true? But nobody has ever pointed it out to me."

Everybody in the world wants to be true, because just to be true brings so much joy and such an abundance of blissfulness – why should one be false? You have to have the courage for a little deeper insight: Why are you afraid? What can the world do to you? People can laugh at you; it will do them good – laughter is always a medicine, healthful. People can think you are mad...just because they think you are mad, you don't become mad.

And if you are authentic about your joy, your tears, your dance – sooner or later there will be people who will start understanding you, who may start joining your caravan. I myself had started alone on the path, and then people went on coming and it became a worldwide caravan. And I have not invited anybody; I have simply done whatever I felt was coming from my heart.

My responsibility is towards my heart, not towards anybody else in the world. So is your responsibility only towards your own being. Don't go against it, because going against it is committing suicide, is destroying yourself. And what is the gain? Even if people give you respect, and people think that you are a very sober, respectable, honorable man, these things are not going to nourish your being. They are not going to give you any more insight into life and its tremendous beauty.

And moreover, everybody is so concerned with their own problems, who cares whether you are laughing, dancing? Who has time for it? It is only your mind that is thinking that the whole world is thinking about you. My own experience is: everybody is so crowded, worried, with the rush of thoughts about himself, his life, his problems – do you think he has time even to look at you, or to think about you?

One Jewish doctor to another: "All day long, I hear stories of pain and suffering: 'Doctor, my back... Doctor, my stomach... Doctor, my wife.' It is awful, I tell you. Tell me, Sam, how come you look so serene after a day listening to the world's troubles?"

Second doctor: "So, who listens?"

You should not be worried at all. Everybody is so concerned with his own world, they don't have time, they don't have energy to bother about you. And even if they have some opinion, it is their problem. You are alone in the world: alone you have come into the world, alone you are here, and alone you will leave this world. All their opinions will be left behind; only your original feelings, your authentic experiences will go with you even beyond death.

Even death cannot take away your dance, your tears of joy, your purity of aloneness, your silence, your serenity, your ecstasy. That which death cannot take away from you is the only real treasure; and that which can be taken away by anybody is not a treasure – it is simply befooling you.

How many millions of people have lived before you on this earth? You don't even know their names; whether they ever lived or not does not make any difference. There have been saints and there have been sinners, and there have been very respectable people, and there have been all kinds of eccentrics, crazy, but they have all disappeared – not even a trace has remained on the earth.

Your sole concern should be to take care of and protect those qualities which you can take with you when death destroys your body, your mind – because these qualities will be your sole companions. They are the only real values, and the people who attain them – only they live; others only pretend to live.

The KGB knocks on Yussel Finkelstein's door one dark night. Yussel opens the door. The KGB man barks out, "Does Yussel Finkelstein live here?"

"No," replies Yussel, standing there in his frayed pajamas.

"No? So what is your name then?"

"Yussel Finkelstein." The KGB man knocks him to the ground and says, "Did you just say that you did not live here?"

Yussel replies, "You call this living?"

Just living is not always living. Look at your life. Can you call it a blessing? Can you call it a gift, a present of existence? Would you like this life to be given to you again and again? It is so empty. Because of its emptiness, your prayers are empty. You cannot fill your prayers with gratitude. Gratitude for what? You are doing no more than acting parts in a drama; you are not being yourself.

I am reminded…a very beautiful young woman had gone to see the great painter, Picasso. And she saw there a photograph of Picasso hanging on the wall. She asked Picasso, "Is that your photograph? Is that you?"

Picasso said, "No."

The woman said, "Strange. It looks exactly like you. Do you have a twin brother? It is so absolutely alike."

Picasso said, "It may be like me but it is not alive. And if it were me, it would have come out of the frame to give you a kiss. It is certainly not me."

Are you really yourself, or just pretending to be somebody that the crowd around you wanted you to be?

As far as I am concerned, a seeker of truth should begin by dropping all that is false in him, because the false cannot seek the truth. The false is the barrier between you and the truth. If all that is false is dropped, you need not seek the truth – truth will come to you. In fact, it is only words when I say, "Truth will come to you." When all that is false is dropped, you are the truth.

Nothing comes; nothing goes.

There is no journey.

Beloved Bhagwan,

At the risk of sounding ridiculous,
in the midst of all this gloom about the future of the world,
I honestly don't care if the world ends tomorrow.
So what is the point of talking about it
and fueling the already massive fire of doom which seems
to burn eternally in the depressing mind of mankind?
Enough is enough.
I understand that it's "now or never," so let's do it now. Let's dance!

Vimal, it is easy to say "I do not honestly care about the world," but let your heart feel it. The world is not something that is only outside you; the world is within you too. You are the world.

And this issue of the darkness that is coming closer and closer has to be given significance, so that your choice becomes "now" and you stop postponing. It is true – "Now or never" – but there are so few people in the world who live now. They are always living either in yesterdays or in tomorrows.

Why am I insisting that there is, for the first time, a possibility that there will not be any tomorrow at all? There is an old proverb: Tomorrow never comes. But the old proverb has been only a proverb and in spite of that proverb, tomorrow has kept on coming. It may not come as tomorrow; it will always come as today – in that sense the proverb is right.

But today the situation is totally different: Tomorrow really may not come.

I want it to sink deep in your being that we have come to the very end of the road – and there is nothing left except dancing and rejoicing. To make it *now*, I am destroying your tomorrow completely. I am taking it away from your mind – which is deeply involved with tomorrows. Even if you say you understand that perhaps tomorrow the world will end, deep down your mind goes on saying, "There have been thousands of wars, and the world has survived. One war more is not going to make much difference."

Mind is very clever in finding excuses, that something or other will prevent the destruction. And I am not saying that the destruction should not be prevented. What I am saying is that in your mind, there should be no excuse left for postponement – so your whole energy gathers in the now; it is not spread in the future. And if the whole energy is concentrated in this point, then this moment can become the moment of enlightenment.

Enlightenment is nothing but your consciousness being concentrated on a single point – now and here.

You are saying, "Enough is enough." No, Vimal. Looking at the human mind, nothing is enough. People will go on living in their old unconscious ways – hoping against hope that although there have always been people like Jesus and Buddha predicting the end of the world, the world is still there. But this time the situation is totally different. I am not predicting the end of the world; it is simply becoming so certain, so logically certain, that there seems to be no possibility to avoid it.

But my interest is not in avoiding it – if it can be avoided, it will be avoided – my interest is to make it so clear to you that it cannot be avoided, and that you don't have any future to invest your energy in, that you have to pull all your energy back to the present moment. And the moment the whole energy becomes a pool, here and now, the explosion of light happens and you are, for the first time, absolutely yourself – an eternal being, an immortal being, who knows nothing of death, who has never come across any darkness.

You are saying, "So let us do it now. Let us dance." But your dance has to be total – because you can dance and still think of the future; you can dance and still think that tomorrow we will be dancing again.

Dance as if this is the last dance.
Dance with abandon, holding nothing back.
That will bring transformation to your being, and a possibility of transformation for other people too.

A politician is making a speech and says: "Fellow electors, we must restore the status quo." A man shouts from the audience, "What does 'status quo' mean?"

The politician replies, in a rare fit of honesty, "Actually, it is Latin for 'the mess we are in.'"

On the surface it seems everything is going perfectly well, but deep down there is great turmoil in the unconscious layers of human beings. You are not even aware of your own unconscious nightmares, but humanity is suffering as it has never suffered before.

It is restless as it has never been before. It has forgotten the language of relaxation, it has forgotten the language of totality, it has forgotten the language of intensity. And all those qualities are needed to make your meditation a revolution in your being. It is not a question of morality, not a question of character, not a question of virtue – religions have been concerned with all those things for thousands of years, and they have not been successful in changing man. It is a totally different approach, a different dimension: the dimension of energy and the concentration of energy.

And just as atomic energy is the explosion of a small atom into its constituents of electrons, protons and neutrons – it is not visible to the eyes, but the explosion is so vast that it can destroy a great city like Nagasaki or Hiroshima – exactly parallel is the inner explosion of the living cell. The atomic energy is outside and destructive – objective and destructive. The inner energy, the subjective cell of your being, has the same qualities, the same tremendous power once it explodes – but it is creative.

It is a chain reaction: one cell inside you explodes, and then other cells inside you start exploding in a chain. The whole of life becomes a festival of lights. Every gesture becomes a dance; every movement becomes sheer joy.

My emphasis that there is no future has nothing to do with gloom; it has something to do with you. If you can drop the idea of future completely, your enlightenment becomes immediately possible. And it is a good opportunity to drop the idea of future because the future itself *is* disappearing. But don't even in any corner of your mind, go on carrying the idea that perhaps this too is a device. These are the strategies of the mind to keep you the same old zombie.

Mind is clever. If you want to get up early in the morning, you put on an alarm clock, and you hear the alarm...the mind is so clever, it may start dreaming that you are in a church and church bells are ringing. The poor alarm clock cannot do anything more than that; the mind has created a dream and made it possible for you to go on sleeping.

The old religions were basically insistent on one thing, and that was future. You should note it: not only future in this life, but after life; their whole program was to take your whole energy as a project for a future life, after death, in paradise far, far away. This strategy worked; it took away the very juice of human life. People were simply waiting to live in paradise; this place, this earth, became just like a waiting room in a station.

Everybody is waiting for the train. And the train never comes, and people go on consulting the timetable. And they don't improve the waiting room because it is a waiting room – particularly in India. I have been traveling so much – almost hundreds of waiting rooms – and I saw why people behave in a waiting room differently than they behave in a house. They go on eating bananas and throwing banana peels all over the waiting room – after all, it is a waiting room; they are not going to live here. Their train is going to come and they will be gone. The waiting rooms are so dirty, their bathrooms are so impossible, and nobody takes any care not to make them more dirty – because everybody's eyes are hooked on the future. They are consulting their timetables, when their train is to come, and they will go.

All the religious scriptures say this world is nothing but a waiting room; your real home is far away, above the clouds. *There* is real living; *here* is only waiting.

I am trying to change the whole pattern of religious thinking. I am trying to say to you: *This* is your home; this very moment is your paradise. It all depends on you. You do not need to be virtuous to dance totally; you do not need to be learned to dance totally; you do not need to be pious to dance totally. To dance totally, all that is needed is that we accept the reality only of this moment. We will accept the reality of the next moment when it arrives, but we will not be waiting for it.

All the religions have been teaching you to wait. I am teaching you to live, to love, to dance, to sing – and don't wait.

It is Easter and a priest is getting cost estimates for the church flower arrangements. A Catholic florist says, "Three hundred dollars."

"Much too much," says the priest...but the florist is one of the flock.

A Protestant florist offers to do the arrangements for two hundred and fifty dollars.

"Cheaper," thinks the priest, "but he is not of the flock, and the difference is not that great."

While he is pondering, Solly Goldberg gives him a price of seventy-five dollars.

"That settles it; Solly gets the contract."

On Easter morning, the flock files into a church filled with magnificent azaleas, camelias, carnations and roses, and above the altar, spelled out in daffodils is the Easter message:

"Christ has risen, but Goldberg's prices never vary."

Okay, Vimal?

Yes, Bhagwan.

Session 16

Love
Is Always an Emperor

*Be more meditative,
become more conscious of your being.
Let your inner world become more silent, and love will be flowing through you.
People have all these problems. The problems
are different – violence, jealousy, misery, anxiety – but the medicine
for all these illnesses is only one, and it is meditation.*

March 20, 1987
Morning

Beloved Bhagwan,

A short time ago You said
that spring has come and many sannyasins are ready to flower.
Do "flowering," "awakening" and "self-realization" all
mean enlightenment, the ultimate truth?
or is there a difference? And can a person, after attaining,
fall back into identification with the mind?

Mukto, there is a difference between flowering, awakening, self-realization, and enlightenment. Enlightenment is the ultimate truth – the seeker disappears but the truth is found. The pilgrim disappears but God is found. It is important to understand the differences....

From enlightenment there is no possibility of falling back, because you are no longer there to fall back. As long as you *are*, there is a possibility. Only your absence is the guarantee that you cannot fall back.

Flowering is just the beginning of entering within yourself – just as you enter into a garden. It is immensely important, because without entering you are never going to reach to the center. But in flowering, for the first time you recognize your potential, your possibility. In flowering is the transition period, from human to divine. But one can fall back, because the flowering is so new and so fragile and your past is so old and so strong – it can pull you back; it is still there.

Awakening is getting very close to your center. And as you get closer to the center, falling back becomes more and more difficult because your new experience is gathering power, strength, experience, and the old is losing. But the old is still there; it has not disappeared. Ordinarily people don't fall from awakening, but the possibility remains: one can fall.

Self-realization is reaching to your center. Many religions have believed that self-realization is the end – for example, Jainism – you have come to your ultimate truth. It is not true.

Self-realization is only a dewdrop which has become aware, alert, contented, fulfilled. It is almost impossible to fall back from self-realization – but I am saying *almost* impossible, not absolutely impossible, because the self can deceive you; it can bring your ego back.

The self and the ego are very similar. The self is the natural thing and the ego is the synthetic, so it happens sometimes that a self-realized man becomes a pious egoist. His egoism is not going to harm anyone, but it certainly prevents him from dropping into the ocean and disappearing completely.

Enlightenment is the dewdrop slipping from the lotus leaf into the vast, infinite ocean. Once the dewdrop has fallen into the ocean, now there is no way even to find it. The question of turning back does not arise. Enlightenment, hence, is the ultimate truth. What begins as flowering moves on the path of awakening, reaches to self-realization. Then one quantum leap more – disappearing into the eternal, into the infinite.

You are no more, only existence is.

I have told you about Kabir, India's greatest mystic. When he was young, he became self-realized and he wrote a small couplet:

Herat, herat he sakhi
Rahya, Kabir, herai

"Searching and searching and searching, oh my friend, the searcher is lost. Seeking and seeking and seeking, the seeker is lost."

Bund samani samund mein
Sokat herijai

"The dewdrop has slipped into the ocean; now there is no way to get it back."

But it was too early to say that. The dewdrop was still there, slipping towards the ocean, but it had not yet fallen into the ocean.

When Kabir was dying, he became enlightened. He called his son Kamaal and told him, "I have written something wrong. At that moment, that was my feeling – that I had come to the ultimate. Before I die, you write this down, and change it."

The change is very small in words, but in experience it is tremendous. He has used again the same words:

Herat, herat he sakhi – "Oh beloved, seeking and searching, the seeker is lost."

Samund samund bund mein
Sokat herjai – "And the ocean has fallen into the dewdrop; now it is impossible to find it."

Just a little difference in the words... "The dewdrop has fallen into the ocean" – something of the self has remained in it. But "the ocean has fallen into the dewdrop"...that is the tremendous experience and explosion of enlightenment. The first statement was about self-realization; the second statement is about enlightenment.

From enlightenment, falling is simply impossible. You are gone – and gone forever; not even a shadow or a trace of you is left behind.

Up to self-realization the possibility remains – it becomes less and less, but it remains. You can start being egoistic about your self-realization: "I have known, I am a realized person. I am a saint, I have encountered God" – but that "I" is there, howsoever pious. Even its shadow is dangerous; it can pull you back.

I have heard a very beautiful story about Jesus....

Jesus was walking through Jerusalem when he saw an angry crowd shouting and screaming at a woman. He came closer and heard the mob accusing the woman of adultery. Jesus strode to the front of the mob, held up his arms and said, "Let him who is without sin cast the first stone."

The crowd fell silent, but one little old lady pushed to the front, picked up a huge rock, and hurled it at the sobbing woman. Jesus gently took the old lady by the arm and said quietly, "Mother, why do you always embarrass me?"

Jesus' mother! She is a virtuous woman – so virtuous that she has given birth to Jesus without any contact with another human being. She stands alone in the whole of history with the claim – even after the birth of the son, of being the *Virgin* Mary. That idea must have got into the old woman's mind too much. Her virtue, her piousness – God has chosen her to be the mother of his only begotten son – has become a subtle ego in her. The others were not pious. The moment Jesus said, "The first stone has to be hurled by one who is virtuous," the mob stopped. They were all in the same boat.

And you can see it in your saints…a strange but very subtle ego. Spirituality has become their achievement. Somebody has all the riches of the world, somebody is the most beautiful person, somebody is the strongest, and somebody is the most pious. The question is not *what* it is by which the ego can get nourished – *any* idea can make you fall.

One has not to stop until he has reached the point when he is not: when there is no claimer, when one has moved the full circle and has come back to the world, just nobody. Perhaps people may not recognize him as a great saint…and this is my understanding, that the greatest of saints have remained unrecognized, because you understand only the language of the ego. You don't understand the language of egolessness.

The greatest sage will appear to you just an ordinary man, nothing special, with no claim for any talent, for any possession, for any power, for any genius, for any knowledge – no claim at all. He has become absolutely a zero. But the zero is not negative, it is full of godliness, overflowing with godliness.

Beloved Bhagwan,

Though Your emphasis has been for us, as individuals,
to go within to save ourselves,
I guess I am still naive enough to feel that our love,
our dancing, our joy could still save this beautiful planet.
Can You please say something about this?

Devaprem, the question is meaningful, but very complex to understand. You are asking, "Though your emphasis has been for us, as individuals, to go within to save ourselves, I guess I am still naive enough to feel that our love, our dancing, our joy, could still save this beautiful planet."

It *may* save the beautiful planet, but you should not carry the idea within you; otherwise it will destroy your love and your dance and your joy. If deep down you are guessing that "my love, my dancing, my joy can save the whole planet," it is the strategy of the ego. You are becoming a savior. You are becoming so great that you can save the whole planet, just by your love and just by your dancing, just by your joy.

Try to understand the complexity. It is possible, if individuals are full of love, full of joy, and their life is not a drag, but a dance...as a by-product it is possible the planet may be saved. But *as a by-product* – you cannot take the credit for saving the world.

This is the trouble: if you start thinking that you are dancing to save the world, your dance is destroyed. Then you are not dancing totally, then you are not dancing here and now; then your dancing has become a means to save the world. Then your love is not pure love – it is just another means, but the end is to save the world. It will be easy for you to understand if I tell you a Sufi story....

One Sufi mystic was so full of love, and so full of joy – his whole life was laughter, music, dancing. And the story says God became very interested in him because he never asked anything, he never prayed. His whole life was a prayer, there was no need to pray.

He never went to the mosque, he never even uttered the name of God; his whole existence was the argument for the presence of God. If anybody asked him whether God exists or not he simply laughed – but his laughter was neither yes nor no.

God himself became intrigued with that strange mystic and he came to the mystic and said, "I am immensely happy because that's how I want people to be – not that they should pray for one hour and do everything against it for twenty-three hours. Not that they should become very pious when they enter the mosque, and when they go out they leave their piousness in the mosque and they are just their old selves: angry, jealous, full of anxiety, full of violence.

"I have watched you and I have loved you. This is the way: you have become the prayer. You are, right now, my only argument in the world that something more than man exists – although you have never argued, you have not even uttered my name. Those are superfluous things...but you live, you love, you are so full of joy that there is no need for any language; your very presence becomes the argument for my existence. I want to give you a blessing. You can ask for anything."

The sage said, "But I don't need anything. I am so joyous, and I cannot conceive there can be anything more. Forgive me, I cannot ask because I really don't need anything. You are generous, you are loving, you are compassionate; but I am so over-full, there is no space within me for anything else. You will have to forgive me, I cannot ask."

God said, "I had thought that you would not ask, so don't ask for yourself – but you can ask for others, because there are millions of people who are miserable, sick, have never known anything for which they can be grateful. I can give you powers to do miracles, and you can change the lives of all these people."

The sage said, "If you are insistent, then with a condition I can accept your gifts."

God said, "With a condition? You really are strange. What is the condition?"

He said, "My condition is that I should not become aware of what is happening through me, by you. It should happen behind my back; it should happen through my shadow, not through me. I may be passing and my shadow may fall on a dead tree, and the tree may become alive again – again lush green, again heavy with flowers and fruits – but I should not know it, because I don't want to fall back.

"If I know it – that I have done it, or even that God has chosen me as the instrument to do it – it is dangerous. So my condition is: a blind man may start seeing, but neither should he know that it is because of me, nor should I know that it is because of me. My shadow behind my back will do all the miracles.

"If you can accept my condition, and remember that I should not know at all...because I am so full of joy, so blissful. Don't drag me back into the miserable world. Don't drag me back to become again an 'I.'"

And it is said that God said to him, "You are not only strange, you are unique and rare. And this will be so: you will never know what things are happening around you. Miracles will be happening around you – wherever you will go, miracles will happen. Neither those people will know that you have done those miracles, nor you will know that you have done those miracles. I will remember the condition."

Devaprem, there is a possibility: the individual coming to enlightenment and celebration is bound to affect the whole destiny of humanity. But it is going to be a by-product. It is going to happen behind your back, through your shadow – not by you. Even guessing is dangerous, because that guessing can give you the ego and can destroy your joy, can destroy your dance. And if your joy and your love and your dance are destroyed, then there is not going to be any by-product to save the planet.

None of my sannyasins are to become saviors. The world has known many saviors, and the world is not saved. And the reason is that they were not as alert as the Sufi mystic; they started bragging about their miracles, they started nursing their egos through their miracles. Then their miracles became only magic, just tricks practiced well. There is nothing like a miraceous in it.

The greatest miracle in the world is that you should dance and disappear in the dance – then let the dance do whatever it can do. That you should love and disappear in the love – then let the love do whatever it can do. You cannot claim that you are doing it – you have already disappeared.

In your disappearance is the whole possibility of some miracle happening. So please don't guess; otherwise deep inside your love will remain half-hearted – you are doing it for some purpose. And when love becomes a purpose it is no longer love. Your joy will become phony, because if you are joyful so something can happen in the world, you are not really joyful – you are using joy. And if your dance is a means towards an end, it cannot be total. Unless your dance is an end in itself, there is no possibility of its being total.

And only a total dance, an authentic love, a wholehearted joy, perhaps may create some miracles around you. But you will not be the one who has done them; you will not be the one who can brag about them. They will happen only when you are not.

God happens only when you have moved out of the way and left yourself totally empty, spacious. It is a very strange phenomenon: The guest only comes inside the house when the host disappears.

Beloved Bhagwan,

Sometimes after moments of clarity and lightness,
it seems old intimates like violent feelings,
jealousy, feeling furious, etcetera, come
back even stronger than before,
as if they were just waiting around the corner
to have their chance again.
Can You say something?

Devam Kranti, I can say something, but those feelings of violence and jealousy and furiousness will still be waiting by the corner. Just by my saying something, they are not going to disappear – because without knowing, you are nourishing them; without knowing, your desire to get free of them is very superficial.

You are not doing exactly what I have been emphasizing continually; you are doing just the opposite. You are fighting with the darkness, and you are not bringing the light in. You can go on fighting with the darkness as long as you want – you are not going to be victorious. That does not mean that you are weaker than darkness, it simply means that what you are doing is irrelevant to darkness.

Darkness is only an absence.

You cannot do anything directly to it – just bring light in.

And it is not that when you bring light in, darkness will rush outside through all the doors. Darkness is an absence – light comes...there is no question of absence anymore. Darkness does not go anywhere, it has no existence of its own.

I will read your question: "Sometimes after moments of clarity and lightness, it seems old intimates like violent feelings, jealousy, feeling furious, etcetera etcetera, come back even stronger than before, as if they were just waiting around the corner to have their chance again."

Your clarity and your lightness are only momentary. If you bring in the light for a moment and then blow out the candle, the darkness will be back again – not that it was waiting by the corner; you have again created the absence of light.

Your torch of consciousness should be burning continuously; then there will not be any darkness.

These feelings that you think are very dangerous are almost impotent. Violence is there because you have not grown your potential for love – it is the absence of love. And people go on doing stupid things. They try to be nonviolent: they repress the violence, they make tremendous efforts to be nonviolent.

But there is no need for anybody to be nonviolent because you are moving in a wrong direction. Violence is a negative thing, and you are trying to destroy violence and become nonviolent. I would say, forget about violence. It is the absence of love – be more loving.

All the energy that you are putting into repressing violence and becoming nonviolent – pour it into being love.

It was unfortunate that Mahavira and Gautam

Buddha both used the word *nonviolence*. I can understand their difficulty. Their difficulty was that by "love" people understand biological love; to avoid that misunderstanding they used a negative term: nonviolence. It gives the appearance that violence is the positive thing and nonviolence is the negative thing. In fact, violence is the negative thing and love is the positive thing, but they were all afraid of using the word *love*.

And because of their fear that "love" may create in people's minds the idea of ordinary love, they used an unfortunate word – nonviolence – and for twenty-five centuries, that nonviolence has been practiced. But have you seen in any follower of Gautam Buddha or Mahavira, the quality of love, the presence of love around him? – he is practicing nonviolence, and there is where he has gone wrong. You will find them shrunken and dead: their intelligence does not seem to have blossomed, their consciousness does not seem to have blossomed. Just the mistake of using a wrong word has created twenty-five centuries of immense torture, in thousands of people.

I want you to know that love is the positive thing, and love does not mean only biological love. And you also understand it: you love your mother, you love your brother, you love your friend, you love your master; there is no biology involved. These are ordinarily available experiences of non-biological love. You love a roseflower – is there any biology involved? You love a beautiful moon, you love music, you love poetry, you love sculpture – is there any biology involved? And I am taking these examples from ordinary life, just to show you that love has many, many dimensions.

There is a love which is between two bodies; then it is biological. There is a love between two minds; then it is the love of two friends. There is a love between two hearts – then it is the love between the disciple and the master. And then there is the love between two beings. Then it is the love between the devotee and the master.

Love has these four dimensions, and each dimension has many, many possibilities.

So rather than having just moments of clarity and lightness, be more loving – loving to the trees, loving to the flowers, loving to music, loving to people. Let all kinds of love enrich your life, and violence will disappear. A man of love cannot hurt anybody. There have been even very rare and unique examples....

One of the Sufi mystics, Sarmad, had in his chest a wound – the orthodox Mohammedans had tried to kill him. They could not kill him, but they wounded him very badly, and the wound became so dangerous....there were small but visible parasites in the wound, who were sucking his blood.

Mohammedans, when they do their *nimaj*, their prayer, bow down to the earth, get up, and then bow down again many times. So those parasites would fall from Sarmad's wound, and he would take them up and put them back in the wound. People said, "Are you mad or something?"

He said, "My body is going to die anyway, the poison has spread all over the body. These poor parasites, why should they die as long as I can help them to live? And anyway they are parasites of my wound – I am not the body. It is going to be the food of animals. So while I am alive, it hurts me that some parasite is going to die. At least as long as I am alive I will continue to put them back."And finally he stopped praying. He said, "Prayer I can do without the ritual, but I cannot hurt these creatures."

But strangely enough, he did not die from the poison that was spreading through his body – perhaps his tremendous love became an antidote

– and the Mohammedans had to cut off his head on the steps of Jamma Masjid in New Delhi. And his only crime was...Mohammedans have a prayer which consists of a simple sentence: "One God; one holy book, *Koran*; one messenger of God, Hazrat Mohammed." These three names come into that prayer.

But Sufis simply repeat the part which talks about one God. They don't bring "one holy *Koran*" and "one messenger of God" into their prayer. They say that there have been other messengers, it is not a monopoly; and there are other holy statements, the *Koran* cannot be the only one. And in the future there will be other messengers and there will be other holy statements. All that we can say is: Existence is one God.

That was their crime, and the orthodox Mohammedans forced Sarmad: "You have to say the whole prayer; this is sacrilegious to pray only half the prayer."

He said, "You cannot force me. As far as prayer is concerned it is my freedom, it is my individual concern with God. If I am answerable, I am answerable to God, not to you. I am not praying to you, I am praying to God, and if I am praying wrongly, it is a matter to be settled between me and God. Who are you?" But they were powerful – the king was Mohammedan – and they were all angry, and they cut off his head.

There are many steps in the mosque in New Delhi...and when they cut his head he laughed, and his head rolled down the steps. And a strange phenomenon was witnessed by thousands of people, because thousands of people had gathered to see: the head was coming down the steps...the blood was flowing from the head, and the body was standing on top of the steps – and the head was still repeating the half-prayer.

That does not seem to be historical; it seems to be a mythology, but there are so many contemporary reports about it – from people who were not Mohammedans – that they have seen it and they have heard it....

Perhaps love can speak even without the body. Perhaps love does not need the body as a necessary medium. Whether it is historical or not is insignificant to me; to me, what is significant is that although he was killed by cutting off his head, there was no anger, no complaint, no ill-will, no curse.

And he was absolutely innocent; to pray is absolutely an individual affair. But even while his head is rolling down the steps, there is only prayer, the half-prayer.

Love knows how to forgive.

Love cannot hurt and cannot be violent.

Devam Kranti, these violent feelings will not disappear unless their energy is transformed into love. And the true love knows nothing of jealousy. Any love that is followed by jealousy is certainly not the true love, it is biological instinct.

The higher you move – from body to mind, from heart to being – all these crude feelings disappear. Love from being to being knows no jealousy.

And how are you going to find such love?

It is a radiation of your silence, of your peace, of your inner well-being, of your blissfulness. You are so blissful that you want to share it – that sharing is love.

Love is not a beggar.

It never asks, "give me love."

Love is always an emperor.

It only knows to give. It never even imagines, expects, anything in return.

Be more meditative, become more conscious of your being. Let your inner world become more silent, and love will be flowing through you. People have all these problems. The problems are different – violence, jealousy, misery, anxiety – but the medicine for all these illnesses is only one, and it is meditation.

And I would like you to be reminded that the word *medicine* and the word *meditation* come from the same root. Medicine means something that can cure your body, and meditation means something that can cure your soul.

Meditation is meditation only because it is a medicine for your innermost illnesses.

A man selling Vaseline Petroleum Jelly had gone around a number of houses in town a week before and had left some samples, asking people to see if they could find an ingenius use for it. Now he went around to the same houses, asking people what uses they had found for Vaseline.

The man in the first house, a wealthy city gent, said, "I used it for medicinal purposes. Whenever my children scraped their elbows or knees, I would rub it on."

The man in the second house said, "I used it for mechanical purposes, such as greasing the bearings of my bicycle and lawnmower."

The man in the third house, a scruffy, unshaven, working-class fellow, said, "I used it for sexual purposes."

In a shocked voice the salesman asked, "What do you mean?"

"Well," said the scruffy man, "I put a whole lot of it on the handle of my bedroom door to keep the kids out!"

You can give the same thing to different people and they will come out with different uses, according to their own unconsciousness. But if they are conscious, they will find only one use.

A man, an archbishop in Japan, went to one very great master, Nan In, with the New Testament. He was certain that by listening to the beautiful statements of Jesus, particularly on the sermon on the mountain, Nan In would be converted to Christianity.

The archbishop was received with great love and he said, "I have come with my holy book, and I want to read a few sentences...perhaps they will change your whole life."

Nan In said, "You have come a little late, because I am changed completely, the transformation has happened. But still, you have come a long way – you can at least read a few sentences."

So he read a few sentences, and just after two, or three sentences, Nan In said, "That's enough. Whoever has written these sentences will become a buddha in some future life ."

The archbishop was very much shocked – he is saying, "In some future life – this man shows a potentiality – he will become a buddha." He said, "But he is the only son of God!"

Nan In laughed. He said, "That is the trouble. That's what is preventing him from becoming a buddha. Unless he drops such nonsense ideas, he will not blossom to his whole potentiality.

"He has beautiful ideas but side by side, he has some stupid ideas too. There is no God, so the question of being the only begotten son does not arise. In some future life – you don't be worried – he will drop them; he seems to be a man of intelligence, and he has suffered enough for his stupid ideas. He got crucified; that was enough punishment. But you should not cling to the stupid part of his statements."

The archbishop said, "But they are our basis, the foundation of our religion, that Jesus is the only begotten son of God, that there is a God who created the world, that Jesus was born of a virgin girl."

Nan In laughed and he said, "This poor fellow, if he could drop these small fictitious things, he would have already become a buddha. If you find him somewhere, bring him here, and I will put him right. There was no need to crucify him – all that he needed was a right master, someone who could have introduced him into the mysteries of meditation."

Meditation is perhaps the master key for all our problems. So rather than fighting with problems separately...which will take lives and still you will not be out of their grip. They will stand by the corner, waiting for their chance – and naturally, if they had to wait too long, they will take as much revenge as possible.

Meditation is not doing anything directly to your violence, not doing anything to your jealousy, to your hate. It is simply bringing light into your house, and the darkness disappears.

(A duck appears in the garden outside the hall, and quacks long and loudly.)

It is just the reincarnation of the Japanese archbishop. And it is natural that he is protesting – this is what happens to archbishops; I have again provoked him....

Should I provoke him again?

Okay, Vimal?

Yes, Bhagwan.

Session 17

Watchfulness...
Your Gift to Yourself

*Tremendous is the splendor
of a person who has come to know everything that goes on within him,
because by being aware, all that is false disappears
and all that is real is nourished.
Except this,
there is no radical transformation possible.*

March 20, 1987
Evening

Beloved Bhagwan,

Is it possible that things are happening inside me
that I am not aware of?
Is it possible for growth to happen in this way?
I have heard You say, "I've been watching you" to people.
Have You been watching me?
How am I doing? Am I missing something?
Should I be doing something that I'm not already doing?

Veet Niten, it is possible that things may be happening within you of which you are not aware, because your awareness is very small, and you are very big. Your whole consciousness is ten times bigger than your awareness, and that ten-times-bigger consciousness is absolutely in darkness. Much continues to happen in your dark inside. You become aware only when it surfaces and comes into the area of your awareness – which is very small.

In fact, it is part of your biology, physiology, that you should not be aware of most things when they are happening because your awareness can become a hindrance to their happening. You eat food, but do you know how it is digested? When it is digested, when your food becomes your blood and your bones?

Up to three hundred years ago, for centuries man had thought that blood is static in the body. The idea of the circulation of blood was non-existent all over the world. Just three hundred years ago, physicians became aware that blood is constantly moving at a fast speed – the blood that is in your feet, within seconds will be in your head, and it goes round and round. Its circulation is absolutely necessary to clean all dead cells from your body, to take them away, to bring new oxygen to your cells, because each cell needs oxygen for its life.

But you are not aware of it all, and in fact if you were aware, you would go mad. So much is happening inside you that it would be impossible for you to maintain your sanity.

The child in the mother's womb sleeps twenty-four hours a day, for the simple reason that in those nine months more things happen in his body than will happen in the seventy years which are to follow after his birth. Much more is happening in those nine months than is going to happen in the body between his birth and death. Hence, he has to remain constantly asleep – no awareness at all.

When you are tired, when you feel spent, you need a good sleep – have you ever thought why? You need a good sleep so that your awareness does not interfere with the rejuvenating of your body. In the morning you feel fresh, again ready to work. What a miracle sleep has done to you! On a greater scale, when it becomes almost impossible for the body to rejuvenate itself, death happens. Death is nothing but a long sleep, a deep sleep, so that your soul can move into another body, into some womb. But your awareness can be a disturbance, so your death almost always happens in a deep sleep. Before you die, you fall asleep; you lose all consciousness, all awareness – it is the greatest surgery that nature does.

What is true about the body and about your physiology is also true about your psychology – much is happening of which you are not aware. You become aware only when a certain situation arises: you are a peaceful man, but somebody insults you and anger arises in you, of which you were not aware. It has always been there, in the darkness of your unconscious, but if somebody insults you, immediately it is ready to react.

I am reminded of one of the most beautiful stories, historical. A great Japanese emperor wanted to see Nan In, a Zen master. Because he was the ruler over all Japan, he thought that Nan In could be ordered to come to the court.

His prime minister advised him, "Don't be foolish. You may be the emperor of the whole of Japan, but there are a few people in the country who are beyond your domination – or anybody's domination. You cannot order Nan In; you can kill him, but you cannot force him to do anything against his will. And he has not left his monastery for thirty years. If you want to see him, you will have to go to the mountains to his monastery."

The emperor said, "If that is the situation, then I will go. I don't want to kill him. I have a question, and many people have suggested to me that there is only one man, Nan In, who can answer the question."

He went to Nan In; he was sitting just in front of his house, on the lawn. The emperor bowed down, sat in front of Nan In, and asked him, "I have come to get an answer: What is hell and what is heaven? I have asked many people, but all that they give as an answer is not their own experience. They are not eyewitnesses, they are only scholars – they have read about it. That I can do myself, but how can I know hell really exists? or heaven?"

At that very moment Nan In said, "You are such an idiot – who made you the emperor of the country?"

The emperor could not believe it! He had never expected, never dreamt that he would be received with such rudeness. And he has not done anything wrong – just asked a question. He was a warrior. He pulled his sword out of its sheath, and was going to kill Nan In, then and there. When the sword was just hanging over the head of Nan In, Nan In said, "This is hell. You are standing exactly at the door of it."

Suddenly, a great realization...and all anger settled; a silence descended. He put back his sword, and Nan In said, "You have turned your back towards hell, and in front of you is the gate of heaven. This is my answer."

The emperor had never thought that answers can be given through situations too; in fact, real answers can only be given through situations. But he became perfectly aware that anger, violence, rage, jealousy and the whole gang of these kinds of qualities are what constitutes hell. And love, silence, blissfulness, compassion, joy...a moment-to-moment living in gratefulness towards existence, is what heaven is constituted of.

He touched the feet of Nan In and he said, "You have answered me – and this is not the answer of a scholar, this is the answer of a man who knows. I am immensely grateful. But you really shocked me, I am still trembling! You are a dangerous man; I had come for a philosophical discussion."

Nan In said, "We are not concerned with philosophy, we are concerned with reality. Philosophy is a game, children's play; reality is a risk, an adventure. Only those who are courageous enough travel on the razor's edge to find the truth."

In your psychology also, much is continuously happening. Even when you are asleep, your mind goes on working. Only a man who enters into meditation, slowly, slowly becomes aware of things which are happening in the mind, of which he was never before aware. And the miracle of meditation is that as you become aware of things, that which is wrong disappears and that which is right becomes tremendously strong. There is only one criterion, according to me, which decides what is right and what is wrong: that is your depth of meditation.

If you are going deeper into silence and something disappears – you saw it receding, evaporating into the air – you can be certain it was wrong, because the false cannot face you; it has not the guts. It cannot come in front of you, it cannot encounter you. And that which is real, good, becomes stronger, becomes more a part of your actions, of your thoughts, of your being.

A moment comes in the life of the meditator when his meditation has reached the point where his whole mind is silent and there is not even a fragment of darkness anywhere inside him – all is light. Then, whatever that person does is right, and whatever that person does not do is wrong. In that state, one never thinks about what to do; what is right, what is wrong are no longer alternatives. The right becomes spontaneous action, and the wrong simply becomes impossible – even if you want to do it, you cannot.

Veet Niten, you are asking, "Is it possible that things are happening inside me that I am not aware of?" Yes, things are happening within you and you have to make your awareness more sharp, more deep, more clear – so that you can become aware. Otherwise, all your actions come out of an unconscious state; you don't know exactly why you are doing it, why there is such a deep urge to do it, because the urge comes from the unconscious where never a ray of light has entered.

In psychoanalysis you have to drop completely whatever you say in your waking hours – it is not trustworthy. Psychoanalysis trusts your dreams more than it trusts you, because your consciousness is so small and it is not aware of all that is happening underneath. But when this consciousness goes to sleep, in your dreams the unconscious starts coming onto the screen of your mind. To know about your dreams is to know much more about you than you know yourself. Your dreams are more reliable because in your dreams you don't deceive; there is no question. Your dreams are so private, nobody is going to know – why deceive?

In your waking hours, you have a certain personality to maintain to live in the society – a certain morality, a certain code of conduct. In your dreams, all codes of conduct, all moralities, all principles disappear – you are simply natural.

Whatever is within you comes in its reality, as it is.

The only problem with dreams is that the unconscious knows no language; it is still the mind of the child. The child thinks in pictures – his language is pictorial, not alphabetical – so you dream in pictures. And that has created a great problem: who is going to interpret those pictures? What do they mean? – because there are many interpreters, many schools of psychoanalysis with different explanations, and all their explanations seem to have some truth.

The East has never tried anything like psychoanalysis, and the West has never tried anything like meditation. The East has been working for almost ten thousand years, single-pointedly, on meditation. And meditation means going beyond the mind – not getting involved in the mind, not being bothered by the mind, not being interested in its dreams – simply transcending it, simply becoming a watcher.

The West has become too involved in the games that mind goes on playing – and those games are very complicated, and they are endless. There is not a single man alive in the world who is completely psychoanalyzed, and there are people who have been in psychoanalysis for fifteen, twenty years, working hard to bring out their dreams to the psychoanalyst. Whichever dream is psychoanalyzed, disappears, but other dreams go on coming – it seems an unending process.

Perhaps somewhere far away in the past, of which no record exists, the East may have encountered something like psychoanalysis and found that it is a futile exercise. You explain one dream, another dream arises. You go on, and dreams go on arising. The East drops the whole mind with all its dreams, all its activities. They change their focus completely to a new area, a new space. Just be a watcher; don't interpret.

Sigmund Freud's whole contribution is interpretation of dreams, analysis of dreams. And the Eastern experience, which is very long, says, don't get involved in analysis or interpretation – just watch. Don't judge, and don't try to find the meaning of it. Don't condemn either, don't appreciate – just be absolutely indifferent, a pure witness who has nothing to do with it. If you become a witness, you will become aware that the mind starts functioning less and less; dreams start disappearing, thoughts are no longer so much, the crowd goes on becoming less and less. A moment comes when you are there, just a witness – and there is nothing to be witnessed. The mind is utterly silent: all dreams, all thoughts, all feelings, are gone.

This is the moment when you will become absolutely aware of who you are. Retrospectively, you will be able to see what you have been doing, and what has been happening inside you. But you are out of it; it is just a fading memory…slowly, slowly it fades away.

To live in silence, in serenity, is a totally different dimension of life where joy is simply natural; where life is in its absolute beauty, in its utter purity and aliveness; where love is so abundant that it goes on overflowing – you cannot contain it, it is a bigger reality than you are. Life becomes a smaller phenomenon than love, and love becomes a smaller phenomenon than light. These three L's contain the whole discipline of inner revolution.

Veet Niten, just being here, things are bound to happen within you of which you may not be aware, because you have not yet learned the art of watchfulness.

You are asking, "Is it possible for growth to happen in this way?" Yes it is possible, but only up to a point. It cannot happen the whole way without your becoming a watcher, so be concerned about *that*.

Instead of that you are asking me, "I have heard you say, 'I've been watching you' to people. Have you been watching me? How am I doing? Am I missing something?" Rather than being concerned whether I am watching you or not, your concern should be: are you watching yourself?

I am certainly watching. The moment I see you, I see you in your totality. To me you are transparent – I even see that which you may not be aware is within you. And I am continuously watching my people, how they are growing or not growing.

You are doing perfectly well, but something is certainly missing. And the thing that is missing is that you are not getting into the space of watching yourself. You cannot depend on me forever. In the beginning it is good, in the beginning it is helpful, but if it becomes a dependence, then it is dangerous. And I don't want anybody to be dependent on me, so my whole effort is to push you – as quickly as possible – into watching, into witnessing, into being a free individual, a free seeker, a searcher with total freedom.

All the religions of the world have been committing one of the great crimes: they want people to be dependent on them. They never want people to become independent, because that means losing customers. You are not my customers; to teach you is not my profession, it is simply my joy. I don't want any reward for it; just that you allowed me to share my heart with you is reward unto itself.

But the conditioning of the mind is so old, the conditioning that you go on hoping that somebody is going to save you: some savior, some messenger of God, but it is somebody else's business. You want to throw the responsibility on somebody else. Veet Niten, that will not be the right thing – at least here in this place with me.

A young Irish girl was talking to the Reverend Mother about her ambitions in life. "When I grow up," she announced, "I want to be a prostitute."

The Reverend Mother gasped and threw up her hands in horror. "Did I hear you rightly? What was it you said you wanted to be?"

"A prostitute."

The Reverend Mother sighed with relief, "Oh, praise the Lord," she said. "I thought you said a Protestant."

That has been the attitude of all the religions. Here, I want you to be just yourself. And that is possible only if you become a watcher. The deeper and sharper your watching, the greater is your individuality, the more is your human dignity.

Tremendous is the splendor of a person who has come to know everything that goes on within him, because by being aware, all that is false disappears and all that is real is nourished. Except this, there is no radical transformation possible.

No religion can give it to you, no messiah can give it to you. It is a gift that you have to give to yourself.

But the unconscious creates difficulties. Not that they cannot be dissolved, but you need a little patience, a little trust in existence. Difficulties will be there but don't take them as difficulties, only as challenges. It is a great adventure to go into your own being, to the very center of your existence – because that is the center of the whole of existence too.

Mrs. Rappaport advertised a new Cadillac for fifty dollars. Goldstein answered the ad and the first thing he asked was, "What is wrong with the car?"

"Nothing," she replied. "If you don't want it, please don't waste my time."

Goldstein asked for the keys and went to the

garage. He backed the car out, parked in front of the house, counted out fifty dollars, and handed it to the owner. "Now you have your money, what is the catch?"

"My husband just died," she said, "and in his will he instructed that the Cadillac be sold and the proceeds be given to his secretary."

You will find mind playing many games. It has been with you for so long, it will not be easy for it. If you simply drop it without giving a second thought, it will struggle to cling to you. But the secret is in watching. Don't fight with it, don't try to throw it away, don't condemn it. Just watch, like a mirror, with no opinion about it – that is the greatest weapon in your hands. If you can remain just like a mirror, your mind soon disappears, and the whole sky of your inner world becomes so silent...and the silence is not dead, it is alive. It has a music of its own. It blossoms, it has a fragrance of its own. It is radiant with light – it has a light of its own.

And it is part of the eternal source from where everything has come, and to where everything has to return.

Once knowing it, you are no longer the same old man. Your whole life will have a new dance, a new song, a new freshness, a new youthfulness, a new playfulness, a new laughter.

But *my* watching you will not help; you have to do it yourself.

Whatever you are doing is perfectly good, but not enough – because one of the most essential things is missing. And that is, you have not yet started on the path of a watcher.

Beloved Bhagwan,

These mornings, sitting in front of You,
when You look at me I feel so completely seen,
so understood and accepted.
And yet when I look at You, all I am aware of
is my blindness, my fear and ignorance.
Can You please comment?

Prem Vasumati, the observation in your question is very accurate. You say, "These mornings sitting in front of you, when you look at me I feel so completely seen – so understood and accepted. And yet when I look at you, all I am aware of is my blindness, my fear and ignorance." It is immensely significant to see your blindness, because that is the beginning of getting out of it. The moment a madman knows he is mad, he is no longer mad.

You can go into madhouses and you will be surprised to know that not a single madman accepts that he is mad. He may condemn the whole world for being mad, but he is not mad. The moment he accepts, even suspects "Perhaps I am mad," the madness starts melting, because it is a quality of sanity, of intelligence. Madness cannot accept that "I am mad" – that will be a contradiction. The mad person tries to prove in every possible way that he is absolutely sane.

I have heard about a man who had gone mad – and not an ordinarily mad person; his madness was unique. He started thinking that he was dead. He would not go to the office...his family would tell him, "Go to the office; otherwise how are we going to survive?" But he would say, "Have you ever heard of any dead man going to the office? Have you ever heard of any dead man helping his relatives, his family, his friends to survive? I am absolutely helpless, what can I do? Nobody has any control over death; I am dead."

People tried in every way: "You are talking and you are eating and you are sleeping and you are walking – and still you go on insisting that you are dead?"

He said, "I know more about myself...I don't need anybody's advice. I feel absolutely certain that I am dead, and if a dead man feels hungry – he eats. What is wrong with it?"

Finally they took him to a psychiatrist, and the psychiatrist said, "I will settle him. He is a little rare; I have never come across.... There have been many kinds of people, but he surpasses them all."

He talked with the dead man, and the dead man's arguments to prove that he was dead were perfectly rational. Not only that: when his family left and he was alone with the psychiatrist, he pulled his chair close to him and told him, "You are also dead. I did not say it in front of those people; otherwise your whole profession would be disturbed. We are in the same boat; just as I died, you died."

The psychiatrist said, "This is too much. You are trying to convince me."

He said, "It is not a question of conviction: once dead, dead forever. Do you think somebody convinced me? I discovered myself that I am dead – and because I know how to discover it, I have discovered that you are dead too. It is good that they brought me here; otherwise you would have lived with the wrong conception – that you are alive."

The psychiatrist thought, "What to do with this man?" He took out his paper knife, to cut the man on his hand. Before cutting the man – just to bring a little blood – he said, "Have you ever heard that dead men don't bleed?"

The man said, "Yes, when I used to be alive, I heard the saying that dead men don't bleed."

The psychiatrist said, "Okay, now this will be decisive." He cut a little on the man's hand and blood came out, and he said, "What do you say now?"

The man said, "What is there to be said? It means the proverb is wrong: dead men *do* bleed. Now just give me the paper knife and I will show you." He cut the hand of the psychiatrist and blood came out, and he said, "Look! There is not only one piece of evidence; now we are both proofs that the proverb is wrong. It seems nobody has ever checked, and some idiot must have spread the idea that dead men don't bleed. Why shouldn't they bleed? They have every right to bleed; it is not the monopoly only of the living ones."

The psychiatrist said, "You take your fees back and you go home before I become convinced, because I have a wife and two small kids, and I have to take care of them. And you are so logically convincing that once in a while the suspicion arises in my mind too: Who knows? perhaps he is right. What proof have I got that I am alive – except that I have never thought about it. You are a great thinker, but go – before it is too late!"

Vasumati, if you see your blindness, that is good news: it means you are starting to see.

The blindness will disappear. If you see your ignorance, that brings an alchemical change. The moment you see your ignorance it becomes innocence – it is ignorance only while you remain unaware of it. The moment you understand that "I don't know," the doors of knowing have opened; if you see your fear, that's a good sign. All these things have to be brought before your consciousness. Fear exists in darkness, and seeing your fear means it is coming into light – in the light it cannot exist.

So remain alert about your blindness, about your fear, about your ignorance, and just your alertness will dispel the whole darkness of blindness, of fear, of ignorance. They are not separate things; they are separate aspects of a single unconscious mind – they all exist together and they all disappear together.

It is a good beginning. As far as I am concerned, my acceptance of everybody is total. Whoever you are, whatever you are, wherever you are, I don't want to impose any ideal on you that you should be something else. If you grow into something else, that is another thing, but I don't want to give you any "shoulds" – that you must be this, that you should be this, that "unless you achieve this ideal you are unworthy of being called human." No, as you are, you are perfectly worthy. Existence accepts you, life accepts you – and I am not against life, I am not against existence; I simply follow the way the river of life moves. If life accepts you, I accept you.

People have conditions when they accept....

I have heard about two lovers sitting on the sea beach on a fullmoon night, and they were discussing marriage.

The woman asked, "Will you always love me – always?"

The man said, "I have told you a thousand and one times that I will love you always, always – but because of your question, a question has arisen in my mind. In your old age, will you look like your mother? Then I cannot love you. If you are determined to become like your mother, then forget all about marriage."

In old age, far away in the future...nobody can predict how that woman will look – like the mother or like the father, or like the chauffeur – nobody knows! But even that far away there is a condition, and that future condition can disturb even the present. In the present, people are continually looking at you with all kinds of prejudices, judgments: how you should be, how you should behave, your etiquette, your manners, your morality.

Small things are enough to create barriers, and we are all living with our defenses so that others cannot know exactly what we are. We allow them to know only that part of our being which is acceptable to them. This is one of the foundations of our misery. People are different, and we should enjoy and rejoice in their differences, in their variety. Your judgment is not going to change anybody; perhaps your judgment may create a stubbornness in the other person not to change. Who are you to change the person?

These are the secrets of life. If you accept somebody with totality, he starts changing, because you give him total freedom to be himself. And a person who gives you total freedom to be yourself – you would like that person to be happy; as far as you are concerned, he has given you the dignity and the honor of accepting you. It is very natural that if you see something in yourself which is not right – although the other person accepts you as you are – you would like to be even better, just for him; to be softer, to be more loving, to be more tender, just for him.

I accept you as you are. I don't have any

expectations of you; I don't want you to be molded into a certain idea, into a certain ideal. I don't want to make you a dead statue. I want you to be alive, more alive, and you can be alive only if your totality is accepted – not only accepted, but respected.

I have a deep reverence for everything that is alive, a reverence for life itself.

If my reverence changes you, that is another thing; I am not responsible for it. And it is going to change you – I warn you beforehand; you cannot blame me later on.

You are fortunate, Vasumati, that you feel completely seen, so understood and accepted. If we could accept people with whom we are in some way related – friends or lovers – and understand them, and allow them not to have any defenses so they can be completely natural, the world would be so beautiful and people would be so happy. But up to now we have lived under very wrong conceptions, and those wrong conceptions have to be dropped.

Two disciples of a famous rabbi came to visit him, and while they were waiting to be ushered into his presence, the rabbi's wife brought them two cups of lemon tea and a plate with two cakes on it – one small, one big.

"After you," said one disciple to the other, offering him the plate.

"No, after you."

"No, no, I insist. After you."

"No, you take first."

Eventually one of the two helped himself first – to the bigger cake. The other was outraged: "What! You helped yourself first, and took the bigger cake!"

"So?" said the other. "If you had chosen first, which cake would you have taken?"

"Why, the smaller one, of course!"

"Well, what are you complaining about? You have got the smaller one!"

All our manners, all our etiquette is so phony – we don't mean what we say, we don't mean what we show.

The whole of humanity has become part of a single ideology, and that is hypocrisy. One may be Christian, one may be Hindu, one may be Jaina, one may be Buddhist – it does not matter; they are all hypocrites.

I want my people to be simply themselves, absolutely natural...and allowing the other also to be natural, accepting each other, trying to understand each other's mystery and helping in every way so the other can become more and more authentic.

Only authentic human beings can create a society which will be joyous, ecstatic, and in the real sense, human.

Beloved Bhagwan,

You say, first jump and then think.
But this is what mankind is doing. First going to the moon,
and then realizing that rockets have made holes
in the ozone layer, for instance.
Sometimes it can be too late to think.
On the other hand, if one thinks too much,
one will never jump – jumping implies risk
and unknown consequences.
I am confused: Can jumping and awareness go together, and how?

Anand Prema, my statement, "Jump before you think," was not concerned with outer reality, it was concerned with your inner space. This is how your mind can change the context and then create unnecessary problems.

As far as the outside is concerned, think first, think twice – only then jump. Even if the risk is that too much thinking may not allow you to jump at all, this is perfectly acceptable to you because in the outside world, what is there to lose? Doing anything without thinking in the outside world is simply stupidity.

But the laws of the outer and the inner are opposite. In the inner world, if you go on thinking you will never jump, because the inner is absolutely unknown. On the outside you are not alone; there are thousands of others. The outer world is objective, visible, and if you are not going to jump, somebody else will jump.

Albert Einstein was asked, "If you had not discovered the theory of relativity, what do you think – would it have ever been discovered?"

Albert Einstein said, "At the most three months later...most probably three weeks later" – because all the facts were there, and thousands of scientists around the world were working on those facts. It was only a question of who solved the puzzle first. And later on it was discovered that a German scientist had discovered the theory of relativity *before* Albert Einstein, but he had not published his paper. He was just going to publish it, but because it was so outrageously against all the old scientific findings, he went on thinking about whether to publish it or not..."I may become a laughingstock, I am going to say something absolutely contradicting the whole of scientific progress."

Albert Einstein's theory of relativity goes against the logic of Aristotle; it goes against the geometry of Euclid, which was well established for two thousand years. And it goes against so many things which have been accepted by scientists as facts – who ever doubted that two plus two is equal to four? Even a man like Bertrand Russell, who wrote one of the greatest treatises on mathematics, took nearabout two hundred and thirty-five pages to prove that two plus two is *really* four. But against all these comes the theory of relativity. It says two plus two can be anything – but never four.

Albert Einstein took the risk, and jumped ahead. But he was aware that if he did not take the jump, somebody else, within three weeks or at the most three months...how long can you prevent it?

In the outside world, there are millions of people, and everything is objective. In the inside world, you are alone – you cannot take anybody as your guide, as your friend; no map exists, no guidebook exists. If you go on thinking, perhaps you will never enter into it.

My statement was about the inner world. Against the old proverb, "Think before you jump," I had said, "Jump before you think." What is the worry? You will be inside; you can go on thinking later on – first jump. And you are not jumping from a hilltop, you are jumping inside yourself. I don't think that there is any possibility of having fractures, or falling into an abysmal ditch, or falling so deep that you cannot come out – it has not happened up to now. Thousands of people have jumped in, and they all have come out in far better shape than they have ever been.

There is no risk. The inner journey is really the safest journey – absolutely insured – because not a single case exists in the whole of history when somebody jumped inside and came out having multiple fractures. Those who have jumped in, have come out with such tremendous joy, with such deep sensibility, with such great understanding...they have found the greatest treasure which exists in existence.

Mr. Cohen comes home one night and starts to pack his bags. "So, where are you going?" asks his wife.

"To Tahiti."

"Tahiti? Why Tahiti?"

"Simple. Every time you make love there, they give you five dollars."

Then Mrs. Cohen starts packing her bags.

"So where are you going?" asks Mr. Cohen.

"I'm going to Tahiti."

"Why?"

"I want to see how you're going to live on ten dollars a year."

Okay, Vimal?

Yes, Bhagwan.

Session 18

Inside You God is Hidden

*To be alone is a great opportunity, a blessing,
because in your aloneness you are bound
to stumble upon yourself and for the first time remember
who you are.
To know that you are part of the divine existence
is to be free from death, free from misery,
free from anxiety; free from all that has been
a nightmare to you for many many lives.*

March 21, 1987
Morning

Beloved Bhagwan,

When You talked about the ultimate death of this world,
I got suddenly in touch with deep aloneness,
and this voice inside me said, "Remember: each single moment,
remember that you are alone."
My beloved Master,
after our death will You still be, in some mysterious way,
with our wandering consciousness?

Prem Amiyo, aloneness is the ultimate reality. One comes alone, one goes alone; and between these two alonenesses we create all kinds of relationships and fighting, just to deceive ourselves – because in life also, we remain alone. But aloneness is not something to be sad about; it is something to rejoice in. There are two words – the dictionary will say they have the same meaning, but existence gives them totally opposite meanings. One word is loneliness and the other word is aloneness. They are not synonymous.

Loneliness is a negative state, like darkness. Loneliness means you are missing someone; you are empty, and you are afraid in this vast universe. Aloneness has a totally different meaning: it does not mean that you are missing someone, it means that you have found yourself.

It is absolutely positive.

Finding oneself, one finds the meaning of life, the significance of life, the joy of life, the splendor of life. Finding oneself is the greatest finding in man's life, and this finding is possible only when you are alone. When your consciousness is not crowded by anything, by anybody, when your consciousness is utterly empty – in that emptiness, in that nothingness, a miracle happens. And that miracle is the foundation of all religions.

The miracle is: when there is nothing else for your consciousness to be conscious of, the consciousness turns upon itself. It becomes a circle. Finding no obstacle, finding no object, it comes back to the source. And the moment the circle is complete, you are no longer just an ordinary human being; you have become part of the godliness that surrounds existence. You are no longer yourself; you have become part of the whole universe – your heartbeat is now the heartbeat of the universe itself.

This is the experience which mystics have been searching for all their lives, down the ages. There is no other experience which is more ecstatic, more blissful. This experience transforms your whole outlook: where there used to be darkness, now there is light; where there used to be misery, there is bliss; where there used to be anger, hate, possessiveness, jealousy, there is only a beautiful flower of love.

The whole energy that was being wasted in negative emotions is no longer wasted; it takes a positive and creative turn. On the one hand you are no longer your old self; on the other hand you are, for the first time, your authentic self. The old is gone, the new has arrived. The old was dead; the new belongs to the eternal, the new belongs to the immortal.

It is because of this experience that the seers of the *Upanishads* have declared man as *amritasya putrah* – "sons and daughters of immortality."

Unless you know yourself as eternal beings, part of the whole, you will remain afraid of death. The fear of death is simply because you are not aware of your eternal source of life. Once the eternity of your being is realized, death becomes the greatest lie in existence.

Death has never happened, never happens, never will happen, because that which is, remains always – in different forms, on different levels, but there is no discontinuity.

Eternity in the past and eternity in the future both belong to you. And the present moment becomes a meeting point of two eternities: one going towards the past, one going towards the future.

Amiyo, you are asking, "When You talked about the ultimate death of this world, I got suddenly in touch with deep aloneness, and this voice inside me said, 'Remember: each single moment, remember that you are alone.'" The remembrance has not to be only of the mind; your every fiber of being, your every cell of the body should remember it – not as a word, but as a deep feeling.

The English word *sin* has been corrupted by Christianity – they have given it a wrong meaning. Its original meaning is forgetfulness. Forgetfulness of yourself is the only sin there is, and to remember yourself is the only virtue.

Gautam Buddha emphasized one single word continually for forty-two years, morning and evening; the word is *sammasati* – it means "right remembering." You remember many things – you can become an *Encyclopedia Britannica*; your mind is capable of remembering all the libraries of the world – but that is not the right remembering. There is only one right remembering – the moment you remember yourself.

Gautam Buddha used to illustrate his point with the ancient story of a lioness who was jumping from one hillock to another hillock, and between the two hillocks a big flock of sheep was moving. The lioness was pregnant, and gave birth while she was jumping. Her cub fell into the flock of sheep, was brought up by the sheep, and naturally, he believed himself also to be a sheep. It was a little strange because he was so big, so different – but perhaps he was just a freak of nature.... He was vegetarian.

He grew up, and one day an old lion who was in search of food came close to the flock of sheep – and he could not believe his eyes. In the midst of the sheep, there was a young lion in its full glory, and the sheep were not afraid. He forgot about his food; he ran after the flock of sheep...and it was becoming more and more puzzling, because the young lion was also running away with the sheep. Finally he got hold of the young lion. He was crying and weeping and saying to the old lion, "Please, let me go with my people!"

But the old lion dragged him to a nearby lake – a silent lake without any ripples, it was just like a pure mirror – and the old lion forced him to see his reflection in the lake, and also the reflection of the old lion. There was a sudden transformation. The moment the young lion saw who he was, there was a great roar – the whole valley echoed the roar of the young lion. He had never roared before because he had never thought that he was anybody other than a sheep.

The old lion said, "My work is done; now it is up to you. Do you want to go back to your own flock?"

The young lion laughed. He said, "Forgive me, I had completely forgotten who I am. And I am immensely grateful to you that you helped me to remember."

Gautam Buddha used to say, "The master's function is to help you remember who you are." You are not part of this mundane world; your home is the home of the divine. You are lost in forgetfulness; you have forgotten that inside you God is hidden. You never look inside – because everybody looks outside, you also go on looking outside.

To be alone is a great opportunity, a blessing, because in your aloneness you are bound to stumble upon yourself and for the first time remember who you are. To know that you are part of the divine existence is to be free from death, free from misery, free from anxiety; free from all that has been a nightmare to you for many many lives.

Amiyo, it was good that you became aware of a deep aloneness – don't lose track of it; become more centered in your deep aloneness. That's what meditation is: becoming centered in one's own aloneness. The aloneness has to be so pure that not even a thought, not even a feeling, disturbs it. The moment your aloneness is complete, your experience of it will become your enlightenment. Enlightenment is not something that comes from outside; it is something that grows within you.

To forget your self is the only sin. And to remember your self, in its utter beauty, is the only virtue, the only religion. You need not be a Hindu, you need not be a Mohammedan, you need not be a Christian – all that you need to be religious is to be yourself.

It has been immensely good that your whole being resounded with these words: "Remember: each single moment, remember that you are alone." You are also asking, "My beloved Master, after our death will you still be, in some mysterious way, with our wandering consciousness?"

We are not separate, even now – nobody is separate; the whole existence is one organic unity. The idea of separation is because of our forgetfulness. It is almost as if every leaf of the tree started thinking it is separate, separate from other leaves... but deep down they are nourished by the same roots. It is one tree; the leaves may be many. It is one existence; the manifestations may be many.

I am with you right now. I have been with you forever, and I will be with you for eternity – there is no other way.

Knowing oneself, one thing becomes absolutely clear: no man is an island – we are a continent, a vast continent, an infinite existence without any boundaries. The same life runs through all, the same love fills every heart, the same joy dances in every being. Just because of our misunderstanding, we think we are separate.

The idea of separation is our illusion.

The idea of oneness will be our experience of the ultimate truth.

I have heard...there are six people on an aircraft: the pilot, Gorbachev, Ronald Reagan, Rajiv Gandhi, the Catholic pope, and a young hippie. When something goes wrong with the plane, the pilot announces that he is taking one of the five parachutes and that they must decide among themselves who will take the remaining four.

Gorbachev declares that since he is the only hope for the spread of communism, he must jump, and taking a parachute jumps out of the plane.

Ronald Reagan declares that he is the only hope for the defense of the free world against the spread of communism, and he too takes a parachute and jumps.

Then Rajiv Gandhi gets up. "I am the leader of the greatest nation and the greatest democracy of the world, India, and I am the most intelligent and youngest world leader; I must jump." And he too jumps out of the plane.

Then the pope rises and says to the young man, the hippie, "My son, I am old and have lived my lifetime. Take the last parachute and jump." But the young hippie protests, "Father, hurry up. There are two parachutes left, one for each of us. Put on one of them and jump."

"But how is that?" asks the pope. The young man replies, "That guy who said he is the most intelligent and youngest world leader – he took my sleeping bag!"

Just a little more intelligence is needed and you can come out of the gloom, the misery, the hell in which the whole humanity is living. The secret of coming out of this hell is to remember yourself. And this remembrance will become possible if you understand the idea that you are alone. You may have lived with your wife or with your husband for fifty years; still, you are two. Your wife is alone, you are alone. You have been trying to create a facade that "We are not alone," that "We are a family," that "We are a society," that "We are a civilization," that "We are a culture," that "We are an organized religion," that "We are an organized political party." But all these illusions are not going to help.

You have to recognize, howsoever painful it appears in the beginning, that "I am alone and in a strange land." This recognition, for the first time, is painful. It takes away all our illusions – which were great consolations. But once you have dared to accept the reality, the pain disappears. And just hidden behind the pain is the greatest blessing of the world: You come to know yourself.

You are the intelligence of existence; you are the consciousness of existence; you are the soul of existence. You are part of this immense godliness that manifests in thousands of forms: in the trees, in the birds, in the animals, in human beings...but it is the same consciousness in different stages of evolution. And the man who recognizes himself and feels that the god he was searching and looking for all over the world resides within his own heart, comes to the highest point of evolution. There is nothing higher than that.

It makes your life for the first time meaningful, significant, religious. But you will not be a Hindu, and you will not be a Christian, and you will not be a Jew; you will be simply religious. By being a Hindu, or a Mohammedan, or a Christian, or a Jaina, or a Buddhist, you are destroying the purity of religiousness – it needs no adjectives.

Love is love – have you ever heard about Hindu love? Mohammedan love? Consciousness is consciousness – have you ever thought about Indian consciousness or Chinese consciousness? Enlightenment is enlightenment: whether it happens in the white body or in the black body, whether it happens in the young man or in the old man, whether it happens in a man or in a woman, it does not make any difference. It is the same experience, the same taste, the same sweetness, the same fragrance.

The only person who is not intelligent is one who is running around all over the world in search of something, not knowing exactly what; sometimes thinking perhaps it is money, sometimes thinking perhaps it is power, sometimes thinking perhaps it is prestige, sometimes thinking perhaps it is respectability.

The intelligent man first searches his own being before he starts a journey in the outer world. That seems to be simple and logical – at least first look inside your own house before you go searching all over the world. And those who have looked within themselves have found it, without any exception.

Gautam Buddha is not a Buddhist. The word *Buddha* simply means the awakened one, who has come out of sleep. Mahavira, the Jaina, is not a Jaina. The word *Jaina* simply means one who has conquered – conquered himself.

The world needs a great revolution where each individual finds his religion within himself. The moment religions become organized, they become dangerous; they become really politics with a false face of religion. That's why all the religions of the world go on trying to convert more and more people to their religion. It is the politics of numbers; whoever has more numbers will be more powerful.

But nobody seems to be interested in bringing millions of individuals to their own selves. My work here consists of taking you out of any kind of organized effort – because truth can never be organized. You have to go alone on the pilgrimage, because the pilgrimage is going to be inside. You cannot take anybody with you. And you have to drop everything that you have learned from others, because all those prejudices will distort your vision – you will not be able to see the naked reality of your being. The naked reality of your being is the only hope of finding God.

God is your naked reality – undecorated, without any adjective.

It is not confined by your body, not confined by your birth, not confined by your color, not confined by your sex, not confined by your country. It is simply not confined by anything. And it is available, so close:

Just one step inside and you have arrived.

You have been told for thousands of years that the journey to God is very long. The journey is not long, God is not far away. God is in your breath, God is in your heartbeat, God is in your blood, in your bones, in your marrow – just a single step of closing your eyes and entering within yourself.

It may take a little time because old habits die hard: even if you close your eyes, thoughts will go on crowding you. Those thoughts are from the outside, and the simple method which has been followed by all the great seers of the world is just to watch your thoughts, just to be a witness. Don't condemn them, don't justify them, don't rationalize them. Remain aloof, remain indifferent, let them pass – they will be gone.

And the day your mind is absolutely silent, with no disturbance, you have taken the first step that takes you to the temple of God.

The temple of God is made of your consciousness.

You cannot go there with your friends, with

your children, with your wife, with your parents.

Everybody has to go there alone.

Amiyo, don't forget the experience that has happened to you – the feeling of deep aloneness and a voice inside saying to you, "Remember: each single moment, remember that you are alone."

The day of your glory will not be far away.

Beloved Bhagwan,

You shower me with love and I am so ashamed,
I can't look at You sometimes.
Inside I know I don't have anything to give You,
and what little there is feels so inadequate.
Master, my heart is broken. Please help me.

Milarepa, your question surprises me, because you give so much love to me. You have given yourself to me – your music, your poetry, your dance. What can be more valuable? You have trusted me – a stranger. What more can there be that you should feel ashamed? You should rejoice, because all that you had, you have given to me, without holding anything back. You have given your heart.

But perhaps you don't think that your songs, your music, your dance, your love, your trust, have any value. They certainly are of the greatest value – although they don't have any price.

You are not poor. Just not to have money does not make a man poor; not to have power, not to be a president or a prime minister of a country, does not make a man poor.

What makes a man poor is not to have a soul. And your soul is so full of songs, so full of dance, so full of laughter – there is no question of your feeling ashamed. You have given to me the richest gifts that anyone can give. But perhaps you have not thought of it in this way.

There are some of the richest people in the world who are so poor inside that all their money cannot make any difference. Their money is outside, and their poverty is inside – anything from the outside cannot destroy the inner poverty. The inner poverty is destroyed only by inner values: love, compassion, silence, prayer, meditation – these are the things that make a person really rich. He may be just a beggar on the street, it does not matter, but even emperors will find themselves jealous of him.

You are misunderstanding. Put things right.

I have heard that Adolf Hitler dies and goes to heaven. He behaves so well that St. Peter tells him he can go back to earth again for a week as a treat. After twenty-four hours, he is back, hammering at the pearly gates to get in.

"What is the matter, Adolf?" asked St. Peter, "you have got six more days."

"Let me in, let me in!" cries Hitler. So St. Peter unlocks the gate, lets him in and asks him, "Adolf, what is the matter? Didn't you enjoy it?"

"Enjoy it?" says Hitler. "Enjoy it? Everyone has gone mad down there since I left. I come back, and what do I find? The Jews are fighting, and the Germans are making money!"

Certainly Adolf Hitler must have been shocked. His old idea, that Jews make money and Germans fight, is no longer relevant. Now Jews are having a tough fight and Germans are making more money than anybody else in Europe.

Milarepa, you also have the old idea that the man of possessions is rich, and the man who does not possess anything is poor. It is not true. The man of inner possessions is the real rich man, and the man of outer possessions is simply deceiving himself that he is rich, but deep down he knows he is a pauper.

I have known the richest people, and when they expose their hearts, their eyes are full of tears – because they have all the money the world can afford...but the money cannot purchase love, the money cannot purchase peace, the money cannot purchase silence, the money cannot purchase prayer, the money cannot purchase God. So what is the use of it? Their inner being remains dark, empty.

And it is the inner being that counts finally, because death will take away everything else and leave you only with that which is inner. Death should be accepted as the only criterion to decide what is richness and what is poverty. That which death can take away is not richness; that which death cannot destroy is the real richness.

And Milarepa, you *are* a rich man. You can become even richer. There is no end to it until you become enlightened, until you have reached to the highest peak of the Himalayas of consciousness.

That should be the goal for every human being who has any intelligence.

Beloved Bhagwan,

Can You talk about the difference
between so- called self-consiousness and self-awareness?
Is self-consciousness a form of unawareness,
or is there something of awareness in it?

Prem Anudeva, self-consciousness is a disease, it is sickness. Self-awareness is health – it is wholeness. Both words appear to be the same, but in fact, because language is created by unconscious people, they cannot make the fine demarcations.

Self-consciousness simply means ego consciousness and self-awareness means soul consciousness. Your ego is a false entity. Because you have so much money, because you have so much power, because you are born in a very respected family...your education, your position in life – all these things constitute your ego. But your soul comes with you when you are born, it has nothing to do with anything. Whether you are educated or uneducated – Kabir was not educated; Jesus was not educated – whether you come from a respectable family or not, does not matter.

It is not known whether Kabir was born from a Hindu family or a Mohammedan family. He was found on the bank of the Ganges by a sannyasin, Swami Ramananda; a small child whose parents had left him there. Perhaps he was illegitimate. But Kabir became one of the richest human beings the world has known. No family, no certainty of what religion he belonged to, no education, no riches – he remained a weaver his whole life. He would weave and go every market day into the market to sell his clothes; that was his whole earnings, enough for seven days.

But you cannot find a richer man; so full of bliss that each of his songs still carries something alive in it. After centuries have passed, just the words of Kabir can echo something within you – as if Kabir were present. He has poured his heart in his words; those words are of gold.

Jesus was a carpenter's son – very poor, absolutely uneducated, had no idea about scriptures, learning, scholarship – but still he had a richness, a consciousness, so that even on the cross he did not forget to pray to God. His last words on the earth were: "Father, forgive these people who are crucifying me, because they know not what they are doing; they are unconscious people." Such compassion comes out of self-awareness. And self-awareness does not depend on anything outside you, it depends only on you. The soul is there; you have just to wake it up. It is an awakening.

Avoid self-consciousness – that is sickness of the soul; and go deeper into self-awareness – that is your authentic reality.

One morning a young woman got out of bed, slipped into her robe, raised the shade, uncovered the parrot, put on the coffee pot, answered the phone, and heard a masculine voice say, "Hello, honey. My ship just hit port and I am coming right over." So the young lady took the coffee pot off the stove, covered up the parrot, pulled down the shade, took off her robe, got into bed, and heard the parrot mumble, "Christ, what a short day that was!"

Man is not even that much alert. You go on living like a zombie – a routine life, every day repeating the same – without ever thinking that you have not yet done the most important thing: you have not encountered yourself. You have not attained to self-awareness; you are engaged in making your ego as big as possible.

But the ego is your enemy, not your friend. It is the ego that gives you wounds and hurts you. It is the ego that makes you violent, angry, jealous, competitive. It is the ego that is continuously comparing and feeling miserable.

Self-awareness is awareness of your inner world, the kingdom of God. As you become aware of the tremendous beauty of your own being – its joy, its light, its eternal life, its richness, its overflowing love – you feel so blessed that you can bless the whole world without any discrimination.

Kill the ego, because that is hiding your authentic soul. And discover your soul; that will be your self-awareness.

Self-awareness, Anudeva, is the way to your kingdom, which is also the kingdom of God.

It is within you.

You are not to go anywhere; you have to come back home.

Okay, Vimal?

Yes, Bhagwan.

210

Session 19

At the Maximum You Disappear

*The people who know the secret of the open heart,
the secret of being nobody,
are the most deserving of all that is beautiful,
of all that is divine,
of all that transcends our mundane existence.
Nothing else is needed...just that you should be absent,
a pure space,
and you are ready to receive the guest.*

March 22, 1987
Morning

Beloved Bhagwan,

As I walk to discourse each morning,
this thought comes before me:
What have I done to deserve this blissful experience
of sitting at Your feet?
Joyfully, sometimes tearfully, awaiting Your glance upon me
and then longing for the next day to dawn
and bring with it yet one more opportunity
of being in Your presence....
Beloved Master, is this not also a type of greed?

Zareen, existence is so generous, life is so bountiful that one need not deserve, need not be worthy to receive its gifts. On the contrary, one has to be absolutely humble, a nobody – receptive, available, with all the doors of the heart open, trusting – and existence showers on him flowers, like rain. The experience deepens one's humbleness and creates a new quality in one's being, of which one is generally not aware – that of gratefulness, gratefulness to all, gratefulness to the whole.

Do we deserve life? Do we deserve love? The very idea of deserving has been implanted in us by the marketplace. What do these trees deserve? But the sun comes every day and the stars come every night, and the trees are constantly in silent meditation. They are also waiting.

And waiting is not greed, waiting is simply our nature, waiting means that our doors are open and we are ready to welcome the guest whenever he comes.

A beautiful poem by Rabindranath Tagore, "The King of the Night".... There used to be a very huge temple, so huge that there were one hundred priests to worship the statues of gods in the temple. One night the chief priest dreamt, and the dream was such that it made him wake up – he could not believe it, but he could not disbelieve it either.

In the dream he saw God himself saying to him, "Tomorrow is the fullmoon night. Clean the whole temple, get ready – I may come any moment. For thousands of years this temple has been calling me, but the call was professional; hence it was not heard. Your call is not professional. You are the first chief priest in this temple whose heart is full of longing, full of prayer, full of waiting. You are not simply doing the rituals, your whole life is in it. So don't forget: tomorrow I am coming and I am giving you an advance notice, so that the temple is ready to receive the guest for which it was made many, many centuries before."

It was difficult to believe that God would speak to him – he is nobody, he does not deserve it. On the contrary, he has so many weaknesses, so many frailties which every human being is prone to...but on the other hand, how to disbelieve? The dream was truer than our so-called true life.

He was worried about what he was going to say to the other priests, because they will make him a laughingstock. The temple has been there for centuries and God has never come. But even if it looks awkward, embarrassing, he has to tell them, because he alone cannot clean the whole temple; it is so big, so huge....

He woke up all the priests and said, "Forgive me for disturbing your sleep. I am in a dilemma: I have seen this dream...."And all the priests laughed – because priests are the only people who don't believe in God. They know perfectly well that God is a strategy to exploit people.

They said, "It was just a dream, go back to sleep." But the chief priest could not sleep. In the morning he said, "It may have been just a dream, but who knows? If God comes and finds us unprepared, it will be such a shame. So I order you, as the chief priest, to clean the temple, to decorate the temple with flowers, with candles. Make it fragrant with incense, and let us wait. Even if it was only a dream, and God does not turn up, there is no harm. The temple needs cleaning, and it is a good opportunity."

The whole day the temple was cleaned, decorated. Delicious food was made for God, but the whole day passed and there was no sign. And the chief priest was standing at the door, looking far away where the sky seems to meet the earth – the temple was in a very lonely place – but the road remained empty; nobody came.

The day disappeared into night. They were all hungry because they were waiting: first God should be served. And then all the other priests said, "We had told you, a dream is just a dream. Who has ever heard of God coming to the temples? You are very naive, very simple, very innocent. Now let us eat – we are feeling hungry and tired – and go to sleep."

So they closed the doors, and ate the food that they had made for God. And because they were tired from the whole day's cleaning and decoration and preparation, they immediately fell asleep.

In the middle of the night a golden chariot came on the road leading to the temple. The sound of the chariot coming... and the chief priest was deep down still feeling that God cannot be so deceptive, particularly to a man who has never done any harm to him. He heard the sound of the chariot. He woke up the priests, and he said, "He is coming! I have just heard the sound of the chariot, listen."

And they were half asleep and they said, "Just go to sleep! You are going mad, just because of a dream. This is not a chariot, this is just the clouds thundering." He was alone. They silenced him.

The chariot came to the door. God stepped onto the long steps reaching upto the temple. He knocked on the door. Again the chief priest said, "I have heard somebody knocking on the door! Perhaps God has come." And now it was too much. Annoying them in the middle of the night...utterly tired and exhausted priests. Somebody shouted at him and said, "You shut up and just go to sleep! It is nothing but the breeze hitting the doors. No God has come and no chariot has come; it has never happened."

They again silenced him.

In the morning when the chief priest...he could not sleep; the waiting kept him awake, the longing kept him awake. He got up early and opened the door – "My god!" he said, "He *has* come" – because on the road there were signs of a chariot coming up to the door, and on the steps he could see the signs of someone reaching the door. He looked carefully...because dust had gathered on the steps and there were perfect impressions of the feet. It was no one other than God, because the impressions in the dust were exactly the same as had been described in the ancient scriptures; exactly how the feet of God would make an impression.

With tears in his eyes, he ran inside and made all the priests wake up. And he said "You did not listen to me – it was not clouds thundering in the sky, it was the chariot of God. And it was not the wind knocking at the doors it was God himself who knocked. But now it is too late."

This beautiful poem has immense significance. God comes to every heart – because that is the temple, the only temple – and knocks on the heart. But you go on rationalizing, and your doors are closed.

Zareen, you are asking, "As I walk to discourse each morning, this thought comes before me – what have I done to deserve this blissful experience of sitting at your feet?" Just to be, and just to be nobody is all that one needs, to deserve. No other virtues, no other qualities but just a simple and loving heart – a heart that is open and ready to receive the guest.

"...Joyfully, sometimes tearfully, awaiting your glance upon me, and then longing for the next day to dawn and bring with it yet one more opportunity of being in your presence.... Beloved Master, is this not also a type of greed?" No. Greed is violent, greed is demanding.

It is simply a loving, longing, waiting. And how can one avoid the waiting and longing? The difference between greed and longing is very clear: greed is aggressive, it has to be so; it is a demand and an expectation, and then it becomes ugly. But if your heart is simply waiting, with no demand, then there is no question of greed.

The people who know the secret of the open heart, the secret of being nobody, are the most deserving of all that is beautiful, of all that is divine, of all that transcends our mundane existence. Nothing else is needed...just that you should be absent, a pure space, and you are ready to receive the guest.

But man has believed in God in as ugly a way as possible, because his God is nothing but all his desires, all his demands. It is not a humble prayer, a humble invitation.

A man is sight-seeing in the mountains and is marveling at the wondrous beauty of nature. At one point he gets so absorbed in the beautiful view of the mountains that he forgets what he is doing and walks over the cliff. As he is falling, he sees a branch sticking out from the wall of the cliff. He reaches out and manages to grab the branch. As he hangs there he begins to pray, "Oh, Lord, please help me. I'm losing my strength and I can't hold on much longer. Please God, save me."

Suddenly the heavens part, and a voice comes booming down, "I am the Lord!"

"Oh Lord," cries the man, "please save me!"

"I will save you," booms the voice. "All you have to do is prove your faith in me by letting go of the branch."

The man looks down at the two-hundred-foot drop below him, thinks for a moment, then says, "Is there anybody else up there I can talk to?"

Our so-called idea of God is just a means to serve us. You may not have ever thought about it, that your God is nothing but a servant. He has to do this, he has to do that. The true religious man is a servant to God; he has no demand. He has only one longing: that God may use him for His purposes. He wants to become nothing but a hollow bamboo flute, so God can sing His song through him. He simply wants not to obstruct but to remain absolutely empty, so God can make of his emptiness whatsoever He wants.

This is trust.

And there is no value higher than trust, because trust is the purest form of love.

Zareen, your tears are tears of love, and your waiting for tomorrow is just a longing of the heart – but not desire, because there is no demand.

Just become more and more humble, more and more nobody, more and more spacious – because when I see you, I am not there; I have departed from myself long ago. I have allowed God to take possession of me. I have allowed him to do whatsoever he wants to do with me. I don't know even what the next word is going to be, because it is not coming from me – it is coming only *through* me.

Just look at my eyes…somebody else is looking through my eyes.

Look at my gestures…they are not mine.

Look at my signatures…they are not mine.

I have lost track of myself so long ago that even if I meet myself, I don't think I will be able to recognize him. And just being a vehicle of God, a vehicle of existence, has been such a fulfillment, such a contentment, such a benediction, that I don't think there can be anything more, deeper, higher.

I am absolutely blessed.

I was also not the deserving one.

I have never practiced any religion, I have never been part of any religious organization, I have never entered temples, churches, or mosques. One thing from the very beginning was clear to me: that there is no way for me to find God, because I don't know his address, I don't know his home. In this vast universe, where am I going to find him? All that I can do is create a longing, a thirst, in every cell of my body and being, and wait.

If God wants to find me, he will find me.

Only he can find me; I cannot find him.

And now, I can say it with absolute authority – that whenever God has happened to anybody, it was not the person's search for God; it was simply the person's waiting and longing. And when the thirst became so much that it was impossible for God to go on hiding…this is the only quality that makes a really religious person deserving. He is a silent waiting, a silent prayer, and a peaceful spaciousness. God comes.

Just don't rationalize when he comes, that it may be the thunder of the clouds, or it may be the wind striking against the doors. Keep the doors open. Keep your eyes open, keep your heart open. He comes. He comes surely, because he has been coming to thousands of people in the whole history of humanity.

And I don't remember a single mystic saying, "I found God because I deserved." The very idea of deserving is of the ego. All the mystics are agreed on the point that God found *them*, because they cried too much, they longed too much.

Their longing was heard; their tears reached God.

Prayers may not reach, but tears certainly reach.

Beloved Bhagwan,

Whenever my energy is overflowing,
which happens very often,
most of the time people give
me the feeling of being too much.
Then I feel guilty and the German heaviness comes back.
Could You please comment?

Prem Bhagvato, there is no possibility that the feeling of *being* can be too much. The being is so infinite...your being is not *your* being, your being is the being of the whole universe. So your feeling of it is always too little; it can never be too much.

Can you love too much? Can you be blissful too much? Can your ecstasy be too much? Those words – love, ecstasy, blissfulness – are just aspects of your being, and it has many more aspects to it.

You cannot feel it too much; that is a misunderstanding. You are asking, "Whenever my energy is overflowing, which happens very often, most of the time people give me the feeling of being too much." Who are the people? Perhaps it appears to them too much because they have not even experienced as much as you are experiencing.

You must have heard the old parable of Aesop. A frog from the ocean was on a religious pilgrimage. On the way he came near a well – he was feeling thirsty. He looked inside the well; there was another frog inside. He said, "I am very thirsty, can I come in?"

He was allowed. The frog in the well asked the stranger, "From where are you coming?"

The stranger said, "It will be very difficult for you to conceive from where I am coming."

The frog of the well laughed, and he said, "You have some nerve. Is your place bigger than this well?" He hopped across one third of the well and he said, "Is your place this much?"

The frog from the ocean was in immense difficulty – what to say to this poor frog? He said, "No, it is bigger."

He jumped two thirds and said, "This much?" The frog from the ocean said, "Forgive me, it is very big."

The frog of the well jumped across the whole well, from one side to the other side, and he said, "What do you say now? Is it still bigger?" The stranger said, "I am sorry to offend you, but your well cannot be a means of measuring the place from where I am coming. It is too big."

And the frog who had never left his well laughed and said, "You seem to be mad! Just get out of here. I have seen many frogs, but I have never seen such a mad one. They come to the well – and I am always happy to have a visitor, just to have news about the world. I have been so generous to you, and you are behaving so uncourteously."

The stranger said, "You just forgive me, perhaps I *am* mad. But I invite you to my place, because that is the only way you can be convinced. Unless you see the ocean, you cannot believe...and I can understand why you are annoyed with me and thinking that I am mad. I must look mad to you; I can think of myself in your place."

So the people you must be meeting, Prem Bhagvato, don't have energy as such. Or maybe they have their energy at the minimum, so when you start overflowing with energy, they start feeling afraid. And their saying to you that you are sometimes "too much" is a condemnation. They are annoyed with you; you have touched their weakest point.

They are living just as survival, and my people are making every effort to live at the maximum.

Why live at the minimum? When life gives you the opportunity to live at the maximum, then sing and dance with total abandon.

Still, I say to you: whatever you do, it is never "the feeling of being too much." That is simply not possible. Your well can become bigger and bigger and bigger, but still, it can never become the ocean. And unless you become oceanic, you don't know what it means to be too much.

But the problem is, the moment you become oceanic, you are no more – only pure energy, vibrating all over the existence.

As long as you *are*, you are always falling short of your maximum.

At the maximum, you disappear.

Then it is only a pure dance of energy.

And the pure dance of energy brings all your potentialities to their fullest expression. Only then can you say the spring has come, because you are blossoming in every dimension of your being.

So don't be bothered by the people who say that your energy, your being, your feeling is too much. It is comparative. Just tell them, "You are poor, you are living at the survival level. You have not known love and you have not known dance and you have not known celebration. You have not known life as such; you are simply vegetating, from cradle to grave, just dragging yourself somehow."

A teacher, standing in front of her class, asks, "Children, what part of the human anatomy expands twelve times when it is directly stimulated?"

Little Susie, in the front row, starts giggling and laughing, trying to cover her mouth with her hand. In the back row, Johnny raises his hand. The teacher says, "Yes, Johnny?"

Johnny stands up and says, "Teacher, the iris of the human eye expands twelve times when it is directly stimulated by light."

The teacher says, "Very good, Johnny. That is the correct answer. And Susie, you have a very dirty little mind, and when you grow up you are going to be very disappointed."

Beloved Bhagwan,

Eight years ago I saw You on TV.
There was a report about the Poona ashram.
I saw You doing the energy darshan, putting Your finger
onto the third eye of some people, causing them to fall down.
At that moment I recognized You.
It took me six years to sit in front of You.
The first time You looked at me, I fell down,
and there was a flash in my brain.
Now, sitting in front of You,
closing my eyes, I see a big, black spot.
Inside this black spot there is a white one.
This white spot comes nearer and nearer, whirling in a circle.
But just before the black spot disappears totally,
I open my eyes.
Please say something about what is going on.

Deva Jagat, what happened to you was tremendously significant, rare and unique. It is one of the contributions of the East to the world: the understanding that between these two eyes, there is a third eye inside which normally remains dormant. One has to work hard, bring his whole sexual energy upwards, against gravitation, and when the energy reaches the third eye, it opens. Many methods have been tried, to do that, because when it opens there is suddenly a flash of light and things which have never been clear to you suddenly become clear.

For example, yoga has tried *shirshasana,* the headstand, standing on your head. The basic purpose was to use gravitation to bring your energy to the third eye. Perhaps even the so-called yoga teachers of today are not aware of it, because it is not written in any scripture. It was given as one of the secrets from the master to the disciple, whispered in his ear.

There have been other methods. When I emphasize watching, witnessing...that is the finest method to bring the third eye into action, because that watching is inside. These two eyes cannot be used, they can only look outward. They have to be closed. And when you try to watch inside, that certainly means there is something like an eye which sees. Who sees your thoughts? Not these eyes. Who sees that anger is arising in you? That place of seeing is called symbolically "the third eye."

Witnessing is the most refined method, because depending on the gravitation of the earth can prove dangerous. If the energy comes flowing too much, as a flood, it can destroy the very small nerves in your brain. And they are so delicate that even to imagine their delicacy is difficult. In your small skull there are millions of nerves, not visible to the eyes, and they are so delicate, so sensitive that if a flood of energy comes, many of them will be washed away, broken.

One day science is going to enter into this field. They have already begun work to discover why animals have not developed the brain. The reason is that the animal's body is horizontal to the earth, so the animal's energy flows all over his body in the same proportion. Those delicate brain cells cannot evolve.

It was all due to man standing on his two feet, because his brain is not so much affected by gravitation, and very little energy reaches there. It became the opportunity for the delicate cells to improve. And you can see it in your so-called yogis: you will never find a very sharp, intelligent man. They may be able to do many distortions of the body, but you will not see in their faces the aura of intelligence. They have not contributed to human consciousness in any way.

What has happened to them? They themselves are not aware. Each person has to find out the right time, how long he can stand on his head without destroying his brain system. According to my findings, three seconds is more than enough. Less will be better – just a little rush and you are back on your feet. Just a little rush will nourish your brain, will not destroy the delicate structure and will help to open your third eye.

But it is dangerous. You know perfectly well: in the night when you go to sleep you need a pillow. Have you ever thought why? It is a protection for your brain, because if you lie down without a pillow, the energy flow will be horizontal, like the animals, and in eight hours of sleeping it can destroy your brain system completely. Even three seconds can be too much, it depends on how delicate a system you have.

The idiot can stand on his head for three hours and nothing will happen, because there is nothing to destroy.

The more intelligent you are, the less time is needed. For a genius it is very dangerous to stand on the head, even for a single second. That's why I say I don't use that method.

Witnessing is the best: you close your eyes and you start watching. In that very watching, your third eye starts opening.

I used to touch people's third eyes with my fingers, but I had to stop it for the simple reason that I became aware that stimulating the third eye from the outside is good if the person continues to meditate, continues to watch – then the first experience coming from the outside will soon become his inside experience. But such is the stupidity of man that when I can stimulate your third eye, you stop meditating. You rather start asking more and more for energy meetings with me, because you have not to do anything.

I also became aware that for different people, a different kind and different quantity of energy is needed from the outside – which is very difficult to decide. Sometimes somebody falls completely into a coma; the shock is too much. And sometimes the man is so retarded that nothing happens.

Because you had seen on T.V. that by touching them with my finger on the third eye, people were going into some inner space, for these six years you must have been thinking to know that inner space yourself. So when you came here and I saw you for the first time, the experience happened without my even touching your third eye. You were almost ready, just on the verge of it.

To see you is also a way of touching you. It is a remote way of touching.

Psychologists have found through many,

many experiments that if you look at someone for three seconds it is not offensive. It is casual – you are passing on the road, you look at someone. But more than three seconds and it becomes offensive because your eyes start – without your knowing, and without the knowledge of the other – stimulating his third eye. And if he has no idea of it, it feels as if something crazy is going on.

In Hindi, words are very significant because they have been coined very consciously. In Hindi, eyes are called *lochan* and the man who looks at somebody for more than three seconds is called *luchcha* – that is from *lochan*. A man who looks at a thing critically is called *aalochak*; that is also from the same root, *lochan*. So it may have just been a coincidence: for six years it was lying like a seed, in your unconscious, and when you came here and I looked at you, suddenly there was a flash and you fell down. But it is a tremendously fortunate state; it means your third eye can function very easily.

Just try to watch with your eyes closed, and the third eye will become more and more active. And the experiences of the third eye are the door to higher spirituality.

The third eye is the sixth center, the seventh is the highest. Six is very close to the highest center of your experience; it prepares the ground for the seventh. At the seventh center you become not only a flash of light, but just light itself. That's why the person who reaches the seventh center...his experience we call "enlightenment." His whole being becomes just pure light, with no fuel – because any light that needs fuel cannot be immortal. There is no fuel; hence the light has an eternity. It is the experience of your very being and the being of the universe.

The second thing you say: "Now sitting in front of you, closing my eyes I see a big, black spot. Inside this black spot there is a white one. This white spot comes nearer and nearer, whirling in a circle, but just before the black spot disappears totally, I open my eyes."

Why do you do that? Are you asking me, or should I ask you? That is the point when you should *not* open your eyes.

But sometimes it happens in spite of you. I have told my people to meditate with a blindfold on your eyes, so when in spite of you, your eyes want to open, they cannot open.

Let the black spot disappear completely, and you would have moved into a new consciousness, into a fresh space.

Deva Jagat, everything is going perfectly good, only you should not open your eyes. Perhaps you become afraid: "My god, all darkness is disappearing! Just let me see, by opening eyes, what is happening." But by opening the eyes, you destroy the whole experience. That is the moment to resist the temptation of knowing what is happening. Let it happen, because you will know only when it has happened.

And once you have known the black spot disappearing...that black spot is you and that white spot is your consciousness. The black spot is your ego, and the white spot is your being. Allow the being to spread and let the ego disappear.

Just a little courage...it may look like death, because you have been identified with the black spot and it is disappearing. And you have never been identified with the white spot, so something unfamiliar, unknown, is taking possession of you. These are the reasons why you open your eyes. Don't open your eyes.

Your mind may give any rationalization – don't listen to the mind. When you have come to me, give me a chance; listen to what I am saying to you.

If your mind comes in between, put it aside.

Your mind is your misery, your mind is your bondage.

An old retired Jewish widow is strolling on the beach in Miami when she suddenly spies an old Jewish man lying alone in the sun. Excitedly she trots over in his direction, stops in front of him and says, "I have never seen you around here before. What is your name?"

"Max," he replies, "and you don't see me because I'm rarely around anywhere!"

"Why, what do you mean?" asks the widow.

"Because I just got out of jail – that's what I mean!" he replies. "I was in for a year."

"Jail!" The old widow steps back a pace and surveys him critically. "What did you go to jail for?"

"Oh, just petty theft," the old man says, and shrugs.

"Ah, I see." The woman takes a step back to him. "That's a small crime, no big deal. All the same, you should be ashamed."

"Not nearly as ashamed as I was when I got the ten-year jail sentence," the old man sighs.

"Ten years!" the widow, in alarm, stumbles back a few more paces. "God! what did you do to get ten years?"

"Oh – just armed robbery." The old man shrugs and rolls over on his beach towel.

"Armed robbery! – that is serious. I hope to God you are sorry for such a thing," the widow scolds him, while at the same time returning a little closer to get a better look at him.

"I was sorry alright – I'd just finished twenty years in the slammer when I picked up that sentence. I had hardly seen the light of day!" The old man sighs heavily in remembrance.

"Twenty years! What kind of man are you?" The widow, panicking, leaps several yards away from him, ready to run. "What on earth did you do to get twenty years in jail?"

"I murdered my wife," the old man replies.

"You are single?" she says, as she unrolls her beach towel beside him.

Just a little courage...the moment you see the black disappearing completely, just a little courage. Keep your eyes closed, and it may bring you a great transformation that comes to people after lives of effort. That it is coming to you so easily can mean only one thing: in your past lives you must have worked. But the work has remained incomplete. This time, don't leave it incomplete. Let this life be your last life in the body.

When the whole universe can become our body, why should we be confined to the small body? It is imprisonment.

Okay, Vimal?

Yes, Bhagwan.

Session 20

Your Longing Is the Seed

*It is good that love fails,
because the failure of love is bound to take you
on a new pilgrimage.
The longing will haunt you until it brings you
to the temple where the meeting happens – but the meeting
always happens with the whole...in which your lover will be,
but in which the trees will also be,
and the rivers and the mountains and the stars.*

March 22, 1987
Evening

Beloved Bhagwan,

This morning, again You came to me and I wonder:
I know how the sun touches me,
how Your face enters my eyes, Your voice my ears.
I know those five doors to the world.
But I wonder what this sixth sense is that feels You.
What door do You pass to reach me so deeply, and why
is it always in the morning that You touch me the most?
Is openness related to the rhythm of the day?
Would You please speak on senses and openness?

Atit Parampara, we are part of a tremendously huge, organic unity of existence. Everything in us is related to the grass, to the trees, to the stars. Nothing is unrelated. The sunrise is not only something that happens outside – something happens within you too. As the sun rises, there is a rhythmic awareness all over the planet: the trees wake up, the flowers blossom, the lotuses open their petals, the birds suddenly start singing. Something within you also starts awakening.

The night is over: a part of your consciousness which was asleep again becomes awake, fresh, rejuvenated, cleaner, younger, after the rest. Hence, it is easy in the morning to be open and to be available. It is a little more difficult in the evening. As the night deepens, it becomes more and more difficult.

Most of the children are born in the morning, just before sunrise or just after sunrise.

But once you become capable of being open and available and receptive, it is not impossible to be receptive in the evening or even in the middle of the night.

It is because of this reason that Sufis have chosen the middle of the night as the time for meditation, because if you can meditate in the middle of the night then the whole day, any time, morning, afternoon, evening, will become very easy. They start from the hardest point. It takes a little longer but their arithmetic is correct: the person who can meditate in the middle of the night when the whole existence is falling deep into sleep...and he remains awake, just like an island in the ocean. In the beginning it may be difficult, but later on he will find it is immensely rewarding because then at any time, any hour, meditation is absolutely simple.

But most of the religions have chosen the morning – just before the sunrise is the best time because the whole of nature is supporting you. You are not in any conflict with existence. The whole of nature is awakening, and you can simply flow with its awakening energy. Except the Sufis, all the religions have chosen the morning to begin with. That too is correct. Why not begin from the simplest and then slowly, move towards the harder?

So you are right, that "it always happens in the morning that You touch me the most." I am touching you all the time. It is just that in the morning you feel me the most.

The sun may have risen but if you keep your doors closed, for you it is still night. It may be that the whole world is full of light... but you can keep your eyes closed and remain in darkness. So remember, everything depends on you. I am available twenty-four hours, exactly the same.

You are sayng, "This morning again you came to me and I wonder: I know how the sun touches me, how your face enters my eyes, your voice my ears. I know those five doors to the world but I wonder what this sixth sense is that feels you. What door do you pass to reach me so deeply?"

In fact, in the East, we have always thought about the sixth sense. There are five senses to go out of yourself, to go to the world, to the objective reality around you. The sixth sense, which has been called in other words the third eye, is to go inwards. If you feel me deeply, it means your third eye receives me – that is the door about which you are wondering. It is exactly between the two eyebrows and has been known for at least ten thousand years in the East.

You will be surprised...and the Indians will be shocked: we have used, for the women when they are married, a red mark on the third eye center – nobody has ever bothered why – and that red mark which is used for a married woman is removed if she becomes a widow. That red mark is to prevent the woman from coming in contact with the divine. Her God is her husband. And if she comes in contact with the divine, then her husband is almost meaningless.

Man has used every kind of strategy against women. He has used even spiritual discoveries to enslave the woman.

The red color is significant. The psychology of color and the science of color is that whichever color you see – if you see something red, then one thing is certain, that that thing is not red; it *appears* red. The sun rays have all the seven colors of the rainbow, and when the sun rays fall on anything, if all the rays are absorbed then you see the thing as black. If all the rays are reflected back and nothing is absorbed, then you see the thing as white. It is because of this reason that black has some connotation with the devil, with death, and white has become symbolic of renunciation, of simplicity, of purity.

If the red ray is reflected back, is not absorbed, if the other rays are absorbed and only the red is not absorbed, then you see the thing as red. If blue is not absorbed then you see the thing as blue because the returned ray falls on your eye and makes the thing appear of a particular color.

Why has the red mark been used for women? It is a simple science: the red ray is the most powerful in awakening that which is asleep. It is the most powerful ray; it hits deeply and wakes the dormant energy. It can open the third eye. Using a red mark on the third eye is preventing the red ray, so the woman remains unrelated to the divine. This door to the beyond is closed.

This is sheer male chauvinistic attitude. The moment a woman becomes a widow, immediately the first thing to be removed is her red mark because now the idea is that the woman should not come in contact with another man. And the best way to prevent her is to bring her in contact with godliness because then there will be no interest for the lower kinds of love relationship; she will know the higher quality of love, prayer, trust.

The widow in India is not allowed to use any other color of clothes – only white, as a symbol that she has renounced the world. Although living, she is no longer part of life.

When the master initiates the disciple, he touches the disciple's third eye with his fingers. The fingers are the most significant parts as far as energy is concerned. Energy cannot move from anything that is round – for example, energy cannot move out of your head. In the whole body, energy can either move through the toes of the feet or through the fingers of the hand. Energy needs finger-like, pointed instruments to move out.

The disciple touches the master's feet – that is one of the places where the master's energy is available. And the master touches, with his hand, the disciple's head. In this way, the bioenergy of the master and the disciple becomes a circle. And this circle has a tremendous feeling of blissfulness, of sweetness, of love that is not biological, that is spiritual.

The West has missed it completely. Now it is recognized, at least by Western science, that human energy is also a special kind of electricity. It is bioelectricity; its specialty is that the electricity you see outside is material, and the electricity that moves in your body is spiritual. It is alive, it is a living energy; hence they have given it a name: bioelectricity, living electricity.

It is your third eye...and the morning is the most potential time for it to be receptive. You should be more alert now when it happens. Close both your eyes so that no energy moves out, and the whole energy becomes available to the third eye. And when it is happening, allow it without any fear, because it cannot do any harm to you. It has never done any harm to anyone, ever.

If you give your whole support, the third eye can make you related with the whole existence. Your center of being will come, for the first time, in touch with the center of the universe. It is a great ecstatic experience.

At first it will happen only in the morning. Then slowly, slowly, as you become accustomed to it, it may happen at other times. But whenever it happens, allow it without any reluctance, without any resistance, because just a little fear and the door will be closed. Be loving and be trusting and the door will remain open.

And you have to bring this experience to the middle of the night. When you reach the same experience in the middle of the night, as it happens in the morning, you have conquered almost a new world, a new space. Now twenty-four hours a day, you will remain available to that which is beyond you.

A subtle current of freshness, of music, of dance, will go on moving within you. A joy will pervade your twenty-four hours. Even in sleep it will be there. You will go to sleep full of joy and you will wake up with the same fullness of joy.

A simple secret has to be remembered: your last thought in the night when you go to sleep is always your first thought in the morning when you wake up. You can watch it and you will be surprised – why is it so? You have been asleep for six hours, seven hours or eight hours. The last thought, whatever it was, the last mood, the last feeling is always going to be the first feeling in the morning. You may be asleep, but that which you have left while you fell asleep remains standing at your door. When you wake up, that visitor is still there; it has not gone.

It is because of this reason that many religions have chosen a time for prayer just before you are going to fall asleep. Because if you can fall asleep with a prayerful mood, peaceful, silent, that mood will pervade your night. Your whole night will become prayerful. If you fall asleep meditating, your whole night becomes a meditation.

People have been telling me that they don't have any time to meditate. And whenever anybody has told me that, I have suggested to him, "You can meditate at least eight hours every day." And he will look at me shocked: "What are you saying, eight hours? I don't even have eight minutes." And I have to explain to him, "I don't mean in the day: start your meditation while you go into your bed and, meditating, slowly slowly fall asleep. But meditation should be the last thing when you drown in sleep. Then in the morning, the first thing you will remember will be a deep meditative state." And to remain eight hours in meditation is of tremendous importance. It will transform your whole life.

The pope and a famous Jewish rabbi die and come to the Pearly Gates at the same time. Saint Peter greets them, hands the pope a ticket, and sends him to stand in line for a motel room.

With the pope watching in astonishment, Saint Peter then escorts the Jewish rabbi to a waiting chauffeur-driven limousine which drives the man to an exclusive luxury villa.

After a few days, the pope can't take it anymore and goes to Saint Peter to complain. "Hey, Pete. I have been your faithful, celibate servant all my life. I finally get to heaven and you send me to a queue for a motel room which I end up having to share with Mother Teresa. But you send this crooked Jewish rabbi in a limousine, to a villa with air-conditioning, beautiful young girls serving him all day. How come?"

"Look, Polack," says Peter. "You don't understand. We have never had a Jewish rabbi here before. This is for the first time; that's why he's being given a special welcome."

Heaven is so close by that you can step into it right now. But very few people will ever be able to make it, for the simple reason that they don't know the door.

All the religions that have developed outside India have no idea of the third eye. In their scriptures there is not a single mention. And without the third eye opening, your doors to paradise are closed – because the paradise is in your very being. You can be very learned, a great rabbi; you can be a pope, very respected. Millions follow you. But you don't know that exactly the paradise you have been seeking is not outside you.

It is something within you.

And my effort here is to knock on your third eye. It is just knocking on the right door, and once you become aware that this is the door from where you can get connected with the whole...or you can call it "God" but with the door closed, God may be standing at your door and still you will not be connected.

I have my own ways to go on knocking on your third eye; I have my own subtle ways. And it is a very accurate observation on your part, Atit Parampara – what door am I using to enter in you? You say, "I know how the sun touches me, how your face enters my eyes, your voice, my ears. I know those five doors to the world but I wonder what this sixth sense is that feels you?"

It is just between your two eyebrows. Next time when you feel me touching you, watch carefully: you will feel something opening between your two eyes – a sensation that goes on deepening inwards and finally reaches to your very being.

And once this door starts opening again and again, from the same door many other things will start entering you. You have seen the rose with your outer eyes but you have not seen it from the door of your third eye.

From your third eye, the rose is psychedelic; it has rays all around you, it radiates. It is so alive that you cannot think that you have ever seen it before.

The green of the trees becomes so much greener that one is simply surprised at everything, feels full of wonder all around. Ordinary colored stones on the sea beach look like diamonds and rubies and emeralds because they are all radiating; it is just that we have to see them from the right sense.

The sixth sense is the sense which has made man aware of the existence of godliness in the world. And that is the only sense which makes a disciple graduate into a devotee. That is the sense which allows the master to enter in the innermost core of the disciple; that is the center which makes the master and the devotee one soul between two bodies.

And that is the center which makes you finally aware that your being and the being of existence are not separate – they are one. You have come back home.

Beloved Bhagwan,

Lately, I have begun to realize how
even my lover is a stranger to me.
Still, there is an intense longing to overcome
the separation between us.
It almost feels as if we are lines
running parallel to each other but destined never to meet.
Beloved Bhagwan, is the world of consciousness
like the world of geometry – or is there a chance
that parallels can meet?

Dhyan Amiyo, it is one of the great miseries that every lover has to face: there is no way for lovers to drop their strangeness, unfamiliarity, separation. In fact, the whole functioning of love is that lovers should be polar opposites. The farther away they are, the more attractive. Their separation is their attraction. They come close, they come very close, but they never become one.

They come so close that it almost feels like just one step more and they will become one. But that step has never been taken, cannot be taken out of sheer necessity, out of a natural law.

On the contrary, when they are very close, immediately they start becoming separate again, going farther away. Because when they are very close, their attraction is lost; they start fighting, nagging, being bitchy. These are ways to create the distance again. And as the distance is there, immediately they start feeling attracted. So this goes on like a rhythm: coming closer, going away; coming closer, going away.

There is a longing to be one – but on the level of biology, on the level of the body, becoming one is not possible. Even while making love you are not one; the separation on the physical level is inevitable.

You are saying "Lately, I have begun to realize how even my lover is a stranger to me." This is good. This is part of a growing understanding. Only childish people think that they know each other. You don't know even yourself, how can you conceive that you know your lover?

Neither the lover knows himself nor you know yourself. Two unknown beings, two strangers who don't know anything about themselves are trying to know each other – it is an exercise in futility. It is bound to be a frustration, a failure. And that's why all lovers are angry at each other. They think perhaps the other is not allowing an entry into his private world: "He is keeping me separate, he is keeping me a little far away." And both go on thinking in the same way. But it is not true, all complaints are false. It is simply that they don't understand the law of nature.

On the level of body, you can come close but you cannot become one. Only on the level of the heart can you become one – but only momentarily, not permanently.

At the level of being, you *are* one. There is no need to become one; it has only to be discovered.

Amiyo, you are saying, "Still there is an intense longing to overcome the separation between us." If you go on trying on the physical level, you will go on failing. The longing simply shows that love needs to go beyond the body, that love wants something higher than the body, something greater than the body, something deeper than the body.

Even the heart-to-heart meeting – although sweet, although immensely joyful – is still insufficient, because it happens only for a moment and then again strangers are strangers. Unless you discover the world of being, you will not be able to fulfill your longing of becoming one. And the strange fact is: the day you become one with your lover, you will become one with the whole existence, too.

You are saying, "It almost feels as if we are lines running parallel to each other but destined never to meet." Perhaps, Amiyo, you don't know non-Euclidian geometry because it is still not taught in our educational institutes. We are still taught, in the universities, Euclidean geometry which is two thousand years old.

In Euclidian geometry, parallel lines never meet. But it has been found that if you go on and on and on they meet. The latest finding is that there are no parallel lines; that's why they meet. You *cannot* create two parallel lines.

New findings are very strange: you cannot even create a line, a straight line, because the earth is round – if you create a straight line here, if you go on drawing it from both the ends and go on and go on, finally you will find it has become a circle. And if a straight line drawn to the ultimate becomes a circle, it was not a straight line in the first place; it was only part of a very big circle, and a part of a big circle is an arc, not a line. Lines have disappeared in the new, non-Euclidian geometry and when there are no lines, what to say about parallel lines? There are no parallel lines, either.

So if it were a question of parallel lines, there is a chance that lovers could meet somewhere – perhaps in old age when they cannot fight, they don't have any energy left; or they have become so accustomed...what is the point? The same arguments they have had, the same problems they have been having, the same conflicts; they both are bored of each other.

In the long run, lovers stop even speaking to each other. What is the point? Because to start speaking means to start an argument, and it is the same argument; it is not going to change. And they have argued it so many times and it comes to the same end. But even then, parallel lines as far as lovers are concerned...in geometry they may start meeting, but in love there is no hope; they cannot meet.

And it is good that they cannot meet because if lovers could satisfy their longing of becoming one at the level of physical body, they would never look upwards. They would never try to find that there was much more hidden in the physical body – the consciousness, the soul, the god.

It is good that love fails, because the failure of love is bound to take you on a new pilgrimage. The longing will haunt you until it brings you to the temple where the meeting happens – but the meeting always happens with the whole...in which your lover will be, but in which the trees will also be, and the rivers and the mountains and the stars.

In that meeting, only two things will not be there: your ego will not be there, and your lover's ego will not be there. Other than these two things, the whole existence will be there. And these two egos were really the problem, were what was making them two parallel lines.

It is not love that is creating the trouble, it is the ego. But the longing will not be satisfied. Birth after birth, life after life, the longing will remain there unless you discover the right door to go beyond the body and to enter the temple.

An old couple of ninety-three and ninety-five go to their lawyer and say that they want a divorce. "A divorce!" exclaims the lawyer. "At your age? But surely you need each other more than ever now, and anyway, you have been married so long, what is the point?"

"Well," says the husband, "We have been wanting a divorce for years now but we thought we would wait until the children are dead." They really waited! And all the children are dead; now there is no problem, they can have the divorce – still no meeting, but divorce.

Just keep your longing burning, aflame; don't lose heart.

Your longing is the seed of your spirituality.

Your longing is the beginning of the ultimate union with existence. Your lover is just an excuse.

Dhyan Amiyo, don't be sad but be happy. Rejoice that there is no possibility of meeting on the physical level. Otherwise, lovers will not have any way of transformation. They will get stuck with each other, they will destroy each other. And there is no harm in loving a stranger. In fact, it is more exciting to love a stranger.

When you were not together, there was great attraction. The more you have been together, the more the attraction has become dull. The more you have become known to each other, superficially, the less is the excitement. Life becomes very soon a routine.

People go on repeating the same thing, again and again. If you look at the faces of people in the world, you will be surprised: why do all these people look so sad? Why do their eyes look as if they have lost all hope? The reason is simple; the reason is repetition.

Man is intelligent; repetition creates boredom. Boredom brings a sadness because one knows what is going to happen tomorrow, and the day after tomorrow...until one goes into the grave, it will be the same, the same story.

A Jewish man and a Polack are sitting in a bar watching the news on television. On the news, they are showing a woman standing on a ledge, threatening to jump. The Jewish man says to the Polack, "I will tell you what. I will make a bet with you: If she jumps, I get twenty dollars. If she does not, you get twenty dollars. Okay?"

"Fair enough," says the Polack.

A few minutes later the woman jumps off the ledge and kills herself. The Pole gets out his wallet and hands twenty dollars to the Jewish guy.

A few minutes later the Jewish guy turns to the Polack and says, "Look, here I can't take this twenty dollars from you. I have a confession to make: I saw this on the news earlier this afternoon. This was a repeat."

"No, no, "says the Polack," You keep the money, you won it fair and square. You see, I saw this on TV earlier in the day, too."

"You did?" says the Jewish guy. "Well, then why did you bet that the woman would not jump?"

"Well," says the Polack. "I didn't think she would be stupid enough to do it twice!"

But life is such....

This sadness in the world, this boredom and this misery can be changed if people know that they are asking for the impossible.

Don't ask for the impossible.

Find the law of existence and follow it.

Your longing to be one, is your spiritual desire, is your very essential religious nature. It is just that you are focusing yourself on the wrong spot.

Your lover is only an excuse. Let your lover be just an experience of a greater love – the love for the whole existence.

Let your longing be a search of your own inner being; there, the meeting is already happening, there, we are already one.

There, nobody has ever separated.

The longing is perfectly right; only the object of longing is not right. That is creating the suffering and the hell. Just change the object and your life becomes a paradise.

Okay Vimal?

Yes, Bhagwan.

Session 21

The Greatest Misfit In the World

*If you cannot feel comfortable here, you will not find another place
in the whole earth to be comfortable.
Nowhere else is the uniqueness of the individual respected;
nowhere else are you loved as you are;
you have to prove, you have to deserve.
Here you don't have to prove anything,
and you don't have to deserve anything.
You don't have to be worthy of anything.
This is the way you are and everybody is
in a tremendous, accepting, awareness.*

March 23, 1987
Morning

Beloved Bhagwan,

As another of Your communes takes off the ground,
I strongly develop symptoms of a misfit. India, and even a commune,
just does not seem to be the place where I feel comfortable.
Is there such a state as "doing your own thing, content and full of gratitude"
that is not just an ego trip?

Prem Leeladhar, I myself am an *un*fit. And this place here has gone far beyond being a commune. The commune was an alternative society. But it has its own organization, its own rules, regulations. Seeing that for misfits it will be difficult to be part of even a commune, I have dropped the idea of a commune too.

Here, now only individuals are living together. Nobody here is expected to be a permanent resident; whenever he feels, he can be here and whenever he feels, he can move. We are trying to give every misfit all the space that is possible. One of my sannyasins – Veeresh, in Europe – is creating "Rajneesh Misfit Cities."

I think you have carried the idea from the American commune. It must have been difficult for you there, because whenever thousands of people live together, they have to follow certain rules. Otherwise it will become impossible to live.

Here there is no permanent residentship. As long as you feel good, you can be here. The moment you feel uncomfortable, the whole world is available to you; wherever you want, you can go and be comfortable. But I want to remind you: if you cannot feel comfortable here, you cannot feel comfortable anywhere else either.

I will read your question. "As another of your communes takes off the ground..." That is not right. No commune is taking off the ground. I have tried hard and found it impossible...if the commune has to exist, the individual has to compromise. That's absolutely natural and necessary. And I am so much in favor of the misfit people, that rather than dropping the misfits, I have dropped the idea of the commune itself. Now there are only misfit people here.

The misfit people obviously understand each other's needs. The need is just to be yourself, and doing your own thing. That's why we are not developing any kind of productive activity here. Neither roads have to be made, nor houses have to be made. Because if you have to make roads and you have to make houses and you have to do farming, and you have to have milk products of your own, then naturally a certain organization becomes necessary.

Leeladhar is a plastic surgeon. Here we are not going to have even a medical center. There was in the old days before the American commune happened, a medical center, but that needs organization.

Now I want this place just to be a paradise – a holiday resort where you can relax, have a massage...soon there will be swimming pools, larger gardens and lawns. You can play on your instruments whenever you want, at whatever time you want. You can do your own thing.

Just remember that your thing should not be an interference in somebody else's life structure, because he also wants to be independent, just as you do. That is the only agreement: that everybody is free to the limit that he does not interfere with anybody else. This much of a limit is absolutely necessary.

Just think – you are sleeping and a few misfits come and start doing dynamic meditation in your room. They are doing their thing; they are not telling you to do the dynamic meditation. And by the time they have left, other misfits come and start playing on their musical instruments. Nobody is bothering you; you can go on sleeping or whatever you want to do! So this line has to be remembered....

Otherwise there is no interference at all. Work I have dropped completely, unless you want to do it, unless it is your thing. In the commune, work was absolutely necessary to survive. Here, you come whenever you can manage financially, for as long as you can manage to live here, but there is no question of any work being imposed on you. You can choose if you want to do something or you simply want to rest, swim, do a few groups, meditate – or not to do any group, not to do any meditation, just to be.

You are saying, "I strongly develop symptoms of a misfit." Again you are wrong: Leeladhar, you are a *born* misfit. It is not something that you are developing. I know you perfectly well.

It was I who was forcing you to remain in the hospital unit in the commune, in spite of yourself. Because I wanted you to remain in the unit, you remained – but you *are* a misfit.

The misfit has to accept one thing: that he will not be respected by the ordinary society. He will not get recommendations and honors and awards for being a misfit. I am certainly thinking to create an award, a world award each year, to be given to the greatest misfit in the world. And Leeladhar, your name is the first on my list.

But the discomfort is not coming from the outside, because outside I don't see that you are expected to do anything. You are feeling uncomfortable as an inner tension; you don't want to be a misfit, and you are. You have not accepted your misfitness with total love and joy.

There is nothing wrong in it; the society needs a few misfit people. They are the people who carry the torch of freedom and consciousness from generation to generation.

Do you think Gautam Buddha was not a misfit? Or Mahavira was not a misfit? The son of a king goes naked – his father was ashamed, his family was ashamed. They were willing – "You can renounce the world...but what is the need to go naked?" But Mahavira never felt uncomfortable; he accepted himself as he was.

The misfitness does not come alone; it will bring disrespect from people.

You have to accept it.

The society is made by the people who are square, absolutely fit people. Any misfit is a disturbance. That society creates in every child the idea: never be a misfit, otherwise you will be dishonored, disrespected, rejected. And those ideas are still in your mind. Misfitness is your nature, and the discomfort is arising because the ideas that society gives to everybody, have been given to you too. You are not together; there is a split. Deep down you don't want to be a misfit.

I would like to suggest, drop those ideas. All respectability, all honor is meaningless if it drives you against your nature. What can you do if you are not a lotus flower, but just a marigold? Enjoy being a marigold.

Existence has no disrespect for misfit people. The sun makes no difference, the moon does not discriminate; the whole existence accepts you as you are. But deep down within you there is a rejection, so you are in a split, in a dilemma. With this dilemma, wherever you go you will feel uncomfortable – more uncomfortable than you are feeling here, because here nobody is interested in condemning, in judging. Nobody will say, "Leeladhar, you are not what you should be." There is no "should" here.

In the American commune, you were not willing to remain a plastic surgeon. Now is the chance – nobody is telling you to be a plastic surgeon; even if you want to be, nobody is interested in plastic surgery here. If somebody's nose is a little long, nobody objects. Or a little smaller...a nose is just functional. With the long nose or the small nose, if breathing is going well, there is no problem. Here nobody is interested in changing from a man into a woman, or from a woman into a man.

This is not a commune, this is simply a gathering of all kinds of misfit people who cannot fit anywhere else. Here they can celebrate their misfitness without losing respect and honor and dignity.

You say, "India, and even a commune, just does not seem to be the place where I feel comfortable."

India is the oldest country which has allowed all kinds of misfit people. It is unbelievable that Indian society down the ages has never crucified a Jesus...and there have been many who were claiming *"Aham Brahmasmi"* "I am a god" – Jesus was only saying "I am the only begotten son of God" – and nobody has objected. If they are enjoying and feeling blissful, they are not doing any harm to anybody.

Gautam Buddha did not believe in God. Mahavira absolutely rejected the very idea of God. But they were not crucified, they were loved as they were.

And even before them, a long passage of ten thousand years...you will find all kinds of people. Somebody is standing on his head; nobody even takes any note of it, nobody says that you are mad or something. Somebody has been standing for years, has been sleeping standing, with the support of a wooden structure; – he is keeping his hands on the structure and is fast asleep – and people always give the freedom: if he decides to be this way, this is his business. It is between him and God; who are we to interfere?

I have seen a man who has been standing for so many years that the upper side of his body has become thin, and all the blood has gone into the legs. In medical science it is called elephantiasis; it is a certain disease. Now even if he wants to sit, he cannot sit. Those legs are so thick, and they have lost the quality of elasticity; they have become almost solid. But nobody condemns him. On the contrary, people bring sweets to him, somebody brings flowers to him...the poor fellow is doing something great, suffering too much, unnecessarily. But if it is natural to him, then it is perfectly okay.

No Socrates was ever poisoned in India, and India has known more Socrates' than any other country – thousands of them, of the same caliber, with the same logic, sometimes even with a more subtle logic, very destructive to people's prejudices. But people have enjoyed them. Whether you agree with them or not, that's one thing, but you have to appreciate their sharpness, their intelligence.

I am reminded of Ramakrishna. He was uneducated, and you will not find another misfit like him. Yet this country has accepted him as one of the incarnations of God.

When he was nine years old, he had an experience of deep meditation. He was not looking for it. He was just a boy coming back from the field to his home, and just on the way there was a lake, a beautiful lake. It was sunset time and there were black clouds in the sky. The rains were just to come. And as he came by the side of the lake, a line of white cranes, who must have been sitting on the bank of the lake, were disturbed by his coming. They flew across the black clouds.

The white crane is snow white, and twelve or fifteen cranes in a line, moving across the black clouds...and the sunset on the lake, spreading gold all over. The beauty of the moment was such that Ramakrishna could not contain it; he fell into unconsciousness. It was too much for his conscious mind, just to say that "It is beautiful" and go home.

When he did not come home, people went to search for him. His father said, "He left the field before me." They looked around the lake and they found him unconscious – but with such a joy on his face. When he came back to consciousness, the first words he said were, "I have known life for the first time. Up to now I have been unconscious; these few hours I was *conscious*."

The parents became afraid – any parents would have become afraid – that this boy was showing symptoms which could lead him to becoming a sannyasin, a seeker. And for centuries parents have thought, and thought rightly, that it would be good to arrange a marriage. The woman will put him right.

They were afraid: perhaps he will say no. But when his father asked, "Would you like to be married?" he said, "Great! I have seen many marriages in town; it is such a joy, riding on the horse like a king."

The father thought, "He does not understand what marriage is, he has simply seen the marriage processions. But it is good that he is ready."

So they found a beautiful girl in a nearby place, and when he was going there – it was summertime – to see the girl, his mother put three rupees in his pocket. She told him, "If you need, you use them, but there is no need to waste them. We are poor people."

And this is the way in India, which still persists over almost ninety percent of India: you can see the girl only as a glimpse. She will come and serve tea – and that is the moment when you see her for a few seconds – and she is gone.

Sharda, who was going to become his wife, came to put some sweets on his plate when they were taking their breakfast. He said to his father, "My god, the girl is so beautiful!" He took out the three rupees and put them at her feet, and touched her feet and said, "Mother, you are one in millions. I am going to marry you."

The father said, "Idiot! First you call her 'mother,' touch her feet...and you have put your offering also, three rupees. And you are going to marry her?"

Even the girl's parents became a little afraid, because this boy seems to be a little crazy. But Ramakrishna said, "I don't see any problem in it. She is so beautiful, that's why I touched her feet. Beauty should be respected. And she is so motherly; you can see it even in her face. That's why I called her 'mother'. Every girl is going to be a mother, so why are you freaking out? And I have decided that if I am going to marry anyone, this girl is the one; otherwise I will remain unmarried."

Both the families managed, convinced each other that he is not mad or anything, just a little outlandish a little eccentric, but he is not harmful. He does things which should not be done, but he never harms anybody.

They were married and the first night Ramakrishna said to Sharda, "It is private, don't say it to anybody; I have accepted you as my mother. Let the whole world think you are my wife. I know you are my mother, you know I am your son. And this is going to be our relationship." And this remained their relationship their whole life. But rather than being criticized he is being respected for this strange relationship. His wife is his mother, and there was never any husband and wife relationship between them.

There are so many stories of unfitness.... One sudra queen – she was a queen, but by the Hindu caste system she was the lowest, untouchable – made a very beautiful temple on the banks of Ganges near Calcutta, in Dakshineshwar. No brahmin was ready to be a priest in her temple. The temple made by a sudra, by an untouchable, had also become untouchable; and the god inside had also become untouchable. In the whole of Bengal, only Ramakrishna, when he heard it, said, "This is a perfectly good chance." He went to the queen and said, "I am ready to be the priest" – and he was a high caste brahmin.

She said, "Have you thought about it? Your society may discard you, expel you."

He said, "I don't have any society. And what does it matter if they expel me, if they make me an outcaste? I am not dependent on anyone. I am going to be the priest in this temple." And he was expelled, condemned.

People tried to persuade him, "If you leave this job we can give you a better job in a high-caste Hindu temple. You will get more money." But he said, "It is not a question of money. I love the temple, I love the place, I love the silence surrounding it, the trees...and I love the goddess inside the temple."

He was expelled, but he never cared about it. Even his family stopped visiting him – because they would be expelled – and they told him that he could not come back home. He said, "It is perfectly okay."

And his worshiping was so strange: sometimes he would worship from morning till evening, dancing and singing madly. People would come and go, and sometimes he would lock the temple and would not open it for a few days. It was reported to Rashmani, the queen: "What kind of priest have you found? Every priest worships for half an hour at the most. This man seems to be mad: when he worships, then time stops; then he goes on dancing and singng from morning till evening. And sometimes, which is absolutely sacrilegious, he locks the temple. Neither does he worship, nor does he allow anybody else to enter!"

The queen called him and said, "Ramakrishna, what kind of worship is this?"

He said, "Who says it is worship? It is a love affair. And in a love affair it is natural: sometimes I get angry, sometimes she gets angry." He is talking about the goddess of the temple. "And when I get angry I lock the door and I say, 'Now live for three days, four days, without food, without worship, and you will come to your senses.'"

Rashmani said, "But we have never heard of this kind of worship!"

Ramakrishna said, "There has never been a priest like Ramakrishna."

In the temples, when priests worship, the food is presented to the god or the goddess and then it is distributed. And Ramakrishna would spoil it completely. First he would taste everything inside the temple. Before offering it to the goddess, he would taste everything, and then he will offer it. Again he was called: "You are doing something very wrong. It has never been done."

He said, "I am not concerned whether it has been done or not. I know only one thing: my mother used to taste everything first and then she would give it to me. If it was really delicious, she would give it; if it was not, she would prepare it again. And if my mother can do that for me...I cannot give anything to the goddess without knowing whether it is worth eating or not."

Rashmani must have been a very intelligent woman to tolerate this misfit man. Instead of condemning him, people started coming to pay respect to him. His love for the goddess was so genuine, although it was not ritualistic. And anything genuine *cannot* be a ritual.

One of the great logicians of Bengal, Keshav Chandra, heard about thousands of people going to Ramakrishna. He was an atheist and a great philosopher, and a very sharp logician. He challenged Ramakrishna: "I am coming on a certain day to discuss matters with you."

All the followers of Ramakrishna were very much afraid – afraid because they knew that Ramakrishna knows nothing, no scripture; he makes his own songs that he sings in the temple. He is uneducated, he has never heard anything about logic, philosophy. It is not a question of mind to him.

They were afraid: "It will be very embarrassing to us all, because Keshav Chandra can defeat Ramakrishna within seconds."

And Keshav Chandra came with his own disciples. He had his own society, and he was a very egoistic man. Ramakrishna jumped up from where he was sitting under a tree, hugged Keshav Chandra, and said, "I am feeling so happy that you also have come to me."

Keshav Chandra said, "I have come here to defeat you."

Ramakrishna said, "It does not matter whether you defeat me or I defeat you. From this moment our love will remain. You start defeating – I am ready."

Keshav Chandra said, "Start defeating? First you have to propose your philosophy."

Ramakrishna said, "I don't know anything about philosophy. You will have to do both things yourself – propose my philosophy and defeat it."

Instead of Ramakrishna looking embarrassed, Keshav Chandra started looking embarrassed – where have I come? But something had to be done, so he said, "Okay, do you believe in God?"

So Ramakrishna said, "Believe? I *know* him. Why should I believe? Only ignorant people believe." Now what to do with this man? A belief can be criticized, but the man says he knows!

Still, Keshav Chandra made great arguments against God; he said "It is all hallucination, illusion, imagination, that you think you know God." And each time he would make a good argument Ramakrishna would stand up and hug him again and say, "You are so beautiful, Keshav Chandra; I love the way you talk, although it does not change anything. In fact, your intelligence is a proof to me that God exists, because your intelligence is derived from existence. It cannot come from nowhere, and all that we mean by

God is that the universe is intelligent. I am a poor fellow, uneducated. I am not a proof for God, but you are."

The authority and the authenticity and the sincerity...for the first time in his life, Keshav Chandra felt defeated, although the man has not argued. He touched the feet of Ramakrishna and said, "Accept me also as your disciple. Seeing you, seeing your behavior, seeing your joy, is enough to prove that dry arguments are not going to transform me. But you are a transformed man. Most probably you are right and I am wrong. I can prove myself right – but to prove oneself right is one thing, and to be right is another thing. Your presence is the argument."

This country has accepted and loved all kinds of unfit people, and if you feel that India is making you uncomfortable, you have to be here a little longer to feel the atmosphere.

I have been around the world. No country has such a groovy atmosphere. They are scientifically developed, technologically very progressive. They are rich, they are educated. This country is poor, hungry, with no science, no techonology. But this country has a certain vibe which has been created by thousands of mystics.

You need to be here, Leeladhar, for a little longer, so that you can start feeling the subtle vibe.

My experience is...in America we created the commune, but in the American atmosphere the commune was, as a whole, out of place. There was no supporting nourishment as far as atmosphere is concerned. And then I moved around the world. I have been talking in every country, and the strangest fact is that I was talking with my own sannyasins, with whom I talk here, but something was missing.

I was there, my people were there, but in the air, something was missing.

Back to India, the same people...but nothing is missing. A subtle juice surrounds, a certain noosphere, a very deep and ancient flavor of mysticism, an inner richness. Communication is easier.

To adapt to the Indian atmosphere it takes a little time, and perhaps that also is making you uncomfortable. It is just as if you are coming from a desert into a garden. It will take a little time to feel the greenness, to feel the fragrance of the flowers. The contrast is so big.

And you have been brought up in the West. Your whole make-up is that of a scientist, and this country knows nothing of science. This is the most unscientific country in the world. But it is the most religious, mystic, heartful land. It has its own juice. Give it a chance.

Certainly you are not a bigger misfit than I am.

In India I feel at ease. The Western tension is not there; neither is the Western speed. I am reminded when, for the first time, the British Empire was laying rails for railway trains.

A British officer was looking at an Indian sannyasin who used to come every day, sit under a tree or lie down under a tree, and watch the people working, putting down the rails, making the arrangements. He had never seen such a lazy man: he never did anything, he just rested there.

One day the officer approached him. He had learned a little bit of Hindi because of working with Indian workers, laborers, for years. So he asked the man, "You come every day. Before we come you are here, and when we go, *then* you go. Why are you wasting time just lying down under the tree, lazy? You can earn money, you can become a laborer. We are in shortage of laborers. I can give you a good job."

The man was not even bothering to sit up. He was lying down and talking with the officer. He said, "The idea is good, but I don't need money. I get food two times a day. My other brothers work on the farm. I have always been this way. And even if I earn money, what am I going to do with it?"

The officer said, "When you earn enough money, then you can retire and rest." And the man said, "This is strange, I am already retired, and I am resting! Why take this unnecessarily long route? First earn money, then get retired, then rest – I am retired from the very beginning. And I am resting; I don't do anything except rest."

There is no speed in the Indian atmosphere. Things move very slowly. You cannot even see the movement, they move so slowly. Centuries pass....

If a man in Europe wakes up from his grave after two thousand years, he will not be able to understand what is happening, because in two thousand years the West has changed so much. But if an Indian comes to visit India after two thousand years, he will be perfectly at home. Almost nothing has changed!

Leeladhar, your discomfort is coming from your own conditioning, one thing. Second, you have not accepted your unfitness in its totality; otherwise why should one be uncomfortable?

And you can be free to do anything you want, anywhere. For example, I have not been uncomfortable anywhere around the world. I was not uncomfortable in the American jails. I was not uncomfortable in different cultures, different countries, different religions. I accept my unfitness with absolute joy.

After the first three days in the American jail, the sheriff of the jail came to see me. He wondered what kind of man I am, because the inmates had become my disciples! I was talking to them about meditation. The nurses and the doctor – because I was in the hospital section – had also joined. Finally, the sheriff brought his wife and his children also: "We may not be able to see this man again, and what he is saying makes sense."

And the doctor – a woman, very beautiful woman – used to come to the hospital section only one time in seven days; otherwise she was engaged in other parts of the jail. It had seven hundred inmates. But for those three days, all the nurses were there, the doctor was there, the whole staff was there. The doctor said to me, "It has never happened. You have turned my office into your class! Otherwise my office is always empty."

Because my cell was very small...it was meant only for two persons. And there were twelve inmates in the hospital section. They all wanted to be with me as much as possible – six nurses, four staff people, the sheriff, the assistant sheriff, the doctor – so they moved me to the doctor's room. And she told me, "You need not use the bathroom that is meant for the prisoners. My bathroom is for you as long as you are here."

Nirupa is here, David is here. They were staying in town to take care of me, to bring new clothes, or anything I needed. The sheriff told me in front of them, "I would like to come to see your commune where such silent, beautiful young people – intelligent, loving – are living with you and growing with you."

He said to me, "Just David and Nirupa are enough proof that man can be transformed." Otherwise, American kids – even the primary school kids – are taking drugs...thirteen and fourteen year-old young boys have been found committing murders, rape, suicide. That is the American atmosphere.

The jails are so full that the magistrate has to think before he sends another prisoner to the jail, because some old prisoner has to be released. The jails are packed. You can bring a new prisoner, but you have to release an old prisoner.

My attorneys who used to come there – Niren was my chief attorney; he is here – they could not believe I was looking so happy and so at ease and at home. I said, "I have never been able to rest so much. The inmates are taking care, the nurses are taking care, the doctor is taking care. And they are all interested in only one thing: the moment I am released and I go back to the commune, they all want to stay in the commune for a few days."

The first day, the sheriff received a phone call from Germany asking about me, and saying that "You must be surprised, because this may be the first time that you have a man like Bhagwan in your jail." He was not acquainted with me. He said, "No, but we have had cabinet ministers, great politicians, so it is not new to us."

But on the third day he came with tears in his eyes when I was leaving and he said, "I don't know who has phoned, but I want to apologize, because I gave him the wrong answer. In these three days so many flowers have come that we don't have any space to keep them; so many telegrams, so many phone calls that we have to keep two extra phone receivers.

"If you find the man just ask him for me, to forgive me. The great politicians and cabinet ministers don't matter. I never in my whole life had a prisoner like you – and I don't think I ever will have, in my remaining years in the service – for the simple reason that you have changed the whole atmosphere of my jail.

"If you are allowed to be here for three or four months this will be your commune. You are really dangerous because all the people of my staff are coming with their wives and with their children to have a photograph taken with you."

The poor prisoners could not manage. They were coming with photographs cut from newspapers just to get my signature: "We will remember our whole life that for three days we were with you, and in three days we have felt a change." People were not making noise. Everybody was saying, "Don't make noise, he will be disturbed."

I have never felt uncomfortable anywhere.

The question, basically is to accept yourself. It is an inner feeling, nothing to do with anything outside you. And I repeat: if you cannot feel comfortable here, Leeladhar, you will not find another place in the whole earth to be comfortable. Nowhere else is the uniqueness of the individual respected; nowhere else are you loved as you are; you have to prove, you have to deserve. Here you don't have to prove anything, and you don't have to deserve anything. You don't have to be worthy of anything. This is the way you are and everybody is in a tremendous, accepting, awareness. Just give it a little time.

"Is there such a state as doing your own thing, content and full of gratitude?"

Yes. That's my whole approach towards life: "doing your own thing content and full of gratitude..." It is not an ego trip. It is your nature, wanting to be left undisturbed.

And here we are not engaged in any kind of work which has to be forced on you. This place has to leave in you a memory of sheer enjoyment, of silence and beauty. And people who are non-interfering with you, are happy in your happiness. Nobody is jealous, nobody is competitive. Nobody is even comparing.

But it all depends on you.

I have created the space here.

Now how you use it, is up to you.

During the second world war, at the Russian front, an Italian and a German general are preparing an attack. When all the preparations are ready, and the attack is ready to be launched, the German general calls his servant: "Heinz, bring me my red coat."

"What, a red coat?" says the Italian general surprised. "How come?"

"Well, during the battle I may be hurt; blood may be flowing, and my soldiers, seeing blood, might get demoralized. So I always wear a red coat during battle."

"What a great idea," says the Italian general and calls his servant.

"Giuseppe, quick, bring my brown trousers!"

Beloved Bhagwan,

I blew it today.
One moment of unawareness feels like it wipes out those moments of awareness.
While pruning in Your garden I cut deeply into a living tree
that I thought was dead. The very moment the axe made its death blow I knew,
You knew, existence knew, I had taken life.
Feeling guilt, fear, stupidity, I finished cutting the tree, carrying it out of Your garden.
Bhagwan, I have cut thousands of trees and killed many, many animals in my life,
but never before felt hurt as much as I did, and do, about this tree.
Mukta is afraid You'll cut off her head.
Spare her head and cut mine, along with my unawareness. I'm sorry.

Anand Vibhavan, it is something tremendously beautiful that reverence for life is arising in you. But don't feel any guilt, neither fear nor stupidity, because these are parasites. Just do one thing: become more alert and remember: before you cut another tree, make sure that it is dead.

There is no hurry. It is simply unconsciousness; otherwise you would have found that it was alive. Perhaps the leaves had fallen and the tree was waiting for new leaves to come. And you could have waited and watched...but guilt is not the right thing. You hurt the tree; now you are hurting yourself.

Reverence for life does not mean reverence only for others' life. It also includes reverence for your own life too.

Guilt is not reverence. Neither are you stupid – because you became aware; not only aware, but you felt hurt that a life is unnecessarily destroyed. It shows intelligence.

And as far as fear is concerned, don't be worried about Mukta. I have chopped her head long ago – she believes she has a head – and I will chop your head too.

But my surgery is not painful. It brings more blissfulness to you than you had ever experienced. So there is no need to have fear. Just have awareness, more alertness, more consciousness.

This garden is not just an ordinary garden. These trees have heard me as much as you have heard me, and these trees have loved me as much as you have loved me. These trees are as much my disciples as you are. So be respectful with them. With loving care, with sensitive alertness, you will not only be a good gardener, you will also become a higher consciousness – more human, more divine.

Shower on these trees all your love. They cannot speak, but they are very sensitive.

The latest experiments about trees are so revealing – they can even read your thoughts. Their sensitivity is far greater than man's sensitivity.

Scientists have developed certain instruments like the cardiogram. They put the cardiogram on a certain tree and the cardiogram starts making a graph of how the tree is feeling. The graph is symetrical, and then suddenly they bring a woodcutter with an axe, and the moment the tree sees the woodcutter the graph changes. It goes berserk, the symmetry is lost. Nothing has been done to the tree, it is just that the woodcutter has come with the idea to cut it. That idea is being caught by the sensitiveness of the tree, and now, there are scientific ways to find it out.

The strangest thing is that if the woodcutter is just passing without any idea of cutting the tree, the graph does not change. It depends on his idea – his thought creates a certain wave. Every thought is being broadcasted from your mind, creating waves around you, and those waves are picked up by the sensitiveness of the tree. They are very much alive.

It is good that you have become aware of it.

Don't lose this awareness, because it will not only help the trees, it will help you too. It will become your meditation.

Everything that is being done here has to become your meditation.

This is a temple, and we are here just for a single reason: to transcend our darkness and our unconsciousness.

A man goes into a men's toilet, holding his hands outstretched, as if they are paralyzed. In the urinals, he taps another man on the elbow.

"Excuse me, I wonder if you could help me. I have a problem with my hands and need assistance in using the urinal. Would you be so kind as to open my zipper?"

The other man is very embarrassed, but obliges. The first man says, "Thank you very much. Now I have another favor to ask. Would you mind helping me to aim?"

The second man blushes, but helps him aim. After he has relieved himself, the first man says, "You don't know how grateful I am. Now please just do me up again." Nearly at the end of his patience, the second man does so.

The first man turns to leave, and looking at his awkwardly-held hands, says, "Good. I think my nail polish is dry now."

Okay, Vimal?

Yes, Bhagwan.

Session 22

What More Do You Want?

*You have to remember that trust does not mean
that you are not supposed to do anything.
Trust simply means that whatever you are doing
is in the right direction, because the man you trust in
cannot take you in a wrong direction.
But you have to do the walking.
I can only show you the path,
I cannot walk for you.*

March 23, 1987
Evening

Beloved Bhagwan,

As a child, one of my favorite games
was to imagine I was going to die in the next minute.
I enjoyed feeling the tension build up until it reached a peak
and then slipped into relaxation,
and I felt as if I was bubbling with happiness.
Later, when I was a teenager, for a period of six months, I would frequently
be awoken by a feeling of panic and fear, a sense of impending death.
I would struggle to prevent my dying by hanging on
to the thought of somebody or something I wanted to live for.
Then the panic would subside and the fear would gradually go.
The last time this happened to me as a teenager,
I woke feeling the fear of death the strongest I ever had.
But this time, instead of panicking,
without any conscious decision, I found myself accepting death, and relaxing.
Immediately, there was an explosion of light
and a sense of being uplifted by bliss.
It was not until some years later, when I took sannyas
and one day was meditating alone, that the fear of death returned.
I was overwhelmed by the intensity of it, and could do nothing
to transform it or even repress it:
I jumped up in a panic and tried to shake it off.
Why has this fear been a constant companion throughout my life,
and what is its significance for me?

Dhyan Amiyo, meditation and death are very similar experiences. In death, your ego disappears; only your pure being remains. The same happens in meditation too: the disappearance of the ego and the presence only of pure *isness*, of your being. The similarity is so deep that just as people are afraid of death, they are also afraid of meditation. On the other hand, if you are not afraid of meditation, you will not be afraid of death either.

Meditation prepares you for death.

Our whole education is only for life. That is only half an education, and the other half – which is far more important, which comes as the crescendo of life – is completely missing from all systems of education that have existed before or are now in existence.

Meditation prepares you for the other half; it helps you to know death without dying. And once you have known death without dying, the fear of death will disappear forever. Even when death comes, you will be silently watching it, knowing absolutely that it cannot even make a small scratch on your being. It is going to take away your body, your mind, but not you.

You belong to the immortal life. Your experience was good; you are saying, "As a child, one of my favorite games was to imagine I was going to die in the next minute. I enjoyed feeling the tension build up until it reached a peak and then slipped into relaxation, and I felt as if I was bubbling with happiness."

Unknowingly, you were doing a simple exercise of meditation. Perhaps from your past life, you may have carried the knowledge, the experience of the meditation, but it is one meditation amongst hundreds of methods – this is one of the methods. And it is not only you, Dhyan Amiyo; many children go on playing things which are of immense importance. But they cannot understand the importance, they can only play them as a game.

For example, all over the world, children like to twirl, to whirl, and naturally the parents will stop them: "Don't do that, you may get dizzy. You may fall, you may hurt yourself." But all over the world, children enjoy it. And it was from seeing children enjoying whirling that Jalaluddin Rumi got the idea that there must be something... because whenever you see a child whirling, his face changes. A strange grace comes to his face; he starts radiating a certain aura, and when he stops he is so full of joy....

Jalaluddin Rumi tried – in the forest, so nobody makes a laughingstock of him – just to know what these children find in twirling. And he was amazed: he discovered one of the greatest methods of meditation, and for twelve hundred years after him, his school has been a living school. His school is called the Whirling Dervishes; in their temple, that is their prayer, that is their meditation. That is their whole religion. They go on twirling for hours together.

Jalaluddin himself became enlightened after thirty-six hours of continuous, nonstop twirling. And when he was asked, "There is no scripture describing this meditation; how have you found it?" He said, "Just by looking at children. I tried it myself, and I was amazed because the more you twirl, the faster you go, soon you become aware that something deep inside you is absolutely still and unmoving. The whole body is moving and the faster it moves, the more is the contrast between the unmoving and the moving. And the unmoving consciousness within is my soul. That is the center of the cyclone."

Man has much to learn from children – but who cares about children? Everybody is trying to teach them without ever thinking about a simple thing: they are coming out of life's source, fresh. They must be carrying something which we have forgotten.

If you go backwards and remember, you cannot go farther back than your fourth year, or at the most your third year. Suddenly there comes a wall; your memory cannot penetrate farther back. What happened? You lived those four years – and in fact, those four years were the happiest that you had known. But your experience somehow has been blocked by the society.

It is dangerous for the society that people should be so innocent, like children. Your parents, your teachers, your leaders – with all the good intentions in their hearts – are doing immense harm. They repress the child in you, and the child in you is closer to God than anything else.

This is why so many mystics have insisted: "Unless you are born again, unless you become childlike again, you will not know the truth and you will not know the beauty and you will not know the mystery of existence."

You can go backwards, remembering, and then suddenly comes a China wall: that is the time when your parents and your teachers started destroying your childhood, making you civilized, making you social, teaching you manners and etiquette, sending you to school, teaching you language and all other worldly ways. And making every effort that you forget completely your innocent days, your days of paradise.

Everybody forgets, but somewhere deep down in the unconscious, the experience of those days goes on echoing. It is this echoing of those experiences that sends you in search, because you cannot accept your miserable life – full of anxiety and tension and psychological sickness – as the meaning of your being here. Vaguely, somewhere, you know that there have been golden moments also. You cannot exactly remember, but an undercurrent in your unconscious goes on creating a longing in you to find those lost moments again.

Religion is basically the search for childhood: the same innocence, the same joy in things, the same fearlessness...those magical eyes, that heart which was able to dance with the trees, the heart that was enchanted with the moon and the stars. That space in which existence was nothing but sheer glory, pure splendor....

Dhyan Amiyo, either accidentally or out of some experience from the past life, you were doing a method of meditation. And that's why, as the tension grew...there is a limit, and the next moment is going to be the moment of death. You became totally concentrated. And from the highest peak of your tension, suddenly comes relaxation. In that relaxation, you found yourself bubbling with happiness.

If you had continued to do that, your life would have been immensely rich. You would not have known sadness, unhappiness. You would not have known anger, jealousy. You would have known only love, silence, joy – and for no reason at all. It is our natural state.

Tension is not our natural state. That's why, after a certain moment, tension has to disappear. For example, you can keep your hand open for as long as you want, it is its natural state. But if you make a fist, and the harder you make your fist, how long can you keep it? It is a state of tension. Soon you will find it is tiring, exhausting and in spite of you, your fist will open. There is a certain energy that is exhausted.

The open hand is relaxed; no energy is being spent. Tension is just like a fist – too much energy is being spent. Soon, you will find yourself utterly exhausted and the tension will disappear. And in its wake, there will be deep relaxation.

This relaxation is the space in which happiness grows, and again I repeat: *for no reason at all*. It is not that you are happy because of something. You are simply happy.

Happiness is your nature.

Unhappiness is something nurtured, you have learned it. Every credit goes to you for all your misery, but for happiness, you cannot have any credit. It is natural. You were born happy. You were happy in your mother's womb....

Sigmund Freud has a great insight; what he says comes very close to the truth. But he was only a thinker and not a meditator; that's why although he is very close to the truth, he misses the experience of truth himself.

It is his observation, objective observation, that the search for religion, the search for God, or the search for paradise is nothing but the search for the mother's womb – because those nine months were sheer silence, utter joy, a peace that passeth understanding. And to us those are nine months, but to the child it is eternity, because the child knows no dates, no days, no weeks, no months, no calendar.

Each moment is so full of joy, and nine

months...it is almost an eternity to the child.

That experience also remains with you, deep in your unconscious. And even after the birth, that experience continues for at least three to four years – in the girls, three years; in the boys, four years. It is strange but about everything, girls are always one year ahead. They become sexually mature at the age of thirteen. Boys become sexually mature at the age of fourteen. In life, too, the girls learn better; they learn with more concentration.

You can see in the schools, in the colleges, in the universities – the boys are scattered all over, their minds are always in fragments. They want to do many things. The girls are more together and more concentrated in whatever they are doing. They learn better, they learn early, and it is a historical fact that in the past, there used to be wise women who were more deeply experienced about life.

Christianity destroyed thousands of wise women, burned them alive. Even the name "witch" – which means "a wise woman" and nothing else – became so condemnatory...and the same happened in the East. All the religions prohibited women, and I can see that the reason is a great fear that if women are allowed the same opportunity as is given to men, they will be far ahead in the experience of God. And that is against the ego of man.

The male ego has done such great harm. Half of humanity has been completely prevented even from entering the area of religion. This was done out of fear. So you have Gautam Buddha and you have Jesus and you have Mahavira and you have Lao Tzu, but you don't have women of parallel height, because all chances were taken away, all possibilities were destroyed.

My own experience is that women can enter into meditation more easily than men. Man has a better head – logically, intellectually, he can go far in search in the outer world – but the woman has a better heart. She's more introvert; she can go easily, very easily, to the innermost center of her being.

Self-knowledge, enlightenment, will be far easier to a woman. For a man, it is easier to become Alexander the Great, Adolf Hitler, Genghis Khan, Nadir Shah. These thousands of wars would have been avoided if the woman had not been completely ignored, repressed, forced to live like a slave. And she constitutes half of humanity.

I want to say to the women of the whole world that your liberation movement has not done anything, because it is in the hands of very stupid women. They are reactionaries, not revolutionaries. Otherwise, the simple and the most important thing, the first priority, is that the women should demand a separate vote, so that women can only vote for women and men can only vote for men. Just a simple and single step, and all the parliaments of the world will be half filled with women. And the women will be naturally in power because man by nature has a tendency to fight. He will create parties, political parties, religious ideologies – on small, minor, trivial things.

So if the women in a parliament are one single whole, the other half, of men, will be divided into at least eight or ten parties. The whole world can move into the hands of women. And women are not interested in wars, women are not interested in nuclear weapons, women are not interested in communism or capitalism.

All these "isms" are from the head. Women are interested in being joyful, in small things of life: a beautiful house, a garden, a swimming pool. Life can be a paradise, but it is going to remain a hell unless man is removed from power altogether.

And he can be removed so easily.

I have so many women sannyasins – more than men. And the strangest thing is that once a woman becomes a sannyasin, she remains a sannyasin. Once she starts meditating, it becomes her devotion, a part of her heart – it is not so with the man; it remains only an intellectual search. There are exceptions, but as a rule....

I have seen men betraying me but not women. And the reason is that the man is intellectually convinced. He is with me...but I am still alive, I am not dead. So tomorrow, I may say something with which his mind does not agree. And just a small disagreement in his mind, and his path separates from mine. He is with me only to the extent that his intellect is nourished by what I am saying. The moment he feels something I am saying is not rational, he is no more with me. All connections have dropped. And my problem is, that my work is not to feed your intellect. If I talk intellectually, that is simply to persuade you towards something that goes beyond intellect, that goes beyond reason.

For the woman the problem is not the same. She is with me not because she is intellectually convinced by me; she is with me because she is nourished on a deeper level than intellect. Her heart sings with me, beats with me, dances with me. Her connection is not superficial: it is that of trust, not of intellectual conviction. Hence, in the whole of history you will find a Judas around every great mystic and great teacher, but you will not find a single woman who has been a Judas. It is strange, in a long history....

Mahavira has his own Judas; his own son-in-law remained with him just with that male ego, hoping that he would be the successor of Mahavira because he was his son-in-law. Mahavira had only one daughter, and the daughter and the son-in-law both had become sannyasins. For twenty years, they remained with him, but the son-in-law was insisting again and again: "You are getting old. Before anything unfortunate happens, you should make it known to your millions of disciples who is going to be your successor."

Mahavira said, "Whoever is capable will succeed me. I don't have to declare his name. Who am I? I am not a king; my treasure is not of this world. Whoever is enlightened will be recognized by the people as my successor, you need not worry about it." Frustrated, he went against Mahavira and took away with him five hundred followers. And he made many attempts on Mahavira's life. Gautam Buddha had his own Judas, and the same story is repeated again and again.

As far as women are concerned, the situation is just the opposite. When Jesus was crucified, all the twelve apostles escaped. They were afraid that somebody in the crowd might recognize them because they were always moving with Jesus, and everybody knew them: "And now there is no point in being here, unnecessarily getting caught. You could be in trouble. Your master is being crucified; they might at least give you a good beating." But three women remained just at the foot of the cross, not even hiding in the crowd – and one of them was a prostitute, Mary Magdalene; a prostitute rises higher than your twelve apostles. They have become great saints, but Mary Magdalene is not remembered, is not counted amongst the apostles.

The second was another woman, Martha. And the third woman was Jesus' mother, Mariam, whom even Jesus had been insulting because she was a woman. In a crowd, Jesus was speaking and his mother was standing outside the crowd. Somebody shouted, "Jesus, your mother is here and she has not seen you for years; you have been traveling all over the place. Tell the people to make way for her to come in. She just wants to see you."

And the answer that Jesus gave is ugly. He said, "Tell that woman" – he could not even say "tell my mother" – "Tell that woman that my father is in heaven and except my father in heaven, I don't have any relation with anybody else."

This is the man who is talking about love. This is the man who is even saying "Love your enemy." But don't love your mother.

Dhyan Amiyo, you should start your childhood's accidental meditation, because it will suit you immediately. And it has happened here also: "One day I was meditating alone and the fear of death returned. I was overwhelmed by the intensity of it and could do nothing to transform or even repress it. I jumped up in panic and tried to shake it off."

You missed a great opportunity. Again, the same space was opening up but you behaved like a grown-up, not like a child. A child is not afraid. He knows nothing about death: he is so close to life that death is a faraway thing, inconceivable to him.

You also remember that "The last time this happened to me as a teenager, I woke feeling the fear of death the strongest I ever had. But this time, instead of panicking without any conscious decision, I found myself accepting death and relaxing. Immediately there was an explosion of light and a sense of being uplifted by bliss."

You know the secret: you have to accept the fear. In acceptance, it disappears. In rejecting it, in escaping from it, you are nourishing it. You are feeding it.

There is no fear, because there is no death. Death is a fiction and fear is the shadow of the shadow. And you have experienced it accidentally, without doing meditation you have known, that if you remained in the space that was opening up, without fear and without panicking but accepting it, accepting even death and relaxing – immediately there was "an explosion of light and a sense of being uplifted by bliss."

You need not be told; you know already what has to be done. So when meditating, if you come close to the same space again and fear arises, rejoice that you are close to the death of the ego. The death of the ego is another name of relaxation, because the ego is your tension. The ego is your anxiety, the ego is your anguish. The ego is your angst.

The moment you are relaxed, you are not. There is simply relaxation – an immense peace and joy. And if it happens in meditation, consciously, and if you have to go through it again and again – because such an experience has to be lived again and again; that's the only way to deepen it – soon you will find there is no fear, there is nothing to panic about. On the contrary, you are entering into the most blissful experience ever. You are entering into your childhood again, in deep innocence, a freshness and a joy, and a music that is absolutely silent, without any sound.

If this experience goes on growing, it will become your enlightenment one day. You will be uplifted to your highest potential. All darkness will disappear; there will be only light and there will be only ecstasy. Then there is no need to meditate. Then it becomes your natural state, just like breathing, just like heartbeats.

Amiyo, you are fortunate because it rarely happens on its own. But we are so unconscious – do you see your unconsciousness? You passed through everything – you knew fear, you accepted fear, you experienced great relaxation, you experienced bliss, you experienced being uplifted by light – and still you are afraid to go into the same space.

But such is our unconsciousness. We are behaving like drunkards, not knowing what we are doing, not knowing what is happening to us, why it is happening to us. And even when we are very close to something great – we go on missing.

Just be a little more alert, a little more aware. You have the key and that key will work to open all the doors of the mysteries of your inner being.

A nervous young priest, about to deliver his first sermon, asks an older priest how he might calm down a bit. He advises the young priest to fill his water jug with martinis.

Well, the new priest preaches up a storm and afterwards, he asks the older priest what he thought.

"You did very well, but I have just a few criticisms: there are ten commandments, not twelve; there are twelve apostles, not ten. David slew Goliath, he did not kick the shit out of Goliath. Next week, there is a toffee-pulling contest at St. Peters, not a peter-pull at St. Toffee's. The Holy Cross is not to be referred to as the 'Big T.' Please do not refer to our savior Jesus Christ and the apostles as 'J.C. and the boys.' And restrain yourself from calling the father, the son, and the holy ghost, 'Big daddy, junior and the spook.' "And lastly, kindly do not call the Blessed Virgin Mary, 'Mary with the cherry.'"

Beloved Bhagwan

There is immense trust inside me
that being with You everything happens so right
that there is nothing more to do but let it happen.
So I'm not forcing anything and more and more there is only
this sweet, painful love for You
and more silence and more laughter and more love.
Yet sometimes when You speak about "doing everything for enlightenment,"
a doubt arises in me that maybe I'm cheating myself:
Am I not doing enough?

Shantam Shivano, your question is "There is immense trust inside me." But immense trust does not mean absolute trust. Howsoever immense it may be, there is space enough for doubts. So first you have to understand: just trust is enough. Don't make it immense.

Just trust is absolute.

And remember, trust is not belief. Belief is in ideas, in ideologies, in doctrines, in theologies, in philosophies. Trust is just the purest form of love; it has nothing to do with any ideology. Doubt can arise if you have a belief – these are subtle connections – doubt is connected with the belief. Doubt has no possibility in trust.

In fact, belief is nothing but a method of repressing doubt, and when you repress a doubt then there is always a possibility: any weak moment, and the repressed will spring up with great vengeance and destroy your whole belief system. But trust is not repressing any doubt. Trust has no connection with any kind of belief system.

Trust is falling in love – not the biological love, but the love that can exist between two beings, two souls, two consciousnesses.

You say, "Being with you, everything happens so right that there is nothing more to do but let it happen." So I am not forcing anything; that's perfectly right. Forcing is violence, forcing is repression, forcing is dangerous. Whatever you force will take its revenge.

My whole teaching can be reduced into two words: Let Go. Just go with the stream and you are doing perfectly well.

"And more and more there is only this sweet painful love for You, and more silence and more laughter and more love. Yet, sometimes when You speak about 'doing everything for enlightenment,' a doubt arises in me that maybe I am cheating myself: Am I not doing enough?"

This doubt arises only because there is some space left empty, not filled with trust. "Immense" is your trust, but immense does not mean total. And less than total is going to have, once in a while, this doubt, that doubt.

Otherwise, there is nothing to doubt. You are growing in silence, you are growing in love, you are feeling more and more laughter – these are the signals that you are on the right path.

And when I speak of doing everything for enlightenment, you and everybody have to remember that I am speaking to so many people – not only to those who are present here, but also to those who are spread all over the world. If you take every statement personally, you will be unnecessarily getting into trouble.

I have to take care of so many people who are so different from each other, and I am answering different people in different stages, in different situations. You have to remember always, to look at your own growth: if it is going towards love, compassion, silence, blissfulness, joy, laughter, celebration, and silence, then remember that I must have answered somebody else. You are doing perfectly well. And sometimes these kinds of doubts can disturb your growth.

Whenever I had said, "Do everything for enlightenment," I must have been answering some – and there are many – who are so lazy, that what to say about everything, they are not even ready to do *anything*. They are simply waiting for me to do something. If it were possible, if nature allowed, I would have done it, but it is against the law of nature itself.

You have to find your truth yourself. And for that, you have to risk everything. Truth cannot be anything else but your first priority. It cannot be one amongst many desires. It is not a desire, it is a wholehearted longing, as if you are lost in a desert and for days you have not been able to find water. Now, thirst is not a desire; now every cell of your body is crying "thirst." There are not even words to say, it is just an experience: you are burning with thirst, you are on fire.

Enlightenment is the greatest experience in human life. Certainly you have to leave your trivial engagements – but remember that I am talking to so many people that everything is not for you. You have to choose.

One thing you have always to remember: if symptoms of love and joy and laughter are growing in you, then there is no need to worry. And there is no need to be in a hurry, either. It is better to go at your pace, slowly but very centered and grounded, so that you don't have to take any step backwards. You don't have even to look backwards.

Drop your doubt. And remember, I am saying *drop*, I'm not saying repress. I am not saying fight with it. I am not saying that you have to do anything with it. Simply drop it. It has no business in your beautiful, slow growth.

Remember one thing: there are seasonal flowers; within six weeks they are there but within six weeks they are gone, too. And there are trees like Cedars of Lebanon, four thousand years old, two hundred feet high. They don't grow in six weeks. Their growth is very slow. But their beauty, their longing to touch the stars, is almost like the human longing to find the divine in existence.

Drop the doubt and always remember that I am talking to so many people…their needs are different, their sicknesses are different, they need different medicines and different treatment.

Whenever you have any problem, you can ask. It is good that you have asked rather than carrying it within your heart. Doubt is as dangerous to spiritual growth as cancer is to the body.

Abie made a small fortune in California in the wholesale clothing business. After he provided for his family, he gave all his wealth to the local temple. He slept well at night knowing that his family was secure and that God was looking after him, so he had not a care in the world.

Imagine how surprised Abie felt when his Malibu beachfront home was endangered by an oncoming hurricane. First, the local fire department came and evacuated Abie's family. But Abie told the fire chief: "I will not leave my home. You cannot help me, only God can save me." The waves began to crash against the shore. The road around Abie's home was engulfed in water. Without fear, Abie decided to wait out the storm.

The Navy sent in a Coast Guard cutter to rescue Abie, as the waves were now crashing against his huge front window. The captain ordered, "Abie, please!"

But Abie insisted, "You cannot help me, only God can save me."

Now Abie was alone on the roof. In the distance, a tidal wave was fast approaching the shore. A US Air Force helicopter hovered above Abie's head. But Abie refused help, such was Abie's faith in his lord and master. Well, the tidal wave did its thing, and Abie looked up at the Pearly Gates, soaking wet and totally pissed off at God.

"But Abie," the gatekeeper said, "God wants to see you right away." Abie's response was, "Tell God to go to hell."

The gatekeeper suggested to Abie that God is not a saint and to give God a second chance. Abie relented and was shown into God's room. God was so pleased to see his beloved Abie.

"Abie, why are you so mad at me?"

Abie said, in a cool, distant voice, "Because when I needed you the most down on earth, you did not lift a finger to help me."

God said, "You've got to be kidding, Abie. I sent the fire department, The US Navy, and the US Air Force. What more do you want?"

You have to remember that trust does not mean that you are not supposed to do anything. Trust simply means that whatever you are doing is in the right direction, because the man you trust in cannot take you in a wrong direction. But you have to do the walking.

I can only show you the path, I cannot walk for you. And there are so many paths and there are so many different people who need different paths, so each one of you has to remember: all that I am saying is not for you.

You have to be very alert: whatever helps to strengthen your progress is for you. Whatever weakens your progress is not for you; it must have been said to somebody else. On some other path it may be helpful. To somebody else, it may be immensely needed.

Okay, Vimal?

Yes, Bhagwan.

Session 23

Love...
Not a Relationship
But a State of Being

*I don't want the family to exist,
I don't want the nations to exist – I don't
want the world to be divided into parts.
I want one world consisting of free individuals
living in spontaneous love,
living in silence, playfulness, without any condemnation
of pleasure, without any fear of hell
and without any desire for reward in heaven –
because we can create the paradise here.
We have every potential to create it,
but we are not using it.*

March 24, 1987
Morning

Beloved Bhagwan,

I heard You say the other day
that You want no part of any relationship
we might imagine we have with You – certainly not our hate,
but not even our love. And I can't say I blame You.
Nevertheless, when You stand before us, dancing,
I feel like a fountain that leaps into life at the sight of You,
and tumbles to Your feet as if it knows
that is where it belongs.
I know my love is riddled with all sorts
of undesirable things; but it rushes towards You
without even stopping to ask my permission.
Bhagwan, please excuse the mess, but I can't help it.

Maneesha, the word "love" can have two absolutely different meanings – not only different, but diametrically opposite. One meaning is love as relationship; the other meaning is love as a state of being.

When I said I don't want any relationship – at least from my side, because I cannot interfere with you, so I cannot say anything from your side; that you have to understand yourself – I was denying love as relationship.

The moment love becomes a relationship, it becomes a bondage, because there are expectations and there are demands and there are frustrations, and an effort from both sides to dominate. It becomes a struggle for power.

Relationship is not the right thing, at least for my people. But love as a state of being is a totally different word. It means you are simply loving; you are not creating a relationship out of it. Your love is just like the fragrance of a flower. It does not create a relationship; it does not ask you to be a certain way, to behave in a certain way, to act in a certain way. It demands nothing. It simply shares. And in sharing also there is no desire for any reward. The sharing itself is the reward.

When love becomes like a fragrance to you, then it has tremendous beauty. And something that is far above the so-called humanity – it has something of the divine.

You are saying, "I cannot help...." Neither can I. When love is a state, you cannot do anything about it. It will radiate, but it will not create any imprisonments for anybody, nor will it allow you to be imprisoned by anybody else.

Your question is significant. I will go into it point by point. You say, "I heard you say...." This is to be remembered: whenever you state anything that I have said, never say, "You said it." Say it exactly the way Maneesha is doing. She has learned in many years' time that it is not necessarily the same, what I say and what you hear.

You hear according to your own prejudices, according to your own mind. You interpret and then you project that meaning, as if I have said it. The right way is, "I heard you say...." All the Buddhist scriptures start with the same sentence: "I have heard Gautam Buddha say...."

I asked one very respected Buddhist monk – world famous because of his writings about Gautam Buddha – why every scripture begins with, "I have heard Gautam Buddha say...."

He said, "You bring strange questions. I have been translating these scriptures my whole life but I never thought about it. Do you think it has any meaning?"

I said, "It has not only meaning, it has tremendous meaning. Whoever was writing it was absolutely aware that, at the most, he could say, 'I have heard...perhaps Buddha was saying something else. Perhaps he was saying what I have heard, but I cannot impose my meaning, my projection on him. I can be wrong.'"

And this is true, because as Gautam Buddha died.... He never wrote anything, and he never allowed in his life that anything he said be written, for a simple reason: If you are listening, there is no need to make any notes. And if you are making notes, you are not listening; your whole mind is concerned with writing the notes. You are behaving like the modern tourist, who is a cartoon character, rushing from one place to another place with a camera hanging on one shoulder, a telescope hanging on another shoulder, many kinds of lenses in a bag. Even standing before the Taj Mahal, he is not seeing it. He is photographing it. Back home when the album is ready, he will look at it with great joy from the golden memories of his tour. But he has never really seen – his being was diverted by the camera.

When I was a teacher in the university, I never allowed any student to take notes – because the moment you start taking notes, you stop hearing. You know that later on you can read your notes, so there is no need to be in the present. That psychological truth is the reason why Buddha did not allow anybody to write down what he was saying. He said, "When I am dead you can write anything you want."

And the first thing that his disciples did was collect forty-two years' discourses, morning and evening, personal interviews given to emperors, to kings and to disciples. And you will be surprised to know that there were thirty-six schools immediately, saying that he has said *this*, not *this*. Their only difference was.... They were all devoted to Gautam Buddha, but they were saying that he has said *this* – and there were thirty-six versions.

So there are thirty-six versions of Buddhist scriptures. They are not reporting Buddha, they are reporting what they have heard – according to their consciousness, according to their intelligence, according to their presence.

So it is not just in beginning the question; it has to be a deep understanding in you: always remember to make it clear that you are reporting what you have heard. It is not necessarily synonymous with what I have said.

Maneesha is saying, "I heard you say" – and I appreciate her understanding in using the words "I heard" – "the other day that you want no part of any relationship we might imagine we have with you."

You have heard rightly, Maneesha. I don't want any part of any relationship, imagined or not imagined. It may be very real to you – it may not be your imagination, it may be factual. You are accustomed to creating relationships from your very childhood. A strange man, and you have to create a relationship with him as your father. You cannot ever be certain that he is your father....

I have heard about one palmist who used to read people's hands. An atheist, a young man who does not believe in God and does not believe in any kind of bullshit – palmistry, astrology – went to the palmist and said, "If your science is true, just read my hand and tell me where my father is right now."

The palmist looked at his hand and said, "Your father has gone fishing." The atheist laughed. He said, "That's what I say: it is all nonsense. My father has been dead for three years; how can he go fishing today?"

The palmist said, "That is not my business, but the truth is, the man who died was not your father. Your real father is fishing. You go to your mother and ask. If she is sincere and honest, she will tell you that the man who died was not your father – although you had created a relationship because you were told that he is your father."

Your whole life is surrounded by many kinds of relationships. I don't want any kind of relationship. Relationship as such, real or imaginary, is a very subtle kind of psychological slavery. Either you enslave the other, or you become a slave yourself.

Another point to be noted is that you cannot enslave somebody without becoming a slave yourself. Slavery is a double-edged sword. One may be stronger, one may be weaker, but in every relationship you become the jailer and the other becomes the prisoner. From his side, he is the jailer and you are the prisoner. And this is one of the fundamental causes of humanity living in such sadness, in such a sorrowful state.

You have heard me rightly: I don't want any part of any relationship, "...certainly not our hate, but not even our love." From my side, I will not allow any relationship; I will not nourish any relationship. But you are free to suffer – that is your birthright.

How can I prevent you, if you start having a relationship of hate with me? And hate is much stronger a relationship than your love, because your love is very superficial. Your hate is very deep. Your hate is your whole animal heritage. Your love is only a potential for the future; it is not an actuality, but only a seed.

But your hate is full-fledged, fully grown – thousands of years of your past moving through different life forms. It has had time and space to grow. It is only in man that the change starts happening.

I cannot prevent anybody from hating me, so how can I prevent anybody from loving me? All that I can do is to explain that the moment hate or love or anything becomes a relationship, it loses its purity.

Let your love be your state of being. Not that you fall in love, but just that you are loving. It is simply your nature. Love, to you, is just the fragrance of your being. Even if you are alone you are surrounded by loving energy. Even if you touch a dead thing, like the chair, your hand is showering love – it does not matter to whom.

The loving state is unaddressed. And I am not preventing you from being in the state of love, but you can be in the state of love only if you drop the old mind pattern of relationships. Love is not a relationship.

Two persons can be very loving together. The more loving they are, the less is the possibility of any relationship. The more loving they are, the more freedom exists between them. The more loving they are, the less is the possibility of any demand, any domination, any expectation. And naturally, there is no question of any frustration.

You say, "And I can't say I blame you." You understand it rightly. I have allowed people to have their real or imaginary love relationship with me – for the simple reason that unless they are with me, there is no possibility of transforming their relationship into a state of being – knowing perfectly well that their relationship is not reliable. No relationship is reliable, and particularly with a man with whom the relationship is one-sided. It is like a bridge which is supported only by one bank of the river, and the other bank does not support it. It is hanging in the air; it is going to fall.

And I have burned my fingers thousands of times, because the people who thought they loved me…I have seen them change to hating me, for some trivial reason.

Love is beyond reason.

Relationship is part of the business world. Just a slight change in the situation, and it evaporates. It has no solidity.

I have showered my love without any conditions, and yet there have been many people who have taken advantage of it, in many ways. And because of their loving imagination, they were expecting something from me. Man is so blind, he cannot see it. When I don't expect anything from you, at least remember that you cannot expect anything from me either.

And when their expectations are not fulfilled – and they are not going to be fulfilled – then immediately love turns into hate. And it has left wounds in my heart, because I have simply given love, never expected anything from them, and they have turned into enemies because of their expectations – in which I have no part. I have never promised them anything. Expectations are there, frustrations are there – but first they were projecting expectations; now they are projecting frustrations. Neither could they see last time, nor are they able to see this time, that they are surrounded with their own unconscious ideas. And they are suffering.

And, just as when they were imagining love, they were appreciating me, not knowing me at all, now they are condemning me. And to condemn me they are creating lies – and perhaps in absolute unawareness. Just as they believed their imagination before, the same game continues; still they go on believing in their lies. I have been asked to refute them. That is not possible. I have loved them; they have been my disciples. It is below me to criticize their lies or to expose their lies.

That's why I want you to remember: don't have any expectations. Love because love is your own inner growth. Being loving, you are calling your spring closer. Your love will help you to grow towards more light, towards more truth, towards more freedom. But don't create a relationship.

"Nevertheless, when you stand before us, dancing, I feel like a fountain that leaps into life at the sight of you, and tumbles to your feet as if it knows that is where it belongs."

I have not been prohibiting you. If love comes as a spontaneity, suddenly, like a fountain, asking nothing in return, then it is one of the greatest treasures.

"I know my love is riddled with all sorts of undesirable things, but it rushes towards you without even stopping to ask my permission."

Love is a fire. The more pure it is…all the riddles, all the problems will be burned. It is love as relationship which will go on creating more problems, "riddled with all sorts of undesirable things." But a spontaneous love is a totally different thing. We don't have another word, that is the difficulty.

"Bhagwan, please excuse the mess. But I just

can't help it."

There is no need to be worried about the mess. Just remember one thing: love is capable of destroying everything else, just don't let it become a relationship – then love will disappear, and in the name of love, domination, politics will take place. Then problems will go on increasing.

I am against all kinds of relationships. For example, I don't like the word "friendship," but I love the word "friendliness." Friendliness is a quality in you, friendship again becomes a relationship.

Maneesha, there is nothing wrong with love. In fact, without love everything is wrong. But love is so valuable that it should be protected from any kind of pollution, contamination, any kind of poisoning. Relationship poisons it. I want the world to consist of individuals. Even to use the word "couple" hurts me. You have destroyed two individuals, and a couple is not a thing of beauty.

Let the world be only of individuals, and whenever love spontaneously blossoms, sing it, dance it, live it; don't create chains out of it. Neither try to hold somebody in bondage, nor allow anybody to hold you in bondage.

A world consisting only of free individuals will be a truly free world.

It is one of the greatest needs of man to be needed. Hence I cannot conceive of any time when love will not be in existence. As long as there are human beings, love will remain their most cherished experience. And it is something that is available on the earth, but does not belong to the earth. It gives you wings to fly like an eagle across the sun.

Without love you are without wings.

But because it is such a nourishment and such a need, all the problems have arisen around it. You want your lover or your beloved to be available to you tomorrow too. It has been beautiful today, and you are worried about tomorrow. Hence marriage came into existence. It is just the fear that perhaps tomorrow your lover or your beloved may leave you – so make it a contract before society and before the law. But it is ugly – it is absolutely ugly, disgusting. To make love a contract means you are putting law above love; it means you are putting the collective mass above your individuality and you are taking the support of the courts, of the armies, of the police, of the judges, to make your bondage absolutely certain and safe.

Tomorrow morning…one never knows. Love comes like a breeze – it may come again, it may not come. And when it does not come, then just because of law, because of marriage, because of social respectability, almost all the couples in the world are reduced to prostitution.

Living with a woman that you don't love, living with a man that you don't love, living for safety, living for security, living for financial support, living for any reason except love, makes it nothing but prostitution.

I would like prostitution to disappear completely from the world. All the religions have been wanting that – that there should be no prostitution. But this is how human stupidity is: these same religions that want there to be no prostitution are the causes of prostitution, because on the one hand they support marriage, and on the other hand they are against prostitution.

Marriage itself is a prostitution. If I trust my love, why should I get married? The very idea of getting married is a distrust. And something that is coming out of distrust is not going to help your love grow deeper and higher. It is going to destroy it.

Maneesha, I am not preventing you from being loving. In fact, that's my whole religion: to love, but not to destroy love by something fake – marriage or any other kind of relationship.

Love is authentic only when it gives freedom. Let this be the criterion.

Love is true only when it does not interfere in the privacy of the other person. It respects his individuality, his privacy. But the lovers that you see around the world, their whole effort is that nothing should be private; all secrets should be told to them. They are afraid of individuality; they destroy each other's individuality, and they hope that by destroying each other, their lives will become a contentment, a fulfillment. They simply become more and more miserable.

Be loving, and remember: anything real is always changing. You have been given wrong notions that a true love remains forever. A true roseflower does not remain forever. A living being himself has to die one day.

Existence is a constant change. But the notion, the idea that love should be permanent if it is true...and if love disappears one day, then the natural corollary is that it was not true.

I want you to know: love came suddenly; it was not because of any effort on your part. It came as a gift of nature. At that time you would not have accepted it if you had been worried about its going suddenly one day. The way it comes, it goes.

But there is no need to be worried, because if one flower has faded, other flowers will be coming. Flowers are going to come forever, but don't cling to one flower. Otherwise soon you will be clinging to a dead flower, and that's what the reality is: people are clinging to a dead love that once was alive. Now it is only a memory and a pain and you are stuck because of respectability, because of law.

Karl Marx had the idea, the right idea, that in communism there would be no marriages. And when revolution happened in Russia, in the first four, five years, they tried to make love a freedom. But then they became aware of practical difficulties of which Marx was not aware – he was only thinking – and the greatest difficulty was that if there is no marriage, family disappears, and family is the backbone, the very spine of the society, of the nation. If the family disappears, then the nation cannot last long.

And after just five years of revolution the Communist party of Russia changed the whole idea. Marriage was again supported; divorce was allowed, but very reluctantly – every obstacle was created for divorce, so that the family unit remains, because now they were interested in having the nation. Without the nation there would be no politicians, there would be no government.

And since then they have never talked about it – that one of Marx's fundamental ideas was that marriage came into existence because of private property, so when private property disappears, marriage has to disappear. Nobody talks about it. I have been talking to communists, but they have fallen into the same trap as all religions. Karl Marx' *Das Kapital* has become their *Holy Bible*, holy *Koran;* you cannot change anything in it.

I said, "That's true, I am not saying to change anything in it – but follow it!" They are not following it either. They have started worshiping it. That is the whole strategy of man to avoid any authentic revolution in the world: worship.

I don't want the family to exist, I don't want the nations to exist – I don't want the world to be divided into parts. I want one world consisting of free individuals living in spontaneous love, living in silence, playfulness, without any condemnation of pleasure, without any fear of hell and without any desire for reward in heaven – because we can create the paradise *here*. We have every potential to create it, but we are not using it. On the contrary, we are creating every hindrance: the earth should not become a paradise.

I am not against love. I am so much in favor of love; that's why I am against relationships, against marriages. It is possible that two persons may live their whole lives together. Nobody is saying that you have to separate, but this living together will be only out of love, without interfering and trespassing into each other's individuality, into each other's private soul. That is his dignity.

You can be loving, you can be love, so don't feel worried about it. But if you are simply loving, if you are simply love, then there is no possibility of you turning to hate. Because there is no expectation, you cannot be frustrated.

But I am talking about love as a spiritual phenomenon, not as biology.

Biology is not love, it is lust. Biology is interested in continuing all the species; the idea of love is just a biological bribe. The moment you have made love to a woman or to a man, suddenly you find you are no longer interested, at least for twenty-four hours. And it depends on your age – as you become older, forty-eight hours, seventy-two hours....

There is a new commander of a base of the French Foreign Legion, and the captain is showing him around all the buildings. After he has made the rounds, the commander looks at the captain and says, "Wait a minute. You haven't shown me that small blue building over there. What's that used for?"

The captain says, "Well, sir, you see, that is where we keep the camel. Whenever the men feel the need for a woman...."

"Enough!" says the commander in disgust.

Well, two weeks later, the commander himself starts to feel in need of a woman. He goes to the captain and says, "Tell me something, captain." Lowering his voice and glancing furtively around, he asks, "Is the camel free anytime soon?"

The captain says, "Well, let me see." He opens up his book. "Why, yes, sir, the camel is free tomorrow afternoon at two o'clock."

The commander says, "Put me down."

So the next day at two o'clock the commander goes to the little blue building and opens the door. Inside he finds the cutest camel he has ever seen. He closes the door.

The captain hears a great roaring and screaming, so he runs up and bursts into the hut. He finds the commander naked, covered in camel hair and mud.

"Ahem, begging your pardon, sir," says the captain, "but wouldn't it be wiser to do as all the other men do – ride the camel into town and find a woman?"

Beloved Bhagwan,

Does joy arise out of the heart or out of the being?
If it comes out of the heart,
does it drop away when one reaches the being?
If so, how come You are radiating so much joy?
Bhagwan, I am so attached to joy and grace.
Do I even need to drop them?

Satyam Prema, it is a beautiful question. "Does joy arise out of the heart or out of the being?" Joy arises out of the being, but passes through the heart.

The heart is the first to receive the joy of the being. And the heart is the vehicle to express the joy to the outside world; hence the misunderstanding can be there, that perhaps joy arises out of the heart. It only comes *through* the heart; it arises out of being. But being is deeper inside. Heart is only an instrument, a medium, a vehicle.

So you need not be worried, as your question shows. "If it comes out of the heart, does it drop away when one reaches the being?" The expression of joy from the heart becomes fuller as one reaches the being, it does not drop. In reaching the being, the passage of the heart becomes cleaner, wider, more expressive. You need not be afraid that you will have to drop joy also.

We are in search of joy, and the greatest joy is when you have reached the being. Then the heart will be expressing it at the maximum; right now once in a while a ray of joy passes the heart.

"If so, how come you are radiating so much with joy?" I am not radiating with joy. Once you are centered in your being, you *are* joy, you *are* love, you *are* blissfulness, you *are* ecstasy. These are no longer happening to you; these are your natural qualities.

"Bhagwan, I am so attached to joy and grace. Do I even need to drop them?" If you are attached, you will not get them in the first place; dropping is out of the question. You have to drop attachment. The moment you drop attachment, you will have joy and you will have grace.

But such questions go on in everybody's mind. They are simple, but our understanding is not deep enough to see that which is very clear. I am talking against attachment; it is attachment that is destroying your capacity to express joy and grace. But rather than dropping attachment, you are becoming attached to joy and grace.

How can you be attached to something that you don't have? You don't have joy, you don't have grace – just ideas, empty containers with no content. Because once you know joy, you know there is no need to be attached; it is impossible to be without joy. Once you know grace, there is no question of attachment or dropping the attachment; grace becomes your natural expression in every gesture – from your eyes, from your face, from your hands. Whatever you do, there will be grace and there will be joy.

Your attachment to joy and grace makes me wonder: perhaps you have seen people like me who are joyous...even if I try to remember, I cannot remember what misery used to be. The very language is almost forgotten. Seeing joyous people you want to imitate them. You want to grab joy and cling to it. But remember, all great values are killed the moment you cling to them. And no great value can be imitated.

You see beautiful people, joyous people, loving people, silent and serene people, and a greed arises in you: "These are the qualities I must have." That is the fear that has come into your question. You don't have them, so the question of dropping them does not arise. First *have* them and then try to drop them! Nobody has ever succeeded. You will be a unique person if you find enlightenment and can drop it.

A French couple, an Irish couple, and a Polish couple are having dinner together. The Frenchman says to his wife, "Pass me the sugar, Sugar."

Not to be outdone, the Irishman says, "Could you pass me the honey, Honey?"

Most impressed by these clever endearments, the Pole leans over to his wife and says, "Pass me the pork, Pig."

Avoid copying; otherwise you will do something stupid. But everybody is imitating everybody else in the world.

It is very strange to see why people imitate. Can't they find their own individuality? And can't they enjoy being themselves?

Any kind of stupid fashion and people will imitate, thinking that "perhaps if all these intelligent people are doing it and I am not doing it, I will be thought unintelligent." But imitation is unintelligent.

It is perfectly good to be in search of your being, which is the source of joy and bliss and truth and love and all that is valuable in existence. Of course it needs the heart for a few values to be expressed, and mind for other values to be expressed. Your being is utterly intelligent, but intelligence can be expressed only through the mind. And your being is immensely loving, but love can be expressed only through the heart.

Right now you have forgotten about the being and you are only carrying instruments with nothing to express. It is just like carrying a guitar, and you don't know why you are carrying this thing and what it is all about.

An ancient story is.... In India there are very refined instruments of music; nowhere else in the world has such refinement happened. Just one single man – who lives in the Himalayas and comes once in a while to the plains – plays a special *veena* which used to exist in the past. And many musicians used to play it, but now only one person knows how to play it. It is called *rudra veena*. Rudra is another name of Shiva; Shiva used to play it. To play it needs such a long discipline, four or five hours' practice every day for years; then only can you bring those subtle notes out of it.

The ancient story is that in one house there was a strange musical instrument which had been there for generations. Nobody knew what to do with it, and it was a nuisance. It had to be cleaned, dust would gather on it, and it was taking up space in the room. And sometimes in the middle of the night a rat would jump on it and create noise.

Finally they decided, "It is useless for us; it is better to get rid of it." So they went out and threw it on the garbage pile by the side of the road.

They had not even reached back home and they heard such sweet music...they had never even imagined. So they turned back – a beggar was playing the instrument, and a crowd had gathered.

The beggar knew, he was a musician, but a musician of such old and ancient instruments that even to find people who could understand it was difficult, so there was no possibility for him to earn anything. He had become a beggar so that he could continue discovering old, ancient instruments about which we have completely forgotten. And as he saw this instrument he could not believe it, because he had been in search of this instrument for years.

There was utter silence in the crowd – everybody who was passing on the road stopped. The people of the house came back, and when he stopped playing they said, "That instrument belongs to us."

The beggar said, "Remember one thing: a musical instrument belongs to one who knows how to play it, there is no other kind of ownership. You have thrown it in the garbage. You have insulted an immensely valuable thing.

"And what will you do with it? Again it will gather dust and you will have to clean it. Again rats will make noise in the night and disturb your sleep. This instrument can be played only if one knows how to play a few other instruments. They are the steps, and this is the end, and I have been searching for it. All other instruments I have found, but this, the final instrument, was missing. You cannot claim ownership of it.

"If you can play it here, before the crowd, it is yours. Otherwise, it belongs to me."

Music is not property; it is art, it is love. It is devotion, it is prayer. You cannot possess it.

The same is my feeling about your being.

You have it, but you don't possess it because you don't know how to play the instrument of your being. All that you know is the mind, which is only a vehicle; the heart, which is only a vehicle. But they are empty. Your thinking leads nowhere. Your heart remains at the point of lust, and never gets to know love.

Search for your being and everything else will follow it on its own accord. You don't have to drop anything – you cannot drop anything. They are your innermost qualities; they will radiate on their own. Your heart will be full of love; your mind will be full of intelligence.

Okay, Vimal?

Yes, Bhagwan.

Session 24

All Our Doings Are Disturbances

*Only in relaxation can you find your center of being.
If you go on making effort
and running after some goal, to achieve awareness,
you will go farther and farther away from your reality.
Just don't do anything.
At least for a few moments every day, simply be.
The heart will be beating, the breathing will be going on –
you are not doing anything, not even thinking.
And in these moments, the whole sky opens up.*

March 24, 1987
Evening

Beloved Bhagwan,

I find that the true moments of joy and peace in my life
come when I am the witness.
Witnessing seems to come easier when I make some effort for it,
such as now, in Vipassana group.
You talked recently about the futility of will,
but for me, it seems some effort or will is needed
for the growth of awareness.
Would You please comment?

Ramfakeer, it is possible to create a certain awareness through effort and through will but it will not be the true awareness.

That which is created by you cannot be eternal. That which is forced by you, will immediately disappear the moment you drop the effort. You forget...and you cannot will twenty-four hours a day. Will needs tremendous energy; the effort will be very tiring.

And after the awareness that is created by will disappears, you will fall deep into unawareness, deeper than you were before. Will is an instrument for creating false things. You can create an ego through will power because ego is false. But you cannot create your being, it is already there. And so is the case with awareness: the authentic awareness is not created by you, it is discovered by you. And the discovery needs no effort on your part because *you* are the problem, your efforts are the hindrances.

You have to be absent – with all your will power, with all your efforts. You simply have to give way, and then there will be a totally different quality of awareness – spontaneous, joyous, relaxing, rejuvenating, and you can never be tired of it. It is simply your nature. Even in your sleep it will remain there, burning like a small candle in the darkness of sleep.

That which is created by will cannot be of the beyond, it can only be something below you. It is your creation – it cannot be bigger than you. And that which you are creating has a cause: your will, your effort. The moment the cause is removed, the flame of awareness will be gone. Your will was functioning like a fuel.

I will not support it. It is fake. And because you don't know the authentic, you cannot make the distinction.

Please try to be in touch with the spontaneous – even a moment's glimpse and you will see: the difference is so vast.... One is just manufactured by you, with all your weaknesses, with all your frailties, with all your unconsciousness – and the other comes from the beyond. The other is divine, and only the divine can liberate you. Only the divine can be your eternal peace, silence, blissfulness.

You are saying, "I find that the true moments of joy..." Have you ever known untrue moments of joy? Either joy is, or is not. Have you ever experienced untrue moments of joy? What do you mean by "true moments of joy"?

Certainly, you are comparing with your moments of hypocrisy, when you try to appear to be happy, joyful, and you know you are not; your smile is just an exercise of the lips. The heart is not behind it; most probably it is just a way to hide your tears. You are afraid if you don't start laughing, you may start crying; it is better to laugh so you are not exposed to others.

People try in every way to hide their misery, their pain, their anguish. Just go to a Lions Club or a Rotary Club and see people – everybody seems enlightened, and the same idiots, for twenty-four hours a day in life, are behaving as unconsciously as anybody else. But they are simply following a ritual. You are supposed to smile, you are supposed to look happy. Slowly, slowly, you simply become a supposition.

Mrs. Reagan boarded a train in Washington late one night and was escorted to an upper berth. Nancy climbed up, stretched out and tried to sleep. However, a man in the lower berth was snoring intolerably. His loud snores became so unbearable, the President's wife leaned over and jabbed the man with her umbrella.

He awoke immediately, looked up at her and said, "It won't do you no good, lady, I had a good look at you when you got on the train." People are showing one thing, thinking something else. Now when he was looking at Nancy, he was not showing what was going on in his mind.

We have become so pseudo, and to a pseudo personality, nothing of value can ever happen.

Ramfakeer, I would like you to remember that either you have moments of joy or you don't have. There is no third alternative because the third alternative will be simply fake, untrue, dishonest. And once you become accustomed to the dishonest, to the insincere within yourself, then your darkness will start getting darker. Rather than moving towards light, you will be moving towards darker spaces of your being.

You are saying, "I find that the true moments of joy and peace in my life come when I am the witness." You have never experienced the witness, because to experience the witness is to go beyond peace, is to go beyond joy, is to go beyond everything into absolute nothingness and silence. There is no experience.

Witnessing is not an experience. Witnessing is going beyond all experiences. Experiences are other than you; witnessing is your very being. Experiences are like clouds in the sky – sometimes very beautiful – white clouds, black clouds with silver lines shining through them, or rainbows passing through them, or at the time of sunrise or sunset, when the whole sky becomes psychedelic.... But the clouds are not the sky.

You are not your experiences. Your experiences are just clouds in the sky of your being. When all the clouds are gone and the empty space remains, you will know what witnessing means.

"Witnessing," according to you, "seems to come easier when I make some effort for it, such as now in Vipassana group. You talked recently about futility of will, but for me, it seems some effort or will is needed for the growth of awareness."

In a way you are right, because you don't know the real awareness. So by effort, by will, you force yourself into some kind of alertness. This alertness is almost like when you come home and find your house is on fire: suddenly, you will find a great awareness in you which has never been there. But it is because the house is on fire; the shock is so much that it has made you a little awake, has brought you out of your sleep. But you cannot go on putting houses on fire just to be a little awake.

And this kind of awareness is very costly and very dangerous – costly, because it can deceive you and you can start feeling that you have become aware, and dangerous because it will take you away from the authentic experience.

Try to relax; don't make any effort, because never in the history of man has anybody become awakened through effort or will. Those who have become aware have always become aware when they had dropped all their efforts and all their will. But man's blindness knows no limits.

In the life of Gautam Buddha, who can be said to be the most well-known historical figure who reached to the highest peak of awareness.... But his followers around the world and in the East – except for India, the whole East is Buddhist; it is the third greatest religion in the world – still go on missing. I have been looking into hundreds of books from Korea, from China, from Japan, from Sri Lanka, from Burma, from Tibet – but I have not found a single mention of the most important thing that happened in Gautam Buddha's life.

For six years, he made every effort. He brought his whole will power to becoming aware, he left no stone unturned. Naturally, this intensity of work, effort, this arduous journey, made him so tired and so frustrated.... Finally, one fullmoon night sitting by the side of a small river, Niranjana in Bihar, he decided, "I have renounced the world, I have renounced my kingdom. Today I renounce even my effort and my will – even the desire to find the truth. I am so tired, so utterly frustrated that this is my second renunciation." He dropped all methods that he had been trying and after six years, for the first time he relaxed and had a good sleep, without a dream. Otherwise, his sleep had been full of nightmares, because on the one hand he had renounced everything and on the other hand, all efforts had led only to failure...or fake experiences.

In the morning, as the last star was disappearing in the sky, he opened his eyes and he could not believe: this is the space he has been looking for! As the star disappeared, his ego disappeared too. As the sky became utterly empty – the stars are gone, the moon is gone and the sun has not come yet – just in that gap, he also became just the same silence, uncluttered with anything. And this was what has been known down the ages as his enlightenment.

Buddhists around the world go on saying, go on writing that he found his enlightenment after six years of arduous effort. The reality is just the opposite. He found enlightenment after he renounced all his efforts.

It is true that you cannot renounce if you have not made any effort. So, Ramfakeer, you are in a good position: you are making effort and you are making use of your will power. But remember, all these will lead you to fake experiences. And when the time comes, don't be a coward: renounce all these experiences of joy and peace and awareness, because they are produced by will and effort. Then is the real miracle, because your very being is eternally awake. It has never fallen asleep, but you have lost the track to reach to it.

Only in relaxation can you find your center of being. If you go on making effort and running after some goal, to achieve awareness, you will go farther and farther away from your reality. Just don't do anything. At least for a few moments every day, simply be. The heart will be beating, the breathing will be going on – you are not doing anything, not even thinking. And in these moments, the whole sky opens up.

It is one of the greatest wonders that what we are seeking and searching for lives together is just present, eternally present within ourselves. But because of our efforts and because of our mind to achieve, we go on missing it.

Our life is a very stupid mess. And the same life can be a great splendor, but we won't allow it. We go on doing something or other, and all our doings are disturbances. This is the greatest lesson in life to learn: that the ultimate phenomenon happens only when we are not doing anything, when we are almost absent, when we are just an open door and the sun rays come dancing in and the fresh breeze passes through us. Suddenly, the whole existence starts helping us to be our true self.

Witnessing is the quality of our true self. It is not a question of creating it, it is a discovery.

I have heard…God is making all the creatures of the earth and is giving out sex lives to each animal. First he turns to the human. "I am giving you ten years of good sex life," says God.

The man's face falls. "Is that all?" he asks.

"I only have so much to go around, fella," says God. He then turns to the monkey and says, "I'm giving you twenty years of a good sex life."

The monkey says, "Oh, I don't really need that much. Ten years would be more than enough for me."

The man, standing nearby, overhears this and says excitedly, "I will take it! I will take those extra ten years."

"All right," says God. "You got it." He then turns to the lion. "I'm going to give you twenty years of good sex life."

The lion replies, "You know, God, I really think I would be happier with just ten."

The man starts hopping up and down. "I will take them! I will take the other ten years!"

"You can have them," says God to the man.

He turns to the donkey and says, "Now, I am going to give you twenty years of a good sex life. Is that all right with you?"

"To tell you the truth," says the donkey, "I would also be satisfied with just ten." God gives the man the other ten years too.

This story explains why a man has ten years of a good sex life, ten years of monkeying around, ten years of lyin' about it, and then ten years of making an ass out of himself.

We are not satisfied with anything, and we go on asking for more, and we go on making our life more of a confusion.

It is true in every dimension of life – even when you start meditating, you are the same man, with the same mind. Your whole life you have been creating false, pseudo, dishonest, inauthentic experiences. You know perfectly well that they are not true, but at least you can deceive others.

But you don't know a simple law: if you can deceive many people, you will be deceived in turn. By their being deceived, you will start thinking there must be something in it; otherwise, so many people cannot be deceived. Start by telling a lie and by the evening – when your wife will tell it to you – it will have gone around the city. You know perfectly well: you started it in the morning. But if the whole city is agog about it, then perhaps there is something in it!

Such is the madness of man that he can

believe even in his own lies, and can believe so totally that you cannot suspect.

One man played the role of Abraham Lincoln for one year continuously. One hundred years had passed since Abraham Lincoln was assassinated, and in his honor and in his memory, a whole year was devoted to celebrate it. A drama was prepared and all over America, a great search was made to find a man who could play the part of Abraham Lincoln. Strangely enough, they managed to find a man who looked like Abraham Lincoln – the same height, the same weight.

They trained him…because Abraham Lincoln used to stutter a little, so they trained him to stutter. One of Abraham Lincoln's legs was a little longer than the other, so they put the poor fellow on a traction machine and pulled one leg a little longer so he started walking like Abraham Lincoln, with a walking-stick in his hand.

For one year, morning, afternoon, evening, three times a day, he was playing the role. And he was doing it so perfectly that people were amazed: it seemed as if Abraham Lincoln had come back. One year is a long time. He became more and more perfect, and when the year ended, he was awarded a first prize.

He came home, but he continued to stutter. His wife said, "Now, there is no need to stutter."

He said, "No need? What do you mean by no need? Abraham Lincoln has to stutter."

The wife said, "Whom are you trying to befool?"

First, they thought that he was just joking, but then the joke went on so long…he would walk like Abraham Lincoln, he will talk like Abraham Lincoln. He would behave as if he were the president. Finally, they thought, "He has gone crazy. He believes it. Three hundred sixty-five days, three times every day, going through the same role…."

At that very time, scientists had discovered the lie detector machine. You stand on the machine – you don't know; it is hidden underneath the ground – and they ask you a few questions: a clock is hanging in front of you on the wall and they ask, "What time is it on the clock?" You cannot lie, you say, "It is ten o'clock" or "twelve o'clock." And the machine goes on marking whether you are right or wrong. They go on asking a few more questions: "How many people are here?" Now, how can you lie? Four persons are there, so you say "four" and the machine makes the point again – "right." So four or five questions are asked about which you cannot lie. And then they asked him, "Are you Abraham Lincoln?"

And he was tired. His family was after him, his friends were after him, he was being taken to this psychologist to that psychologist.…

And finally he had decided to drop this idea, to just accept what these idiots are saying. Although he *is* Abraham Lincoln, what to do? If nobody is ready to believe it, how long can he argue with these people? So when they asked, "Are you Abraham Lincoln?" he said, "No."

And the machine said, "He is lying!" Because deep in his heart, he knew perfectly well – and the machine functions according to the heart. When you lie, your heartbeat loses its symmetry. When you say something true, the heartbeat goes on in the same rhythm, but when you lie, just a little jerk – and the machine catches that jerk.

And the poor man was saying, "I am not Abraham Lincoln" and the machine is saying he is! When the result came out, the scientist said, "Now, there is no way. Unless he gets assassinated, he will not understand."

Don't believe in this joy and in this peace that you are feeling. And don't think that it is witnessing. It is not.

I give you the criterion: in witnessing, there is

nothing to witness. That is a simple criterion: as long as there is something to witness, witnessing has not come in.

When there is nothing to witness and only a pure awareness remains, just the mirror, not reflecting anything, you have found yourself. Of course this finding will radiate joy, but it will not be your experience. *Others* will experience it; to you, it will be just like breathing, just natural. You will be in constant ecstasy, but others will feel it.

You will radiate a new presence, a new charisma, but others will feel it.

To you, it will be just like you accept your body, you accept your eyes, you accept your hair, you accept your hands; there is nothing special about it.

The moment joy is no more anything special, the moment peace is no more anything to brag about, the moment ecstasy is just like breathing – you have arrived home.

Beloved Bhagwan,

Today, I had a unique experience.
After siesta, I felt myself begin waking up.
I opened my eyes and next to my head I saw my hand.
I got my watch to look at the time but the watch was dark:
there was no time.
I turned the watch towards the window's light but – darkness again.
I stood up and I felt the floor under my feet.
But suddenly I saw my hand, unmovable, next to my head.
I got scared. But immediately a voice inside told me,
"You are dreaming, with open eyes!"
I relaxed and decided to continue the game; looking
at my hand, I could see my whole body moving.
At the end, my hand was always at the same position.
Then I decided to wake up and I moved my hand and my whole body.
I think I experienced something of death.
Would You please comment?
If it happens again, can You suggest something for me to do?

Bodhi Anand, it was nothing but a nightmare – not an experience, special and unique. Neither was it anything to do with death. It was just your mind.

Everybody has experienced nightmares, dreams which are insane. But what happens more often is that you don't remember them. In eight hours of sleep, you dream six hours, but you don't remember six hours of dreaming. You remember only the last dream, when you are half awake and half asleep, just coming out of sleep. Your memory starts functioning and you catch hold of the last dream that is fleeting by.

If a nightmare happens in the morning hours, then there is a possibility that you may remember it. If it happens in the middle of the night, you will not remember it – unless it is really a nightmare; something like the concentration camps of Adolf Hitler, or the gas chambers of the second world war. If it is too dangerous, then it can wake you up – just the very danger of it. But it has nothing to do with death.

It is just your mind which goes on collecting a thousand and one things, unnecessarily. It is a junkyard. You have seen a film in which there are dangerous scenes, you have read a novel in which there are murders and rapes and all kinds of crimes. You have been reading the newspaper every day. All this goes on collecting inside your mind, and in your sleep time, the mind wants to unload itself. Your dreams are nothing but an unloading of the mind.

If you don't collect unnecessary junk, you won't have dreams.

I have not dreamt for years, and not to dream gives a different quality to your sleep. It is light and very sweet, almost musical, a poetry without any words, a meditation of immense silence and serenity.

But your dreams say much about you. This kind of dream shows that you are collecting unnecessary information, and all that gets jumbled, piled up. And your unconscious is not very reasonable, it knows nothing of reason, so everything gets mixed up. These mixtures create nightmares.

It happened that Charles Darwin had become very old and his friend thought, "Perhaps this birthday is going to be his last; we will not be able to celebrate his next birthday." He was feeling weak and doctors were saying that he could not last long. So all his students and all his friends gathered. And he was one of the most respected men of his times; he had given the theory of evolution which had helped humanity in many ways to grow.

Children he loved very much, and the children of the whole neighborhood were thinking what to present him on his birthday. Finally, they decided on a novel idea....

Charles Darwin's whole life was in studying animals, insects, birds, and he had gone around the world to study all kinds of species and how they have evolved up to man. He wanted to know each step. So the small children of his neighborhood, who were his friends, made a very beautiful present: they collected as many insects as they could find in his garden and they cut those insects – some insect's head, some other insect's body, some other insect's legs, some other insect's other parts – many insects they cut and glued them into one, new insect. They did a really good job, and on the birthday when all his great scientist friends were there, they also came with their present and they said, "We would like to know to what species this insect belongs."

Charles Darwin looked at it. In his whole life, he had never seen such a thing. He remembered that he had seen the the head...he had seen the body...but not with this head. He had seen the legs, but not with this body.

But he was a genius. He said to the children, "Yes, I know this insect. Its name is humbug."

Your mind creates many humbugs – a head from somewhere, a body from somewhere, legs from somewhere else, a tail from somewhere else. And then you have a ready-made nightmare. This is not what you are thinking – a "unique experience" – it is simply a humbug experience. And there is no need to be worried about such experiences. They are just dreams, soap bubbles.

But it is good to understand one's mind, that you have made it just a wastepaper basket. You go on throwing into it anything. You never think, "Is this novel worth reading? Is this film worth seeing?"

Whatever you see is going to be collected in your memory. You are not very intelligent about what kind of information should be allowed to enter into your mind. That information is going to make your dreams; it can even affect your actions.

I have been reading data that in California, whenever there is a football match or a boxing match, crime rates rise up to fourteen percent higher, immediately. It takes seven days for them to come back down slowly to the average. And what kinds of crime rates? – murders, suicides, rapes. And not only young people but even children, seeing the boxing or seeing the football match, are getting a certain feedback and they start behaving in the same way.

And in fact you cannot make a successful film without murders, without racing cars at a dangerous speed, without suicides, without rapes. If you make a film without all these things, nobody is going to see it, it is going to be a flop. If you want it to be a full-house success, then make it as criminal, as ugly as possible. But you don't know that you are feeding all that to the people who are seeing it.

And there are special blue films for rich people who can afford a theater in their own house and can invite their friends to see sex orgies, perverted sexual scenes, pornography. But a simple thing is not understood: that all this is going inside your brain. You are poisoning yourself: your dreams will reflect it, your actions will reflect it. Your life will be molded by what you collect in your memory.

So if you come across such dreams, it is an indication that you have to be more careful of what goes in your mind, because it will come out in some way or other. In fact, its coming out through dreams is the most harmless way, because it does not harm anybody. But it can come out through your actions, too.

Stopping to pay a call on some of his suburban flock, the priest discovered they were having a party and offered to come back at a more convenient time.

"Don't go," implored the host, "we are playing a game you might like. We blindfold the women and then they try to guess the identity of the men by feeling their genitals."

"How dare you suggest such a thing to a man of my dignity and stature!" roared the priest.

"You might as well play," said the host, "your name has been guessed three times already."

You are living in a society which is one thing from the outside and just totally different from inside. This is not just a joke. These kinds of games have been happening down the ages, but they were happening only at the highest level of society – the super-rich, the kings, the priests. They have a beautiful facade to show to the world. They will teach morality and they will teach everything against obscenity, pornography, but in their own life, hidden behind the curtains, totally different things are happening.

It is a very hypocritical world. In this world, to be interested in truth, to be interested in the search of your own being, should be conceived of as already a great blessing. A Sufi saying is that before you choose God, God chooses you. Before you begin to search for him, he has already started searching for you; you are always number two.

Even in this country which is poorest of the

poor, there are ugly films, obscene films, pornographic magazines – and they all exist because all the religions go on insisting on repression. So everybody goes to the temple, to the mosque, to the church to pay respect to God – but in his heart, in his mind, there is all kinds of crap.

If he is a little intelligent, he should not enter any temple, because he is carrying such crap inside him that he should not think himself worthy. He should just be outside the temple.

The country may be poor; people cannot afford to eat, but still they will go to see the film. Hungry – but they cannot miss the film and its sexuality, its sensuality. And if you look into their dreams, you will find all that they have repressed, all that they have collected.

Ronald Reagan comes to God and says, "Tell me, God, how many years before my people will be happy?"

"Fifty years," God replies.

Reagan weeps and leaves.

Thatcher comes to God and asks, "Tell me God, how many years before my people are happy?"

"A hundred years," replies God.

Thatcher weeps and leaves.

Rajiv Gandhi comes to God and says, "Tell me God, how many years before my people will be happy?"

God weeps and leaves.

Okay, Vimal?

Yes, Bhagwan.

Session 25

The Watcher Is Always in the Now

Don't be serious;
meditation is not a serious affair.
Don't try to be a saint;
meditation has nothing to do with pious egoism.
Meditation is as simple as these trees growing,
these birds singing.

March 25th, 1987
Morning

Beloved Bhagwan,

There is confusion in me that keeps coming again and again.
The message I have got from You more and more
is to relax with myself, to watch and wait,
but I also feel this urgency to wake up now;
and then another part screams, "But how?"
What do I need to do?
Do I need to 'push' myself through this wall?
Could You make this clear to me?

Masti, *mind* is confusion; it is not that *you* are in confusion. And there is no way for the mind to be not in confusion. Mind's whole structure is based on confusion.

Mind is a duality; it is always split. There is no single point on which the mind agrees in totality. Half of the mind will agree and half of the mind will disagree, and whatever you choose, you are choosing only the half. The remaining half is going to take revenge. The unchosen part, the left over, will wait for its chance to show you that whatever you have chosen is wrong. But it does not matter which part you choose.

Choice itself is wrong.

So the first thing to be understood is that there is no mind which has ever been without confusion.

One very learned American rabbi, Joshua Liebman, has written a book, *Peace of Mind*. It is one of the best-sellers: Liebman is a good writer, and the book is well presented.

I wrote him a letter, asking, "Have you ever considered that peace of mind has never existed? Peace of mind is intrinsically impossible. Peace happens only when mind is not. It is not peace of mind; it is peace beyond mind."

It is almost like a lotus flower: it grows in mud and water; it is a miracle of nature that out of dirty mud and water it brings out one of the most beautiful flowers in existence. But mud and water are not the lotus flower. The lotus flower blossoms only when the lotus plant has gone beyond the mud, beyond the water, has transcended both – then it opens up to the sun, to the sky, and releases its fragrance to the wind. Although it comes from the mud, it is not mud anymore. It is transcendence.

The same is true about peace. Mind is muddy;

all kinds of relevant and irrelevant thoughts are jumbled there. It is a crowd, with so many fragments fighting with each other that you can call it a battleground. Mind cannot be at peace. But you can go beyond mind because you are not the mind. You can transcend and become a lotus flower. And then there is peace, there is beauty, there is bliss, and all that you have always dreamt about but have had no experience of.

I will read your question: "There is a confusion in me that keeps coming again and again." Unless you resolve it, it does not have to come, it is *always* there. It is only that whenever you are unoccupied, it surfaces. It does not go and come, it is embedded in your mind.

"The message I have got from You more and more is to relax with myself, to watch and wait." The message remains the same, because that is the only way to transcend the mind. The watcher is always above the mind. The watcher is never part of the mind.

The mind is just like a TV screen on which thoughts, dreams, imaginations, projections, desires, and a thousand and one things go on passing. The watcher is not on the screen, he is sitting in the movie hall. But the problem arises when the watcher becomes identified with something on the movie screen.

You must have seen yourself sometimes crying, sometimes laughing, sometimes becoming sad…and you know perfectly well that there is nothing on the screen. It is empty, and all that you are seeing is only a projection, just a film being projected through light.

I have heard that when for the first time the silent movies came into existence, the first show happened in London, and a man watched the movie in the matinee showing. Everybody left, but he remained. The manager came to him and said, "The show is over."

He said, "I want to see the second show also." The manager said, "What is the point? You have seen it."

He said, "It is none of your business. This is the money for the ticket. I am not going to leave."

He saw the second show, and the manager was thinking, "What happens after the second show?" He came back again; the crowd had gone, but the man was still there, because there was still a third show. The manager said, "Do you want to see the third show also?" He said, "Yes. This is the money."

The manager said, "But you have seen it twice!" He said, "You don't understand a thing. There is a scene in which a beautiful woman is undressing. She is just about to become nude and jump into a beautiful lake to swim. At that very moment a train passes by, and that train becomes a curtain, and when the train has gone, the woman is already in the water."

The manager said, "But I still don't understand the point."

The man said, "The point is, the train is going to be late sometime!"

Now the projected film has taken on a reality in his mind. He has become identified; it is no longer a film, he is part of it. He is not waiting, he is not watching; he is participating.

It happened that one of India's very learned men, Ishwar Chandra Vidyasagar was invited to inaugurate a drama. He inaugurated the drama, and of course he was sitting in front.

In the drama there is a character – a very cunning man, ugly and disgusting – who is after a beautiful woman, harassing her in every possible way. And one day he finds the woman alone, passing on a path that moves through a thick forest. He takes the opportunity, catches hold of the woman – he wants to rape her. This was too much: Vidyasagar completely forgot that it was a drama. He jumped on the stage, took out one of his shoes, and started beating the poor character, the actor!

But the actor proved to be far wiser than Vidyasagar. He took the shoe in his hands with great respect, touched the shoe to his head, and told Vidyasagar, "This is my greatest prize. I have been winning many prizes in my life, but this is my greatest prize. I could have never believed that a man of your understanding should take a drama as if it were real."

Vidyasagar woke up as if from a sleep. He said, "I am sorry, but I went on becoming hotter and hotter, and when I saw that you were going to rape the woman I could not resist the temptation to prevent you. It was my moral duty, and I completely forgot that this is not a real rape, it is just acting."

I have seen the shoe. In the family of that actor, they are keeping it in a beautiful glass box. It has become a historical thing. Now it must be the fourth or fifth generation, but they say, "This is our most prized treasure. One of our forefathers received this award from the hands of Vidyasagar himself." And certainly this proves that the man was a perfect actor: he created the situation such that Vidyasagar became identified and forgot it was just a drama and he was there to watch it, not to participate in it.

This is happening continuously in your mind. The whole confusion is that you jump into the drama of the mind, which is just a screen.

I have been telling you again and again just to watch. Every drama has its end, and no thought in the mind remains for long. If you can keep alert not to become a victim of your thoughts, soon less and less thoughts will be moving on the screen. And when the watching becomes perfect, the screen becomes empty. When you are ready to witness, there is nothing to witness.

It is your identification with thoughts that is creating the confusion: it brings you down into the mind; otherwise your watcher is far above it. And to get centered in your watching is the only way for peace.

There is no such thing as peace of mind.

There is only one peace, and that is when there is no mind. When there is only a watcher and nothing to watch, suddenly everything becomes calm and quiet.

Hence I repeat again, Masti: relax, watch, and wait patiently. But you are saying, "I also feel this urgency to wake up now." That's what I mean by jumping into the drama and becoming a participant. The watcher is always in the now. The watcher knows no other tense – neither past nor future, but only the present.

Only this moment is all for the watcher. It is the imagination that needs future, it is memory that needs past, but the watcher is neither imagination nor memory. It is always in the now.

And your urgency is simply another name for impatience. You are hiding your impatience behind a beautiful word, urgency. What urgency is there?

You cannot force things to happen before their time. The spring will come and the flowers will blossom, but you cannot force the spring. The rain will come, the clouds will cover the sky, the whole thirst of the earth will be gone – but you cannot force it, you have to be patient.

And this is the beauty, that the more patient you are, the quicker is the coming of the spring. If you can be absolutely patient, this very moment spring can come.

Your urgency is creating a trouble for you because it is making you more and more confused, more and more restless, in a hurry. I can understand; the whole Western tradition has taught you only one thing, and that is speed.

I have heard about a pilot who was a lover of flying. He had taken his girlfriend for a flight, and he was going at full speed, maximum. The girl was a little afraid. Finally she asked, "Where are we going?"

The pilot said, "Don't ask unnecessary questions. The real question is, we are going at full speed. Who cares where we are going? The going in itself is so good."

The speed has become such a problem because for centuries in the West the mind has been conditioned to do things quickly: "Don't be lazy, be efficient." But all this has created a turmoil in the mind.

Everybody is trying to become rich as quickly as possible, and naturally if you want to be rich quickly you have to find some immoral means – maybe heroin money. All the Western religious leaders are against drugs, but they don't understand that the idea of speed, that everybody has to be fast enough...and millions are competing for the same place; naturally there is competition, there is jealousy, there is violence. It does not matter, means don't matter; the end is to reach quickly – either to a powerful position, or to become world famous, or to have all the riches possible.

But these trees don't grow impatiently. They move with a grace, with patience, with trust. There is no hurry anywhere else except in your mind. If you really want to be in a state of peace and joy, you will have to unlearn your old habit for achieving things quickly, fast.

Just the other day I was informed that in Japan, they have invented a train that moves four hundred miles per hour. Up to now the record was two hundred fifty miles per hour; they have broken all records. And because the train moves four hundred miles per hour the very speed of the train creates a cushion of air, and raises the train above its rails one foot. It is no longer on the rails. It is very comfortable because it is moving in the air, almost like an airplane, just one foot above the earth.

And they forgot completely that Japan is such a small country. They have recognized it only *now*, and for years they have been inventing the train. Now they have recognized – where are we going? – because the country is so small that you can have at the most two stations: one from where the train begins and the other where it stops. So the train is now ready, but the land is not big enough to use it! But one wonders...for years they have been working and they never thought about the fact that four hundred miles in Japan is absurd. Japan consists of two small islands. Where will you be going with such speed?

You are saying, "And then another part screams, 'but how?'" Urgency naturally creates the question: "How?" If speed is needed, then the technology is needed. "How" means technology.

Meditation is not a by-product of any technology. It does not need any technology.

It does not need any "how."

It simply needs *now*.

And in meditation you are not going anywhere. You are simply being here, relaxed, utterly centered in yourself. Everything stops. For this, no "how" is needed.

But because one question leads to another question, urgency creates the question "how," and then the question comes: "What do I need to do? Do I need to push myself through this wall?"

There is no wall!

These are our unconscious confusions. Somehow we make them appear rational.

One drunkard reached his home one night. His wife was tired – every day a fight in the middle of the night, and the whole neighborhood was complaining. The man was not going to change.

So she had given him the keys, saying, "Don't wake me up and don't create any noise, because the neighbors are getting very angry. They want to throw us out. So silently open the door and go to your bed."

He came in the middle of the night, absolutely drunk. His hands were shaking, so he was holding the key, but to put the key in the lock was a problem. He kept missing the target. He said, "This is strange. This has never happened; certainly there must be an earthquake, the whole house is in such trembling state."

Rather than looking at his own hands, rather than remembering his own drunkenness, the whole earth is having a great earthquake and the house is moving – that's why the lock is moving.

A policeman was watching him from the street. He laughed. He came and he said, "Can I help you?" The man said, "It would be great of you if you could help me. Just hold the house for a moment so that I can put this key into the lock."

The policeman said, "It is better that you give me the key and I will open the lock." There was no need to argue with him that the house is not shaking, that there is no earthquake happening, that it is simply that you are absolutely unconscious.

The man entered the house very cautiously because the wife has said.... And whenever a drunkard comes close to his wife, half of his drunkenness is gone. The wife is such a cure...nothing else works, but the closeness of the wife is enough.

She was snoring in her room. He remembered what she had said: "Don't create any noise." So silently he went into the bathroom, but he was very much puzzled because his whole face was scratched. There was blood oozing from a few places.

Then he remembered that on the way home he had been fighting with another drunkard. So he tried to find some ointment to put on his face; otherwise the wife in the morning will create trouble for him. So very carefully and silently, he put the ointment on every scratch. He was very satisfied, and went silently to bed.

In the morning the wife screamed from the bathroom, "Who has spoiled my mirror, and destroyed my ointment too? Who has painted the mirror with the ointment?"

He said, "My god...." He had thought he was putting the ointment on his face, but he was putting it on the reflection of his face; he was putting it on the mirror.

The unconscious mind goes on doing things and creating problems. There is no wall at all that you have to push through. The real thing is that you want to push, you are in a hurry. And because you want to push, you have to imagine a wall. It is your imagination.

Just try to laugh at your imagination, at your hurry, because this is not the way meditation happens. Laugh, relax, and just be in the moment – watching whatever is going on, outside or inside, in the world or in the mind. You are neither the world nor the mind. You are behind all, just a pure watching consciousness.

You are asking me, "Could you make this clear to me?" There is nothing to be made clear. Only one thing is harassing you: your own idea of achieving things as quickly as possible. But meditation is not to be achieved; it is already there. It has only to be discovered. And discovery needs only one thing: a silent watcher – just for your laughter, so that you can relax.

Don't be serious; meditation is not a serious affair. Don't try to be a saint; meditation has nothing to do with pious egoism. Meditation is as simple as these trees growing, these birds singing.

One night in Washington, when Nixon was

president, there was a heavy snowfall. When the president woke up in the morning, he looked out of the window and saw a beautiful blanket of snow covering the White House lawn. He snapped out of his beautiful reverie when he noticed, written on the lawn in yellow snow, "Dick Nixon is an asshole."

The president got very angry and summoned the FBI and CIA. "I want that urine to be analyzed," he ordered them. "And I want to find out who the culprit is right now, without delay! This is top priority!"

Early in the afternoon a representative of the two agencies reported back to Nixon. He said, "We have tested the urine and we know whose it is. However, there is some good news and some bad news; which would you like first?"

"Oh no," said Nixon. "Guess you had better give me the good news first."

"Well, sir," said the man. "We analyzed the urine, and it is Henry Kissinger's."

"Oh no," cried Nixon, and then suddenly the realization hit him. "That's the *good* news? What could the bad news possibly be?"

The man answered him, "It was in your wife's handwriting."

Beloved Bhagwan,

Please could You talk about
the subtle differences between instinct and intuition?

Yogeshwar, your individuality can be divided – just for the purpose of understanding it; otherwise there is no division. It is one single unity, whole: the head, the heart, and the being.

Intellect is the functioning of the head, instinct is the functioning of your body, intuition is the functioning of your heart. And behind these three is your being, whose only quality is witnessing.

The head only thinks; hence it never comes to any conclusion. It is verbal, linguistic, logical, but because it has no roots in reality, thousands of years of philosophical thinking have not given us a single conclusion. Philosophy has been the greatest exercise in futility.

Intellect is very clever in creating questions and then creating answers, and then out of those answers, more questions and more answers. It can make palaces of words, systems of theories, but they are all just hot air.

The body cannot rely on your intellect, because the body has to live. That's why all essential functions of the body are in the hands of instinct – for example breathing, heartbeat, digestion of your food, circulation of the blood – a thousand and one processes are going on inside your body in which you have no part at all. And it is good that nature has given the body its own wisdom. Otherwise, if your intellect were to take care of the body, life would have been impossible. Because sometimes you may forget to breathe – at least in the night, how will you breathe while you are asleep?

You are already so confused just with

thoughts; in this confusion, who will take care about the blood circulation – whether the right amount of oxygen is reaching to your cells or not? Whether the food that you are eating is being analyzed into its basic constituents, and those basic constituents are sent where they are needed? Something is needed by your bones, it goes to the bones; something is needed by your brain, it goes to the brain; something is needed by your skin, it goes to the skin. And continuously, twenty-four hours, dead cells have to be removed; otherwise they will block the passage of blood circulation.

You may never have thought about it; when you cut your hair, why don't you feel pain? Cut your fingers and you will feel pain. Hairs are also part of your body, just as your fingers, but why don't you feel any pain when cutting your hair? Hairs are the dead cells of the body; that's why you don't feel hurt. Nails are also made of dead cells of the body; that's why you can cut them. And this whole, tremendous amount of work is done by instinct. You are not needed. You can remain in a coma; still the body will continue to work.

I have seen one woman who was in a coma for nine months. The doctors had said that she would never revive, and even if she did reveive, she would not be a human being, because such a long period of unconsciousness destroys the very delicate nervous system that makes you a human being, that gives you intelligence. So she would be just a vegetable. But her body was functioning perfectly well. Her intellect had disappeared, her consciousness had not been there for nine months, but her body was perfectly well; there was no disease in the body.

Nature has left all essential functions of your body to instinct. And it has left all that makes your life meaningful – because just to exist, just to survive, has no meaning...to give meaning to your life, existence has given to your heart, intuition. Out of your intuition is the possibility of art, of aesthetics, of love, of friendship – all kinds of creativity is intuitive.

But the marketplace does not need your intuition. It does not deal in love, in your sensibility; it deals with very solid and mundane things. For that, your intellect, which is the most superficial part, functions. Intellect is for the mundane life with others in the marketplace, in the world, to make you capable of functioning. It is mathematics, it is geography, it is history, it is chemistry. All science and all technology is created by your intellect.

Your logic, your geometry, are useful, but the intellect is blind. It simply goes on creating things, but it does not know whether they are being used for destruction or for creation. The nuclear war will be a war created by intellect.

Intellect has its use, but by some misfortune it has become the master of your whole being. That has created immense troubles in the world.

The master is hidden behind these three: the body, the mind, the heart. The master is hidden behind all these three – that is your being. But you never go inwards; all your roads go outwards, all your senses go outwards. All your achievements are there in the world.

Only very few people in the world have traveled the path towards their being, towards their very center. When I insist that you should be only a watcher, only a witness, I am trying to bring you closer to your own being, because that is your life source – and a life source which is eternal and immortal. Knowing it, all fears disappear, because even death disappears.

Knowing it, you know the very heartbeat of existence.

Knowing it, you have known all that is worth

knowing, and you have achieved all that is worth achieving. It opens doors to all the mysteries of existence, to all the treasures of existence which belong to you.

Outside you are simply a beggar. Even your greatest intellectuals are just playing with words.

The father of Western logic, Aristotle, has written in his books on logic that women have one tooth less than men. That was traditionally thought to be true for thousands of years in Greece, because a woman cannot be equal in any way – how can she have the same number of teeth as man? And Aristotle – who is the father of logic – had two wives, not only one. He could have simply told Mrs. Aristotle Number One or Number Two, "Open your mouth, I want to count your teeth." But philosophers are not experimental. He has written that women have one tooth less than men. They have to have less of everything than men.

Intellect is useful in the world, and all your educational systems are techniques to avoid the heart and take your energy directly to your head. The heart can create troubles for the head. The heart knows nothing of logic. The heart has a totally different center of functioning, and that is intuition. It knows love, but love is not a commodity of any use in the world. It knows beauty, but what are you going to do with beauty in the marketplace?

The people of the heart – the painters, the poets, the musicians, the dancers, the actors – are all irrational. They create great beauty, they are great lovers, but they are absolutely unfit in a society which is arranged by the head. Your artists are thought by your society to be almost outcast, a little bit crazy, an insane type of people. Nobody wants their children to become musicians or painters or dancers. They all want them to be doctors, engineers, scientists, because those professions pay. Painting, poetry, dance, are dangerous, risky: you may end up just a beggar on the street, playing on your flute.

The heart has been denied, and by the way, it will be useful to remember: the denial of the heart has been the denial of the woman, and unless the heart is accepted, the woman cannot be accepted. Unless the heart has the same opportunity to grow as the head, the woman cannot have liberation. The woman is heart and the man is head. The distinction is clear.

Instinct, nature has taken in its own hands, and whenever you interfere with instinct you create perversions. All the religions have been doing that. For example, celibacy is interfering with the body and its instinct; then there will be homosexuality, lesbianism, all kinds of perversions. But every religion has been interfering with the body – and the body is absolutely innocent; it has never done anything wrong.

If you accept the body in its absolute naturalness, it will help you tremendously. It will help your heart, nourish your heart. It will help your intelligence to become sharper, because the nourishment for the intellect comes from the body. Nourishment to the heart comes from the body. And if your head, your heart and your body are all in a symphony, then to find your being is the easiest thing in the world. But because they are in conflict, your whole life goes on being wasted in that conflict, conflict between instinct and intellect and intuition.

A wise man is one who creates a harmony between head, heart, and body. In this harmony one comes to the revelation of the source of one's life, the very center, the soul. And that is the greatest ecstasy possible – not only to human beings but in this whole universe, nothing more is possible. It is already too much.

I am not against anything. I am only against disharmony, and because your head is creating the most inharmonious situation, I want your head to be put in its right place. It is a servant, not a master. As a servant it is great, very helpful.

A Dublin milkman has just finished his delivery, so he parks his horse and cart outside the pub and goes in for a drink. Refreshed after an hour, he comes out to find his horse painted bright green. Very angry, he strides back into the pub and demands, "Which of you just painted my horse green?"

A seven foot Irish giant stood up and, towering over him, said, "I did. Want to do something about it?"

The milkman gave a sickly grin and said, "I just came in to tell you, the first coat is dry!"

Intellect is helpful. There are situations where you will be in need of intellect – but only as a servant, not as a master.

Two psychiatrists who are friends happen to run into each other on the street one day. One of them says to the other, "You are fine, how am I doing?"

Intellect can be helpful, but it needs consciousness to be its master; otherwise it can behave in a very stupid way. It can misunderstand things, it can misrepresent things. It needs a master to guide it, to give it a sense of direction. That master is your being.

Valerie, a twenty-three-year-old typist, walked along the beach, despondent. She was flat-chested, and felt totally distraught watching the other big-bosomed girls on the beach surrounded by eligible men. As Valerie strolled on the sand her toe kicked a small bottle. She picked it up and removed the cork, and out popped a genie. "Who are you?" asked the frightened girl.

"I am a genie, and because you were kind enough to give me my freedom, I will grant you any wish you make."

"Oh, that's wonderful," declared Valerie. "I would like the two biggest boobs in the world."

The genie snapped his fingers and there appeared Jimmy Carter and Ronald Reagan.

Okay, Vimal?

Yes, Bhagwan.

Session 26

Life's Aim Is Life Itself

Life is not a static phenomenon.
It is a flux, a riverlike flux;
it needs constant change.
It needs moment-to-moment awareness;
otherwise you will be left behind.
Not to be left behind is one of the most important steps
for the growth of intelligence.

March 25, 1987
Evening

Beloved Bhagwan,

What is the aim of life?

Anwar Aman, life has no aim other than itself, because life is another name for God himself. Everything else in the world can have an aim, can be a means to an end, but at least one thing you have to leave as the end of all but the means of none.

You can call it existence.
You can call it God.
You can call it life.

These are different names of a single reality.

God is the name given to life by the theologians and it has a danger in it because it can be refuted; it can be argued against. Almost half of the earth does not believe in any God. Not only the communists, but the Buddhists, the Jainas and there are thousands of free thinkers who are atheists. The name "God" is not very defensible because it is given by man and there is no evidence, no proof, no argument for it. It remains more or less an empty word. It means whatever you want it to mean.

"Existence" is better. All the great thinkers of this century are existentialists. They have dropped the word "God" completely. Existence in itself is enough for them.

But to me, just as "God" is one extreme, so is "existence" another extreme, because in the word "existence" there is no indication that it may be alive – it may be dead. There is no indication that it is intelligent – there may be no intelligence. There is no indication that it is conscious – it may not have any consciousness.

Hence, my choice is "life." Life contains everything that is needed; moreover, it needs no proof. You are life. You are the proof. You are the argument. You cannot deny life; hence in the whole history of man, there has not been a single thinker who has denied life.

Millions have denied God, but how can you deny life? It is beating in your heart, it is in your breathing, it is showing in your eyes. It is expressing in your love. It is celebrating in a thousand and one ways – in the trees, in the birds, in the mountains, in the rivers.

Life is the aim of everything. Hence, life cannot have an aim other than itself. To say it in other words: life's aim is intrinsic. It has it within itself to grow, to expand, to celebrate, to dance, to love, to enjoy – these are all aspects of life.

But up to now, no religion has accepted life as the aim of all our efforts, of all our endeavors. On the contrary, religions have been denying life and supporting a hypothetical God. But life is so real that thousands of years of all the religions have not been able even to make a dent in it, although they have all been anti-life. Their God was not the innermost center of life, their God was to be found only in renouncing life. It has been a very great calamity humanity has passed through: the very idea of renouncing life means respecting death.

All your religions are worshipers of death. It is not a coincidence that you worship only the dead saints. When they are alive, you crucify them. When they are alive, you stone them to death. When they are alive, you poison them and when they are dead, you worship them – a sudden change happens. Your whole attitude changes.

Nobody has gone deep into the psychology of this change. It is worth contemplating: Why are the dead saints worshiped and the living ones condemned? Because the dead saints fulfill all the conditions of being religious: they don't laugh, they don't enjoy, they don't love, they don't dance, they don't have any kind of relationship with existence. They have really renounced life in its totality: they don't breathe, their hearts no longer beat. Now they are perfectly religious!

They cannot commit a sin. One thing is certain – you can depend on them, you can rely on them.

A living saint is not so reliable. Tomorrow he may change his mind. Saints have become sinners, sinners have become saints – so until they are dead, nothing can be said about them with absolute certainty. That is one of the basic reasons that in your temples, in your churches, in your mosques, in your gurudwaras, in your synagogues...whom are you worshiping? And you don't see the stupidity of it all, that the living are worshiping the dead. The present is worshiping the past.

Life is being forced to worship death. It is because of these anti-life religions that the question has arisen again and again down the ages: What is the aim of life?

According to your religions, the aim of life is to renounce it, to destroy it, to torture yourself in the name of some mythological, some hypothetical God.

Animals don't have any religion, except life; trees don't have any religion except life; stars don't have any religion except life. Except man, the whole existence trusts only in life; there is no other God and there is no other temple. There is no holy scripture.

Life is all in all.

It is the god and it is the temple and it is the holy scripture – and to live it totally, wholeheartedly, is the only religion.

I teach you that there is no other aim than to live with such totality that each moment becomes a celebration. The very idea of "aim" brings future into the mind, because any aim, any end, any goal, needs future.

All your goals deprive you of your present, which is the only reality you have. The future is only your imagination, and the past is just footprints left in the sands of your memory. Neither is the past real anymore, nor is the future real yet.

This moment is the only reality.

And to live this moment without any inhibition, without any repression, without any greed for the future, without any fear – without repeating the past again and again, but being absolutely fresh in every moment, fresh and young, unhampered by memories, unhindered by imaginations – you have such purity, such innocence, that only this innocence I call godliness.

To me, God is not someone who created the world. God is someone that *you* create when you live totally, intensely – with all your heart, not holding anything back. When your life becomes simply a moment-to-moment joy, a moment-to-moment dance, when your life is nothing but a festival of lights...every moment is so precious because once it is gone, it is gone forever.

Living for any aim simply means you are not living in the present. Living for any heaven is simply greed. And you are missing the present, you are sacrificing the real that is in your hands, at the feet of some imaginary heaven, for which no proof exists at all.

Or being afraid of hell.... There are thousands of monks – Christians, Hindu, Buddhist, Jaina. They are all living out of fear and greed. It is strange that nobody sees a simple fact – that they are living for greed to enter heaven and to enjoy the heavenly pleasures, and they are living out of fear that they should not commit anything wrong; otherwise they will have to suffer hellfire for eternity. And these monks, to whatever religion they belong, are worshiped by you.

These are sick people, they need psychiatric treatment. They are so full of greed that this life is not enough for them, they need some heaven. And they are so much afraid, so much fear-oriented, that out of their fear they have created all kinds of hell. Of course, heaven is for those who will follow the path that they think is the path of virtue. And hell is for those who will not follow the path of virtue according to them.

And just a little look around, and you will be very much surprised: the Hindu gods are not celibate, and according to Jainism or Buddhism, or Catholic theology, celibacy is the foundation of all virtue. What about Hindu gods? According to Jainism and Buddhism, drinking any alcoholic beverage is a sin, but according to Christians, even on their holy days they drink alcohol. Even Jesus was drinking alcohol.

Not only that, Christians brag that Jesus did many miracles. One of them was turning water into wine. Turning water into wine is a miracle – or, is it a crime? According to Jainism and Buddhism, Jesus is a meat eater, a drinker of wine; he is not following the path of virtue. Even Hindu gods, according to Jainism and Buddhism, are living the ordinary life of a householder. They are not celibate and they have not renounced life; they cannot be accepted as holy.

Just in the last part of the past century, Ramakrishna was worshiped by Hindus almost as a god, but being a Bengali, his food consisted mainly of rice and fish. According to the vegetarians, a man who is eating fish, destroying life for his food, is not even human, what to say about divine?

Looking from the other side, Christians cannot accept Gautam Buddha as a religious person because he never served the poor, he never opened institutions for the orphans like Mother Teresa does. He never opened hospitals for the sick. He was not concerned at all with human misery, poverty, sickness, disease. He was not in the service of God's creation. He was a selfish man, just meditating, just enjoying his own being, just reaching to the higher peaks of consciousness. But his ecstasy is selfish – it is not in the service of those who are suffering.

Mahavira cannot be accepted as a religious man according to Christianity for the same reasons. These are all very selfish people. All meditators are selfish because they are more concerned about their own growth than they are concerned about the blind and the deaf and the dumb.

What is virtue? Who is going to decide? According to Mohammedanism, animals are created by God for man to eat. There is no question of violence; their very purpose is to be nourishment for humanity – so says the holy *Koran*. Now, no Eastern religion can accept Mohammedanism as a religion. Mohammed married nine wives. He was continuously fighting. His whole life was a life of war, although the word that he has for his religion is *Islam* and Islam means "peace." But a strange man – his religion is peace and his whole life is nothing but violence. Even on his sword it was written, "Peace is my religion." He could not find any other place to write it.

What is the path of virtue? No religion has been able to provide it – not even the criterion by which it can be judged.

As far as I am concerned, I say to live joyously, contented, fulfilled, sharing your love, your silence, your peace, letting your life become such a beautiful dance that not only you feel blessed but you can bless the whole world – that is the only authentic path. Life is itself the criterion; everything else is non-essential.

And each individual is so unique that you cannot make a superhighway on which everybody has to travel to find the aim of life. On the contrary, everybody has to find his life without following the crowd, but following his own inner voice; without moving in a mob, but following a small footpath. That too is not created by anybody else. You create it as you walk.

The world of life and consciousness is almost like the sky – birds fly but they don't leave any footprints. As you live deeply, sincerely, honestly, you don't leave any footprints and nobody has to follow you. Everybody has to follow his own, still, small voice.

My emphasis on meditation is so that you can hear your still, small voice – which will give you the guidance, the sense of direction. No scripture can give it to you. No religion, no religious founder can give it to you because they have been giving it to humanity for thousands of years and all their efforts have failed. They have only created retarded people, unintelligent people, because they insisted on believing. The moment you believe in someone, you lose intelligence. Belief is almost like poison to your intelligence.

I say to you not to believe in anyone, including me. You have to find your own insight, and then follow it. Wherever it leads is the right path for you. Whether anybody else is following that the path or not is not the question. Each individual is unique and each individual life has a beauty in its uniqueness.

Anwar Aman, your question is very significant, perhaps the ancientmost question. Man has asked it since the very beginning. And millions of answers have been provided but no answer has been successful. The question still remains. The question is still relevant. That means...Mohammed, Moses, Mahavira, Buddha, Krishna, Rama – what happened to their answers? Their answers have not satisfied anyone. The question bubbles up again and again, and it will continue to bubble up because it cannot be resolved by wrong answers.

And the right answers they could not give,

because they were all anti-life. They were all escapists; they were afraid to live.

My answer is: life's aim is life itself – more life, deeper life, higher life, but life always. There is nothing higher than life.

And a reverence for life is a necessary corollary. If life's aim is life, then reverence for life becomes your religion. Then respect other people's life. Don't interfere in anybody's life, don't try to force somebody to follow a certain path that you think is right. You can follow it, it is your freedom, but never impose it on anybody else.

The world does not need any organized religion. The world certainly needs religious people – neither Hindus, nor Mohammedans, nor Christians – the world simply needs individuals in search of deeper and richer life. Not God, not paradise, not heaven.... And as life becomes infinitely deep, it *is* the paradise; you have entered the kingdom of God. And the doors are within your own heart.

But people are blind, and tradition has been making them more and more blind. Tradition respects blind people, it respects people who don't think, it respects people who never doubt. It respects people who are not skeptical. It wants people to be just obedient machines. Perhaps machines are, according to the traditional mind, the most religious people in the world because they never disobey.

As far as my insight is concerned, a man who is not rebellious cannot be religious – rebellious against the past, rebellious against organized religions, rebellious against all those people who want to dominate you. And they have found subtle ways to dominate you: "Our religion is the most ancient!" So what? That means your religion is the most rotten! But they are trying to make it "most ancient" so that you feel an awe; if for ten thousand years nobody has disobeyed, there must be some truth in it.

Every religion uses the argument that it is very old, very ancient. Religions which are not very old naturally have to try the opposite argument; for example Sikhism, which is only five hundred years old, or Mohammedanism, which is only fourteen hundred years old. Their argument is, that older religions are older versions of God's message to man: "We are bringing the latest message of God to man."

Hazrat Mohammed has said, "There have been other messengers before, but after me there will be no other messenger, because I have brought the final version of the message." Hence he could say, "There is only one God and one holy book, the *Koran*, and one holy messenger, Mohammed. After me, anybody who claims that he has a direct communication with God is committing the greatest sin possible."

It happened in Baghdad once...a man was brought to the Caliph's court in Baghdad. The Caliph is the chief representative of the messenger of God, Hazrat Mohammed. Omar was at that time the Caliph in Baghdad and the man was brought because he was declaring that he had brought an even fresher version than Mohammed.

The Caliph said, "This is unforgivable, but you look so simple and so innocent: I will give you seven days time to think it over, and simultaneously, you will be punished as much as possible so that you come back to your senses. And after seven days, I will come to the prison myself to ask you what you think now." After seven days, he went there. The man was naked, bound to a pillar, and he had been beaten continually for seven days. He had not been allowed to sleep, had not been given anything to eat. They had tortured him as much as possible.

When Caliph Omar asked him, "What do you think now?" he said, "What do I think? When I was sent by God, he warned me: 'Listen, my messengers have always been tortured.' He was right. Your torture has proved that I am the messenger. Now there is no need of Hazrat Mohammed; I have brought the latest message from God."

And at that very moment, from another pillar, another naked man who had been caught one month before, because he had been declaring himself, "I am God" – for one month he had been tortured – he shouted from the other pillar, "Don't believe this cheat! After Mohammed, I have not sent any messenger to the world. This man is a deceiver."

You will think these people are mad but the same kind of people have become the founders of your religions. Perhaps these people were not very articulate, were not very intelligent; otherwise they might have created a new religion. Mahavira, the twenty-fourth *teerthankara* of the Jainas, declares that he is the last teerthankara; now there will be no other teerthankara...

I used to go to Wardha while traveling around India. In Wardha, there used to live a man, Swami Shakti Bhakta. He was a learned man; he was a Jaina, very scholarly. And just joking with him, I told him, "You are so learned that you can easily declare yourself the twenty-fifth teerthankara of the Jainas." He said, "That idea has come many times to my mind too, but Jainas are not going to accept it."

I said, "They never accepted Mahavira easily. There were eight other contenders, and it was a long, drawn out fight, in which Mahavira succeeded in convincing people that he was the twenty-fourth, the other were fake. So it all depends; if you have the ability, you may convince them."

He said, "I have the ability." I said, "Then this is a good chance!" He declared himself the twenty-fifth teerthankara, and the Jainas expelled him. Now he was very angry with me, saying that "You destroyed my reputation!" I said, "I was giving you the greatest respect possible, making you the twenty-fifth." I said, "You should have thought about it, whether you have guts enough. They are not going to accept you so easily, against the statement of Mahavira, that 'After me there is going to be no teerthankara; my message is complete, entirely complete. Nothing can be added, nothing can be edited out; there is no need for the twenty-fifth.' It was on your intelligence, arguments, scholarship that the whole thing depended. I am not to be blamed.

"Just look at it this way: if Jainas came to me and said, 'You are our twenty-fifth teerthankara,' I am not going to accept, because who wants to be twenty-fifth in a line? I am the first, otherwise forget all about it! You were stupid to accept the idea of being twenty-fifth, standing in a queue, the twenty-fifth. The moment you accepted it, that very moment I understood that now you would be in trouble. You cannot blame me.

"And you had told me that this idea had occured to you yourself, many times. It was just that you had not the courage to say it, and because I supported it, you thought at least there is one person.... I said, "I am still ready to support you, but you will have to fight for it."

He said, "But how can I fight? They have expelled me." I said, "That is your business; you tried and you failed."

All these religions have been doing the same: they closed the doors out of fear, because somebody may come afterwards and may change the structure of their religion, of their disciplines. And certainly it needs constant change, because times go on changing. If Mahavira comes today, he himself will find that everything has changed. It was one thing to walk barefooted on mud paths – it is another thing to walk barefooted in the hot summer days in India on coaltar roads.

Jaina monks and nuns all have their feet burned. And what are they doing? They put towels around their feet. Now I said, "This is stupid, because that is a kind of primitive shoe. Why can't you purchase a shoe made of synthetic leather, in which no violence is involved? Or a rubber shoe in which no violence is involved, or a cloth shoe? That's what you are trying to do, and it looks so awkward – towels around the feet, and then binding them with ropes. You look simply stupid." But the trouble is, Mahavira will not allow any change to happen after him.

Life is not a static phenomenon. It is a flux, a riverlike flux; it needs constant change. It needs moment-to-moment awareness; otherwise you will be left behind.

Not to be left behind is one of the most important steps for the growth of intelligence. The whole world is almost retarded, and the people who are responsible for your retardedness are the people you worship. They have stopped thousands of years before and you are still following them. Meanwhile, everything has changed.

Coming home early from work one afternoon, a man found his wife naked in bed, breathing heavily and quite visibly distressed. "Honey, what is the matter?" he asks. "I...I...I don't know," she cried, "I think maybe I am having a heart attack." The husband freaked, and rushed downstairs to call the doctor. He was in the middle of dialing the number when his young daughter rushed in and screamed, "Daddy, Daddy, there is a naked man in the closet!" The distraught husband threw down the phone, rushed up the stairs again and opened the closet door, only to find his best friend inside.

"For Christ's sake, Ed," the man shouted, "my wife is in the bedroom having a heart attack, and you have got to sneak around naked, scaring the kids!"

Only retarded people are left in the world.

At the beginning of World War II, a Nazi officer is forced to share a compartment on a crowded train with a Jew and his family. After ignoring them for a while he says contemptuously, "You Jews are supposed to be so clever: where does this so-called intelligence come from?"

"It is from our diet," says the Jew, "we eat a lot of raw fish heads." Upon which he opens his basket and saying, "Lunchtime!" and proceeds to hand out fish heads to his wife and children. The Nazi, getting excited says, "Wait a minute, I want some!"

"Okay," says the Jew, "I will sell you six for twenty-five dollars."

The Nazi accepts and begins to chew. He almost throws up, but the children shout encouragement, "Suck out the brains, suck out the brains!"

The Nazi is on his fourth head when he says to the Jew, "Is not twenty-five dollars a lot of money for six fish heads, that are usually thrown out as garbage?"

"See?" says the Jew, "It is working already!"

Beloved Bhagwan,

What is intelligence?
Is it a state far beyond the mind and its limits?
A kind of awareness of what the mind is, without belonging to it?
Is meditation connected with intelligence?
And is intelligence a potential that we all have,
and that simply needs to be awakened?
Can we raise our consciousness with intelligence?

Benoit, the question you have asked is of great significance: "What is intelligence? Is it a state far beyond the mind and its limits?" Yes. Intelligence is not of the mind; intelligence is one of the qualities of your being. But mind is being used as a vehicle for it; hence the confusion. People think intelligence is *of* the mind – it comes *through* the mind. Mind is the instrument for its expression.

Mind itself is only a bio-computer. It has a memory system just as any computer has: you feed the memory system and the mind keeps the memory. But memory is not intelligence.

Intelligence is the clear insight into things about which you don't have any information. Memory can function only about those things which are known to you – but life consists of the known, of the unknown, and of the unknowable. As far as the known is concerned, memory is enough.

That's what all your universities and all your educational systems are doing: they are simply feeding your memory with more and more information, and whatever is known to your memory system, you will answer immediately. That answer does not prove that you are intelligent.

Intelligence is known only when you encounter the unknown, about which you don't have any memory, any knowledge, any information beforehand. When you encounter the unknown, that is the point which is decisive. How do you respond? You can respond intelligently or you can respond stupidly.

For example, Germany is one of the countries where the population is decreasing. And the government is worried, because for every three thousand people who leave or die, thirty thousand people are coming from other countries as immigrants into Germany. The government is afraid that just within a decade Germany will not be the land of the Germans. Their population is decreasing and immigrants are entering into the country.

And here in India in 1947, when India became independent, the population of the country was four hundred million – now the population of the country is nine hundred million – five hundred million people is the increase. Even in 1947 the country was poor, and Britain was in a hurry to give freedom to this country because soon Britain would be blamed for the poverty. The prime minister of England, Atlee, had sent Mountbatten to India with an urgent message: "Whatever happens, before 1948 – the deadline is 1948 – you have to give India freedom. Because we can see what is going to happen, and the whole blame will be on our heads – so be quick!"

And Mountbatten did really a quick job. Even before 1948 he gave India freedom – in 1947, one year earlier. Atlee was very happy. And none of the Indian leaders even thought about what was the hurry. In 1942 Britain was not ready to give freedom to India; when India was ready to fight for freedom, Britain was not willing. Britain crushed India's revolution in 1942 within nine days. And not a single Indian leader, including Mahatma Gandhi and Jawaharlal Nehru, could see the point why Britain suddenly became so much interested to give them freedom.

There was no revolution; after 1942 Indian leaders had lost hope, because their revolution had been crushed in nine days. This was the smallest revolution in the whole history of mankind! And then suddenly out of the blue, Britain itself decides.... If they had been intelligent, they could have seen that there was something unknown: you are not asking for freedom and they are ready to give it to you; what new factors have come into existence? But nobody bothered about it. They were simply happy because they were getting old and if freedom did not come soon, then it would not be in their lifetimes; perhaps in the footnotes of history their names would remain, but they would not be great leaders of the country.

They were so happy, like children, that freedom had come. But they never thought about it: has any empire, any imperialist country, ever, on its own been in such a hurry to give freedom to the slaves, when the slaves are perfectly happy and no revolution is happening? And there was no possibility of any revolution for at least another twenty years.

The situation was clear, but it needed intelligence. There was no question of memory, because the situation was new. India had grown to the point of four hundred million people, and Britain could see by the rate of growth that this country is going to die from hunger and starvation, and they did not want to be responsible for it.

I started saying in 1950 that India needs birth control, and I was condemned: "You are talking against religion. God sends the children – how can we prevent them?"

I argued with them: "When you fall sick, God sends the sickness – why do you call the doctor? If God wants you to be well, he will send the medicine too."

They argued with me. The *shankaracharya* of Puri himself argued with me: "Birth control methods are artificial."

I asked him, "What do you mean by artificial?" He said, "They are not created by God."

I said, "Do you think railway trains are created by God, airplanes are created by God? The medicines you are using are all artificial."

And he was wearing heavy glasses on his nose. I said, "What about this – have you come from God's house? Have you brought these glasses with your birth? God has given you eyes and you should remain with your eyes – what is the need of having these heavy glasses? These are artificial. Everything else artificial is okay, but birth control methods cannot be used because they are artificial."

He became so angry with me that he refused to speak from the same stage, in a meeting, saying "I cannot speak with this man on the same stage. Either he will speak or I will speak."

And I was telling them that soon they would be in trouble, but even today the government is afraid, the religious leaders are afraid. It goes against their memory system; otherwise, a small intelligence would be enough to show them....

Scientists are predicting that by the end of this century, India will have one billion people – that is one thousand million people, and that is the lowest estimate. The more progressive and more intelligent people have estimated that India will have one billion and eight hundred million people by the end of this century, almost the double population of today.

Fifty percent of India is going to die by the end of this century, and when one in two persons, is going to die, what do you think about those who will be left living amongst corpses? Their situation will be worse than being dead. The dead will at least be at rest.

But to talk about birth control or the birth control pill goes against the memory, against the system, against the mind that has been told something for centuries but is not aware that a totally new situation has arisen. India has never been the most populated country – it was China. By the end of this century India will have gone ahead of China. China is behaving more intelligently.

But the real intelligent people you will find in Germany, in Switzerland, where population is decreasing. Increasing the population is increasing death. The situation is new; it needs new methods to face it.

Intelligence means the capability to respond to new situations. It comes from your being – mind is only a vehicle – a kind of awareness of what the mind is, without belonging to it.

You are only intellectually thinking about it. But whatever you are saying, if it becomes your experience, it will transform your whole life.

Intelligence is the quality of the witness; it watches the mind and it gives direction to the mind. Right now, whatever you have in your mind has come from the outside. Intelligence comes from your inside. That used to be the basic meaning of the word education – it means "to draw out." But what is being done in the name of education is just the opposite – it is "to stuff in," to stuff in all kinds of nonsense. Nowhere are efforts being made that your intelligence be drawn out. You have it already, it just needs a passage, a way.

Meditation creates that passage, that way. It makes your being the master and your mind just a servant.

Memory is from the outside, intelligence is from your innermost sources, your very life, responding to situations.

"Is meditation connected with intelligence?"

Meditation is connected with your being, and your being has many aspects: intelligence, blissfulness, grace, gratitude, prayer, love, compassion...infinite is the treasure of your being. Intelligence is only one of the parts.

"And is intelligence a potential that we all have, and that simply needs to be awakened? Can we raise our consciousness with intelligence?"

Everybody is born with the same potential. Differences exist because we are not using our potential to the same extent.

You will be surprised to know that even a man like Albert Einstein, whom you can call an example of genius, uses only fifteen percent of his potential. The people whom you think of as very talented use only ten percent of their potential. And the ordinary masses, the millions of people, use between five and seven percent.

The world would be a totally different place if everybody was using a hundred percent of their potential, in different directions, in different dimensions.

Meditation can only make you aware of your potential, can make the passage in which your potential can grow and can find its expression. And nobody is devoid or unequal as far as intelligence is concerned. The inequality appears only because of our use: somebody uses it, somebody does not use it.

An American, a very devout Catholic, had tried for years to get a private audience with the pope. When his request was finally granted, he flew to Rome, and within the hour was kneeling before His Holiness. Kissing the ring after the pope had blessed him, the man said, "Your Holiness, I want you to know this has been the most inspirational experience of my life. I am deeply grateful. I would like to share my favorite story with you: There were these two Polacks..."

"Excuse me, my son," the pope interrupted, a little offended, "are you aware that I am Polish?"

"Ah yes, Your Holiness, but don't worry. I will tell it very, very slowly."

Okay, Vimal?

Yes, Bhagwan.

Session 27

Harmony
Is Your Reality

Language is created by people for mundane affairs.
For the sacred there is only silence.

March 3, 1987
Morning

Beloved Bhagwan,

Last night whilst lying in bed
and allowing my mind to wander down creative corridors,
I experienced what I can only describe as a mental somersault,
and I looked, for the first time, inside.
I will not attempt to describe how it felt, but I can say
it was more ecstatic than anything I could imagine.
I felt doors that were stuck tight, dissolve,
and in my trembling and astonished innocence
I was aware of Your compassionate presence cushioning me.
Oh my precious and beloved master,
what was this treasure I discovered?
Is this what You call meditation,
and will it be easy to find again?

Parambodhi, it has been a beautiful first glimpse of meditation. But the first glimpse should not be desired; otherwise you will destroy it. Just as it has happened on its own – you were not attempting to achieve it – allow it to come and go; don't be greedy. That is one of the great obstacles on the path of those who are in search of themselves. A glimpse happens, it is ecstatic, and the old mind immediately grabs it and starts thinking in its old pattern: how to get it again.

Mind is not going to get any experience of meditation. And the more greedy the mind becomes, the less is the possibility of that relaxed state when meditation blossoms. So one most important thing to be remembered is: forget all about it. It has come on its own, it will come on its own. It cannot be made a goal. Our mind turns everything into a goal; its whole training is for achieving: if you have achieved this much, you should achieve it again and you should achieve more.

But the very desire of achieving is a disturbance, is a tension, is an anxiety. It happens to almost everybody when for the first time the sky opens inside. You were not asking for it; you were doing something else. But you were relaxed, calm, and quiet. You were ready, but you were not demanding anything from existence.

Existence never yields to any of our demands. It is the demanding mind that has been creating all our misery.

Once you have tasted something that you have never tasted before, it seems absolutely natural to ask for it again and again. But you have to understand that meditation is something not of your doing. It is not your act. It is something that happens to you in a certain space. That space is not of desire, not of demand, but of absolute relaxation and trust in nature. If it has given you one glimpse, it will give you many glimpses of a deeper nature, of a higher quality. Right now you may not be able even to imagine them, because unless you experience something, you cannot imagine it, you cannot dream about it.

This is the very beginning of the journey on the path, but a very beautiful opening. If you don't come in the way, many more experiences will follow.

So the only thing to avoid is yourself coming in the way. Remember always that it is a happening, so when you are not anxious to get it, only then it is possible. Your anxiety, your tension, your greed, make your mind very confused and do not allow the relaxed space where flowers of meditation blossom.

You are saying, "Last night whilst laying in bed and allowing my mind to wander down creative corridors, I experienced what I can only describe as a mental somersault. And I looked for the first time inside." It all happened naturally. It was not preplanned. You were not looking for it.

"I will not attempt to describe how I felt." Even if you do attempt, you cannot describe it. The experience of your inner being, howsoever small, is basically indescribable. There are no words, no concepts into which you can put it rationally. It is an experience where language has never entered, where mind has never entered. It is not a mental experience; otherwise there would be no difficulty to describe it. Anything that can be described is of the mind, and anything that cannot be described is of real authentic value; it is spiritual.

"I will not attempt to describe how I felt, but I can say it was more ecstatic than anything that I could imagine. I felt doors that were stuck tight, dissolve, and in my trembling and astonished innocence..." Remember these words. It was happening in your "trembling and astonished innocence."

"I was aware of Your compassionate presence cushioning me. Oh my precious and beloved master, what was this treasure I discovered?"

You are again asking for a description, for an explanation. And you know perfectly well that even in ordinary life there are many things which cannot be described, but only experienced.

You taste something – is there any way to describe it? Is there any way to give an explanation about it? And it is an ordinary thing. You have tasted something, you have smelled a fragrance, you have heard music…. You experienced it; it thrilled you. You can say what happened to you, but you cannot say what it was exactly. You know perfectly well what it is, but there exists no language. Language is created by people for mundane affairs.

For the sacred there is only silence.

A man came to a Zen master, Rinzai. He was sitting on the beach. The man said, "I have been looking for you, and for many days I have been thinking to come to you. I want to know the essential, the very essence, of all your religious teaching – in short, because I am not a man of philosophical bent. What is it that you are teaching?"

Rinzai looked at him and remained silent. A moment passed. The man felt a little strange. He said, "Have you *heard* me or not?"

Rinzai said, "I have heard you, but have *you* heard me or not?"

The man said, "My god, you have not said a single word."

Rinzai said, "I was sitting silent. That is the essential part of my teaching. I thought that rather than talking about it, it would be better to show it to you. In words, things get distorted; in words, you start interpreting according to your own prejudices."

The man said, "It is beyond me. Please give some words that I can remember."

Rinzai said, "If you insist I will commit the crime of forcing something into words which is not ready, which is absolutely unwilling to be put into words."

He wrote with his finger in the sand where he was sitting: meditation.

The man said, "I have come from very far away and you are making me more puzzled. First you remained silent; now you simply write 'meditation.' That does not make any sense to me. What is meditation?"

Rinzai said, "What is meditation...what is a roseflower? A roseflower is a roseflower. You can see it dancing in the wind and in the rain and in the sun. You can enjoy its dance, you can enjoy its fragrance, its beauty, but what is a roseflower? Don't ask such stupid questions."

He said, "But I have come from so far, with great expectations...just a little more, so that I can understand what mediation is."

So Rinzai wrote with capital letters: MEDITATION.

The man said, "Does it make any difference whether you write in small letters or you write in capital letters?"

Rinzai said, "You are only concerned with *your* difficulty. You are not concerned with *my* difficulty. Even writing it as meditation, I am committing a crime against meditation itself, because it is an experience, not an explanation.

"It is the flower of silence. It cannot be contained in words. Even the word meditation is just utilitarian. People ask and feel annoyed if they are not answered, so we answer, but all our answers are wrong.

"The moment we transform the experience into an explanation, something goes wrong. It is a wordless state of being. If you really want to know it, you sit with me; you be with me for a few days. Perhaps my silence may affect you, because it is contagious."

Don't ask what treasure you have discovered. You have discovered only the door; you have not even entered into the temple yet. But you are on the right path and you are going in the right direction.

If you don't allow greed, if you don't start expecting it to happen every day, according to your desires, you will discover the treasure too. It is inside you.

"Is this what You call meditation?"

Just the beginning.... Meditation is when mind is no more at all.

Meditation is a state of no-mind. Your mind has not dissolved; it was watching, standing by the corner. And it is your mind which is enquiring about what has happened. It is not the business of the mind.

Mind is meant for outward things, for objective reality. In science it is perfectly in its right place, but in religion, in your interiority, in your subjectivity it has no place at all.

"And will it be easy to find it again?"

It all depends on you. If you don't try to find it again, it will be very easy. If you try to find it again, you will make it more and more difficult. The more you try, the less is the possibility.

The American idea of "try and try and try again" will not help. It is good for the outside world; for the inside world, don't try. Just wait, and wait with patience. If it happens, feel grateful. If it does not happen, don't feel sad.

I have heard about a Sufi mystic, Bayazid, who used to say after each prayer, raising his hands towards the sky, "Father, you are so generous. You take care of me so carefully, as if I am the only one to be taken care of." His disciples were very tired of listening to it every day, morning, evening....

Once it happened that for three days...Bayazid obviously was a rebel; no mystic can be otherwise. I have not heard that a mystic can be orthodox, traditional. A mystic is naturally rebellious. His religion is rebellion, rebellion against all kinds of lies that tradition goes on giving from one generation to another generation. And Bayazid had annoyed the orthodox, the so-called religious, the priests, all the vested interests who want man to remain enslaved to the past. For three days they had been passing through villages where no food was given to them, doors were closed in their faces, even water was not given and it was a desert, with no shelter. They were sleeping cold nights on the sand.

And still after every prayer he was saying, "How can you manage? You have to look after such a vast universe, but you take so much care. I cannot ever return it; I don't have anything to give to you."

The disciples finally freaked out! They said, "It is enough. Before it was okay, but for three days no food, no water...we are dying! Cold nights in the desert, hot days in the desert, and you are still telling God, 'You are taking care of us'?

Bayazid said, "He knows what is needed and when it is needed. These three days of hunger and thirst and the cold nights and the hot days must have been absolutely necessary for us. He always takes care."

Such a trust in existence will bring, whenever you are ready, whatever you need. So be grateful if it happens and be grateful if it does not happen. That is real gratefulness.

But don't start asking, "Will it be easy to find it again?" Have you found it in the first place, or has it found you? You have not found it, so how can you find it again?

It has found you. And it will find you again and again, but don't lose your innocence in expectations, in desires. That is one of the very stupid things religious people go on doing.

Two polacks rent a rowboat and go fishing in a lake. They are catching fish after fish, and have almost two dozen by the end of the afternoon.

One man says to the other, "Why don't we come back to the very same place tomorrow?"

"Good idea," his friend answers.

So the first man takes a piece of chalk, and draws an X on the bottom of the boat. "Don't be stupid!" the friend says. "How do you know that we'll get the same boat tomorrow?"

Just remain available and grateful – waiting with a throbbing heart, not with a desiring mind; waiting with an open heart, not with a closed mind, with the idea that "It has to happen. Why is it not happening?"

If you can remember this simple thing, it will happen more often, it will happen more deeply, it will happen in new forms, in new riches, in new colors, with new significance, with deeper meanings, with higher flights.

But it will always happen.

It will not be your doing.

Beloved Bhagwan,

This morning before discourse started, sitting on the marble,
I felt as if we were one mouth singing, one heart beating, one breath breathing.
I felt so much love in my being, as if we were all one being.
I feel like giving a lot;
I feel as if I am taking so much from everywhere, and my being wants to be useful for developing eternal love.
I have the feeling we are holding each other's hands
and starting to flower all together in the spring.
Am I just a dreamer, beloved Bhagwan?

Amrito, Friedrich Nietzsche in one of his statements says, "The greatest calamity will fall on humanity the day all the dreamers disappear." The whole evolution of man is because man has dreamt about it. What was a dream yesterday, today is a reality, and what is a dream today can become a reality tomorrow.

All the poets are dreamers, all the musicians are dreamers, all the mystics are dreamers. In fact, creativity is a by-product of dreaming.

But these dreams are not the dreams that Sigmund Freud analyzes. So you have to make a distinction between the dream of a poet, the dream of a sculptor, the dream of an architect, the dream of a mystic, the dream of a dancer – and the dreams of a sick mind.

It is very unfortunate that Sigmund Freud never bothered about the great dreamers who are the foundation of the whole of human evolution. He came across only the psychologically sick people, and because his whole life's experience was to analyze the dreams of psychopaths, the very word "dreaming" became condemned. The madman dreams, but his dream is going to be destructive of himself.

The creative man also dreams, but his dream is going to enrich the world.

I am reminded of Michelangelo. He was passing through the market where all kinds of marble was available, and he saw a beautiful rock, so he enquired about it.

The owner said, "If you want that rock you can take it for free because it has just been lying around taking up space. And for twelve years, nobody has even enquired about it; I also don't see that there is any potential in that rock."

Michelangelo took the rock, worked on it for almost the whole year, and made perhaps the most beautiful statue that has ever existed. Just a few years ago, a madman destroyed it. It was in the Vatican; it was a statue of Jesus Christ after he was taken down from the cross, and is lying dead in his mother Mary's lap.

I have seen only the photographs of it, but it is so alive, as if Jesus is going to wake up any moment. And he has used the marble with such artfulness that you can feel both things – the strength of Jesus and the fragileness. And the tears are in the eyes of Jesus' mother, Mary.

A madman, just few years ago, hammered the rock that Michelangelo had made, and when he was asked why he had done it he said, "I also want to become famous. Michelangelo had to work one year; then he became famous. I had only to work for five minutes, and I destroyed the whole statue. And my name has gone around the world as a headline on all the papers."

Both men worked on the same marble rock. One was a creator, another was a madman.

After one year, when Michelangelo had finished the work, he asked the shopkeeper to come to his home, because he wanted to show him something.

He could not believe his eyes. He said, "From where did you get this beautiful marble?"

And Michelangelo said, "Don't you recognize? It is the same ugly rock that waited in front of your shop for twelve years." And I remember this incident, because the shopkeeper asked, "How did you manage to think that that ugly rock could be turned into such a beautiful statue?"

Michelangelo said, "I did not think about it. I have been dreaming of making this statue, and when I was passing by the rock I suddenly saw Jesus, calling me, 'I am encaged in the rock. Free me; help me to get out of this rock.' I saw exactly the same statue in the rock. So I have only done a small job: I have removed the unnecessary parts of the rock, and Jesus and Mary are free from their bondage."

It would have been a great contribution if a man of the same caliber as Sigmund Freud, instead of analyzing the sick people and their dreams had worked on the dreams of psychologically healthy, and not only healthy, but creative people. The analysis of their dreams will not show that all dreams are repressions. The analysis of their dreams will show that there are dreams which are born out of a more creative consciousness than ordinary people have.

So don't be worried about being a dreamer. All the people who have gathered around me are dreamers. They are dreaming of a higher state of consciousness, they are dreaming of a possibility to find the eternal source of life. They are dreaming of God. And their dreams are not sick, their dreams are authentically healthy. The whole evolution of man and his consciousness depends on these dreamers.

Amrito, you are saying, "This morning before discourse, sitting on the marble, I felt as if we were one mouth singing, one heart beating, one breath breathing. I felt so much love in my being, as if we were all one being.

"I feel like giving a lot, I feel as if I am taking so much from everywhere, and my being wants to be useful for developing eternal love. I have the feeling we are holding each other's hands and starting to flower all together in the spring."

It is not a dream. It is a dream that is becoming real, a dream that is transforming itself into reality.

And it is not only you. Many people have written to me; in different ways they have felt it, and what they have felt is not their projection. It is our reality, it is our discovery.

The whole existence is one organic unity. You are not only holding hands with each other, you are holding hands with the trees. You are not only breathing together, the whole universe is breathing together.

The universe is in a deep harmony. Only man has forgotten the language of harmony, and our work here is to remind you. We are not creating harmony; harmony is your reality. It is just that you have forgotten about it. Perhaps it is so obvious that one tends to forget about it. Perhaps you are born in it; how can you think about it?

An ancient parable is that a fish who was of a philosophical bent of mind was asking other fish, "I have heard so much about the ocean; where is it?" And she is in the ocean! But she was born in the ocean, she has lived in the ocean; there has never been any separation. She has not seen ocean as a separate object from herself. An old fish caught hold of the young philosopher and told her, "This is the ocean we are in."

But the young philosopher said, "You must be kidding. This is water and you are calling it the ocean. I will have to enquire more of wiser people around."

A fish comes to know about the ocean only when it is caught by a fisherman and drawn out of the ocean, thrown into the sand. Then, for the first time she understands that she has always lived in the ocean, that ocean is her life and without it she cannot survive.

But with man there is a difficulty. You cannot be taken out of existence. Existence is infinite, there are no shores where you can stand aloof and see existence. Wherever you are, you will be part of existence.

We are all breathing together. We are part of one orchestra. To understand it is a great experience – don't call it dreaming, because dreaming has got a very wrong connotation because of Sigmund Freud. Otherwise it is one of the most beautiful words, very poetic.

You are experiencing a reality, because all the people who are here, are here for the same purpose: just to be silent, just to be joyful, just to *be*. In their silence, they will feel they are joined with others.

When you are thinking, you are separate from others because you are thinking some thoughts and the other person is thinking different thoughts. But if you are both silent, then all the walls between you disappear.

Two silences cannot remain two. They become one.

All great values of life – love, silence, blissfulness, ecstasy, godliness – make you aware of an immense oneness. There is nobody else other than you; we are all different expressions of one reality, different songs of one singer, different dances of one dancer, different paintings – but the painter is one.

But this has to be reminded to you, Amrito, again: don't call it a dream, because in calling it a dream you are not understanding that it is a reality. And reality is far more beautiful than any dream can be. Reality is more psychedelic, more colorful, more joyful, more dancing than you can ever imagine. But we are living so unconsciously....

Our first unconsciousness is that we think that we are separate. But I emphasize that no man is an island, we are all part of a vast continent. There is variety, but that does not make us separate. Variety makes life richer – part of us is in the Himalayas, a part of us is in the stars, a part of us is in the roses. A part of us is in the bird on the wing, a part of us is in the green of the trees. We are spread all over. To experience it as reality will transform your whole approach towards life, will transform your every act, will transform your very being.

You will become full of love; you will become full of reverence for life. You will become for the first time, according to me, truly religious – not a Christian, not a Hindu, not a Mohammedan, but truly, purely religious.

The word religion is beautiful. It comes from a root which means bringing together those who have fallen apart in their ignorance; bringing them together, waking them up so that they can see they are not separate.

Then you cannot hurt even a tree. Then your compassion and your love will be just spontaneous – not cultivated, not something of a discipline. If love is a discipline, it is false. If nonviolence is cultivated, it is false. If compassion is nurtured, it is false. But if they come spontaneously without any effort of your own, then they have a reality so deep, so exquisite....

In the name of religion, so much crime has been done in the past. More people have been killed by religious people than by anybody else. Certainly all these religions have been fake, pseudo.

The authentic religion has to be born.

Once H.G. Wells was asked, when he had published his history of the world – a tremendous work – "What do you think about civilization?"

And H.G. Wells said, "It is a good idea, but somebody should do something about it to bring it into existence."

Up to now we have not been civilized, not cultured, not religious. In the name of civilization, in the name of culture, in the name of religion we have been doing all kinds of barbarous acts – primitive, subhuman, animalistic. And sometimes we have passed even beyond the animals: no animal eats its own species, no animal is a cannibal, except man.

And you will be thinking that only in Africa a few people eat human flesh. It is not so simple to throw the responsibility on small tribes in Africa.

Just a few days ago, in Palestine, people asked the government – because so many people are dying from hunger and starvation – "Can we eat human flesh? Of course, of dead people – those who have died of starvation at least can help others to survive a little longer. And the government of Palestine has accepted the idea that it is better to eat human flesh than to die.

The population is growing so fast in the world that it is not just a guess that by the end of this century, millions of people will be eating human flesh. No animal goes that low. He will die hungry, but he will not eat any animal of his own species.

Man has fallen far away from reality. He has to be awakened to the truth that we are all one. And it is not a hypothesis; it is the experience of all the meditators, without exception, down the ages, that the whole existence is one organic unity.

So don't mistake a beautiful experience as a dream. To call it a dream cancels its reality. Dreams have to be made real, not reality changed into dreams.

An old man of eighty-two went to a sperm bank to make a deposit.

"Are you sure," asked the woman at the reception desk, "that you want to do this?"

"Yes," answered the old man, "I feel it is my duty to give something of myself to the world."

The woman handed him a jar, and directed him to a room down the hall. When thirty minutes had passed and he did not return, the girl began to worry. She feared he might have had a heart attack or a stroke.

At that moment the old man came out of the room and approached the young woman. "Listen," he said, "I tried it with one hand, then I tried it with two hands, then I got it up and beat it on the sink. Then I ran warm water on it, then cold water over it....

"And still I can't get the lid off the jar."

Don't guess!

Okay, Vimal?

Yes, Bhagwan.

WORLDWIDE DISTRIBUTION CENTERS FOR THE WORKS OF BHAGWAN SHREE RAJNEESH

Books by Bhagwan Shree Rajneesh are available in many languages throughout the world. Bhagwan's discourses have been recorded live on audiotape from 1974 onwards and on video from 1985. There are many audio recordings of Rajneesh meditation music and of celebration music played in His presence; and beautiful photographs have been taken of Bhagwan. For further information and catalog, contact the closest distribution center:

EUROPE

West Germany

Rajneesh Verlags GmbH
Venloer Strasse 5-7
D-5000 COLOGNE 1
Tel. 0221/574 07 43

Nationwide book-shop distributor
VVA Vereinigte Verlagsauslieferung,
Gütersloh

Italy

Rajneesh Services Corporation
Via XX Settembre 12
I-28941 ARONA (NO)
Tel. 02/839 21 94 (office Milano)

Netherlands

Stichting Rajneesh Publikaties
    Nederland
Cornelis Troostplein 23
NL-1072 JJ AMSTERDAM
Tel. 020/573 21 30

United Kingdom

Rajneesh Media
Manor Garden Enterprise Center
Manor Garden 10-18
LONDON N7 6GY
Tel. 01/281 4892

ASIA

India

Rajneeshdham
Rajneesh Mandir
17 Koregaon Park
POONA 411001
Tel. 0212/60953/4

Japan

EER Rajneesh Neo-Sannyas Commune
Mimura Building 6-21-34 Kikuna
Kohoku-ku, YOKOHAMA, 222
Tel. 045/434 1981

NORTH AMERICA

United States of America

Chidvilas Foundation
P.O. Box 1510
Boulder, CO 80306
Tel. (303)665-6611

Also available in nationwide
bookstores of Walden Books
and B.Daltons

BOOKS BY BHAGWAN SHREE RAJNEESH

ENGLISH LANGUAGE EDITIONS

RAJNEESH PUBLISHERS

Recent Releases

Beyond Enlightenment
Sermons in Stones
That Art Thou
The Last Testament *(Volume 1)*
　　Interviews with the World Press
The Messiah *(Volume 1)*
　　Commentaries on Kahlil Gibran's The Prophet
The Messiah *(Volume 2)*
　　Commentaries on Kahlil Gibran's The Prophet
The Rajneesh Bible *(Volumes 1-5)*
The Rajneesh Upanishad
The Rebellious Spirit
Zarathustra: A God that can Dance *(Volume 1)*
Zarathustra: The Laughing Prophet *(Volume 2)*

Compilations

A New Vision of Women's Liberation
Bhagwan Shree Rajneesh On Basic Human Rights
Life, Love and Laughter
Priests and Politicians - The Mafia of the Soul
The New Man: The Only Hope for the Future

Books on Bhagwan Shree Rajneesh

Bhagwan Shree Rajneesh The Most Dangerous Man
　　Since Jesus Christ *(by Sue Appleton)*
Bhagwan: The Most Godless Yet The Most Godly Man
　　(by George Meredith)
Bhagwan: The Buddha For The Future
　　(by Juliet Forman)

Biographies

Books I have Loved
Glimpses of a Golden Childhood
Notes of a Madman

Photobiographies

The Sound of Running Water
    - *Bhagwan Shree Rajneesh*
    and His work 1974-1978
This Very Place The Lotus Paradise
    - *Bhagwan Shree Rajneesh*
    and His Work 1978-1984

The Bauls

The Beloved *(Volumes 1&2)*

Buddha

The Book of the Books *(Volumes 1-4)*
    - *the Dhammapada*
The Diamond Sutra - *the Vajrachchedika*
    Prajnaparamita Sutra
The Discipline of Transcendence *(Volumes 1-4)*
    - *the Sutra of 42 Chapters*
The Heart Sutra
    - *the Prajnaparamita Hridayam Sutra*

Buddhist Masters

The Book of Wisdom
    (Volumes 1&2)
    - *Atisha's Seven Points of Mind Training*
The White Lotus
    - *the Sayings of Bodhidharma*

Compilations

The Book *An Introduction to the Teachings*
    of Bhagwan Shree Rajneesh
    Series I   from A - H
    Series II from I - O
    Series III from R - Z

Early Discourses and Writings

A Cup of Tea - *Letters to Disciples*
And Now, and Here *(Volumes 1&2)*
Beware of Socialism
Dimensions Beyond the Known
From Sex to Superconsciousness
I am the Gate
Krishna: The Man and His Philosphy
The Long and the Short and the All
The Perfect Way
In Search of the Miraculous *(Volume 1)*
The Silent Explosion

Hassidism

The Art of Dying
The True Sage

Jesus

Come Follow Me *(Volumes 1-4)*
    - *the Sayings of Jesus*
I Say Unto You *(Volumes 1&2)*
    - *the Sayings Of Jesus*
The Mustard Seed - *the Gospel of Thomas*

Kabir

Ecstasy: The Forgotten Language
The Divine Melody
The Fish in the Sea is Not Thirsty
The Guest
The Path of Love
The Revolution

Meditation

The Orange Book
    - the Meditation Techniques
    - of Bhagwan Shree Rajneesh

Responses to Questions

Be Still and Know
My Way: The Way of the White Clouds
The Goose is Out!
The Wild Geese and the Water
Walk Without Feet, Fly Without Wings and
    Think Without Mind
Zen: Zest, Zip, Zap and Zing

Sufism

Just Like That
Straight to Freedom
Sufis: The People of the Path *(Volumes 1&2)*
The Perfect Master *(Volumes 1&2)*
The Secret
The Wisdom of the Sands *(Volumes 1&2)*

Unio Mystica *(Volumes 1&2)*
    - *the Hadiqa of Hakim Sanai*
Until You Die

Tantra

Tantra, Spirituality and Sex
    - *Excerpts from The Book of the Secrets*
Tantra: The Supreme Understanding
    - *Tilopa's Song of Mahamudra*
The Book of the Secrets *(Volumes 4&5)*
    - *Vigyana Bhairava Tantra*
The Tantra Vision *(Volumes 1&2)*
    - *the Royal Song of Saraha*

Tao

Tao: The Golden Gate *(Volumes 1&2)*
Tao: The Pathless Path *(Volumes 1&2)*
    - *the Stories of Lieh Tzu*
Tao: The Three Treasures *(Volumes 1-4)*
    - *the Tao Te Ching of Lao Tzu*
The Empty Boat - *the Stories of Chuang Tzu*
The Secret of Secrets *(Volumes 1&2)*
    - *the Secret of the Golden Flower*
When the Shoe Fits
    - *the Stories of Chuang Tzu*

The Upanishads

I Am That - *Isa Upanishad*
Philosophia Ultima - *Mandukya Upanishad*
The Ultimate Alchemy *(Volumes 1&2)*
    - *Atma Pooja Upanishad*
Vedanta: Seven Steps to Samadhi
    - *Akshya Upanishad*

Western Mystics

Guida Spirituale - *the Desiderata*
Philosophia Perennis *(Volumes 1&2)*
    - *the Golden Verses of Pythagoras*
The Hidden Harmony
    the Fragments of Heraclitus
The New Alchemy: To Turn You on
    - *Mabel Collins' Light on the Path*
Theologia Mystica
    - *the Treatise of St. Dionysius*

Yoga

Yoga: The Alpha and the Omega *(Volumes 1-10)*
    - *the Yoga Sutras of Patanjali*
Yoga: The Science of the Soul *(Volumes 1-3)*
    - *Originally titled Yoga: The Alpha and the Omega*

Zen

Ah, This!
Ancient Music in the Pines
And the Flowers Showered
A Sudden Clash of Thunder
Dang Dang Doko Dang
Nirvana: The Last Nightmare
No Water, No Moon
Returning to the Source
Roots and Wings
The First Principle
The Grass Grows By Itself
The Sun Rises in the Evening
Walking in Zen, Sitting in Zen
Zen: The Path of Paradox *(Volumes 1-3)*
Zen: The Special Transmission - *Zen Stories*

Zen Masters

Hsin Hsin Ming: The Book of Nothing
    Discourses on the Faith-Mind of Sosan
Neither This Nor That
    - *The Sutras of Sosan*
Take it Easy *(Volumes 1&2) - Poems of Ikkyu*
The Search - *the Ten Bulls of Zen*
This Very Body the Buddha
    - *Hakuin's Song of Meditation*

Darshan Diaries
Talks between
Master and Disciple

Hammer on the Rock
    (December 10, 1975 - January 15, 1976)
Above All Don't Wobble
    (January 16 - February 12, 1976)
Nothing to Lose But Your Head
    (February 13 - March 12, 1976)
Be Realistic: Plan For a Miracle
    (March 13 - April 6, 1976)
Get Out of Your Own Way *(April 7 - May 2, 1976)*
Beloved of My Heart *(May 3 - 28, 1976)*
The Cypress in the Courtyard *(May 29 - June 27, 1976)*
A Rose is a Rose is a Rose *(June 28 - July 27, 1976)*
Dance Your Way to God *(July 28 - August 20, 1976)*
The Passion for the Impossible
    (August 21 - September 18, 1976)
The Great Nothing *(September 19 - October 11, 1976)*
God is Not for Sale *(October 12 - November 7, 1976)*
The Shadow of the Whip
    (November 8 - December 3, 1976)
Blessed are the Ignorant *(December 4 - 31, 1976)*
The Buddha Disease *(January 1977)*
What Is, Is, What Ain't, Ain't *(February 1977)*

The Zero Experience *(March 1977)*
For Madmen Only (Price of Admission: Your Mind)
    (April 1977)
This is It *(May 1977)*
The Further Shore *(June 1977)*
Far Beyond the Stars *(July 1977)*
The No Book (No Buddha, No Teaching, No Discipline)
    (August 1977)
Don't Just Do Something, Sit There *(September 1977)*
Only Losers Can Win in this Game *(October 1977)*
The Open Secret *(November 1977)*
The Open Door *(December 1977)*
The Sun Behind the Sun Behind the Sun
    (January 1978)
Believing the Impossible Before Breakfast
    (February 1978)
Don't Bite My Finger, Look Where I'm Pointing
    (March 1978)
Let Go! *(April 1978)*

The 99 Names of Nothingness *(May 1978)*
The Madman's Guide to Enlightenment *(June 1978)*
Don't Look Before You Leap *(July 1978)*
Hallelujah! *(August 1978)*
God's Got a Thing About You *(September 1978)*
The Tongue-Tip Taste of Tao *(October 1978)*
The Sacred Yes *(November 1978)*
Turn On, Tune In, and Drop the Lot *(December 1978)*
Zorba the Buddha *(January 1979)*
Won't You Join the Dance? *(February 1979)*
You Ain't Seen Nothin' Yet *(March 1979)*
The Shadow of the Bamboo *(April 1979)*
Just Around the Corner *(May 1979)*
Snap Your Fingers, Slap Your Face & Wake Up!
    (June 1979)
The Rainbow Bridge *(July 1979)*
Don't Let Yourself Be Upset by the Sutra, Rather Upset
    the Sutra Yourself *(August/September 1979)*
The Sound of One Hand Clapping *(March 1981)*

OTHER PUBLISHERS

UNITED KINGDOM

No Water, No Moon *(Sheldon Press)*
Roots and Wings *(Routledge & Kegan Paul)*
Straight to Freedom *(Sheldon Press)*
Tao: The Three Treasures *(Volume 1, Wildwood House)*
The Art of Dying *(Sheldon Press)*
The Book of the Secrets *(Volume 1, Thames & Hudson)*
The Supreme Doctrine *(Routledge & Kegan Paul)*

Books on Bhagwan Shree Rajneesh

The Way of the Heart: the Rajneesh Movement
    by Judith Thompson and Paul Heelas, Department of Religious Studies, University of Lancaster (Aquarian Press)

UNITED STATES OF AMERICA

Dimensions Beyond the Known
    (Wisdom Garden Books)
Hammer on the Rock *(Grove Press)*
I Am the Gate *(Harper & Row)*
Journey toward the Heart
    (Original title: Until You Die, Harper & Row)
Meditation: The Art of Ecstasy *(Original title: Dynamics of Meditation, Harper & Row)*
My Way: The Way of the White Clouds *(Grove Press)*
Roots and Wings *(Routledge & Kegan Paul)*
The Book of the Secrets *(Volumes 1-3, Harper & Row)*
The Great Challenge *(Grove Press)*
The Mustard Seed *(Harper & Row)*
The Psychology of the Esoteric *(Harper & Row)*
The Supreme Doctrine *(Routledge & Kegan Paul)*
Words Like Fire *(Original title: Come Follow Me, Volume 1) (Harper & Row)*

Books on Bhagwan Shree Rajneesh

Dying for Enlightenment *by Bernard Gunther (Harper & Row)*
The Awakened One: The Life and Work of Bhagwan Shree Rajneesh *by Vasant Joshi (Harper & Row)*
The Rajneesh Story: The Bhagwan's Garden *by Dell Murphy (Linwood Press, Oregon)*

FOREIGN LANGUAGE EDITIONS

Chinese

I am the Gate (Woolin)

Danish

Bhagwan Shree Rajneesh Om Grundlaeggende Menneskerettigheder (Forlaget Premo)
    Bhagwan Shree Rajneesh On Basic Human Rights
Hu-Meditation Og Kosmik Orgasme (Borgens)
    Hu-Meditation and Cosmic Orgasm
Hemmelighedernes Bog (Borgens)
    The Book of the Secrets (Volume 1)

Dutch

Bhagwan Shree Rajneesh Over de Rechten van de
   Mens (Stichting Rajneesh Publikaties Nederland)
   Bhagwan Shree Rajneesh On Basic Human Rights
Volg Mij (Ankh-Hermes), *Come Follow Me (Volume 1)*
Gezaaid in Goede Aarde (Ankh-Hermes)
   Come Follow Me (Volume 2)
Drink Mij (Ankh-Hermes), *Come Follow Me (Volume 3)*
Ik Ben de Zee Die Je Zoekt (Ankh-Hermes)
   Come Follow Me (Volume 4)
Ik Ben de Poort (Ankh-Hermes), *I am the Gate*
Heel Eenvoudig (Mirananda), *Just Like That*
Meditatie: De Kunst van Innerlijke Extase (Mirananda)
   Meditation: The Art of Inner Ecstasy
Mijn Weg, De Weg van de Witte Wolk (Arcanum)
   My Way: The Way of the White Clouds
Geen Water, Geen Maan (Mirananda)
   No Water, No Moon (Volumes 1 & 2)
Tantra, Spiritualiteit en Seks (Ankh-Hermes)
   Tantra, Spirituality & Sex
Tantra: Het Allerhoogste Inzicht (Ankh-Hermes)
   Tantra: The Supreme Understanding
Tau (Ankh-Hermes),
   Tao: The Three Treasures (Volume 1)
Het Boek der Geheimen (Mirananda)
   The Book of Secrets (Volumes 1-5)
De Verborgen Harmonie (Mirananda)
   The Hidden Harmony
Het Mosterdzaad (Mirananda)
   The Mustard Seed (Volumes 1 & 2)
De Nieuwe Mens (Volumes 1 & 2) (Zorn/Altamira)
   Excerpts from The Last Testament (Volume 1)
   Dutch edition only
Het Oranje Meditatieboek (Ankh-Hermes)
   The Orange Book
Psychologie en Evolutie (Ankh-Hermes)
   The Psychology of the Esoteric
De Tantra Visie (Arcanum)
   The Tantra Vision (Volumes 1 & 2)
Zoeken naar de Stier (Ankh-Hermes)
   10 Zen Stories
Totdat Je Sterft (Ankh-Hermes)
   Until You Die

French

Je Suis la Porte (EPI), *I am the Gate*
La Meditation Dynamique (Dangles)
   Meditation: The Art of Inner Ecstasy
L'Eveil a la Conscience Cosmique (Dangles)
   The Psychology of the Esoteric
Le Livre des Secrets (Soleil Orange)
   The Book of Secrets (Volume 1)

German

Und vor Allem: Nicht Wackeln
   (Fachbuchhandlung für Psychologie)
   Above All Don't Wobble
Der Freund (Sannyas Verlag), *A Cup of Tea*
Vorsicht Sozialismus (Rajneesh Verlag)
   Beware of Socialism
Bhagwan Shree Rajneesh: Über die
   Grundrechte des Menschen (Rajneesh Verlag)
   *Bhagwan Shree Rajneesh On Basic Human
   Rights*
Komm und folge mir (Sannyas/Droemer Knaur)
   Come Follow Me (Volume 1)
Jesus aber schwieg (Sannyas)
   Come Follow Me (Volume 2)
Jesus - der Menschensohn (Sannyas)
   Come Follow Me (Volume 3)
Sprung ins Unbekannte (Sannyas)
   Dimensions Beyond the Known

Ekstase: Die vergessenen Sprache (Herzschlag)
Ecstasy: The Forgotten Language
Vom Sex zum kosmischen Bewußtsein)
(New Age/Thomas Martin)
From Sex to Superconsciousness
Goldene Augenblicke:
Portrait einer Jugend in Indien (Goldmann)
Glimpses of a Golden Childhood
Sprengt den Fels der Unbewußtheit (Fischer)
Hammer on the Rock
Ich bin der Weg (Sannyas), *I am the Gate*
Meditation: Die Kunst, zu sich selbst zu finden
(Heyne), *Meditation: The Art of Inner Ecstasy*
Mein Weg: Der Weg der weissen Wolke (Herzschlag)
My Way: The Way of the White Clouds
Nirvana: Die letzte Hürde auf dem Weg
(Rajneesh Verlag/RFE), *Nirvana: The Last Nightmare*
Kein Wasser, Kein Mond (Herzschlag)
No Water, No Moon
Mit Wurzeln und Flügeln (Edition Lotos)
Roots and Wings (Volume 1)
Die Schuhe auf dem Kopf (Edition Lotos)
Roots and Wings (Volume 2)
Spirituelle Entwicklung und Sexualität (Fischer)
Spiritual Development & Sexuality
Tantra, Spiritualität und Sex (Rajneesh Verlag)
Tantra, Spirituality & Sex
Tantrische Liebeskunst (Sannyas)
Tantra, Spirituality & Sex
Tantra: Die höchste Einsicht (Sannyas)
Tantra: The Supreme Understanding
Das Buch der Geheimnisse (Heyne)
The Book of the Secrets (Volume 1)
Die Gans ist raus! (Rajneesh Verlag)
The Goose Is Out!
Rebellion der Seele (Sannyas),
The Great Challenge
Die verborgene Harmonie (Sannyas)
The Hidden Harmony

Die verbotene Wahrheit (Rajneesh Verlag/Heyne)
The Mustard Seed
Das Orangene Buch (Rajneesh Verlag/RFE)
The Orange Book
Esoterische Psychologie (Sannyas)
The Psychology of the Esoteric
Auf der Suche (Sambuddha) *The Search*
Das Klatschen der einen Hand (Edition Gyandip)
The Sound of One Hand Clapping
Tantrische Vision (Heyne)
The Tantra Vision (Volume 1)
Alchemie der Verwandlung (Edition Lotos)
The True Sage
Nicht bevor du stirbst (Edition Gyandip),
Until You Die
Was ist Meditation? (Sannyas)
Compilation about meditation, German edition only
Yoga: Alpha und Omega (Edition Gyandip)
Yoga: The Alpha and the Omega (Volume 1)
Der Höhepunkt des Lebens (Rajneesh Verlag)
Compilation on death, German edition only
Intelligenz des Herzens (Herzschlag)
Compilation, German edition only
Kunst kommt nicht vom Können (Rajneesh Verlag)
Compilation about creativity, German edition only
Liebe beginnt nach den Flitterwochen
(Rajneesh Verlag)
Compilation about love, German edition only
Sexualität und Aids (Rajneesh Verlag)
Compilation about Aids, German edition only

Greek

Bhagwan Shree Rajneesh Gia Ta Vasika
Anthropina Dikeomata (Swami Anand Ram)
Bhagwan Shree Rajneesh on Basic Human Rights
I Krifi Armonia (PIGI/Rassoulis)
The Hidden Harmony

Hebrew

Tantra: Ha'havana Ha'eelaeet (Massada)
　Tantra: The Supreme Understanding

Italian

Bhagwan Shree Rajneesh Parla Sui Diritti Dell'Uomo
　(Rajneesh Services Corporation)
　Bhagwan Shree Rajneesh On Basic Human Rights
Dimensioni Oltre il Conosciuto (Mediterranee)
　Dimensions Beyond the Known
Estasi: Il Linguaggio Dimenticato (Riza Libri)
　Ecstasy: The Forgotten Language
Dal Sesso all'Eros Cosmico (Basaia)
　From Sex to Superconsciousness
Guida Spirituale (Mondadori)
　Guida Spirituale
Io Sono La Soglia (Meditarranee)
　I am the Gate
Meditazione Dinamica: L'Arte dell'Estasi Interiore
　(Mediterranee), *Meditation: The Art of Inner Ecstasy*
La Mia Via: La Via delle Nuvole Bianche
　(Mediterranee), *My Way: The Way of the White
　Clouds*
Nirvana: L'Ultimo Incubo (Basaia)
　Nirvana: The Last Nightmare
Dieci Storie Zen di Bhagwan Shree Rajneesh:
　Ne Acqua, Ne Luna (Mediterranee),
　No Water, No Moon
Philosofia Perennis (ECIG)
　Philosophia Perennis (Volumes 1 & 2)
Semi di Saggezza (Sugarco), *Seeds of Revolution*
Tantra Spiritualita e Sesso
　(Rajneesh Foundation Italy)
　Tantra, Spirituality & Sex
Tantra: La Comprensione Suprema (Bompiani)
　Tantra: The Supreme Understanding
Tao: I Tre Tesori (Re Nudo)
　Tao: The Three Treasures (Volumes 1-3)
Tecniche di Liberazione (La Salamandra)
　Techniques of Liberation
Il Libro dei Segreti (Bompiani)
　The Book of The Secrets (Volume 1)
L'Armonia Nascosta (ECIG)
　The Hidden Harmony (Volumes 1 & 2)
Il Seme della Ribellione
　(Rajneesh Foundation Italy)
　The Mustard Seed (Volume 1)
La Nuova Alchimia (Psiche)
　The New Alchemy To Turn You On (Vol. 1&2)
Il Libro Arancione (Mediterranee)
　The Orange Book
La Rivoluzione Interiore (Mediterranee)
　The Psychology of the Esoteric
La Bibbia di Rajneesh (Bompiani)
　The Rajneesh Bible (Volume 1)
La Ricerca (La Salamandra), *The Search*
La Dottrina Suprema (Rizzoli),
　The Supreme Doctrine
La Visione Tantrica (Riza)
　The Tantra Vision

Japanese

Bhagwan Shree Rajneesh On Basic Human Rights
　(Meisosha Ltd.)
Dance Your Way to God (Rajneesh Publications)
From Sex to Superconsciousness
　(Rajneesh Publications)
Meditation: The Art of Inner Ecstasy (Merkmal)
My Way: The Way of the White Clouds
　(Rajneesh Publications)
Tantra: The Supreme Understanding (Merkmal)
Tao: The Three Treasures (Volumes 1-4), (Merkmal)
The Beloved (Volumes 1 & 2), (Merkmal)

The Diamond Sutra (Meisosha Ltd./LAF Mitsuya)
The Empty Boat (Volumes 1 & 2),
    (Rajneesh Publications)
The Grass Grows by Itself (Fumikura)
The Heart Sutra (Merkmal)
The Mustard Seed (Volumes 1 & 2), (Merkmal)
The Orange Book (Wholistic Therapy Institute)
The Search (Merkmal)
Until You Die (Fumikura)

Korean

Tao: The Pathless Path (Chung Ha)
The Pathless Path (Vol 1&2)
Theory of Happiness (Vol 3&4)
The Art of Dying (Chung Ha)
The Divine Melody (Chung Ha)
The Empty Boat (Chung Ha)
The Grass Grows by Itself (Chung Ha)

Portuguese

Sobre Os Direitos Humanos Basicos (Editora Naim)
    Bhagwan Shree Rajneesh on Basic Human Rights
Palavras De Fogo (Global/Ground)
    Come Follow Me (Volume 1)
Dimensoes Alem do Conhecido (Cultrix)
    Dimensions Beyond the Known
Extase: A Linguagem Esquecida (Global)
    Ecstasy: The Forgotten Language
Do Sexo A Superconsciencia (Cultrix)
    From Sex to Superconsciousness
Eu Sou A Porta (Pensamento), *I am the Gate*
Meditacao: A Arte Do Extase (Cultrix)
    Meditation: The Art of Inner Ecstasy
Meu Caminho: O Caminho Das Nuvens Brancas
    (Tao Livraria & Editora)
    My Way: The Way of the White Clouds
Nem Agua, Nem Lua (Pensamento)
    No Water, No Moon
Notas De Um Homem Louco (NAIM),
    Notes of a Madman
Raizes E Asas (Cultrix), *Roots and Wings*
Sufis: O Povo do Caminho (Maha Lakshmi Editora)
    Sufis: The People of the Path
Tantra: Sexo E Espiritualidade (Agora)
    Tantra, Spirituality & Sex
Tantra: A Suprema Compreensao (Cultrix)
    Tantra: The Supreme Understanding
Arte de Morrer (Global), *The Art of Dying*
O Livro Dos Segredos (Maha Lakshmi Editora)
    The Book of the Secrets (Volumes 1 & 2)
Cipreste No Jardim (Cultrix)
    The Cypress in the Courtyard
A Divina Melodia (Cultrix), *The Divine Melody*
A Harmonia Oculta (Pensamento),
    The Hidden Harmony
A Semente De Mostarda (Tao Livraria & Editora)
    The Mustard Seed (Volumes 1 & 2)
A Nova Alquimi (Cultrix)
    The New Alchemy To Turn You On
O Livro Orange (Pensamento), *The Orange Book*
A Psicologia Do Esoterico (Tao Livraria & Editora)
    The Psychology of the Esoteric
Unio Mystica (Maha Lakshmi), *Unio Mystica*

Russian

Bhagwan Shree Rajneesh On Basic Human Rights
    (Rajneesh Foundation Europe)

Serbo-Croat

Bhagwan Shree Rajneesh (Swami Mahavira)
    (Compilation of various quotations)

Spanish

Sobre Los Derechos Humanos Basicos
  (Futonia, Spain)
  Bhagwan Shree Rajneesh on Basic Human Rigths
Ven, Sigueme (Sagaro, Chile), *Come Follow Me*
  (Volume 1)
Yo Soy La Puerta (Editorial Diana, Mexico)
  I am The Gate
Meditacion: El Arte del Extasis
  (Rosello Impresiones)
  Meditation: The Art of Inner Ecstasy
El Camino de las Nubes Blancas
  (Editorial Cuatro Vientos)
  My Way: The Way of the White Clouds
Solo Un Cielo (Collection Tantra), *Only One Sky*
Introduccion al Mundo del Tantra
  (Rosello Impresiones)
  Tantra: The Supreme Understanding
(Volumes 1 & 2)
Tao: Los Tres Tesoros (Editorial Sirio, Spain)
  Tao: The Three Treasures
El Sutra del Corazon (Sarvogeet, Spain)
  The Heart Sutra
El Libro Naranja (Bhagwatam RMC, Puerto Rico)
  The Orange Book
Psicologia de lo Esoterico: La Nueva Evolucion
  del Hombre (Editorial Cuatro Vientos, Chile)
  The Psychology of the Esoteric
El Riesgo Supremo (Editorial Martinez Roca, Spain)
  The Ultimate Risk
Que Es Meditacion? (Koan/Rosello
  Impresiones/Pastanaga), *What Is Meditation?*

Swedish

Den Väldiga Utmaningen (Livskraft)
  The Great Challenge

RAJNEESH MEDITATION CENTERS ASHRAMS AND COMMUNES

There are many Rajneesh Meditation Centers throughout the world which can be contacted for information about the teachings of Bhagwan Shree Rajneesh and which have His books available as well as audio and video tapes of His discourses. Centers exist in practically every country, including some behind the iron curtain.

Argentina

Niketana Rajneesh Meditation Center
Combate de los Pozos 764
RA-1222 Buenos Aires

Australia

Kalika Rajneesh Meditation Center
25 Martin Street
Cairns 4870

Prabhakar Rajneesh Meditation Center
c/o Post Office
Innot Hot Springs
North Queensland 4872

Rajneeshgrad Neo-Sannyas Commune
P.O. Box 1097
160 High Street
Fremantle WA 6160

Belgium

Indu Rajneesh Meditation Center
Coebergerstraat 40
2018 Antwerp

Suryodaya Rajneesh Meditation Center
Rue de Drapieres 12
1050 Bruxelles

Brazil

Abhudaya Rajneesh Meditation Center
Caixa Postal 2651
Porto Alegre 90000
R/S

Amaraloka Rajneesh Meditation Center
Rua Noel Torezin No. 83
Campo Belo
Sao Paulo SP 04615

Anurag Rajneesh Meditation Center
Avenida Recife 4282
Modulo 4, Apto 314 ES
Tancia-Recife 50000

Jwala Rajneesh Meditation Center
Avenida Nico Pecanta 50, Sala 2315
Edificio Rodoefo
De Padi Centro
Rio de Janeiro

Premadhara Rajneesh Meditation Center
Av. Dep. Paulino Rocha 1001,
Apto 402
Sqn. Bloco H, Castelao
Fortaneza-Ceara 60000

Purnam Rajneesh Meditation Center
Caixa Postal 1946
Rio Grande do Sul
Porto Allegre 90000

Sudhakar Rajneesh Meditation Center
Rua Getulio Vargas 80
Jardim Sao Francisco
Cabo Frio
Rio de Janeiro 28900

Canada

Grada Rajneesh Institute
5161 Park Avenue
Montreal

Samaroha Rajneesh Meditation Center
1774 Tolmie Street
Vancouver B.C. V6R 4B8

Colombia

Padma Rajneesh Meditation Center
Apartado Aereo 4128
Medellin

Denmark

Anwar Rajneesh Meditation Center
Thorsgade 74, 4TV
2200 Copenhagen N

Khalaas Rajneesh Meditation Center
Museumsstien 8
9990 Skagen

Pragya Rajneesh Meditation Center
Kiersplads 6 III TV
8000 Aarhus C

Rajneesh Institute for Spiritual Creativity
Bogballevey 3
Tonning
8740 Braeostrup

Sahajo Rajneesh Meditation Center
Sudergade 26 1
3000 Helsinger

Ecuador

Moulik Rajneesh Meditation Center
Eustorgio Salgado 197, piso 3
Miraflores Quito

Finland

Leela Rajneesh Meditation Center
Merimiehenkatu 16B 24
00150 Helsinki 15

France

Rajneesh Meditation Center
60 Ave. Charles de Gaulle
92200 Neuilly

Greece

Darshan Rajneesh Meditation Center
20 Aribou Street
11633 Athens

Mallika Rajneesh Meditation Center
Nikiforou Ouranour 25-A
11499 Athens

Surya Rajneesh Meditation Center
Oia-Santorini

India

Rajneeshdham Neo-Sannyas Commune
17 Koregaon Park
Poona 411001

Rajyoga Rajneesh Meditation Center
C5/44 Safdarjang Development Area
Opposite ITT, Palam Road
New Delhi 110016

Italy

Devamani Rajneesh Meditation Center
Via Basilica 5
10122 Torino

Divyananda Rajneesh Meditation Center
Pensione Tambo
Alpe Motta

Gautama Rajneesh Meditation Center
Via S. Martino 51
Morosolo Casciago
21020 Varese

Miasto Rajneesh Neo-Sannyas Commune
Podere San Giorgio
Cotorniano
53010 Frosini (SI)

Vishad Rajneesh Meditation Center
Castelvecchio di Compito
55062 Lucca

Japan

Eer Rajneesh Neo-Sannyas Commune
Mimura Building 6-21-34
Kikuna
Kohoku-ku
Yokohama 222

Mahamani Rajneesh Meditation Center
105 Country Heights
635 Shimabukuro
Kitanakagusuku-son
Okinawa 901-23

Sitara Rajneesh Meditation Center
498-218, Teine-miyanosawa
Nishi-ku
Sapporo-shi
Hokkaido

Svagat Rajneesh Meditation Center
1-22-46 Nishi-Nakada
Sendai-Shi Miyagi-Pref. 981-11

Kenya

Archana Rajneesh Meditation Center
P.O. Box 82501
Mombasa

Preetam Rajneesh Meditation Center
P.O. Box 10256
Nairobi

Mexico

Madhu Rajneesh Meditation Center
Rancho Cutzi Minzicuri
San Juan de Vina
Tacambaro
Michoacan

Nepal

Asheesh Rajneesh Meditation Center
P.O. Box 278
Pulchowk
Kathmandu

Rajneesh Teerth Neo-Sannyas Commune
Masina Patan, P.O. Box 91
Pokhara

Satmarga Rajneesh Meditation Center
Mahendra Pul
Pokhara

Netherlands

De Stad Rajneesh Mystery School
Cornelis Troostplein 23
1072 JJ Amsterdam

Mudita Rajneesh Meditation Center
Veldhuizenstraat 2
Gein
1072 Amsterdam

Prakash Rajneesh Meditation Center
Dykhuizenweg 70
9903 AE Appingedam

Alok Rajneesh Meditation and Art Center
Stationsweg 73
2515 BJ Den Haag

Wajid Rajneesh Meditation Center
Prins Hendrikplein 1
2518 JA Den Haag

Rajneesh Humaniversity
Dr Wiardi Beckmanlaan 4
1931 BW Egmond aan Zee

De Nieuwe Mens
Enschedesestraat 305
7552 CV Hengelo (O)

Arvind Rajneesh Meditation Center
Hoge Larenseweg 168
1221 AV Hilversum

Amaltas Rajneesh Meditation Center
Staalwijklaan 4
3763 LG Soest

Padam Rajneesh Meditation Center
Koningsoord 10
9984 XH Oudeschip

New Zealand

Rajneesh Meditation Center
P.O. Box 29132
Greenwoods Center
Epsom
Auckland 3

Shunyadeep Rajneesh Meditation Center
42 Park Road
Mirimar
Wellington

Norway

Devananda Rajneesh Meditation Center
Post Box 177
Vinderen
0319 Oslo 3

Peru

Adityo Rajneesh Meditation Center
Paseo de la Republica 4670 Depto E
Miraflores
Lima 18

Portugal

Karam Rajneesh Meditation Center
Rua Conselhevio Fernando de Mello
3360 Penacova (Coimbra)

Spain

Gulaab Rajneesh Information and
Meditation Center
'Es Serralet'
Estellens
07192 Mallorca-Baleares

Kamli Rajneesh Meditation Center
Apartado de Correos 607
Ibiza-Baleares

Krisana Rajneesh Meditation Center
Futonia S.A.
c/ Juan de Urbieta 61
28007 Madrid

Argayall
Valle Gran Rey
La Gomera-Canary Islands

Sweden

Madhur Rajneesh Meditation Center
Foervattarvagen 40
16142 Bromma

Switzerland

Almasta Rajneesh Meditation Center
9 Av. des Arpilleres
1224 Chene-Bougerie - Geneva

Mingus Rajneesh Meditation Center
Asylstrasse 11
8032 Zürich

USA

Nirakar Rajneesh Meditation Center
2646 Orchard Ave.
Los Angeles, CA 90007

Idam Rajneesh Meditation Center
Sw Moksha Prem (MacGregor)
1151 Raymond (23)301
Glendale, CA 91201

Surdham Rajneesh Meditation Center
The Nest, 75-111
Indian Wells, CA 92210

Nanda Rajneesh Meditation Center
447 Aster St.
Laguna Beach, CA 92651

Chandrika Rajneesh Meditation Center
2477 Louis Road
Palo Alto, CA 94306

Viha Rajneesh Meditation Center
252 Richardson Dr.
Mill Valley, CA 94941

Premsindhu Rajneesh Meditation Center
216 Beryl Street
Mill Valley, CA 94941

Gandharva Rajneesh Meditation Center
121 First Ave.
Santa Cruz, CA 95062

Yakaru Rajneesh Meditation Center
P.O. Box 130
Laytonville, CA 95454

Suranga Rajneesh Meditation Center
5852 Dewey Blvd.
Sacramento, CA 95824

Sukhdhama Rajneesh Meditation Center
1546 28th Street No. 412
Boulder, CO 80303
Chidvilas Foundation Inc.
P.O. Box 1510
Boulder, CO 80306

Vibhakara Rajneesh Meditation Center
P.O. Box 5161
Woodland Park, CO 80866

Devadeep Rajneesh Meditation Center
1430 Longfellow St. NW.
Washington, DC 20011

Dharmadeep Rajneesh Meditation Center
2455 6th Avenue N.
St. Petersburg, FL 33713

Rakesh Rajneesh Meditation Center
P.O. Box 1554
Kapas, HI 96746

Mahima Rajneesh Meditation Center
P.O. Box 1863
Makawao, HI 96768

Virat Rajneesh Meditation Center
Top Floor
2316 W Arthur
Chicago, IL 60645

Hridaya Rajneesh Meditation Center
Rt 4, Box 231
Burnsville, NC 28714

Devatara Rajneesh Meditation Center
155 Spencer Ave.
Lynbrook, L.I., NY 11563

Sangit Rajneesh Meditation Center
2920 Healy Ave.
Far Rockaway, NY 11691

Neeraj Rajneesh Meditation Center
2493 McGovern Drive
Schenectady, NY 12309

Shunyam Rajneesh Sannyas Ahsram
P.O.Box 1197
Post Road
New Paltz, NY 12561

Devadeep Rajneesh Meditation Center
Dicob Road, Box 1
Lowville, NY 13367

Tara Rajneesh Meditation Center
2240 S. Patterson Blvd. 4
Dayton, OH 45409

Ansu Rajneesh Meditation Center
19023 SW Eastside Road
Lake Oswego, OR

Bhagwatam Rajneesh Meditation Center
P.O. Box 21297
Rio Piedras, PR 00928

Fulwari Rajneesh Meditation Center
1726 Hillmont Drive
Nashville, TN 37215

Kafi Rajneesh Meditation Center
1781 Spyglass DT247
Austin, TX 78746

Suravi Rajneesh Meditation Center
1215 E. Aloha
Seattle, WA 98102

Sudhakar Rajneesh Meditation Center
902 S. 11th Street
Wausau, WI 54401

West Germany

Dörfchen Rajneesh Institute for Spiritual
Therapy and Meditation
Dahlmannstrasse 9
1000 Berlin 12

Dharmadeep Rajneesh Institute for Meditation
and Spiritual Growth
Karolinenstrasse 7-9
2000 Hamburg 6

Mani Rajneesh Meditation Center
Johannes-Büll Weg 13 II
2000 Hamburg 65

Mukto Rajneesh Meditation Center
Roonstrasse 79
2800 Bremen

Rajneesh-Stadt
Strickhauserstrasse 39
2882 Ovelgönne

Digant Rajneesh Meditation Center
Philippinenhöferweg 75
3500 Kassel

Purnam Rajneesh Neo-Sannyas Commune
Graf-Adolf Strasse 87
4000 Düsseldorf 1

Uta Rajneesh Institut für Spirituelle
Therapie und Meditation
Venloer Strasse 5-7
5000 Köln 1

Pranada Rajneesh Center for Meditation
and Health
Burgberg 3
5378 Blankenheim-Ahr

Prasuna Rajneesh Meditation Center
Oenekinger Weg 60
5880 Lüdenscheid

Kasha Rajneesh Meditation Center
Eiserne Hand 12
6000 Frankfurt/Main

Nityam Rajneesh Meditation Center
Villa Rödelstein
6551 Altenbamberg

Sirat Rajneesh Meditation Center
Hohbuchstrasse 50
7410 Reutlingen

Rajneesh Academy for Harmonious Integration
and Meditation (RAHIM)
Merianstrasse 12
7800 Freiburg

Sampat Rajneesh Meditation Center
Mendelweg 5
7900 Ulm/Lehr

Geha Rajneesh Meditation Center
Winterstetten 44
7970 Leutkirch

Tao Rajneesh Zentrum
Klenzestrasse 41
8000 München 5

Rakesh Rajneesh Meditation Center
Am Hang 1
8063 Oberumbach

Ansumala Rajneesh Meditation Center
Kaps 1
8219 Rimsting

Nishant Rajneesh Meditation Center
c/o Tassy Family
Hör Rain 6 Weichendorf
8608 Memmelsdorf

Premapara Rajneesh Meditation Center
Asternweg 4
8900 Augsburg 1

For further information contact:
Rajneeshdham
17 Koregaon Park
Poona 411 001 (MS)
India